I0820366

"We're told that biblical studies and systematic theology should be totally separate. But then comes along Guy Waters, a New Testament scholar and a superb systematic theologian. There has never been a greater need for a biblical doctrine of the church. I hope this is read widely for the health of every church not only in the US but in the Majority World."

MICHAEL HORTON,
professor of theology and apologetics,
Westminster Seminary California

"Guy Prentiss Waters provides an insightful, precise, readable, and thorough doctrinal account of ecclesiology. His masterful work encompasses biblical revelation, doctrinal matters, and practical wisdom. While there is much with which I agree, there is one significant point of difference: in contrast to a traditional Reformed continuity perspective, I place the church's inauguration on the day of Pentecost, representing a baptistic discontinuity viewpoint; that is, there is one people of God with two expressions: old covenant Israel (which was not the church) and the new covenant church. However, Waters's clarity in discussing these matters prompts me to use his book when I teach ecclesiology, to serve as a different yet well-articulated and argued position. Highly recommended!"

GREGG R. ALLISON,
professor of Christian theology, The Southern Baptist
Theological Seminary, Kentucky

"In his typically warm and readable style, Dr. Guy Prentiss Waters presents a rich gift to the church. In *One, Holy, Catholic, and Apostolic Church*, he invites us into a sweeping (biblico-theological) survey of the church through Old and New Testaments, and then, while fearlessly probing the perennial questions (including such topics as government, worship, discipline, mission, and church/state relations), draws summary (systematic-theological) conclusions about Christ-honoring principles for the church's life and practice. In this welcome work about the church, Waters has produced a new go-to resource for the church."

DAVID B. GARNER,
chief academic officer, vice president of global ministries, and Charles Krahe Professor of Systematic Theology at Westminster Theological Seminary, Glenside, Pennsylvania

"We welcome another volume in the We Believe series of books edited by Murray J. Smith and John McClean, this one by Guy Prentiss Waters on one, holy, catholic, and apostolic church. This volume displays the interests of the series (in promoting exegetical theology, biblical theology, systematic theology, and history of dogma) while also displaying the special interest Dr. Waters has taken over the years in the areas of ecclesiology and worship. Dr. Waters has consistently and winsomely promoted worship that is regulated by Scripture (i.e. Reformed worship) and he has done so again in this interesting and thorough volume."

T. DAVID GORDON,
professor emeritus of Greek and Biblical Studies, Grove City College, Pennsylvania

"As a Baptist seminary professor, I want my students to read the best from other traditions, which is why I assign Guy Waters's first ecclesiology book on Presbyterian polity, *How Jesus Runs the Church.* Yet now they'll get his full ecclesiology: holy, catholic, and apostolic. In this eminently readable volume, Waters both provides a fuller biblical theology than most ecclesiologies offer. Then he draws on the best of the Reformed tradition to give a straightforward treatment of the traditional systematic categories for a doctrine of the church. It's faithful, reliable, biblical, and, frankly, a joy to read, even if I as a Baptist don't make all the same theological judgments as him."

JONATHAN LEEMAN,
editorial director, 9Marks

"Guy Waters embodies a rare combination of being a sharp biblical scholar, excellent theologian, and clear writer. This addition to what is proving to be an excellent series on the Nicene Creed, develops the doctrine of the church biblically, systematically, and practically. Filled with a robust array of post-Reformation, Scottish, and American sources, he showcases the best of Presbyterian ecclesiology and polity, achieving in a short volume what many authors have taken a long time to say. Summarizing the book's primary arguments with seven theses on the church at the close of the book, Waters presents his material with characteristic clarity and exceptional usefulness."

RYAN M. MCGRAW,
Morton H. Smith Professor of Systematic Theology,
Greenville Presbyterian Theological Seminary

"Guy Waters is one of the most reputable names in Reformed theology for good reason, which this book puts on display in application to ecclesiology. Building further than his previous work about church polity, this book is a more comprehensive statement of the church's origins, calling, attributes, mission, and ordering. Certainly, this volume will enrich its readers. What an honor to commend it!"

HARRISON PERKINS,
pastor at Oakland Hills Community Church (OPC);
author of *Reformed Covenant Theology: A Systematic Introduction*

"This wonderfully wide-ranging and astute study draws on discussion from throughout church history. Waters situates the rise and constitution of the church in God's Old Testament redemptive plan as well as in the work of Jesus and the apostles. He does justice to the church's doctrinal construction, its mission, and its place relative to the state. Students, pastors, and scholars alike will profit from Waters's Christ-centered and Scripture-normed survey and synthetic proposals."

ROBERT W. YARBROUGH,
professor of New Testament, Covenant Theological Seminary,
St. Louis, Missouri

GUY PRENTISS WATERS

is the James M. Baird Jr. Professor of New Testament and academic dean at Reformed Theological Seminary in Jackson, Mississippi. He is the author of *The Sabbath as Rest and Hope for the People of God*, *The Lord's Supper as the Sign and Meal of the New Covenant*, and *How Jesus Runs the Church*.

ONE, HOLY, CATHOLIC, AND APOSTOLIC CHURCH

THE BIBLICAL DOCTRINE OF THE CHURCH

WE BELIEVE

STUDIES IN REFORMED BIBLICAL DOCTRINE

We Believe is a series of eight major studies of the Christian faith's primary doctrines as confessed in the Nicene Creed and guided by the Reformed tradition. In each volume, trusted authors engage a major creedal doctrine in light of its biblical-theological foundations and historical development, drawing out its spiritual, ethical, and missional implications for the church today.

1
One God Almighty
The Biblical Doctrine of the Triune God

2
Maker of Heaven and Earth
The Biblical Doctrine of Creation and Providence

3
The Lord Jesus Christ
The Biblical Doctrine of the Person and Work of Christ

4
For Us and for Our Salvation
The Biblical Doctrine of Humanity and Sin

5
He Will Come Again in Glory
The Biblical Doctrine of the End

6
The Giver of Life
The Biblical Doctrine of the Holy Spirit and Salvation

7
He Spoke through the Prophets
The Biblical Doctrine of God's Self-Revelation

ONE, HOLY, CATHOLIC, AND APOSTOLIC CHURCH

THE BIBLICAL DOCTRINE OF THE CHURCH

WE BELIEVE: STUDIES IN REFORMED BIBLICAL DOCTRINE

VOLUME 8

JOHN MCCLEAN AND MURRAY J. SMITH, SERIES EDITORS

GUY PRENTISS WATERS

One, Holy, Catholic, and Apostolic Church: The Biblical Doctrine of the Church
We Believe, edited by John McClean and Murray J. Smith

Lexham Academic, an imprint of Lexham Press
1313 Commercial St., Bellingham, WA 98225
LexhamPress.com

Print ISBN 9781683598367
Digital ISBN 9781683598374
Library of Congress Control Number 2024951532

Lexham Editorial: Todd Hains, Paul Robinson, Abigail Stocker, Mandi Newell, Danielle Burlaga
Cover Design: Joshua Hunt
Typesetting: Anna Fejes

24 25 26 27 28 29 30 / IN / 12 11 10 9 8 7 6 5 4 3 2 1

Now unto the King eternal, immortal, invisible,
the only wise God, be honour and glory
for ever and ever. Amen.
—1 Timothy 1:17

CONTENTS

BIBLICAL EXPOSITIONS

SERIES INTRODUCTION

Your word is a lamp to my feet
and a light to my path.
Psalm 119:105

The unfolding of your words gives light;
it imparts understanding to the simple.
Psalm 119:130

AN INVITATION TO CONFESSIONAL THEOLOGY

We Believe is a series of eight studies of the primary doctrines of the Christian faith as confessed in the Nicene Creed and received in the Reformed tradition. The series marks the 1700th anniversary of the Council of Nicaea (AD 325) by re-affirming and advancing the Church's confession.[1] The title of our series is drawn from the first words of the Creed—the single Greek verb Πιστεύομεν—which introduces what has become the classic confession of the Christian faith. Since the Church's confession neither began at Nicaea, nor ended with its creed, *We Believe* examines the biblical foundations of the Church's faith, traces its development (especially in the Reformed tradition), and applies its truths to the worship, life, and mission of the Church today. Since true theology begins in prayer and worship of the God who has revealed himself, each volume opens with a theme prayer, shaped by Scripture and the Church's confession. Further,

1. For the history of the Nicene Creed, which received its final form at the Council of Constantinople (ad 381), see D. Fairbairn and R. M. Reeves, *The Story of Creeds and Confessions: Tracing the Development of the Christian Faith* (Grand Rapids: Baker Academic, 2019), 48–79.

since even the deepest truths of the faith need to be simply expounded so they can be clearly grasped and faithfully lived, each volume closes with a series of theses, which summarize the doctrine covered in the book. *We Believe* provides a comprehensive and integrated biblical, theological, and missional treatment of the major doctrines of the Christian faith.

BIBLICAL REVELATION

The Church's confession is rooted in and ruled by God's revelation in Scripture. The Scriptures are "the Word of God written" and "the rule of faith and life" (Westminster Confession of Faith 1:2). The first part of each study, therefore, is devoted to a fresh examination of biblical revelation.

Fundamentally, our studies are tethered to the text of Scripture, and each volume in the series includes expositions of the primary biblical texts which form the doctrine under consideration.[2] Moreover, since Scripture is the only "infallible rule" for its own interpretation (Westminster Confession of Faith 1:9), our studies seek to interpret Scripture by Scripture, initially by embracing the discipline of Biblical Theology.[3] We begin—where God's people have always begun—with the recognition that Scripture is God's inspired and authoritative word. We proceed by tracing God's progressive revelation of himself and his purposes in the organically unfolding canon of Scripture, taking full account of its varied forms, while especially recognizing its fundamental, Christ-centered unity. This procedure is one we learn from Scripture itself. The Bible regularly claims that its revelation forms a single coherent narrative climaxing in the gospel of Christ, even as it also indicates that this narrative has many dimensions and is revealed in a diversity of literary forms.[4] Faithful Christian readings of Scripture—from Irenaeus and Augustine to Calvin and Kuyper—have,

---

2. For convenience of reference, these biblical expositions are highlighted in text boxes. Several key biblical texts are important for more than one doctrine, but to avoid repetition, these are only treated once in the series.

3. We understand this discipline along the lines sketched by Geerhardus Vos in his 1894 Inaugural Lecture at Princeton Theological Seminary. G. Vos, "The Idea of Biblical Theology as a Science and as a Theological Discipline," in *Redemptive History and Biblical Interpretation: The Shorter Writings of Geerhardus Vos*, ed. R. B. Gaffin (Phillipsburg: P & R, 1980), 3–24; *Biblical Theology: Old and New Testaments* (Grand Rapids: Eerdmans, 1948), 3–18.

4. See, for example: Deut 26:5–11; Josh 24; 1 Sam 12:6–18; Pss 78; 105–6; 136; Neh 9:7–37; Acts 7; 13:13–43; Heb 11.

therefore, always recognized a fundamental unity within the rich diversity of Scripture—a unity which is conceptual (in that the Scriptures speak of the same God relating in consistent ways to the same created world), and narratival (in that the Scriptures narrate a single redemptive-history).[5]

In the first part of each study, then, we look for the organic unfolding of God's revelation from its seed form in the garden of Eden (Gen 1–2) to its full flowering in the garden-city of the New Jerusalem (Rev 21–22). As Augustine said, "In the Old Testament the New is concealed, in the New the Old is revealed."[6] So we read Genesis in the light of the Gospels, Exodus in the light of the Epistles, and Ruth in the light of Revelation. We follow the rich network of citations and allusions—the "inner biblical exegesis"—by which Scripture interprets Scripture.[7] We outline the primary biblical themes relevant to each doctrine—God's kingdom and covenant, God's creation and blessing, God's Son and people, God's Spirit and temple—together with their many related sub-themes, as they inform and shape the Church's confession. We use Scripture's own words and categories to trace the drama of redemption from creation to new creation centered on Christ.

Following this approach, we recognize that the Bible fundamentally structures its own unfolding narrative, and organizes all its major themes, around God's two primary covenants with Adam and Christ (Rom 5:12–21; 1 Cor 15:22). Reformed theology came to characterize these as the "covenant of works" and the "covenant of grace," confessing that, from start to finish, God has related to his people and his world by way of covenant (Westminster Confession of Faith 7:1–6).[8] Scripture thus presents each of the major post-fall biblical covenants—God's covenants with Abraham,

---

5. See C. H. H. Scobie, "History of Biblical Theology," in *New Dictionary of Biblical Theology*, ed. T. D. Alexander and B. S. Rosner (Downers Grove, IL: InterVarsity Press, 2000), 11–20.

6. Augustine, Quaest. in Hept. 2: 73: *Novum Testamentum in Vetere latet, Vetus Testamentum in Novo patet.*

7. The phrase "inner biblical exegesis" was coined by M. A. Fishbane, *Biblical Interpretation in Ancient Israel* (Oxford: Oxford University Press, 1985). See further: G. K. Beale and D. A. Carson, eds., *Commentary on the New Testament Use of the Old Testament* (Grand Rapids: Baker Academic, 2007); G. K. Beale, *Handbook on the New Testament Use of the Old Testament: Exegesis and Interpretation* (Grand Rapids: Baker Academic, 2012); G. E. Schnittjer, *Old Testament Use of Old Testament: A Book-by-Book Guide* (Grand Rapids: Zondervan, 2021).

8. See esp. G. P. Waters, J. N. Reid, and J. R. Muether, eds., *Covenant Theology: Biblical, Theological, and Historical Perspectives* (Wheaton: Crossway, 2020); H. Perkins, *Reformed Covenant Theology: A Systematic Introduction* (Bellingham, WA: Lexham, forthcoming).

Israel, David, and the new covenant—as successive administrations of the single covenant of grace: the covenant which was first promised in the garden (Gen 3:15), climactically sealed by the blood of Christ (Matt 26:28 and Mark 14:24 with Exod 24:8), and which ultimately will be fulfilled in the new creation when the Triune God comes to dwell with his people at last (Rev 21:3).[9]

Above all—and consistent with the covenant theology we have just sketched—we take Jesus's own word as our guide, and look for him, the Lord Jesus Christ, "in all the Scriptures" (Luke 24:27). Following Jesus and his apostles, we recognize that God "promised ... the gospel ... beforehand through his prophets in the Holy Scriptures" (Rom 1:3–4; cf. Luke 24:44–49; Gal 3:8; 1 Cor 15:3–5; 1 Pet 1:12). Christ himself—his person, his work, and his kingdom—is the climax and goal of the Triune God's gracious plan to redeem his people and his world. Indeed, Christ is the very "substance" of biblical revelation (Col 2:17; cf. John 5:39; Rom 10:4; 1 Cor 10:4; 2 Cor 1:20; 2 Tim 3:15; 1 Pet 1:10–12). The grace of God in Christ was not merely foreshadowed and prophesied in the Old Testament; it was mediated in advance to the saints of old, by the Spirit, through the "promises, prophecies, sacrifices ... and other types" given to God's people in that period (Westminster Confession of Faith 7:5–6). We therefore affirm that the Old Testament is *both* Christo-telic (in that it points forward to Christ as its goal), *and* Christo-centric (in that its types and promises really mediated God's grace in Christ, through the Spirit).[10] Thus, with John Calvin, we are right to "seek in the whole of Scripture ... truly to know Jesus Christ, and the infinite riches that are comprised in him and are offered to us by him from God the Father."[11]

---

9. For the central covenant promise—"I will be your God and you will be my people" (or variations), see: Gen 17:7–8; 28:15; 31:3, 5, 42; 39:2–6, 21–23; Exod 6:7; 29:45–46; Lev 11:45; 25:38; 26:11–12; Deut 23:15; 26:17–18; 29:12–13; 2 Sam 7:23–24; 1 Chron 17:22; Ps 95:7; Jer 11:4; 24:7; 30:22; 31:1, 33; 32:38; Ezek 14:11; 34:24, 30–31; 36:28; 37:23, 27; Zech 2:11; 8:8; 13:9; Hos 1:8–2:23; Matt 1:23; 18:20; 28:20; 2 Cor 6:16; Rev 21:3.

10. See: P. A. Lillback, ed. *Seeing Christ in All of Scripture: Hermeneutics at Westminster Theological Seminary* (Philadelphia: Westminster Seminary Press, 2016); L. G. Tipton, "Christocentrism *and* Christotelism: The Spirit, Redemptive History, and the Gospel," in *Redeeming the Life of the Mind: Essays in Honor of Vern Poythress*, ed. J. M. Frame, W. A. Grudem, and J. J. Hughes (Wheaton: Crossway, 2018), 129–45.

11. From Calvin's preface to Pierre Olivétan's French translation of the New Testament (1534) in *Calvin: Commentaries*, ed. and trans. J. Haroutunian and L. P. Smith (Philadelphia: Westminster Press, 1958), 70.

In thus seeking Christ in all the Scriptures, we find that later revelation in Scripture interprets earlier revelation in ways that are consistent with its original meaning; the later revelation shows the "true and full sense" (*sensus plenior*) in light of the fulfillment in Christ (Westminster Confession of Faith 1:9). The New Testament offers no radical reinterpretation, much less correction, of the Old, but unfolds the full meaning of God's inspired word. As B. B. Warfield put it, the Old Testament is like a room "richly furnished but dimly lighted," such that "the introduction of light [from the New Testament] brings into it nothing which was not in it before," but "brings out into clearer view much of what is in it but was only dimly or even not at all perceived before."[12] As we read the Scriptures as the unfolding narrative of God's redemptive purpose, we learn to see, again and again, that Christ is the center and substance of the Scriptures, and so the center and substance of the Church's faith.

DOGMATIC DEVELOPMENT

The Church confesses not only what is "expressly set down in Scripture" but what "by good and necessary consequence may be deduced from Scripture" (Westminster Confession of Faith 1:6). The second part of each study in the *We Believe* series, therefore, is devoted to an account of the dogmatic development of the doctrine under consideration. Far from being opposed to each other, Biblical Theology and Systematic and Confessional Dogmatics actually need each other; there is a necessarily reciprocal relationship between the two.[13] While both disciplines deal with God's special revelation in Scripture, they analyze it according to different principles. The primary

12. B. B. Warfield, "The Biblical Doctrine of the Trinity," in *Biblical Doctrines: The Works of Benjamin B. Warfield*, vol. 2 (New York: Oxford University Press, 1932), 141–42.

13. For reflection on the relationship between the two disciples in the Reformed tradition, see esp. Vos, "Idea," 3–24; J. Murray, "Systematic Theology," in *Collected Writings of John Murray: Volume 4, Studies in Theology: Reviews*, ed. I. Murray (Edinburgh: Banner of Truth, 1983), 1–21; R. B. Gaffin, "Systematic Theology and Biblical Theology," *WTJ* 38 (1975–76): 281–99. For review of these contributions and a constructive proposal, see M. Allen, "Systematic Theology and Biblical Theology—Part One," *JRT* 14 (2020): 52–72; "Systematic Theology and Biblical Theology—Part Two," *JRT* 14 (2020): 344–57. Note also: J. McClean, "Of Covenant and Creation: A Conversation between Systematic Theology and Biblical Theology," in *An Everlasting Covenant: Biblical and Theological Essays in Honour of William J. Dumbrell*, ed. J. A. Davies and A. M. Harman, RTR Supplement Series 4 (Doncaster: Reformed Theological Review, 2010), 187–227.

organizing principle for Biblical Theology is history—the organic unfolding of God's work of redemption and his interpretation of the same in his inspired word. The primary organizing principle of Dogmatics is logic—the rational organization of God's revealed truth. As Geerhardus Vos observes, while Biblical Theology constructs a historical "line," Christian Dogmatics constructs a logical "circle."[14] Thus, while Christian Dogmatics, including the Church's creeds and confessions, generally follow the redemptive-historical shape of biblical revelation, it self-consciously sets that redemptive history within the reality of the Triune God and his relations to his world as these are revealed in all of Scripture.[15] In the same way, while Christian Dogmatics fundamentally expresses itself using biblical language, it also employs extra-biblical language to summarize and synthesize biblical teaching, especially where Scripture uses a variety of expressions for the same reality, or where this is necessary to refute error.[16] Since "the word of God is living and active" (Heb 4:12), the God-given language of Scripture remains primary. Faithful Dogmatics rightly recognizes what John Webster calls the "rhetorical sufficiency" of Scripture.[17] Indeed, since "the Old Testament in Hebrew ... and the New Testament in Greek" were "immediately inspired by God," the final court of appeal for all Christian Dogmatics is the words of Scripture in the original languages (Westminster Confession of Faith 1:8). Yet still, the same theological judgment can be expressed in a range of different conceptual and linguistic forms, and the faithful presentation and propagation of biblical truth sometimes requires extra-biblical expression.[18]

There is, moreover, a real history of doctrinal development to be traced through the ages of church history. As the very word of the living God, the Scriptures possess an inexhaustible depth. As the Church reads and re-reads God's word in an ever-changing world, we find that there is always more to confess regarding God and his ways in the world, and always more

---

14. See Vos, "Idea," 23; cf. Murray, "Systematic Theology," 9.

15. Cf. Allen, "Systematic Theology—Part Two," 355–56.

16. Cf. "Systematic Theology—Part Two," 355.

17. J. Webster, "Biblical Reasoning," in *The Domain of the Word: Scripture and Theological Reason* (London: T & T Clark, 2012), 131.

18. See D. S. Yeago, "The New Testament and Nicene Dogma: A Contribution to the Recovery of Theological Exegesis," *Pro-Ecclesia* 3 (1994): 87–100. Compare B. B. Warfield's comments to this effect on the doctrine of the Trinity (Warfield, "Trinity," 133).

to celebrate in the depths of his "being, wisdom, power, holiness, justice, goodness, and truth" (Westminster Shorter Catechism 4). Herman Bavinck states it well:

> Scripture is not designed so that we should parrot it but that as free children of God we should think his thoughts after him. ... So much study and reflection on the subject is bound up with it that no person can do it alone. That takes centuries. To that end the church has been appointed and given the promise of the Spirit's guidance into all truth.[19]

As each generation has read the Scriptures, confessed the faith, proclaimed the gospel, instructed children, discipled converts, and refuted errors, the Church—under the oversight of its living Lord, and by the enabling of his Holy Spirit—has deepened in its grasp of biblical truth.[20] The Church has learned again and again that "the Lord hath yet more light and truth to break forth from His Word."[21] The foundational doctrines of God and Christ were fundamentally established in the Church's early centuries, and codified in the ecumenical creeds, such that they received only incremental refinements thereafter. Other doctrines, however, no less crucial to the life of the Church—for example, the doctrines of Scripture and authority—received considerable development in the medieval, Reformation, and modern periods.

Doctrinal development, however—at least where it can be considered faithful—never moves beyond Scripture; it only ever penetrates more deeply into its truth. Faithful Dogmatics is thus not the imposition of a foreign grid onto Scripture, but a complementary means of interpreting Scripture by Scripture. In doing so, we make use of sanctified human reason. For while the fall has corrupted the human mind (Rom 1:21–23; Eph 4:17–18), that same mind is renewed in Christ and by the Spirit (Rom 12:2; 1 Cor 2:10–13; Eph 4:23), and as such can play the role of servant in the task of theology. Thus Francis Turretin helpfully distinguishes between

---

19. H. Bavinck, *Reformed Dogmatics: Volume 1, Prolegomena* (Grand Rapids: Baker Academic, 2003), 83.

20. The role of the Spirit in doctrinal development is helpfully emphasized by Murray, "Systematic Theology," 1–21, esp. 6.

21. G. Rawson, "We Limit Not the Truth of God" in *Leeds Hymn Book*, 1853, no. 409.

revelation as the "foundation of faith" and reason as the "instrument of faith," which can serve to "illustrate" and "collate" biblical passages or arguments, to draw out "inferences," and to help assess whether various positions agree or disagree with what has been revealed.[22]

The Church has been at this task for nearly two-thousand years, and there is a great deal to be learned from the wisdom of the ages. For this reason, each volume in the *We Believe* series provides a survey of the historical development of the doctrine under consideration. In charting this development, we give the Church's creeds and confessions pride of place. For while Augustine, Aquinas, Luther, Calvin, Turretin, and Bavinck—among a host of others—have provided significant insight into biblical truth, the Church's creeds and confessions reflect the official teaching of the Church *as* Church or—perhaps better—the common teaching of the Church's elders, that is, the teaching of those appointed by the Spirit, and charged with guarding and promoting the apostolic gospel and, indeed, "the whole counsel of God" (Acts 15:1–35; 16:4; 20:27–28; 1 Tim 3:2; 5:17–18; 2 Tim 2:2; Titus 1:9).[23]

The Church's teaching is always subordinate to Scripture. Scripture is the magisterial authority, the "rule that rules" (*norma normans*); the Church's teaching is a ministerial authority, "the rule that is ruled" (*norma normata*). In the order of authority, "the Supreme Judge, by which all controversies of religion are to be determined, and all decrees of councils, opinions of ancient writers, doctrines of men, and private spirits, are to be examined, and in whose sentence we are to rest, can be no other but the Holy Spirit speaking in the Scripture" (Westminster Confession of Faith 1:10). At the same time, in the order of knowing, there is wisdom in beginning with the Church's confession. We rightly take the Church's teaching as our guide in reading, interpreting, and applying Scripture. We learn the truth from our elders as they teach us the truth from God's word. This yields an iterative process: the Scriptures form our confession; our Scripturally-formed confession provides the lens through which we read

22. F. Turretin, *Institutes of Elenctic Theology*, trans. G. M. Giger, 3 vols. (Phillipsburg: P&R, 1992–97), §1.8.3, 6–7; 1.12.15.

23. See M. S. Horton, *The Christian Faith: A Systematic Theology for Pilgrims on the Way* (Grand Rapids: Zondervan, 2011), 211–18.

the Scriptures; and our further reading of the Scriptures further refines our confession.[24]

We Believe stands unashamedly in the Reformed confessional tradition, and seeks to defend and advance it. There are, of course, significant differences between the various Christian confessions. While the whole Church receives the doctrine of the ecumenical creeds (the Apostles', Nicene, and Athanasian creeds, together with the definition of Chalcedon), the later confessions present divergent views on a host of significant matters. It is our conviction that the Reformed confessions, especially the Three Forms of Unity and the Westminster Standards, present the best—that is, the most fully biblical—account of Christian truth. That very tradition, however, has always aimed to contend for "the faith that was once for all delivered to the saints" (Jude 3) and has thus championed a kind of Reformed catholicity.[25] Our approach in the *We Believe* series is therefore irenic, and ecumenical. We write *from* the perspective of the Reformed tradition, but *for* the Church catholic.

Moreover, while the Reformed confessions of the sixteenth century are a high point in the development of the Church's doctrine, they are not the end point. The body of Christ will not "attain to the unity of the faith and of the knowledge of the Son of God, to mature manhood, to the measure of stature of the fullness of Christ" (Eph 4:13) until Christ fully unites us to himself by his Spirit, when he raises his people from the dead and perfects us by his glorious presence (1 Cor 15:42–49; Phil 3:20–21). The bride of Christ will not be fully purified, "without spot or wrinkle," until the Lord returns and presents us to himself "in splendour" (Eph 5:27; Rev 21:2, 9). The city of God will not be complete until God himself comes to dwell among us in all his fullness and illumine us with his light (Rev 21:3, 22–23). A Reformed commitment to the creeds and confessions is, therefore, not an end point, but a stimulus to further biblical exposition and dogmatic clarification.[26] As a work in Christian Dogmatics, *We Believe* does not merely aim to retrieve

---

24. S. Swain, "A Ruled Reading Reformed: The Role of the Church's Confession in Biblical Interpretation," *IJST* 14 (2012): 177–93.

25. Horton, *Christian Faith*, 30–32. Cf. M. Allen and S. R. Swain, *Reformed Catholicity: The Promise of Retrieval for Theology and Biblical Interpretation* (Grand Rapids: Baker Academic, 2015); *Christian Dogmatics: Reformed Theology for the Church Catholic* (Grand Rapids: Baker Academic, 2016).

26. See Bavinck, *Reformed Dogmatics*, 1:31.

or to repristinate the Reformed tradition, but to constructively develop it, always under the authority of God's word. If this series makes a modest contribution to the Church's pilgrimage to maturity in Christ, it will have achieved its goal.

TRUTH FOR WORSHIP, LIFE, AND MISSION

The Church's maturity in Christ involves far more than doctrinal faithfulness and clarity. The drama of redemption, which forms the Church's doctrine, aims ultimately at discipleship and doxology.[27] The third part of each study in the *We Believe* series, therefore, briefly considers the ways in which the doctrine under consideration shapes the Church's worship, life, and mission. While the discussion here is necessarily indicative rather than exhaustive, we aim to demonstrate how biblical doctrine creates a moral vision for all of life. This includes, at the broadest level, observing the way in which the particular doctrine provides the basis for biblical principles for Christian worship, life, and mission, whether these are given explicitly in the biblical text (e.g. Matt 7:12, the "golden rule"), or summarized from biblical revelation as a whole (e.g. "the sanctity of life").[28] It includes, more sharply, consideration of the way in which Christian doctrine grounds the moral law, summarized in the Ten Commandments, and further summarized in the two great commandments of love for God and neighbor (Westminster Confession of Faith 19.2, 5; see esp. Exod 20:1–17; Deut 5:6–21; Matt 22:37–40; Rom 13:8; Gal 5:14; Jas 2:8). It also includes, further, consideration of the wealth of biblical examples which illustrate—both positively and negatively—the wisdom of life according to God's law. Crucially, since Reformed theology has always emphasized the necessity of the work of the Spirit in enabling faith and renewing those who were lost in sin by uniting them to Christ, this section also considers the way in which each doctrine highlights the gracious work of God in enabling his people "to live and work for his praise and glory" (*A Prayer Book for Australia*).

---

27. For this alliterative summary—"drama, doctrine, doxology, and discipleship"—see Horton, *Christian Faith*, 13–27.

28. See J. Murray, *Principles of Conduct: Aspects of Biblical Ethics* (London: Tyndale Press, 1957), 78–140.

Each of the authors for the series subscribes to one or more of the major Reformed confessions, and shares the general approach to Scripture and theology we have just outlined. At the same time, each author has approached the task in their own way, and—within the rich agreement just sketched—there are differences between us at the level of detail. We have deliberately assembled a company of authors who are experts in either Biblical Theology or Dogmatics on the conviction that in the Reformed tradition scholars must have a facility in both, even while maintaining their own expertise. The books aim to show the necessary integrity of Biblical Theology and Systematic Theology, to introduce students to biblical-confessional theology, and to help enrich and expand Reformed theology, while serving as a resource and reference for pastors, elders, and thoughtful Christians. We're thankful to Lexham Press, and especially our expert editor Dr. Todd Hains, for their partnership in this venture. Our hope and prayer is that these eight *Studies in Reformed Biblical Doctrine* might serve to ground the Church more firmly in the truth of God's word, that together we might "glorify God and enjoy him forever" (Westminster Shorter Catechism 1).

Almighty God, you are enthroned on the praises of Israel,
and all nations will worship and glorify your name.
Grant us counsel, instruct us, and reveal yourself to us,
that we would enjoy and glorify you in heart, soul,
and mind in this life and forever.
Through Jesus Christ our Lord,
who lives and reigns with you
and the Holy Spirit, one God,
now and forever.
Amen.

John McClean
Vice Principal and Lecturer in Systematic Theology and Ethics
Christ College, Sydney

Murray J. Smith
Lecturer in Biblical Theology and Exegesis
Christ College, Sydney

PREFACE

I AM GRATEFUL FOR THE opportunity to contribute to the *We Believe* series. Special thanks go to Murray Smith and John McClean, who not only invited me to write this book, but also responded to my questions and edited my submission with patience, care, and grace. I am grateful to Nathan Lee, Erick Kruger, Wyatt Lieberman, and John Fesko, who read through the manuscript in draft form and offered valuable and insightful feedback and suggestions. I am also thankful to Prashant Thakkar, who prepared the list of abbreviations and the bibliography, and to Wyatt Lieberman, who prepared the indices. A form of the last chapter was presented as a seminar during the General Assembly of the World Reformed Fellowship in 2022. I am appreciative of the thoughtful and helpful responses of those who attended that seminar.

I have the privilege of serving at Reformed Theological Seminary as both professor and Academic Dean of the Jackson campus. Particular thanks go to our board of trustees; to our chancellor, Ligon Duncan; and to our provost, Robert J. Cara. Their support, sacrifices, and labors on behalf of RTS make it possible for me to serve through teaching and writing.

Above all, I am grateful to the Triune God who has made me, redeemed me, and placed me in his church to serve. It has been a privilege to get glimpses of his work in the church at home and abroad. "To the King of the ages, immortal, invisible, the only God, be honor and glory forever and ever. Amen" (1 Tim 1:17).

Guy Prentiss Waters

ABBREVIATIONS

ANF	Ante-Nicene Fathers
BCO	*The Book of Church Order of the Presbyterian Church in America*
BECNT	Baker Exegetical Commentary on the New Testament
BSC	Bible Student's Commentary
BST	Bible Speaks Today
BTNT	Biblical Theology of the New Testament
BZNW	Beihefte zur Zeitschrift für die neutestamentliche Wissenschaft
CCC	*Catechism of the Catholic Church*
ESV	English Standard Version
JPS	Jewish Publication Society
ICC	International Critical Commentary
NAC	New American Commentary
NIBC	New International Biblical Commentary
NICNT	*New International Commentary on the New Testament*
NICOT	*New International Commentary on the Old Testament*
NIGTC	New International Greek Testament Commentary
NSBT	New Studies in Biblical Theology
RAD	Reformed Academic Dissertations
SSBT	Short Studies in Biblical Theology
TOTC	Tyndale Old Testament Commentaries
VTSup	Supplements to Vetus Testamentum
WBC	Word Biblical Commentary
WCF	Westminster Confession of Faith

WJE	The Works of Jonathan Edwards
WLC	Westminster Larger Catechism
WSC	Westminster Shorter Catechism
ZECNT	Zondervan Exegetical Commentary on the New Testament

PRAYER FOR THE STUDY OF THE CHURCH

On the holy mount stands the city he founded;
    The Lord loves the gates of Zion
    more than all the dwelling places of Jacob.
Glorious things of you are spoken,
    O city of God. *Selah.*

Among those who know me I mention Rahab and Babylon;
    Behold, Philistia and Tyre, with Cush—
  "This one was born there," they say.
And of Zion it shall be said,
  "This one and that one were born in her";
    For the Most High himself will establish her.
The Lord records as he registers the peoples,
  "This one was born there." *Selah.*

Singers and dancers alike say,
  "All my springs are in you."

Psalm 87

Our Great God and Heavenly Father, we thank you that you have sent your Son, our Savior and Lord, into this world in the fullness of time to save us from our sins. We praise you for the gift of your Spirit, who makes dead sinners alive and grafts your people into Christ. We bless you for the privilege of belonging to your church, and for preserving and prospering your people in every generation. Help us to learn from the Scripture more of your will and ways toward your beloved bride. And grant with that knowledge a deeper desire to serve your people and, in company with your people, to serve the world. May we, in our meditations, grow in our love for the church and, above all, for you, the God who in love, wisdom, and power gathers, defends, and perfects his people. Through Jesus Christ our Lord. Amen.

INTRODUCTION

THE PEOPLE OF GOD

In the face of divisions threatening the church in the fourth century, the Nicene-Constantinopolitan Creed summoned Christians to confess "one, holy, catholic, and apostolic church," and to "acknowledge one baptism for the remission of sins." Since the fourth century, the church has witnessed any number of subsequent disagreements, controversies, and splits, not least concerning the doctrine of the church (and the sacraments of the church). Unfairly labeled as schismatic by their opponents, the Reformers in fact labored to see the church express the unity, holiness, catholicity, and apostolicity that Scripture predicates of the church and calls the church to pursue. The Reformation, in other words, was a fundamentally ecclesial movement, striving to reform the church according to Scripture. And while the Reformed wing of the Reformation and its seventeenth-century heirs would expend considerable energy to frame a biblical ecclesiology, it would remain to a later day for those planted seeds to mature to full flower.

In the nineteenth-century, Presbyterians were conscious that the doctrine of the church was *the* question claiming the attention of the Protestant church. Upon his inauguration in 1858 as the Professor of Ecclesiastical History and Church Polity at Columbia (SC) Theological Seminary, John B. Adger declared, "The question of our age is *the Church*, her nature, her mission, her functions, her powers, her officers, her members."[1] His contemporary, Alexander T. McGill, told his students at Princeton Theological

1. John B. Adger, "Inaugural Discourse on Church History and Church Polity," *Southern Presbyterian Review* 12, no. 1 (April 1859): 163, emphasis original.

Seminary, "Ecclesiology, and especially the department of governmental polity ... is the 'present truth' in which nearly all the unsolved problems of Christianity are to be found."[2] These problems could only be solved, McGill continued, if "theology ... turn[ed] back to the Bible."[3]

In that spirit, this volume begins its explorations of the doctrine of the church in the Scripture. Far from being peripheral to the teaching of Scripture, the church (the people of God) sits at Scripture's heart. At the creation, God called Adam to secure confirmed, eschatological life through continued covenantal obedience. Adam stood not only for himself but for all human beings ordinarily descending from him. Had Adam continued in obedience to God, he would have ushered himself—and his posterity—into unbroken and heightened fellowship and communion with God. But Adam sinned, and, in Adam, we all sinned. Thankfully, God soon revealed his purpose to redeem a people for himself. This work of redemption would be undertaken by the last Adam, Jesus Christ. In Jesus Christ, God is gathering this redeemed people to dwell with him forever. The closing chapters of the Bible portray the consummation in precisely these terms.

Part 1 of this book explores the way in which the Scripture portrays the people of God across human history, from creation to redemption to consummation. Although the form and shape of God's people have undergone changes—even profound changes—across the epochs of redemptive history, God has always had a single people for himself. Far from being random or meaningless, these changes were expressions of the one divine purpose to prepare his people for the coming of Jesus Christ into history to undertake his saving work. The people of God under the last and climactic administration of the covenant of grace, the new covenant, reflect in any number of ways the stamp of their Savior and Lord who has completed his work of redemption. As such, paying careful attention to the people of God throughout the progress of redemptive history affords unique insight into the person and work of Christ, not least through some of the leading metaphors that describe the church (e.g., vine, temple, bride).

---

2. A. T. McGill, *Church Government: A Treatise Compiled from His Lectures in Theological Seminaries* (Philadelphia: Presbyterian Board of Publication and Sabbath Work, 1888), 22. I am indebted to the Rev. Per Almquist for this quote and the Adger quote above.

3. McGill, *Church Government*, 22.

Because the church, Paul tells us, cosmically manifests the "manifold wisdom of God" (Eph 3:10), systematic-theological reflection on the church demands our attention. Part 2 of this book explores the definition, government, worship, life, and mission of the church. In company and conversation with saints of past generations, we will mine the Scripture to uncover biblical answers to questions such as the following: How may we identify the one, holy, catholic, and apostolic church? How does God want his church to be governed? What kind of worship is pleasing and acceptable to God? How is Christ maturing his body? How is Christ growing and expanding his kingdom? As with our biblical-theological reflections upon the church, our systematic-theological reflections upon the church begin with the word of God and lead us invariably to the blessed Triune God, Father, Son, and Holy Spirit.

The points of intersection between the doctrine of the church and our contemporary world are conceivably endless. One perennial and nettlesome issue that has occupied the church from nearly its beginning is its relationship with the state. Part 3 will survey the way that the Reformed church, in the Old World and in the New World, has sought to bring the Scripture to bear upon this question. The fruits of our spiritual ancestors' labors afford biblical wisdom and practical insight to the global church in the twenty-first century.

For all our attention upon the church in the pages that follow, we must never let our attention fall only upon the church. God has designed the church in such a way as to draw the eyes of those who look upon the church heavenward, to himself. As we explore the *people* of God, let us not neglect to gaze upon and to adore the *God* of his people—the church's only Maker, Sustainer, and Redeemer.

PART 1

BIBLICAL REVELATION

1

CREATION: FOUNDATIONS FOR THE CHURCH

To formulate a biblical ecclesiology, one must reach back to the beginning of the Bible. That is to say, the roots of the people of God do not lie ultimately in redemption, but in creation. Exploring the details of the account of God's creation of the world, in general, and of human beings, in particular, affords insights into what God intends for the church in redemption and consummation.[1]

CREATED: CREATION AND RULE BY THE WORD

The creation account highlights a principle that will characterize God's dealings with his people throughout history—God brings life into being and brings order to that life by the power of his Spirit and through his word.

1. Compare the observation of Jonathan Edwards, "It may be ... argued that the creation of the visible world was in order to the work of redemption, that not only the things made do shadow forth things that appertain to this work, but the work of creation itself seems to be so done that it should shadow forth the work of redemption in the manner of doing it." "Miscellany 702," WJE 18:284.

Genesis 1:1–31

The opening verse of the Bible—"In the beginning, God created the heavens and the earth" (Gen 1:1)—declares "that until God spoke, nothing existed."[2] God, then, is the sole author of all created life and being.

Consider how God brings about this work of creation. The initial state of the creation is "without form and void," that is, it lacks structure or order and it lacks fullness (Gen 1:2a). More than that, "darkness was over the face of the deep" (1:2b). The absence of form, fullness, and light will be remedied by the work of God in the course of six days (1:3–31). The reference at the close of Genesis 1:2 to "the Spirit of God ... hovering over the face of the waters" refers to the divine agent by whom form, fullness, and light will come into being in the created order. Although the Spirit is not mentioned again in Genesis 1, we are intended to understand God the Spirit as the author of the work described in the verses that follow.[3]

The account of the creation in the six days of Genesis 1:3–31 goes on to highlight the word of God in the production of form, fullness, and light. This point is underscored by the serial repetition of the phrase, "And God said ..." (1:3, 6, 9, 11, 14, 20, 24; compare 1:26). The fact that this phrase "is accompanied ... in several instances ... by an action on God's part ... clearly indicates that we are dealing with a manifestation of divine power."[4] The "word of God," then, "is the creative and binding force of life."[5]

Genesis 1 shows us that God creates all things by his Spirit and word. And, as Calvin observes from Genesis 1:2 and Psalm 104:29–30, the Spirit not only creates life, but "the power of the Spirit was

---

2. Derek Kidner, *Genesis: An Introduction and Commentary*, TOTC (Downers Grove, IL: InterVarsity, 1967), 43. Compare the testimony of Hebrews 11:3.

3. For a concise defense of "the Spirit of God" as the "Third Person in the Holy Trinity," see Abraham Kuyper, *The Work of the Holy Spirit*, trans. Henri de Vries (London: Funk & Wagnalls, 1900), 28–29.

4. Gerhard Charles Aalders, *Genesis: Volume 1*, trans. William Heynen, BSC (Grand Rapids: Zondervan, 1981), 56.

5. Bruce K. Waltke, *Genesis: A Commentary* (Grand Rapids: Zondervan, 2001), 69.

necessary to sustain" the life that he creates.[6] The creature, once brought into being and given form by the divine power and will of God (compare Gen 2:7), is no less preserved and governed by God at every moment of its existence.

This principle will be no less true of the people of God. God brings his people into being by the almighty power of his life-giving Spirit (John 3:3, 5), who is pleased to grant life on the occasion of the proclamation of "the word of truth" (James 1:18; compare Rom 4:17). The people of God are indwelt by the Spirit (Eph 2:22; 1 Cor 3:16; 6:19), who continues to sustain the life of individual Christians and of the church. But the Spirit no less supplies order to the life of God's people, individually (Gal 5:22–25) and corporately (1 Cor 14:33, 40), even as he directs and governs the life of believers and of the church (see Gal 5:18, 25).[7]

HUMANITY—THE CROWN OF CREATION

Human beings are the crowning work of God in the six days of creation. This point is highlighted in a number of ways in the early chapters of Genesis. First, human beings conclude the account of creation in Genesis 1:3–31. Second, the particular description of the creation of the first man and the first woman is proportionately lengthier than any previous description of God's work of creation. Third, Genesis 2:4–25 offers a parallel and expanded account of the first human beings. Fourth, only in relation to the creation of people does God employ the language of self-deliberation ("Then God said, 'Let us make man,'" Gen 1:26). Fifth, although God is also said to have "blessed" the animals created on the fifth day (1:22), when God "blessed" man, he speaks to them ("And God said to them," Gen 1:28), "thus drawing attention to the personal

6. Calvin, *Commentaries on the First Book of Moses Called Genesis*, trans. John King, 2 vols. (repr., Grand Rapids: Baker, 1996), 1.73. See further Calvin's discussion at *Institutes of the Christian Religion*, I.16.19.

7. Although Paul does not explicitly invoke the Spirit in 1 Corinthians 14:33, 40, it is the work of God the Spirit that is preeminently in view in this chapter (see 1 Cor 14:2; compare 12:1–11). When Paul speaks of God in 1 Corinthians 14:33, 40, therefore, he has in mind especially God the Spirit.

relationship between God and man."[8] Human beings are unique among the creatures listed in Genesis 1 as receptors of divine speech. Sixth, although human beings stand alongside the sea creatures as recipients of the command, "be fruitful and multiply and fill …" (1:22, 28), only human beings are tasked with "dominion over the fish of the sea and over the birds of the heavens and over every living thing that moves on the earth" (1:28), a dominion that extends even to vegetation (1:29). Such dominion constitutes the "glory and honor" that distinguish ruling human beings from the ruled lower creation (see Ps 8:5–8).

This distinguishing function that God assigns to humanity is rooted in a unique human ontology. Human beings alone in Genesis 1 are said to be made after the image and likeness of God: "Then God said, 'Let us make man in our image, after our likeness'" (Gen 1:26). As such, they are to exercise "dominion" over the lower creation (Gen 1:26).

Genesis 1:26–31

Reflection upon human beings as "image" and "likeness" of God, and of the functions that correspond to humans as image-bearers, is critical to understanding the ecclesiology of Scripture. To begin, what does it mean that human beings are said to be made in the image and likeness of God (בְּצַלְמֵנוּ כִּדְמוּתֵנוּ)?[9] Although some have argued for distinct denotations to the nouns "image" and "likeness," they are almost certainly parallel and interchangeable.[10] After all, in Genesis 5:1, Adam is said simply to have been made "in the likeness of God" (בִּדְמוּת אֱלֹהִים).[11] The two terms together convey similarity

8. Gordon Wenham, *Genesis 1–15*, WBC 1 (Waco, TX: Word, 1987), 33.

9. For a recent survey of the "image of God" in light of ancient Near Eastern background, see Catherine L. McDowell, *The Image of God in the Garden of Eden: The Creation of Humankind in Genesis 2:5–3:24 in Light of the* mīs pî, pīt pî, *and* wpt-r *Rituals of Mesopotamia and Ancient Egypt* (Winona Lake, IN: Eisenbrauns, 2015).

10. Arguments for these terms' distinct denotation go back at least to Irenaeus of Lyons, so Wenham, *Genesis 1–15*, 29. As Bavinck notes, Rome's view of the image of God and, in particular, its doctrine of the *donum superadditum* "did not arise from the distinction between 'image' and 'likeness,' although it was later associated with this distinction as well," Herman Bavinck, *Reformed Dogmatics: Volume 2, God and Creation*, trans. John Vriend (Grand Rapids: Baker Academic, 2004), 539.

11. So, rightly, Calvin and many others after him, *Genesis*, 1.94.

or resemblance between human beings and the God who made them.[12] If we were to inquire at what points that similarity obtains, the broader context of Genesis 1:26 affords an answer. This context highlights at least two dimensions or aspects of this image. In the first place, the Creator God is a speaking, communicative God—"by the word of the Lord the heavens were made" (Ps 33:6). Furthermore, God uniquely speaks to human beings among the creatures that he makes in Genesis 1. We are bound to understand the image of God, then, in terms of a human person as a thinking, communicative being. In the second place, God repeatedly surveys his creative works and pronounces them to be "good" (1:4, 10, 12, 18, 21, 25). He concludes his work of creation by pronouncing all he has made to be "very good" (1:31). The goodness of the creation reflects the goodness of the Creator. For human beings to be made in the image of God is to be made morally good or righteous, a point confirmed by Ecclesiastes 7:29 ("God made man upright").

Genesis 1:26–31 shows us that the image of God should be understood both intellectually and morally. Human beings are thinking, communicative, moral creatures and, in this respect, reflect or bear similarity to the God who made them. That we should understand the image of God along these lines is confirmed in the New Testament. The apostle Paul reflects upon how the work of Christ both restores creation from the effects of the fall and advances creation to its intended consummation. This work of restoration encompasses the image of God.

> " ... and to put on the new self (τὸν καινὸν ἄνθρωπον), created after the likeness of God (κατὰ θεὸν κτισθέντα) in true righteousness and holiness." (Eph 4:24)

> " ... and have put on the new self (τὸν νέον), which is being renewed in knowledge after the image (εἰκόνα) of its creator." (Col 3:10)

---

12. "Humanity is a faithful and adequate representation, though not a facsimile," Waltke, *Genesis*, 65.

Here Paul sees fallen human beings, united to Christ, as being restored after "the likeness of God," "the image of its creator." This language refers to the creation of human beings in the image of God.[13] Paul conceives the renewed image (and, therefore, the original image) along three lines—"knowledge," "righteousness," and "holiness." That is to say, there are two points of similarity between human beings and their Creator—intellectual and moral. These two points of similarity constitute the image of God.

It is in light of this anthropological ontology that the creation account of Genesis 1 speaks to the functional dimensions of the image of God.[14] We noted above that "dominion" over the lower creation is immediately associated with human beings as made in the image of God. In exercising rule over the creation, humans imitate or reflect the God who has created all things and rules the works of his hands. The association between rule and fruitfulness in Genesis 1:28 likely indicates that we are also to understand the command to "be fruitful and multiply and fill the earth" as a functional expression of the image of God. In other words, when human beings obey the call to reproduce and, in this respect, to populate the world, they are modeling the God who himself filled and populated a world that was initially "void" (Gen 1:2). This is not to say that dominion and fruitfulness *constitute* or *comprise* the image.[15] It is to say, however, that they *express* what it means to be an image-bearer.

To reflect on the image of God ontologically and functionally, however, does not entirely exhaust the significance of this essential component of our humanity. There is no less a relational dimension to the image of God. In stressing a relational dimension to the image of

---

13. The word translated "image" in Colossians 3:10 is the word rendered "image" in LXX Genesis 1:26—εἰκών.

14. As G. K. Beale has noted, it is these "functional aspects" of the image of God that receive "the emphasis in Gen. 1," *New Testament Biblical Theology: The Unfolding of the Old Testament in the New* (Grand Rapids: Baker Academic, 2011), 32n13.

15. So rightly Calvin, "Nor is there any probability in the opinion of those who locate God's likeness in the dominion given to man, as if in this mark alone he resembled God, that he was established as heir and possessor of all things; whereas God's image is properly to be sought within him, not outside him, indeed, it is an inner good of the soul," *Institutes* 1.15.4.

God, we do not mean to say that the image is essentially relational.[16] But it is to say that image-bearers are necessarily relational beings. As Michael Horton has observed, "To be created in God's image is to be called persons in communion. There was no moment when a human being was actually a solitary, autonomous, unrelated entity; self-consciousness always included consciousness of one's relation to God, to each other, and to one's place in the wider created environment."[17] It is as humans relate to other personal beings that they reflect the relational, Triune God who has created them.[18]

Human relationality runs in basically two directions according to Genesis 1. First, it runs horizontally. Immediately after human beings are said to be created in God's image, they are said to be "created ... male and female" (Gen 1:27). Since the image is rooted in the individual person and is not essentially social (see Gen 5:1), we should not understand Genesis 1:27 to say that a man or a woman is, by himself or herself, less than the image of God. At the same time, God creates humans as biologically gendered beings. Image-bearers necessarily relate to one another as "male" and "female."

As we will see, in Genesis 2 God establishes a unique and permanent union between one man and one woman—marriage. This relationship is the divinely ordained relationship within which childbearing is to occur (see Gen 2:24). Marriage, then, and its

---

16. As Barth, *Church Dogmatics* 3.1, trans. and ed. G. W. Bromiley and T. F. Torrance (Edinburgh: T&T Clark, 1960), 191–206. Referencing this section of Barth, Waltke astutely notes that "Genesis 5:13 and 9:6 show clearly that 'the image of God' pertains to the individual himself or herself, not to relationship. ... Clearly the image of God refers to the structure of the individual, and his or her capacity for companionship with a female or male respectively is an entailment," *Genesis*, 66n50. See the fuller discussion and analysis at G. C. Berkouwer, *Man: The Image of God*, trans. Dirk W. Jellema (Grand Rapids: Eerdmans, 1962), 72–74.

17. Michael Horton, *The Christian Faith: A Systematic Theology for Pilgrims on the Way* (Grand Rapids: Zondervan, 2011), 387.

18. That God himself is relational is evident in several respects from the text of Genesis 1. The word of self-deliberation at Genesis 1:26 ("Let us make man in our image, after our likeness") points to a plurality of persons within the essential unity of the Godhead, a point made more explicit by subsequent revelation, which speaks of Father, Son, and Spirit as active in the work of creation (see, for instance, Ps 33:6; John 1:1–3; Col 1:15–20). Even in Genesis 1, a distinction is drawn between "God" and "the Spirit of God" (compare Job 33:4). We are to understand the relationality of God, then, in terms of his essential triunity. It is as God is an essentially relational being that he comes to his image-bearing human beings along the avenue of the spoken word (Gen 1:28–30).

corresponding fruitfulness is a leading way in which the image of God comes to expression in human relationality.[19]

Second, human relationality runs vertically. God, we have seen, uniquely speaks to his image-bearers in Genesis 1. God therefore establishes a species of relationship with human beings that he does not have with the other creatures. In Genesis 2, as we will see later, God will order and advance this relationship in the covenant that he establishes with Adam. It is in the context of this covenant that the potential of the natural relationship between God and human beings, established at their creation, will be actualized. In covenant with God, human beings can enjoy communion with God and the blessing that comes from that interpersonal fellowship with their Creator.

CREATION AND THE PEOPLE OF GOD

The anthropology of Genesis 1 lays a critical foundation for subsequent biblical reflection upon the people of God. We may offer three such observations, corresponding to the three dimensions of biblical anthropology explored above. First, the image of God, marred by the fall of Adam into sin, is restored only in Christ. Paul reminds the Corinthians that "we all, with unveiled face, beholding the glory of the Lord, are being transformed into the same image from one degree of glory to another" (2 Cor 3:18). Christ is, after all, "the image of the invisible God" (Col 1:15). Paul emphasizes to the Corinthians that this project of transformation is a corporate one ("*we all* … are being transformed"). That is to say, the restoration of the image of God does not transpire outside the context of the people of God.

Given that state of affairs, it is no surprise that the Scripture emphasizes two realities about the life of the people of God. The image of God, we have seen, should be understood partly in terms of the mind of the image-bearer. Mind-renewal according to the word of God, therefore, is both indispensable and fundamental to the ministry of the church (Rom 12:2, Eph 4:24; compare Matt 28:18–20, Acts 2:42). The image of God, furthermore,

19. As Wenham notes, the command of Genesis 1:28 ("Be fruitful and multiply and fill the earth") follows immediately upon the statement that God made his image-bearers "male and female" (Gen 1:27), *Genesis 1–15*, 33. This conjunction confirms our observations above.

has an essentially moral dimension to it. It is as God's people receive and share the word of God among one another that they are to become more and more holy (2 Cor 7:1), and "to grow up in every way into him who is the head, into Christ" (Eph 4:15). At the consummation, Christ will present his church to himself as a "pure virgin" (2 Cor 11:2), "without spot or wrinkle or any such thing ... holy and without blemish" (Eph 5:27). These examples have been drawn from the New Testament but could easily be multiplied with examples from the Old Testament. The ministry of the word of God and the pursuit of holiness are not accidental to, but essential to, the life and character of the people of God in every age.

Second, at the creation, God tasked human beings to "fill the earth," "subdue it," and "have dominion" over the lower creation (Gen 1:28). It is not accidental that Christ's commissions to his church routinely bid them to go out into and among the nations (see Matt 28:19; Luke 24:47; Acts 1:8). The task of the church does not immediately concern the church's sexual fruitfulness.[20] The people of God, rather, go out into the world to "make disciples" of the nations (Matt 28:19). In this way, the church multiplies and expands, as Acts so frequently reminds us (Acts 2:41, 47; 4:4; 5:14; 6:1, 2, 7; 9:31; 16:5). The apostle Paul even speaks of the gospel's advance among the nations in terms of "bearing fruit and increasing" (Col 1:6).

Neither does the task of the church concern subduing the lower creation. Rather, in proclaiming the gospel of Christ to the nations, the people of God gather men and women from among the nations into willing submission to the risen Lord, Jesus Christ (Matt 28:18). Image-bearers, redeemed by the grace of God, gladly serve the Lord who created and redeemed them. In this way the words of the Old Testament prophets Habakkuk and Isaiah come to fulfillment: "The earth will be filled with the knowledge of the glory of the Lord as the waters cover the sea" (Hab 2:14; compare Isa 11:9).[21]

---

20. Although, godly parents are to raise their children "in the discipline and instruction of the Lord" (Eph 6:2). Fruitfulness in the estate of marriage remains a noble calling for believers—a fruitfulness that consists not merely in producing offspring, but in raising those children in the knowledge and direction of God in Christ.

21. These tasks of the people of God were true even under the old covenant, *mutatis mutandis*. The Old Testament's emphasis upon and concern with sexual reproduction in the people of God prior to the new covenant was not an end in itself. God was always concerned that his growing people be "a holy nation" (Exod 19:6), exhibiting to the nations around her the character of their covenant God (Deut 4:4–8). God intended for his knowledge to diffuse from Israel to the nations, in whose midst he had set her (Ezek 5:5). Sadly, the reverse

Third, image-bearers are necessarily relational beings, engaging one another and their God. This consideration alone warrants the conclusion that, from the creation, God had never intended his image-bearers to live in isolation from one another. On the contrary, he intended for them to live in community. Genesis 1:27–28 necessarily implies, and Genesis 2:23–25 explicitly confirms, that marriage is a good instituted at the creation for humanity. Marriage is not a punishment inflicted for sin, but an ordinance of God designed to promote the well-being of his image-bearers and to foster their endeavors in the wider world.

Significantly, the church not only is comprised of men and women who serve the Lord in the estate of marriage, but also is herself constituted as a spiritual family—a family that even includes both unmarried believers and the children of at least one believer. The frequent form of address in the letters of Paul—"brothers"—confirms this reality to the congregations of the early church. It reinforces the indispensably communal character of the lives of God's people. To be united to Christ, God's Son, is to be counted "sons and daughters" in relation to the Father (2 Cor 6:18)—sons by adoption in and for the sake of the Son, Jesus Christ (see Gal 4:4–5). And as sons of God in Jesus Christ, the people of God are brothers and sisters in relation to one another.

These horizontal relationships within the people of God are necessarily joined to and subservient to the vertical relationship that God establishes and maintains with each of his children in Christ. In Christ, and by the Spirit, God's new family now has "access ... to the Father" (Eph 2:18). We have communion and fellowship with the Triune God who, by his sovereign grace and power, has ushered us into the new creation by an act of new creation (2 Cor 5:17; 2 Cor 4:6).

CONCLUSION

Genesis 1 documents God's creation of the world ex nihilo in the space of six days. At its conclusion, there are only two human beings, Adam and Eve. The world is created "very good," and human beings are created in righteous integrity. At first glance, it might appear as though Genesis 1 has little or nothing to do with the

---

happened. Israel sought more and more to conform herself to the nations around her. In judgment, God removed her from the land and dispersed her among those very nations. Only in Christ and his finished work in history do God's purposes for human beings find their intended realization and consummation.

church. In reality, the account of creation in Genesis 1 establishes principles that will surface in God's redemptive work of new creation. The agency of the Spirit and the instrumentality of the divine word are central both to the creation and to the new creation. God's work of new creation fully takes into account the way in which he created human beings as bearing his image—ontologically, functionally, and relationally.

Any survey of creation—and of the church in relation to the creation—would be incomplete without a consideration of Genesis 2. The account of the creation of Adam and Eve in Genesis 2 serves to amplify and to extend some of the very principles we have observed from Genesis 1. In particular, Genesis 2 offers a glimpse into the purpose for which God made the world and the goal that he intended for it. That purpose and goal, we will see, is foundational to a well-formed biblical ecclesiology.

FURTHER READING

Beale, G. K. *New Testament Biblical Theology: The Unfolding of the Old Testament in the New* (Grand Rapids: Baker Academic, 2011). Beale is a leading contemporary Reformed biblical theologian. He especially explores the ways in which the creation narratives of Genesis 1–2 underlie the teaching of the New Testament.

Hoekema, Anthony. *Created in God's Image*. Grand Rapids: Eerdmans, 1994. A contemporary treatment of the doctrine of anthropology that gives particular attention to human beings as made in the image of God.

Kuyper, Abraham. *The Work of the Holy Spirit*. Translated by Henri De Vries. New York: Funk & Wagnalls, 1900. Alongside Bavinck and Warfield, Kuyper was a leading Reformed theologian at the turn of the twentieth century. His discussion of the person and work of the Spirit is valuable for its comprehensiveness, for its integration of biblical theology and systematic theology, and for the way it provides a foundation for thinking biblically about the people of God.

II

EDEN: BEGINNINGS OF THE CHURCH

GENESIS 2:4–25 SERVES AS AN account of the creation that complements that of Genesis 1:1–2:3. It is a closer look at the events of the sixth day of creation, particularly the creation of the first man and the first woman. In this chapter, we will explore two callings that God assigns to human beings in Genesis 2:4–25—labor and marriage. We will furthermore reflect upon how Genesis 1 and 2 together point to the worship of God as the apex of human existence and endeavor. We will also explore the covenant that God establishes with Adam in Genesis 2:4–25 as the mechanism by which humanity was to be eschatologically advanced to the goal of its existence. Each of these three areas—labor and marriage, worship, covenant—is foundational to the way in which we think about the people of God across human history. We will see that the ordinance of labor anticipates the church's identity as a kingdom of priests; the ordinance of marriage anticipates the relationship between Christ and the church; and the ordinance of worship constitutes the foundation for the worship of God's people in every age. We will also see the way in which the covenant of works sets the stage for the covenant of grace, in which God gathers to himself a people in Christ.

LABOR AND MARRIAGE

Labor

IN GENESIS 1, GOD ASSIGNS, in general fashion, the callings of labor and marriage to human beings. In Genesis 1:28, God grants human beings "dominion" over the lower creation, and then immediately tells them, "I have given you every plant yielding seed that is on the face of all the earth, and every tree with seed in its fruit. You shall have them for food" (Gen 1:29). To be sure, the emphasis of this verse is upon the kind provision of God for human beings.[1] Even so, the unspoken assumption is that humans will have to exert planning and effort in order to secure the food that God has graciously provided them. Human beings will need to work in order to eat. Accompanying the call to labor is the call to marriage. In Genesis 1:27, God creates human beings "male and female." In the following verses, he tells Adam and Eve, "Be fruitful and multiply" (Gen 1:28). As Genesis 2 will make clear, the divinely-stipulated context for the command to procreate is the institution of marriage. Labor, then, is not undertaken in solitude but in the context of divinely-appointed relationships.

Genesis 2:4–25 clarifies and amplifies this particular calling of labor. In Genesis 2:8, we learn that "the Lord God planted a garden in Eden, in the east, and there he put the man whom he had formed." There, "the Lord God made to spring up every tree that is pleasant to the sight and good for food" (Gen 2:9). This garden, then, will be a suitable dwelling place for the man whom God has created (Gen 2:7). God does not set Adam free to roam the world. He places him in a habitation that is bounded and set apart from the rest of the world. Here, he will have the food that God has graciously committed to provide (see Gen 1:29).

But Adam is not to be idle in this garden. We read that "the Lord God took the man and put him in the garden of Eden to work it and keep it" (Gen 2:15). God calls Adam to labor in this particular space in the creation. It is in this setting that Adam is to carry out the divine calling to exercise "dominion" over the lower creation (Gen 1:28).[2] Furthermore, as commentators have noted, the verbs "work" (עבד) and "keep" (שמר) in Genesis 2:15 appear "elsewhere in the Pentateuch [to] describe activity only of priests."[3] Even if the text does not explicitly identify Eden as a temple, and Adam as its priest, we must certainly recognize that Moses is consciously describing

1. Derek Kidner, *Genesis*, TOTC (Downers Grove, IL: InterVarsity, 1967), 52.

2. G. K. Beale, *A New Testament Biblical Theology: The Unfolding of the Old Testament in the New* (Grand Rapids: Baker Academic, 2011), 34.

3. Bruce Waltke, *Genesis: A Commentary* (Grand Rapids: Zondervan, 2001), 87. Wenham cites Num 3:7–8, 8:26, and 18:5–6 as texts in which these "two terms are juxtaposed," and that in a specifically cultic context, *Genesis 1–15*, WBC 1 (Waco, TX: Word, 1987), 67.

Eden in terms that will later come to describe the tabernacle and temple, and the priestly service that takes place in them.[4] The effect of this analogy is to underscore Adam's labor as rendered in sincere devotion to the Lord God himself.

The New Testament employs similarly analogous priestly language to describe the this-worldly endeavors of the people of God. Paul tells the Romans "to present your bodies as a living sacrifice, holy and acceptable to God, which is your spiritual worship" (Rom 12:1). Paul's statements in Romans 12:1 are "a development of Rom. 6:13, 16, 19," and, with Romans 12:2, serve as an "antithesis to [Rom] 1:18–28."[5] Given that Paul's descriptions of human engagement in the world in both Romans 1 and Romans 6 are global and wide-ranging, Paul's interests in Romans 12:1 are no less global and wide-ranging. Believers are to conceive of all that they do in God's world in priestly terms.

Significantly, Paul yokes priestly activity in Romans 12:1 to the mind: "Do not be conformed to this world, but be transformed by the renewal of your mind, that by testing you may discern what is the will of God, what is good and acceptable and perfect" (Rom 12:1). Just as Adam's labors in the garden were to be ordered by the express commands of God (Gen 1:28–30; 2:15–16), so believers' labors in "this age" (Rom 12:2, ESV mg) are to be ordered by the express commands of God. Believers learn of those commands through the ministry of the word of God in the church. The church of Jesus Christ proclaims the "whole counsel of God" (Acts 20:27)

---

4. On Eden as a temple, see especially G. K. Beale, *The Temple and the Church's Mission: A Biblical Theology of the Dwelling Place of God*, NSBT 17 (Downers Grove, IL: InterVarsity Press, 2004), and "Eden, the Temple, and the Church's Mission in the New Creation" *JETS* 48 (2005): 5–31, esp. 7–12. For reservations about this identification, see Daniel I. Block, "Eden: A Temple? A Reassessment of the Biblical Evidence," in *From Creation to New Creation: Biblical Theology & Exegesis: Essays in Honor of G. K. Beale*, ed. Daniel M. Gurtner and Benjamin L. Gladd (Peabody, MA: Hendrickson, 2013), 3–29. One compelling reservation against identifying Eden/Adam as temple/priest stems from the fact that priests' labors in Scripture assume sin on the part of those on behalf of whom they serve before God, on which see Geerhardus Vos, *Redemptive History and Biblical Interpretation: The Shorter Writings of Geerhardus Vos* (Phillipsburg, NJ: P&R, 1980), 138–41. Genesis 2 is describing, of course, Adam in his prelapsarian state.

5. Beale, *New Testament Biblical Theology*, 255, 375. See the comparable statement at Hebrews 13:15–16, "Through him then let us continually offer up a sacrifice of praise to God, that is, the fruit of lips that acknowledge his name. Do not neglect to do good and to share what you have, for such sacrifices are pleasing to God."

so that believers may apply that word in the context of their this-worldly callings, not least their labors.

Marriage

GENESIS 1 DOCUMENTS THE CREATION of man "male and female" and the divine command to "be fruitful and multiply" (Gen 1:27, 28). It is in Genesis 2:4–25 that God establishes the framework within which men and women are to carry out that command. In Genesis 2:18 God declares, "It is not good that the man should be alone; I will make him a helper fit for him." For the first time in Genesis, God declares a state of affairs to be "not good" (לֹא־טוֹב). God will therefore make for the man "a helper fit for him" (עֵזֶר כְּנֶגְדּוֹ). This expression indicates that "the man has governmental priority," even as "both sexes are mutually dependent on each other."[6]

When God presents the woman to Adam, Adam responds in poetic rapture (Gen 2:22–23).[7] Neither the woman nor the institution of marriage is a burden to Adam, but rather a delight.[8] The following verse clarifies the prescriptive character of God's action: "Therefore a man shall leave his father and his mother and hold fast to his wife, and they shall become one flesh" (Gen 2:24).[9] The marital union, insofar as it is said to be "one flesh," is unique among all human relationships. This relationship "has priority over the bond of procreation" insofar as it entails a forsaking of one's parents.[10] This union is "exclusive," in that it is not open to any except this one man and this one woman, and it is "permanent" in that within this union the man "hold[s] fast to his wife."[11]

---

6. Waltke, *Genesis: A Commentary*, 88.

7. For poetic analysis of Genesis 2:23, see Wenham, *Genesis 1–15*, WBC 1 (Word: Waco, 1987), 70.

8. Responding to the medieval ideal of the celibate life, Calvin concludes, "To these wicked suggestions of Satan let the faithful learn to oppose this declaration of God, by which he ordains the conjugal life for man, not to his destruction, but to his salvation," *Commentaries on the First Book of Moses Called Genesis*, trans. John King, 2 vols. (repr., Grand Rapids: Baker, 1996), 1.129.

9. See Gordon Hugenberger, *Marriage as a Covenant: Biblical Law and Ethics as Developed from Malachi*, VTSup 52 (Leiden: Brill, 1994), 151–56. This prescription is reinforced by Jesus in his public teaching (Matt 19:4–6), and by the apostle Paul (Eph 5:31).

10. Waltke, *Genesis: A Commentary*, 90.

11. Derek Kidner, *Genesis: An Introduction and Commentary*, TOTC (Downers Grove, IL: InterVarsity Press, 1967), 66. Wenham notes that the verb "hold fast" carries the senses both of "passion and permanence," *Genesis*, 71.

Later revelation characterizes the covenantal relationship between God and his people in marital terms. In fact, the verbs "forsake" and "stick" come to be "use[d] ... in the context of Israel's covenant with the Lord."[12] As we will see in later chapters, God frequently employs the marital analogy when, through the canonical Prophets, he indicts his people, Israel, for covenantal treachery (see, for example, Hos 2:1–23). But the marital analogy is not merely or even primarily a device that God employs to express his displeasure for Israel's sin and rebellion. It is first and foremost an expression of the preeminent, exclusive, and permanent bond that God establishes with his people in a covenant relationship. As such, the institution of marriage in Genesis 2 serves as the foundation of this corporate and covenantal description of the people of God.

The apostle Paul grounds the relationship of the church (as "body") to Christ (as "head") in God's institution of marriage at Genesis 2:24 (see Eph 5:23, 31). After citing Genesis 2:24 in Ephesians 5:31, Paul appends an explanation: "This mystery is profound, and I am saying that it refers to Christ and the church" (Eph 5:32). In describing Genesis 2:24 in terms of a "profound ... mystery," Paul declares that "the pattern wherein a man leaves his family and becomes one with a wife contains within it a reflection of a grander marriage: Christ leaving his heavenly home and Father and becoming one with the church."[13] That is to say, "Christ is the ultimate eschatological 'man' (ideal Adam), and the church is the ultimate, eschatological bride."[14] Such identifications are not *ex post facto* reflections upon Genesis 2. Paul, rather, sees these identifications as eschatologically embedded in the text of Genesis 2 itself, so much so that "Gen 2:24 is not primarily about the relationship of husbands to their wives but rather of Christ to the church."[15]

It is no surprise, then, to see at the consummation of the history of redemption the apostle John witness "the holy city, new Jerusalem, coming down out of heaven from God, prepared as a bride adorned for her husband" (Rev 21:2), followed by an extended description of "the Bride, the wife of

---

12. Wenham, *Genesis 1–15*, 71.
13. Beale, *New Testament Biblical Theology*, 881.
14. Beale, *New Testament Biblical Theology*, 882.
15. Beale, *New Testament Biblical Theology*, 881.

the Lamb" (21:9, 10–21). The consummation, in fact, is termed "the marriage of the Lamb" to "his Bride [made] ready" (19:7).

Marriage, then, is a relationship established at the creation for the good of God's image-bearers. It uniquely bonds one man and one woman together in a permanent, preeminent, voluntary, and exclusive union. It is in light of such characteristics as these that marriage comes to describe the covenantal relationship between God and his people. This description is found in the Old Testament prophets, and it is found within the New Testament. The apostle Paul emphasizes that it is Christ and his church that assign meaning to marriage and not the reverse. The apostle John helps us to see that "marriage" is a strand within a biblical theology of the church that runs directly and explicitly from creation to new creation.

WORSHIP

THE ACCOUNT OF THE CREATION of humanity in Genesis 1 highlights, as we have seen, labor and marriage as standing ordinances for human beings. As important as these ordinances are for human beings to bring to expression the image of God, they are not ultimate with respect to the purposes for which God has created humanity. The opening chapters of Genesis teach that it is worship that is the highest task that God assigns to human beings. It is this point that is underscored in Genesis 2:1–3.[16]

> Thus the heavens and the earth were finished, and all the host of them. And on the seventh day God finished his work that he had done, and he rested on the seventh day from all his work that he had done. So God blessed the seventh day and made it holy, because on it God rested from all his work that he had done in creation. (Gen 2:1–3)

16. The following five paragraphs have been adapted from my *The Sabbath as Rest and Hope for the People of God*, SSBT (Wheaton, IL: Crossway, 2022).

Genesis 2:1–3

THESE VERSES CONCLUDE THE ACCOUNT of God's creation of the world, which began at Genesis 1:1.[17] In the first place, they tell us that the work of creation is completed: "The heavens and the earth were finished, and all the host of them" (2:1; compare 1:2, 30). This work was done in six days; therefore the seventh day will be different. It is not a day of work for God, but rest, for "he rested on the seventh day from all his work that he had done," and "on [the seventh day], God rested from all his work that he had done in creation" (Gen 2:2, 3).

Second, this day is set apart from the previous six days in at least three ways. First, the verb translated "rested" (שׁבת) in Genesis 2:2, 3 is related to the Hebrew noun translated "Sabbath" (שַׁבָּת). There is, therefore, an implicit connection established between God's rest and what later revelation will call the "Sabbath." Second, it is a day that "God blessed" (2:3). Earlier, God is said to have "blessed" the birds and the sea creatures, and to have "blessed" Adam and Eve at their creation (1:22, 28). In each case that benediction is followed by the command, "be fruitful and multiply and fill ..." (1:22, 28). When God blesses the seventh day, our expectation is that this day will be marked by fruitfulness and fullness appropriate to that day. Third, God "made [the seventh day] holy" (2:3) (וַיְקַדֵּשׁ). This is the first time in Genesis that God is said to make something "holy." God, then, makes this seventh day different from the other six days. What distinguishes the "holy" seventh day is that it is set apart for purposes of worship.[18]

This observation raises the question, "What kind of worship is in view?" The answer of Genesis is human beings' worship of the

---

17. The next verse begins with the phrase, "These are the generations ... " Commentators often point out that this clause serves as the marker of a new section within Genesis (see 5:1; 6:9; 10:1; 11:10; 11:27; 25:12; 25:19; 36:1; 36:9; 37:2). The first portion of the section that follows, Genesis 2:4–25, offers a more detailed account of the way in which God created the first humans, Adam and Eve, on the sixth day (compare 1:26–31).

18. Gregory K. Beale, *A New Testament Biblical Theology*, 778. As Beale notes, "The use of the Piel stem of the Hebrew word *qādaš* found in Genesis 2:3, which is used the most throughout the OT, almost always refers to setting apart humans or things for human cultic use. However, the only days said to be 'set apart' or 'holy' in the OT are Sabbaths and various festival days," Beale, *A New Testament Biblical* Theology, 778.

God who made them. As those who bear the image of God, people are uniquely capable among all the creatures mentioned in Genesis 1:1–2:3 of fellowship and communion with God.[19] The worship for which God provides in Genesis 2:1–3 is intended for his image-bearers to have fellowship with him.[20] Thus, "humanity ... is not the culmination of creation, but rather humanity in Sabbath day communion with God."[21]

Genesis 1:1–2:3, in fact, presents a two-fold imitation of God on the part of his image-bearers. As we have seen, God creates human beings to work, and God exercises dominion over the works of his hands. Human beings take up labor in imitation of the God who fills the world and rules over the world. But it would be a mistake to say that Genesis 1:1–2:3 conceives no higher human imitation of God than labor. As human beings imitate God at work, so also they are to imitate God at rest.[22] As God made the world and everything in it within the space of six days, and rested the seventh day, so human beings are to engage in six days of labor and one day of holy resting.

God, then, does not bless the seventh day for his own sake, but for humanity's sake. He is setting apart this one day in seven to be a regular day of rest in the weekly cycle of human existence. He is, in effect, commanding human beings to observe the Sabbath. We have noted above that the word translated "made ... holy" (וַיְקַדֵּשׁ) frequently relates to the worship of God in the Old Testament.[23] This observation clarifies that human beings are to observe this seventh day as a day devoted to the worship of God. As it is dedicated to the worship of God, the Sabbath promises blessing to human beings who comply with this divine command.

While there is an indispensably, even fundamentally, individual dimension to the worship of God, Genesis 1 and 2 gesture to what later revelation will declare explicitly—that God intends for his worship to

19. So rightly L. Michael Morales, *Who Shall Ascend the Mountain of the Lord? A Biblical Theology of the Book of Leviticus*, NSBT 37 (Downers Grove, IL: InterVarsity Press, 2015), 46.

20. "That benediction is nothing else than a solemn consecration, by which God claims for himself the meditations and employments of men on the seventh day," Calvin, *Genesis*, 1.105.

21. Morales, *Who Shall Ascend*, 47.

22. "God rested, then he blessed this rest, that in all ages it might be held sacred among men: or he dedicated every seventh day to rest, that his own example might be a perpetual rule," Calvin, *Genesis*, 1.106.

23. See note 18 above.

be undertaken corporately and publicly. Neither of the other two creation ordinances—labor and marriage—is a solitary enterprise. The divine call to humans to "be fruitful and multiply and fill the earth and subdue it, and have dominion ..." (Gen 1:28) immediately follows the statement that God "created [humankind] male and female" (Gen 1:27). The implication is that labor is something that human beings will undertake together—male and female. This implication is made explicit in Genesis 2:18 when God says, "It is not good that the man should be alone; I will make him a helper fit for him." Eve, then, will come alongside Adam as he "works" and "keeps" the garden (Gen 2:15). Marriage, by definition, is an institution that is non-solitary. It establishes a permanent union between one man and one woman (Gen 2:23–25). Our expectation, then, is that the transcendent ordinance of worship will similarly require the assembling together of human beings.

COVENANT

God created human beings to share in his seventh-day rest. Therefore, he appointed for them at the creation a weekly day of holy resting. By observing this day, humans can come to experience the blessing that God has tied to it.

This weekly cycle orders the temporal life of human beings. But in Genesis 2, God establishes a covenant with Adam that sets before him eternal life consisting in fellowship and communion with God. This covenant, and Adam's breach of it through his first transgression, supplies critical foundational considerations for a biblical ecclesiology.

To assert a covenant in Genesis 2 is a controversial claim. After all, the word "covenant" does not appear in Genesis before Genesis 6:18 ("But I will establish my covenant with you ..."). A *prima facie* reading of the text of Genesis does not appear to support the existence of a covenant in Genesis 2.[24] But although the term "covenant" does not appear in Genesis 2, the concept is very much present in Genesis 2:16–17.[25]

---

24. A point argued with some emphasis by Paul R. Williamson, *Sealed with an Oath: Covenant in God's Unfolding Purpose*, NSBT 23 (Downers Grove, IL: InterVarsity Press, 2007), 72.

25. In this respect, the arrangement that God establishes with Adam in Genesis 2 is comparable to the arrangement that God establishes with David in 2 Samuel 7. The latter text does not refer to God's promises to David as a "covenant," but the absence of the term does not necessitate the conclusion that the arrangement described in this text is not a covenant.

Genesis 2:16–17

Having created Adam and established a relationship with him as his Sovereign, God proceeds to formalize that relationship in solemn terms. He does so by setting before Adam promises and corresponding obligations. He also sets before Adam a visible sign or pledge of what he had promised to Adam in covenant. We will look at these dimensions of this covenant between God and Adam in Genesis 2.

We should first note that the covenant is between God and Adam: "And the Lord God commanded the man, saying …" (Gen 2:16). Eve has not yet been created. Even after God creates her, Eve will not stand in covenantal relationship to God in the way that Adam does. Adam stands as a representative person in covenant with God. That is, Adam's actions will affect the lives and destiny of those whom he represents. The penalty of death (Gen 2:17) is inflicted not only upon Adam ("and he died," Gen 5:5), but also upon all his natural posterity ("and he died," Gen 5:8 *et passim*). The first sin of Adam is so imputed to his natural posterity that they bear the legal consequences for that sin, namely, death.[26] As the apostle Paul pithily expresses the point, "For … by a man came death. … For as in Adam all die" (1 Cor 15:21, 22; compare Rom 5:12–21). Party to this creation covenant, then, are God and Adam, who stands as the representative of his natural posterity.

God introduces his covenantal command by reminding Adam, "You may surely eat of every tree of the garden" (Gen 2:16b). Framing the command, then, is a reminder of God's abundant generosity toward Adam in the garden (compare Gen 2:9). The command proceeds from a God who is both sovereign and benevolent toward his creature.

Subsequent revelation explicitly terms this arrangement as a covenant (see Pss 89:3, 28, 34, 39; Pss 132:11, 12). Further, Hosea 6:7 arguably refers to an Adamic covenant in Genesis 2, on which see Byron G. Curtis, "Hosea 6:7 and the Covenant-Breaking like/at Adam," in *The Law Is Not of Faith: Essays on Works and Grace in the Mosaic Covenant*, ed. Bryan D. Estelle, John V. Fesko, and David VanDrunen (Phillipsburg, NJ: P&R, 2009), 170–209, and Peter J. Gentry and Stephen J. Wellum, *Kingdom through Covenant: A Biblical Theological Understanding of the Covenants*, 2nd ed. (Wheaton, IL: Crossway, 2018), 254–57. The real question is whether the elements essential to a covenant are present in the text of Genesis 2.

26. For a defense of the imputation of Adam's sin to his posterity, see John Murray, *The Imputation of Adam's Sin* (Phillipsburg, NJ: P&R, 1977), and John V. Fesko, *Death in Adam, Life in Christ: The Doctrine of Imputation* (Fearn, UK: Mentor, 2016).

The command itself is a direct one, "but of the tree of the knowledge of good and evil you shall not eat" (Gen 2:17). Adam may eat of any tree in the garden, but he may not eat from "the tree of the knowledge of good and evil." God assigns no reason to the prohibition. "For the simple practical purpose of this first fundamental lesson it was necessary to stake everything upon the unreasoned will of God."[27] This particular command—the distinguishing command of the covenant that God establishes in Genesis 2:16–17—is a supreme test of Adam's obedience and allegiance to God the Lawgiver.

It must be remembered that, while the specific positive command given in the form of a prohibition was the distinguishing command of this covenant, it was not the sole command of this covenant.[28] Adam, created in the image of God, was "righteous" from the moment of his creation. Under this covenant, Adam was to continue in full, willing, conscious conformity to the righteous character of God. The superadded, positive command served, in Tertullian's words, as "the matrix of all God's precepts" insofar as his keeping or breaking it revealed his ultimate allegiance and devotion—to God or to self.[29]

Attending this command is a threatened sanction, "for in the day you eat of it you shall surely die" (Gen 2:17). God here conjoins disobedience with its penalty, death. To be sure, the death threatened is biological—the temporary separation of soul and body (compare Gen 2:7). But biological death hardly plumbs the deepest sense of "death" in Genesis 2:17. In an act of judgment, Adam is banished from the garden of Eden "to work the ground from which he was taken," and judicially barred from re-entry (Gen 3:23–24). The expression "ground from which he was taken" evokes Genesis 3:19, which associates the "ground" from which Adam was "taken" with death.[30]

27. Geerhardus Vos, *Biblical Theology: Old and New Testaments* (Edinburgh: Banner of Truth, 1975), 32.

28. F. Turretin explains that this command is "positive" in that it "did not bind man from the nature of the thing (which was in itself indifferent), but from the mere will of God." "It is also called 'symbolic,'" he continues, "because it was given for a symbol and trial of the obedience of man," *Institutes of Elenctic Theology*, trans. George M. Giger, ed. James T. Dennison, Jr., 3 vols. (Phillipsburg, NJ: P&R, 1992–1997), 1.579 (=L 8.4.4).

29. Tertullian, *An Answer to the Jews* 2, ANF 3:152, cited at Turretin, *Institutes*, 1.579.

30. Vos, *Biblical Theology*, 40.

Therefore, "the root of death is in having been sent forth from God," that is, to be separated from the favorable presence of God.[31]

The covenant that God establishes with Adam is cast in largely negative terms—a prohibition with an attendant threat. It would be a mistake, however, to conceive this covenant in *exclusively* negative terms. Necessarily implied in the prohibition is a promise—had Adam continued in obedience to God during this period of testing, God would have granted him "life." If death is the wage of sin (Rom 6:23), then life is the reward of obedience. In this covenant of "works," Adam would have secured the "life" that God had pledged to give to him for his obedience.

But that raises the question, How could Adam, created a "living creature" (Gen 2:7), receive life as the reward for his obedience? Wasn't he already alive? That "life" was the reward given to a living creature serves to highlight an important feature of Adam's circumstances at the creation. Adam certainly enjoyed fellowship and communion with God in his pre-fallen state. Later in Genesis, and outside Genesis, the "garden of Eden" (Gen 2:15) is called the "garden of the Lord" or the "garden of God" (Gen 13:10; Ezek 28:13, 31:8, 31:9; compare Isa 51:3). That is to say, this garden is characterized by the presence of the God who established it, a point confirmed by the fact that God is described as "walking in the garden in the cool of the day" (Gen 3:8). We therefore should understand the "life" that Adam enjoyed in the garden in terms of his communion with God there.

The "life" that Adam possessed at creation was subject to forfeiture, as events would demonstrate. But the "life" that God held out to Adam in this first covenant was *confirmed* and *unlosable* life and was no less *heightened* life, the fullness of life in eternal communion with God. It is precisely this life that the last Adam, Christ, has won for his people by his obedience and death, and freely gives to them by the Spirit.[32] Had Adam continued in obedience to God, he would have secured this life, according to the terms of the covenant that God established with him. And he would have secured it not only for himself but also for all whom he represented.

31. Vos, *Biblical Theology*, 40.

32. "Since Christ died that through him we might recover what we lost in Adam and merited for us eternal life, it is necessary that it should have been lost for us in Adam and that Adam would have attained it, if he had persevered in obedience," Turretin, *Institutes*, 1.584 (=L.8.6.5).

It is this heightened, eschatological "life" that God set before Adam in this covenant. This positive dimension of the covenant of works is underscored by the presence of another tree in the garden, the "tree of life" (Gen 2:9). As the "tree of knowledge of good and evil" has covenantal significance, so also does the "tree of life"—the only two trees distinguished by name in Eden (Gen 2:9). The "tree of life" points to the "higher, the unchangeable, the eternal life" that God held out to Adam as the reward for his obedience.[33] God's words in Genesis 3:22 ("Now, lest he reach out his hand and take also of the tree of life and eat, and live forever—") indicate that Adam had not eaten of that tree during his period of probation in the garden. The result of eating of the tree—"and live forever"—is "sacramental," but only "for the time after the probation" of Adam.[34] Its presence in the garden during Adam's probation, as Jonathan Edwards notes, was intended "that man might be the more assured of his reward in case of his obedience, and that this consideration might engage his spirit the more earnestly to seek that he might come to taste of it. 'Tis probable that God told Adam of this tree to encourage his obedience."[35]

The covenant of works provides a critical framework to understanding the Scripture's teaching on the people of God. Had Adam sustained his probation in the garden, he would have received "life" as the reward for his obedience. That is to say, he would have entered immediately into heightened and confirmed eschatological life in communion with God. Because Adam was a representative man in covenant with God, his obedience would have been imputed to his posterity. The outcome of Adam's obedience, then, would have been the confirmation of the human race in righteousness and their unbroken participation in fellowship with God.

---

33. Vos, *Biblical Theology*, 28. As confirmation, Vos points to the reappearance of the tree of life in Revelation 2:7: "It is to 'him that overcometh' that God promises to give of the tree of life in the midst of paradise," *Biblical Theology*, 28. On the ways in which seventeenth-century Reformed theologians understood the "tree of life," see Heinrich Heppe, *Reformed Dogmatics Set Out and Illustrated from the Sources*, trans. G. T. Thomson (1950; repr., Grand Rapids: Baker Academic, 1978), 296–98.

34. Heppe, *Reformed Dogmatics*, 296–98.

35. Jonathan Edwards, "East of Eden" (Sermon on Genesis 3:24), *Sermons and Discourses 1730–1733*, WJE 17:338. Edwards clarifies earlier in this sermon that Adam would have eaten of this tree only "after his trial," Edwards, "East of Eden," WJE 17:338.

Even though these reflections are necessarily hypothetical, they serve to underscore an important point about the destiny of the human race (and of the whole creation). As Vos observes, "There is an absolute end posited for the universe before and apart from sin. The universe, as created, was only a beginning, the meaning of which was not perpetuation, but attainment."[36] The creation was destined to be filled with the glory of God, and image-bearers were destined for consummate communion with the Triune God. The institution of the Sabbath at the creation (Gen 2:1–2) was and remains a standing reminder of this goal.[37] Seen from this light, the covenant that God established with Adam (and, representatively, with his natural posterity) was a means to an end—to bring humanity to the eschatological goal set before it.[38] The covenant was designed to bring the human race into perpetual, eschatological life with God. Had Adam sustained his probation in this covenant, the people of God and the human race would have been entirely coextensive.

But Adam fell into sin and, with him, his natural posterity. This sin (and the events that lay in its wake) redirected the human race in profound ways. For one thing, the path to eschatological life via Adam's obedience was now forever closed. After exiling Adam from Eden, God stationed the "cherubim and a flaming sword that turned every way to guard the way to the tree of life" (Gen 3:24). In this way, sinners are judicially barred from attaining eternal life through their own obedience.[39]

Adam was driven from Eden in judgment, banished from the place where "God was uniquely present in all his life-giving power."[40] Human

---

36. Geerhardus Vos, *The Eschatology of the Old Testament*, ed. James T. Dennison, Jr. (Phillipsburg, NJ: P&R, 2001), 73.

37. "The Sabbath finds its prototype in the life and works of God. Thus, it means fulfillment; not cessation and weariness, but consummation. This rest of consummation was introduced into the life of man in order to show him his goal. Even in unfallen man the Sabbath was an eschatological sign because its meaning lies in the relation of man and God," Vos, *Eschatology of the Old Testament*, 75.

38. "The so-called 'Covenant of Works' was nothing but an embodiment of the Sabbatical principle. Had its probation been successful, then the sacramental Sabbath would have passed over into the reality it typified." *Biblical Theology*, 140.

39. Kidner, *Genesis*, 72.

40. Wenham, *Genesis 1–15*, 86. Although, as Calvin notes, "Adam was not so dejected as to be left without hope of pardon. ... He was excommunicated from the tree of life, but a new remedy was offered him in sacrifices," *Genesis* 1.185.

beings, in Adam, are similarly estranged from God. And, estranged from God, they come to be estranged from one another, a point that is vividly demonstrated in Cain's fratricidal murder of Abel in the next chapter. The roots of human enmity and estrangement, then, lie in humans' willful estrangement from God because of their sin. Sin is corrosive and destructive of human community. Left to itself, sin drives human beings into selfish isolation and violent conflict.

In God's mercy, that is not the last word on the human race. God abandons neither the goal that he has set for human beings nor the covenantal mechanism designed to bring human beings to that goal. What Adam failed to do, the last Adam will accomplish. In Adam, sinners have transgressed the law of God and merited the law's just penalty, eternal death (Rom 6:23). In dying on the cross for his people, Christ bears that penalty in his own humanity (Gal 3:10, 13; Rom 8:3; Heb 9:26). Christ's penal and atoning death satisfies the justice of God on behalf of his people. In Adam, sinners have failed to observe the law of God and thus to find life by that obedience (Lev 18:5; Gal 3:12; Rom 10:5). In obeying the law in the place of his people, Christ has fulfilled its requirements and merited its reward, namely, eternal life (Rom 8:4; Rom 5:17, 19). In his death and resurrection, Christ conquered death and entered victoriously into eschatological life (Col 2:13–15; Acts 2:24; 1 Cor 15:54–57). The last Adam, who possesses and is possessed by the life-giving Spirit of God (1 Cor 15:45) fully poured out this Spirit on all kinds of people on the day of Pentecost. Therefore, any sinner, united to Christ by the Spirit and through faith, begins to experience the life of the age to come now, and has the assurance of the consummate experience of life at the resurrection of his body at the last day.

Sinners are saved one by one, to be sure, but each saved person is necessarily engrafted into the people of God (1 Cor 12:13). When a sinner is united to Christ he is at one and the same time united to his body. God, in other words, never deviates from his purpose to bring a *people* into eschatological life and communion with himself. The gospel will produce what Paul terms "fullness" of both Jew (Rom 11:12) and gentile (11:25). That is to say, in Christ, God secures for himself a full, redeemed humanity. Christ has purchased "people for God from every tribe and language and people and nation," making them "a kingdom and priests to our God," who "shall reign on earth" (Rev 5:9, 10; compare Rev 7:9).

CONCLUSION

How, then, does God accomplish this goal? He does it with another covenant, the covenant of grace. He begins by speaking a promise of his Son and his redemptive victory over sin and Satan (Gen 3:15). He then immediately begins to gather a people around that promise, starting with Adam and Eve. Indeed, the rest of the Scripture is taken up with these two realities—the progressive revelation of the saving promises concerning the last Adam; and the divine ingathering and upbuilding of a people set apart for himself and his service in this world. In the next several chapters, we will trace the beginnings of the ways in which God establishes a people for his glory.

FURTHER READING

Edwards, Jonathan. *A History of the Work of Redemption, The Works of Jonathan Edwards*, Volume 9, ed. John F. Wilson. New Haven: Yale, 1989. One of the first comprehensive attempts on American soil to explore the work of redemption diachronically. As such, it anticipates the biblical and theological writings of Reformed authors in the nineteenth and twentieth centuries.

Murray, John. *Principles of Conduct: Aspects of Biblical Ethics.* Grand Rapids: Eerdmans, 1957. Murray was the founding systematic theologian at Westminster Theological Seminary. The opening chapters of this book address in some depth the creation ordinances.

Vos, Geerhardus. *Biblical Theology: Old and New Testaments.* Edinburgh: Banner of Truth, 1975. Vos was the contemporary of B. B. Warfield at Princeton Theological Seminary and a pioneer of the discipline of biblical theology within American Presbyterianism. The early chapters of this work show how integral the covenant of works is to the architecture of the biblical theology of Scripture.

III

ABRAHAM: COVENANTAL ESTABLISHMENT OF THE CHURCH

God's goal in creation is to glorify himself through a people confirmed in their dedication to his worship and service. God establishes the covenant of works with Adam so that Adam might bring himself and his posterity to this goal. At first glance, Adam's fall into sin appears to derail those plans insofar as, in Adam, human beings are estranged from God and from one another. In reality, the fall is God's appointed means to bring his goal to historical realization. It will not be Adam but the last Adam who advances humanity to its eschatological destination. In Christ, God will, in "the fullness of time ... unite all things in him, things in heaven and things on earth" (Eph 1:10; compare Col 1:20).[1] It is Christ, the mediatorial head of a new humanity, who will establish the people of God in the new creation. In this way, God secures for himself a people unreservedly dedicated to his glory (1 Cor 10:31).

1. Note the observations of John Owen on this text, "To answer all the ends of this *new Head* of God's *re-collected* family, all power in heaven and earth, all fulness of grace and glory, is committed unto him. There is no communication from God, no act of rule towards this family, no supply of virtue, power, grace, or goodness unto angels or men, but what is immediately from this new head whereinto they are gathered. In him they all consist, on him do they depend, unto him are they subject; in their relation unto him doth their peace, union, and agreement among themselves consist. This is *the recapitulation of all things* intended by the apostle," John Owen, "Meditations and Discourses on the Glory of Christ," *The Works of John Owen*, ed. William H. Goold, 16 vols. (1850–1853; repr., Edinburgh: Banner of Truth, 1965), 1:371.

Although God saves sinners in every age through the work of Christ, God does not send Christ into the world immediately. Before he sends Christ, God makes promises that progressively reveal Christ with increasing fullness and clarity. In fact, the totality of God's promises in the Old Testament point to the person and work of Jesus Christ (2 Cor 1:20).

The first of these promises appears when God exiles Adam from Eden in judgment. Adam, in other word, leaves Eden with a gospel promise in tow. This promise—*protoevangelium* (the first proclamation of the gospel)—is the seed from which all subsequent promises will blossom and grow.

In this chapter, we will explore that promise and, particularly, its implications for the people of God in this stage of redemptive history. We will then reflect upon the state and condition of God's people between the exile of Adam and the call of Abram. Finally, we will explore the covenant that God makes with Abraham.

PROTOEVANGELIUM

THE FIRST ANNOUNCEMENT OF EVANGELICAL promise in Scripture is in many ways an unexpected one. Having found Adam and Eve "hid[ing] themselves from the presence of the Lord God among the trees of the garden" (Gen 3:8), God asks them a series of questions in what amounts to a formal judicial inquiry (Gen 3:9–13).[2] God then proceeds to address the serpent (Gen 3:14–15), the woman (Gen 3:16), and the man (Gen 3:17–19)—"in the same sequence as that in which the sin had been committed" (see Gen 3:1–7).[3] Of the three, however, only the serpent, is "cursed" of God (Gen 3:14).[4] Adam and Eve will experience the effects of sin, up to and including death (Gen 3:19), but contrary to expectation they do not emerge from this inquiry under the curse of God.

2. Bruce Waltke, *Genesis: A Commentary* (Grand Rapids: Zondervan, 2001), 92. As Waltke notes, the intent of this line of questioning is to "induc[e] them to confess their guilt." Waltke, *Genesis*, 92.

3. Geerhardus Vos, *Biblical Theology: Old and New Testaments* (Edinburgh: Banner of Truth, 1975), 42.

4. The same verb is used in Genesis 3:17 when God speaks to Adam, but it is not Adam who is cursed, but the ground that is "cursed" (אֲרוּרָה).

Genesis 3:15

THE REASON FOR THIS STATE of affairs is found in God's words to the serpent in Genesis 3:15, "I will put enmity between you and the woman, and between your offspring and her offspring; he shall bruise your head, and you shall bruise his heel." The serpent had won the allegiance of Eve away from God, but now God will "put enmity" between them—God does not "merely instigate or promote enmity; He sovereignly *puts* it."[5] This sovereign imposition of enmity will extend to the serpent's "offspring" and the woman's "offspring" (זֶרַע in both instances; in LXX, the word is translated σπέρμα). Paul's reading of this passage in Romans 16:20 confirms that "offspring" should be understood "collectively."[6] And yet, "offspring" should also be understood in reference to an "individual (cf. Gal 3:16)," that is, to "Jesus as the last Adam."[7]

The unfolding of this promise in the remainder of Scripture shows exactly how the individual and collective aspects of this promise are related. The serpent is a reference to Satan (see Rom 16:20; Rev 12:9). By nature, sinners in Adam are spiritually aligned with Satan, who tempted Eve to sin against God. In his sovereign grace, God is going to establish a people who are spiritually aligned against Satan and with God. Although they are the biological offspring of Eve, this biological descent does not account for their alignment with God. It is a spiritual division that accounts for this alignment, a division that is the result of the powerful and sovereign working of divine grace.

These antithetical allegiances will characterize human relationships for the remainder of human history. Cain's murder of Abel (Gen 4:1–26) is a graphic illustration of the outworking of this "enmity." Cain acts as he does, the apostle John explains, because he "was of the evil one" (1 John 3:12), that is, "the devil" (1 John 3:10), and because "his brother's [deeds were] righteous" (1 John 3:12).

---

5. Vos, *Biblical Theology*, 42.

6. Vos, *The Eschatology of the Old Testament*, ed. James T. Dennison, Jr. (Phillipsburg, NJ: P&R, 2001), 77.

7. Derek Kidner, *Genesis: An Introduction and Commentary*, TOTC (Downers Grove, IL: InterVarsity Press, 1967), 71.

But this ongoing struggle or conflict will reach its acme in the conflict of Satan with a single descendent of Eve, Jesus Christ.[8] In this conflict, which the New Testament locates at the cross, Christ, in his death, gets the victory over Satan (see John 12:31; 16:11; Col 2:15; Heb 2:14). Here at the cross, Christ's "heel" is "bruise[d]," while Satan's "head" is "bruise[d]" (Gen 3:15). That is to say, in dying to pay the penalty for his people's sin, Jesus delivers to Satan a mortal blow. Rescued from the guilt and dominion of sin through the work of Christ, the people of God are no longer subject to the tyrannical dominion of Satan.

We have, then, embedded in this first gospel promise the origin of the people of God as the company of the redeemed. God is going to separate from the mass of fallen humanity a single people for himself. That people will be characterized by sincere and prevailing devotion to God himself and, consequently, will suffer the opposition of human beings who remain aligned to Satan. The redemption of this people, however, is not grounded in their devotion or endurance under opposition. It is grounded exclusively in the work of a single descendant of Eve. This promised offspring will, in the act of suffering, conquer the satanic foe. The people of God, on their part, receive in faith the promise of the offspring to come. It is in this respect that Adam and Eve escape the curse—God will remove that curse and will bless them through the work of Christ. And it is as Christ is offered to Adam and Eve in the way of promise that we may speak of this arrangement in Genesis 3 as covenantal. The promise of "offspring" anticipates the later covenantal promises of Christ as "offspring" (see Gen 12:7; 17:7; Gal 3:16). We have in Genesis 3:15, then, the inauguration of a gracious covenant through which God saves a people for himself through the work of his Son, Jesus Christ.

The indications in the text that follow are that both Adam and Eve believingly embraced this first promise of the gospel. When God first encounters Adam and Eve, they are clothed in garments of their own making (Gen 3:7). When God dismisses them from the garden, he makes for them both "garments of skins and clothed them" (Gen 3:21).

---

8. "As at the climax of the struggle the serpent's seed will be represented by the serpent, in the same manner the woman's seed may find representation in the same person," Vos, *Biblical Theology*, 43. Aalders further notes that "the victory in that conflict is not won by the collective seed of the woman, but by that one unique seed of the woman, our Lord Jesus Christ, and by Him alone," G. Ch. Aalders, *Genesis*, 2 vols., BSC (Grand Rapids: Zondervan, 1981), 1.107.

In this act, God "restores the alienated couple to fellowship with him and one another."[9] When Adam "called his wife's name Eve, because she was the mother of all living" (Gen 3:20), he was expressing faith in God's promise. Only God's promise warrants Adam to look for life rather than death to proceed from Eve. Eve's naming of Cain (arguably) and her naming of Seth (more probably) are expressions of faith in the promise of God (Gen 4:1, 25).[10] God has not only spoken a redemptive promise to Adam and Eve, but he has also, by his sovereign grace, brought them to believe and to act upon that promise. Adam and Eve emerge from the garden of Eden as the people of God.[11]

PRESERVATION

Following the first gospel promise, we see God working out his redemptive purpose of saving a people for himself in the ongoing division of humanity. Between the exile of Adam and the call of Abram, Genesis charts the histories of the "seed of the serpent" and the "seed of the woman." The "seed of the serpent"—fallen humanity aligned with Satan in rebellion against God—is committed to violence. Cain slays his brother in cold blood (Gen 4:8). Lamech boasts in bloodshed (Gen 4:23). In the days of Noah, "the earth was filled with violence" (Gen 6:11). In response, God pronounces his curse upon Cain (Gen 4:11), and resolves "to make an end of all flesh" because of humanity's violence (Gen 6:13).

In the face of prevailing violence on earth, God preserves his people. Although Cain slays Abel, God provides another child to Adam and Eve, Seth (Gen 4:25). It is in the generation of Seth's son, Enosh, that "people began to call upon the name of the Lord" (Gen 4:26). While the expression "call upon the name of the Lord" often denotes prayer in the Old Testament, it is likely

9. Waltke, *Genesis*, 95. Waltke tentatively notes that "the killing of an animal necessary to make garments of skin may suggest/imply the image of a sacrifice for sin," *Genesis*, 95n56.

10. See the discussion at Gordon Wenham, *Genesis 1–15*, WBC 1 (Word: Waco, TX: 1987), 100–102, 115.

11. See the testimony of Scots Confession §5, "We most constantly believe that God preserved, instructed, multiplied, honoured, decoired, and from death called to life his Kirk in all ages, from Adam, till the coming of Christ Jesus in the flesh."

that it here "refers to public worship" more generally.[12] In contrast to the seed of the serpent, which exalts itself, the seed of the woman exalts God.[13]

God preserves his people from yet another threat. In Genesis 6:1–4, as people "multiply on the face of the land," the "sons of God" take "wives" from among the "daughters of men" (Gen 6:1, 2; compare 6:4). The identification of "the sons of God" is debated, but the broader context commends taking the "sons of God" to be the godly line of Seth, and the "daughters of man" to be human beings who "remained in their original condition."[14] As the godly line of Seth intermarries with the ungodly line of Cain, the spiritual integrity of the "seed of the woman" is jeopardized.[15] Seen from this perspective, God's resolve to bring global judgment upon humanity (Gen 6:7) is intended to preserve the seed of the woman from utter ruin.

God executes his resolution to judge human beings by bringing a destructive flood of water upon the earth (Gen 6:9–8:19). God spares Noah and his family from this destruction, setting them in an ark. Although numbering only eight people (1 Pet 3:20), the people of God are preserved and delivered through the waters of judgment. Notwithstanding the violence of the seed of the serpent, the folly of God's people intermarrying with ungodly people, and the global judgment of God, God sees to it that his people are not extinguished but preserved.

Noah himself is said to have "found favor in the eyes of the Lord" (Gen 6:8) and, in the next verse, to be "a righteous man, blameless in his generation. Noah walked with God" (Gen 6:9b). Noah's righteousness and blamelessness, however, are not the cause or ground of his finding favor with God. The intervening statement, "These are the generations of Noah"

---

12. G. Ch. Aalders, *Genesis*, 1.135, referencing 2 Sam 6:2; 1 Chr 13:6; Pss 79:6; 116:17; Jer 10:25; Zeph 3:9.

13. Waltke, *Genesis*, 101.

14. Calvin, *Commentaries on the First Book of Moses Called Genesis*, trans. John King, 2 vols. (repr., Grand Rapids: Baker Academic, 1996), 1.238. See Calvin's defense of this interpretation at *Genesis* 1.237–39. Another interpretation sees the "sons of God" as angels. One obstacle to this interpretation stems from Jesus's statement that angels "neither marry nor are given in marriage" (Luke 20:35; compare 20:36). Another problem with this interpretation is that it fails to explain why God, in light of the intermarrying of Genesis 6:1–4, proceeds to bring judgment exclusively upon human beings in the verses that follow (Gen 6:5–8).

15. A point that is brought up subsequently in redemptive history, both under the old covenant (Deut 7:3–4) and the new covenant (1 Cor 7:39; compare 2 Cor 6:14). A believer marrying an unbeliever is not only an act of disobedience to God's express will but also an enticement to the believer to forsake God and cling to the gods of his or her spouse.

(Gen 6:9a), serves as a "heading" to "narratives" that follow (compare 2:4; 5:1; 10:1; 11:10; 11:27).[16] That is to say, the statement of Genesis 6:9a marks the conclusion of the previous section and the introduction of a new section. Among the wicked people of that generation (see Gen 6:5), Noah finds mercy and grace from the Lord (Gen 6:8). His righteousness and blamelessness are the fruit of that grace, not its ground or cause.[17] Entry into the people of God is not merited or earned by one's character. It is the gracious gift of the sovereign God.

Both before and after the flood, God is said to "establish [his] covenant with [Noah]" (Gen 6:18; compare 9:9). The verb "establish" (קוּם) at Genesis 6:18 is best translated "confirm" or "establish."[18] The previous covenant that God is confirming or establishing is "the historic inauguration of the covenant of grace and the institution of common grace" at Genesis 3:14–19.[19] We have, then, an extension and expansion of the covenant inaugurated with the first proclamation of gospel promise in Genesis 3:15. In keeping with his covenant commitments, God pledges himself to two works. First, he will deliver his chosen people from the judgment that they otherwise deserve and that justly falls upon ungodly human beings (Gen 6:9–8:19). Second, he will preserve or spare the world from a second diluvial judgment (Gen 8:20–9:17). God does this, in part, by reasserting and extending many of the provisions and ordinances that he established at the creation of the world.[20]

We may, therefore, speak once again of the people of God as the covenant community. They are called out of the world by the sovereign grace and mercy of God. Looking in faith to the redemptive promise, they evidence

---

16. Wenham, *Genesis 1–15*, 49.

17. Similarly, in Genesis 7:1, when God says, "Go into the ark, you and all your household, for I have seen that you are righteous before me in this generation," God is not promising to save Noah on the basis of Noah's antecedent righteousness. Noah's righteousness, rather, is evidence of the prior work of sovereign grace in Noah's life, on which see Calvin, *Genesis*, 1.265.

18. See the argument of W. J. Dumbrell, *Covenant and Creation: A Theology of the Old Testament Covenants* (London: Paternoster, 1984), 15–26 and, more recently, Gentry and Wellum, *Kingdom through Covenant*, 187–95.

19. So Miles V. Van Pelt, "The Noahic Covenant of the Covenant of Grace," ed. Guy Prentiss Waters, J. Nicholas Reid, and John R. Muether. *Covenant Theology: Biblical, Theological, and Historical Perspectives* (Wheaton, IL: Crossway, 2020), 119–20. Van Pelt, however, sees the covenant of Genesis 6:18 as distinct from the covenant of Genesis 9:9. On a single, Noahic covenant, see O. Palmer Robertson, *The Christ of the Covenants* (Phillipsburg, NJ: P&R, 1980), 110n2.

20. On which, see Van Pelt, "The Noahic Covenant," 124–27.

that faith in lives of righteousness and obedience.[21] God commits himself, by covenant, to save his people from judgment and to preserve the world so that he may bring his redemptive promises to their purposed fulfillment.

ABRAHAM

God's covenant with Abraham is foundational to what follows in redemptive history in at least two respects. First, the New Testament writers repeatedly appeal to the promises of the Abrahamic covenant as finding their intended fulfillment in the person and work of the coming Messiah, Jesus (see representatively Matt 1:1–17; John 8:31–59; Acts 3:25–26; Rom 4:1–25; Gal 3:1–29; Heb 11:8–19).[22] Second, the Abrahamic covenant, which administers the promises that God made to Abraham and to his offspring, is an "ecclesiastical covenant."[23] That is to say, it embraces not only Abraham but also Abraham's household. In doing so, it orders and directs the life of the people of God in ways that will characterize the people of God for the remainder of redemptive history.

We also see lines of continuity with the way that God has formed and sustained his people in previous periods of redemptive history. God's call of Abram—like the call of Adam and of Noah—is a gracious call, as Abram is brought from a life of idolatry (see Josh 24:2) into fellowship with the one, true God. Divine, redemptive promises similarly comprise the heart of God's relationship with Abram. These promises are delivered to Abram in connection with his call (Gen 12:1–3) and are reiterated to him and to his descendants repeatedly in the Old Testament. God administers these gracious promises to Abram in a covenant that he establishes with Abram and his descendants (Gen 15:1–20; 17:1–14). God institutes a sign in the context of this covenant in order to provide his people with a visible representation of what God has already promised them and what they may possess through faith in the word of promise (Gen 17:9–14; compare Gen 9:12–17).

---

21. Note the way in which the God's words in Genesis 3:14–19 inform the meaning of Noah's name (Gen 5:29).

22. "All subsequent covenants are but the confirmation and further elucidation of this [covenant with Abraham]," Stuart Robinson, *The Church of God as an Essential Element of the Gospel* (1858; repr., Willow Grove, PA: The Committee on Christian Education of the Orthodox Presbyterian Church, 2009), 43.

23. John Mitchell Mason, *Essays on the Church of God* (1832; repr., Taylors, SC: Presbyterian Press, 2005), 47, emphasis removed.

The Divine Promises

It is within the context of these basic similarities with previous covenantal administrations that we see at least two important lines of development that will bear upon all of God's subsequent dealings with his people. The first concerns the promises that God makes to Abram, "I will make of you a great nation, and I will bless you and make your name great, so that you will be a blessing. I will bless those who bless you, and him who dishonors you I will curse, and in you all the families of the earth shall be blessed" (Gen 12:2–3). Five times in these verses some form of the word "bless" appears, corresponding to the five instances of the word "curse" in Genesis 1–11 (3:14; 3:17; 4:11; 5:29; 9:25).[24] The Abrahamic promises, then, stand in the line of God's plan to bring accursed sinners into divine blessing, but lend that blessing more specificity.

What is striking about the form of this particular promise is that the blessing in view is intended for "all the families of the earth" (Gen 12:3; compare Gen 28:14). God makes Abram to be a blessing so that he in turn may be a blessing to the nations. For the first time an explicit mission is attached to God's redemptive promises. Abram will be both the recipient and conduit of divine blessing to human beings from all the nations.

If we ask what in particular the promised "blessing" is, the answer comes later in the narrative—God pledges to Abraham "to be God to you and to your offspring after you. ... I will be their God" (Gen 17:7, 8). The blessing is the presence and possession of God himself.[25] This global or universal promise stands in relief against the immediately preceding narrative of Babel (Gen 11:1–9).[26] The inhabitants of Babel united in sinful pride to "build ... a city and a tower with its top in the heavens," to "make a name for ourselves, lest we be dispersed over the face of the whole earth" (Gen 11:4). In other words, the seed of the serpent strives to climb into heaven, to establish a "name" for themselves, and to disobey the divine command to "fill the earth" (Gen 1:28). In judgment, God "confuse[s] their language"

24. So Gentry and Wellum, *Kingdom through Covenant*, 279.

25. "[T]he blessing of God [is] God's bestowal of himself upon mankind. To be blessed, then, is to enjoy the very presence of God, to have fellowship with him, and to be enriched by all that God is and offers as he gives himself to Abraham," Gerard van Groningen, *Messianic Revelation in the Old Testament*, 2 vols. (Grand Rapids: Baker Academic, 1990), 1.133–34.

26. The genealogy spanning from Shem to Abram intervenes between these two accounts (Gen 11:10–32).

and scatters the inhabitants "over the face of all the earth" (Gen 11:9). In the succeeding narrative, God comes down to Abram, pledges to "make [his] name great," and to disperse "blessing" through him to "all the families of the earth" (Gen 12:2, 3). What the seed of the serpent cannot and will not accomplish, God is pleased to do through the seed of the woman.

The particular promise that God will make Abram a "great nation" is lent further specificity in Genesis 13:16, "I will make your offspring as the dust of the earth, so that if one can count the dust of the earth, your offspring also can be counted" (compare 22:17). There is an undeniable biological component to this promise—Abraham will have many physical descendants. But the New Testament confirms that this is neither the heart nor the substance of the promise. Referencing the Abrahamic promises, Paul highlights the singularity of the word "offspring," insisting that it refers to Christ (Gal 3:16). As Gentry and Wellum note, "Here Paul is picking up the promise theme from Genesis 3:15, traced through a distinctive line of seed, beginning with Adam, running through Noah, Abraham, Isaac, Israel, and David, and eventually culminating in Christ. In Christ, we have the promised seed, the mediator of God's people, the one who fulfills all God's promises, not least the Abrahamic promises."[27]

At the same time, Paul is aware of the collective dimension of the word "offspring." It is for this reason that he declares that those who "are Christ's ... are Abraham's offspring, heirs according to promise" (Gal 3:29). Those who are united by faith to Jesus Christ, whether Jew or gentile, are the authentic offspring of Abraham, the proper recipients of the promised Abrahamic blessing.[28]

Ancillary to this promise of offspring and blessing is the promise of land, "Lift up your eyes and look from the place where you are, northward and southward and eastward and westward, for all the land that you see I will give to you and to your offspring forever" (Gen 13:14–15). In light of the apostle Paul's interpretation of this promise in Romans 4:13 ("For the promise to Abraham and his offspring that he would be heir of the world," compare Heb 11:9–16), one may not restrict this promise to the land of

---

27. Gentry and Wellum, *Kingdom through Covenant* (Wheaton, IL: Crossway, 2012), 630.

28. "The immediate particularism" of God's election of Abraham "is for the sake of an ultimate universalism," Patrick Fairbairn, *The Typology of Scripture*, 2 vols. (New York and London: Funk and Wagnalls, 1911), 1.291, emphasis removed.

Palestine. The promise, no less than the corresponding promise to raise up from Abraham a universal family, is universal in scope. It encompasses nothing less than the whole creation, even new heavens and earth (Rev 21–22).[29] In keeping with his creational purposes, God will have a global humanity glorifying his name in all creation.

These expansive promises are objective in nature and rest entirely upon God's sovereign initiative and power to implement. But that is not to deny that there is a corresponding and necessary subjective response on the part of the covenant partner to those promises. The overwhelming response emphasized in Genesis, and picked up by the apostle Paul, is "faith"—Abraham is "the man of faith" (Gal 3:9), the "father of us all [who] shar[e] the faith of Abraham" (Rom 4:16). Faith is emphasized particularly in its receptivity. Abraham does not contribute anything but receives everything that God offers in promise to him, "and [Abram] believed the Lord, and he counted it to him as righteousness" (Gen 15:6; compare Gal 3:6; Rom 4:9, 21, 22). As Abram beholds the night sky, a picture of the divine promise of offspring (Gen 15:5), he believes that promise. Trusting in the Messiah, Abram has confirmed to him the gifted, imputed righteousness of Christ, on the basis of which alone God has declared him righteous before God.[30]

Abraham's faith "grew strong" (Rom 4:20), but Abraham was not free from temptations to doubt God's promises. In many respects the Abrahamic narrative (Gen 12–24) documents a series of temptations and threats that Abraham faces with respect to God's promises, and to which he often responds in unbelief. And yet, in mercy, God reaffirms his promises to Abraham, and does so in such a way as to strengthen his faith in God (see Gen 15:1–20). Faith, in other words, is both created and sustained by the word of God.

Abraham's faith is evidenced by his obedience to God, a point that the apostle James underscores (James 2:21–23).[31] In fact, Abram demonstrates his faith in the initial divine promise to him by obeying the command, "Go from your country and your kindred and your father's house to the land

---

29. On which, see Gentry and Wellum, *Kingdom through Covenant* (2012), 707–16.

30. On which, see Douglas J. Moo, *Galatians*, BECNT (Grand Rapids: Baker Academic, 2013), 187–91; and Thomas R. Schreiner, ZECNT (Grand Rapids: Zondervan, 2010), 190–92.

31. D. Douglas Bannerman, *The Scripture Doctrine of the Church, Historically and Exegetically Considered* (1887; repr., Grand Rapids: Baker Academic, 1976), 22.

that I will show you" (Gen 12:1; compare 12:4).[32] It is by complying with the divine command in faith that Abraham comes to experience the blessing that has been freely offered to him in the divine promise.

The Covenant Community

The second important line of development with respect to the people of God in the days of the patriarchs concerns the form and shape of the people of God. Up until the days of Abram, Geerhardus Vos observes, "the [human] race as a whole had been dealt with." Even "in Noah's case," he continues, "there had been election of a new race out of an old one given over to destruction."[33] But with Abram, God begins a new and ultimately enduring pattern of dealing with human beings. "Here one family is taken out of the number of existing Shemitic families, and with it, within it, the redemptive, revelatory work of God is carried forward."[34]

Having chosen one family in the interests of advancing his redemptive purposes, God proceeds to order the life of that family in unprecedented fashion.[35] We can see the way in which God does this by exploring the testimony of Genesis 17.

Genesis 17

God now explicitly takes Abraham *and* his household into covenant relationship with him: "And I will establish my covenant between me and you and your offspring after you throughout their generations for an everlasting covenant, to be God to you and to your offspring after you" (Gen 17:7). Consequently, they are to "keep [God's] covenant"—Abraham and his "offspring after [him] throughout their generations" (Gen 17:9).

---

32. See also Gen 13:14–17 with 13:18; Gen 14:22–24; Gen 17:1–14 with 17:22–27; Gen 22:1–19.

33. Vos, *Biblical Theology*, 76.

34. Vos, *Biblical Theology*, 76.

35. "[T]his calling of Abraham may be looked upon as a kind of new foundation for a visible church of God in a more distinct and regular state, to be upheld and built upon this foundation from hence forward till Christ should actually come, and then through him to be propagated to all nations," Jonathan Edwards, *A History of the Work of Redemption*, ed. John F. Wilson, WJE 9 (New Haven: Yale, 1989), 160.

The covenant community is distinguished or set apart in at least two respects. In the first place, they are to be marked by their covenant fealty to God. Abraham himself is to "walk before [God], and be blameless" (Gen 17:1), that is, sincere in heart and faithful in mind and life. The purpose of God's election of Abraham, God says, is "that he may command his children and his household after him to keep the way of the Lord by doing righteousness and justice, so that the Lord may bring to Abraham what he has promised him" (Gen 18:19).[36] The covenant community, then, is to be characterized by conformity to God's character. It possesses a familial government, with Abraham at its head, that fosters and promotes holiness.

Second, the covenant community is set apart by an ordinance that God institutes and imposes—circumcision. God tells Abraham that circumcision is "a sign of the covenant between me and you" (Gen 17:11), and goes so far as to identify his covenant with circumcision (17:10, 13). Paul speaks of circumcision as both "sign" and "seal" (Rom 4:11). It is a sign of the covenant promises that God has already made to Abraham, and it is a seal, or confirmation, of "the righteousness that he had by faith while he was still uncircumcised" (Rom 4:11). Circumcision must not be mechanically identified with God's covenant. Neither must it be understood to convey *ex opere operato* the gracious benefits signified. God intended circumcision to be a help to faith—to point faith to, and to confirm faith in, the promises of the covenant.[37]

What, in particular, was the meaning or signification of circumcision? Circumcision testified to a heart that was unclean by nature (Lev 26:41; Deut 10:16, 30:6; Jer 4:4, 6:10, 9:25, 26; Ezek 44:7; Rom 2:25–29, 4:11; Eph 2:11; Phil 3:3; Col 2:11–13).[38] Even as circumcision pointed to the imputed righteousness of Christ (Rom 4:11; Gen 15:6), it also pointed to the recipient's need for that righteousness. "Circumcision teaches that physical descent from Abraham is not sufficient to make

36. As Calvin notes, the concluding final clause ("so that the Lord may bring to Abraham what he has promised him") sets forth "the consequence rather than the cause" of our salvation, since "the grace of God alone begins and completes our salvation," Calvin, *Genesis*, 1.483.

37. Note Calvin, "We now consider how the covenant is rightly kept; namely, when the word precedes, and we embrace the sign as a testimony and pledge of grace; for as God binds himself to keep the promise given to us; so the consent of faith and of obedience is demanded from us," *Genesis*, 1.452.

38. Cited by Vos, *Biblical Theology*, 90.

true Israelites. The uncleanness and disqualification of nature must be taken away."[39] Salvation was not by birthright or physical descent. Salvation was solely by the sovereign grace of God.

God commands that "every male" in the covenant community "be circumcised" (Gen 17:10). Male infants who are born into the household of Abraham are to be circumcised the eighth day (17:12–13). The covenant sign is placed upon them no less than adult members of the covenant community. This command, then, is a recognition that Abraham's "children, in successive generations, are recognized as having a birthright, not only in its general privileges, but as born members of the great visible community which this covenant, as a charter, founds and organizes."[40] Circumcision, then, does not make them members of the covenant community. It is a recognition that they are already, by birthright, members of the covenant community. As such, they belong to God and are obliged to believe the promises signified to them, and to walk in faith before God.

Furthermore, males who are "bought with your money from any foreigner who is not of your offspring" are to be circumcised as well (17:12; compare 17:13). This command shows that the covenant community was not restricted to Abraham's biological descendants.[41] Neither, then, may circumcision be defined as or reduced to a "badge of national membership"—non-Jewish males brought into the covenant community were to be circumcised no less than their Jewish counterparts. Circumcision, then, "functions as the sign of the covenant."[42]

Seen in a distinct light, circumcision is an act of the worship of God. Abraham is set before us in Genesis as a man who repeatedly offers God worship. To be sure, as Calvin notes, Abram "bore an altar in his heart."[43] Even so, Abram's heart devotion came to outward expression. That outward expression assumes two related features. The first

39. Vos, *Biblical Theology*, 90. In this respect, Vos notes here, circumcision represents the graces of justification, regeneration, and sanctification.

40. Stuart Robinson, *Discourses of Redemption*, 4th ed. (Richmond: Presbyterian Committee of Publication, 1866), 86.

41. The males of Genesis 17:12,13, were they to remain uncircumcised, were to be "cut off" from the people of God and counted as those who have "broken [God's] covenant." This sanction assumes their membership in the covenant community.

42. O. Palmer Robertson, *The Christ of the Covenants* (Phillipsburg, NJ: P&R, 1980), 157.

43. Calvin, *Genesis*, 1.377, referenced at Bannerman, *Scripture Doctrine*, 46.

is the construction of altars (Gen 12:7, 8; 13:18), and the second is the offering of sacrifices (Gen 15:9–10; 22:1–8).[44] This pattern serves as a reminder that God establishes covenant with human beings in order to glorify himself when they approach him in fellowship and communion. Tellingly, on both occasions when Abram constructs altars, he does so in response to the promissory word of God (Gen 12:7a; 13:14–17). The church's worship is not an attempt to extract something from or to manipulate God. It is, rather, the grateful and obediential response to a God who demonstrates his goodness in covenant with human beings.

Sacrifice, an established component of the relationship between God and his people (Gen 3:15; 8:20–22), points to the acceptance of God's covenant partners solely on the basis of the mediation of Christ. Although he is not termed a priest, Abraham performs what we may term a priestly function in offering sacrifices to God. Abraham also performs an additional priestly function, intercession, on more than one occasion (Gen 18:22–33; 20:7, 17). In this respect, Abraham foreshadows the high priestly work of Jesus Christ.[45]

Abraham foreshadows Christ in two other respects. In speaking to Abimelech, God terms Abraham a "prophet" (Gen 20:7). This description—"the first time [it] is used in the Bible"—characterizes Abraham not only as an intercessor but also one who, "having received revelation, mediates God's word."[46] Although Abraham is not called a king, he executes the royal function of leading an army victoriously into battle to deliver his nephew, Lot (Gen 14:1–16). Abraham's priestly, prophetic, and royal activity, then, foreshadow the redemptive work of his messianic offspring, Christ.

CONCLUSION

When God called Abram into covenant relationship with himself, he extended and expanded the promise of an offspring who would bring salvation to sinners. These promises, the New Testament reminds us, find their direct fulfillment in the person and

---

44. Note the expression at Genesis 12:8, "and called upon the name of the Lord," an echo of Genesis 4:25.

45. A point made independently at Genesis 14:17–24, according to Hebrews 7:1–10.

46. Waltke, *Genesis*, 286.

work of Christ. God formalized the community of people that he had gathered around those promises. They are chosen by God for blessing, set apart for holiness in fellowship with God, marked by circumcision as sign of covenant promise, and committed to the worship of God in obedience to and in grateful response to his word. As we will see in the next chapter, these features continue to characterize the people of God as they grow and expand in successive generations. And, as Abraham dimly foreshadowed the work of the Mediator to come, so the covenant community under Moses will, under God's direction, point to the Christ as prophet, priest, and king of his church.

FURTHER READING

Bannerman, D. Douglas. *The Scripture Doctrine of the Church, Historically and Exegetically Considered.* 1887. Reprint, Grand Rapids: Baker Academic, 1976. The son of James Bannerman, D. Douglas Bannerman was a late nineteenth-century Scottish Presbyterian who authored a comprehensive and insightful biblical theological survey of the doctrine of the church.

Redd, J. Scott. "The Abrahamic Covenant." In *Covenant Theology: Biblical, Theological, and Historical Perspectives,* edited by Guy Prentiss Waters, J. Nicholas Reid, and John R. Muether, 133–48. Wheaton, IL: Crossway, 2020.

Robertson, O. Palmer. *The Christ of the Covenants.* Phillipsburg, NJ: P&R, 1980. An influential late twentieth-century presentation of Reformed covenant theology. Its treatment of the Abrahamic covenant and its engagement of Dispensationalism have important implications for ecclesiology.

Robinson, Stuart. *The Church of God as an Essential Element of the Gospel.* 1858. Reprint, Willow Grove, PA: The Committee on Christian Education of the Orthodox Presbyterian Church, 2009. A prominent American Presbyterian of the nineteenth century, Robinson gave particular attention to the doctrine of the church. This valuable work offers a biblical theological survey of the church across redemptive history.

IV

MOSES: TYPOLOGICAL ORGANIZATION OF THE CHURCH

When God made a covenant with Israel at Mount Sinai, much had changed in the life of the people of God from the days of the patriarchs. The offspring of Abraham had been sojourning in the land of promise before living in bondage in a foreign land, Egypt. At Sinai God is poised to bring redeemed Israel back into the land of promise, this time to possess it. Israel had once been a large family—several dozen went down to Egypt in the days of Joseph (Gen 46:6–27; Acts 7:14). Israel is now a sizeable nation—well over a million come out of Egypt under Moses (see Num 1:1–46).

The Sinaitic covenant will order the life of God's people in ways that reflect these new circumstances. And yet, there is a basic and underlying set of similarities between the people of God in the days of Abraham and the people of God in the days of Moses. God continues to administer his promises of salvation by the coming Seed of the Woman. Looking in faith to the promised Messiah, Israel pursues holiness according to the laws that God has given her.

In this chapter, we will look at the foundational covenant that God established with his people on Mount Sinai. In particular, we will explore the ways in which God, through that covenant, ordered the life of this elect and redeemed nation. We will highlight developments with respect to the form and pattern of God's people since the days of Abraham, and we will look at ways in which Israel's polity and worship anticipated the coming Messiah.

THE SINAITIC COVENANT

The founding event of Israel, in her national existence, is the exodus from Egypt. As God tells his people, gathered on Mount Sinai, "You yourselves have seen what I did to the Egyptians, and how I bore you on eagles' wings and brought you to myself" (Exod 19:4); "I am the Lord your God, who brought you out of the land of Egypt, out of the house of slavery" (Exod 20:1). God, then, has redeemed his people from a state of bondage for his own purpose. He has gathered them to himself, to be God's "treasured possession among all peoples," "a kingdom of priests and a holy nation" (Exod 19:5–6).

Previous chapters of Exodus emphasize that God was already in relationship with Israel when they were enslaved in Egypt. In particular, it was God's covenant with Abraham that gave form and direction to this relationship. God calls Israel in Egypt his "firstborn son" (Exod 4:22).[1] God had "heard their groaning, and God remembered his covenant with Abraham, with Isaac, and with Jacob. God saw the people of Israel—and God knew" (Exod 2:24–25). But the Abrahamic covenant not only explains God's compassionate redemption of Israel from bondage in Egypt, it also explains God's purposes for Israel after he has redeemed them. In particular, God will fulfill his promises to Abraham to give the land of promise to Israel "for a possession" (Exod 6:8; compare 3:8, 17).

The Sinaitic covenant, then, should be understood as an extension and expansion of the Abrahamic covenant. As Herman Bavinck has noted, "This covenant with the ancestors continues, even when later at Sinai it assumes another form. It is the foundation and core also of the Sinaitic covenant (Exod 2:24; Deut 7:8). The promise was not nullified by the law that came later (Gal 3:17). The covenant with Israel was essentially no other than that

1. As J. A. Motyer notes, "Here in Exodus ... Israel is for the first time called the Lord's son," which means that "the relationship is not one of 'natural' descent but had a beginning in history and is contemporary with the Lord's acts of deliverance and redemption (Exod 6:6)," *The Message of Exodus*, BST (Downers Grove, IL: InterVarsity Press, 2005), 91.

with Abraham."[2] The promises that God made to Abraham—blessing, offspring, and land—are administered to the people of God under the Sinaitic covenant as well.[3] The preeminent promise that God will be Abraham's God and that he and his offspring will be his people (see Gen 17:8) is reiterated in Egypt (Exod 6:7) and then again at Sinai (Exod 19:6).[4]

How, then, are we to understand the condition attached to the promises of Exodus 19:5–6 (emphasis added), "Now, therefore, *if you will indeed obey my voice and keep my covenant*, you shall be my treasured possession among all peoples, for all the earth is mine"? We should note, in the first place, that such a condition is not unique to this covenant. It finds parallel in God's words to Abraham in Genesis 17:1–2, "I am God Almighty; walk before me, and be blameless, *that I may make my covenant between me and you, and may multiply you greatly*" (emphasis added; compare Gen 18:19, 22:16–18). In light of the unmerited character of the promises that God makes to Israel and to Abraham in these passages, "God cannot mean that Abraham's and Israel's obedience is a procuring precondition for God's promises. ... Covenant obligations in no way *merit or earn* God's covenant promises, but they are the way in which God has appointed [his people] to *experience and enjoy* the blessings that he freely gives us in his promises."[5]

THE MOSAIC LEGISLATION

THIS DYNAMIC LEADS TO A second point of continuity with the Abrahamic covenant. If the Sinaitic covenant is founded upon gracious promises (the very same promises that God extended to Abraham and to his offspring), then the Sinaitic covenant no less calls God's people to lives of holiness in

2. Herman Bavinck, *Reformed Dogmatics: Volume 3, Sin and Salvation in Christ*, trans. John Vriend (Grand Rapids: Baker Academic, 2006), 220.

3. On which, see Bavinck, *Reformed Dogmatics*, 3:221–22. Bavinck perceptibly notes while the Sinaitic covenant sets forth various "natural" and "temporal" blessings, these blessings not only accompany "spiritual" blessings but also shadow them: "The natural is first, then the spiritual. All spiritual and eternal benefits are therefore clothed, in Israel, in sensory forms," 221.

4. A number of voices within the Reformed tradition have maintained that the Mosaic covenant is, in some sense, a republication of the covenant of works, on which see the "Report of the Committee to Study Republication, Presented to the Eighty-third (2016) General Assembly of the Orthodox Presbyterian Church," https://www.opc.org/GA/republication.html, accessed December 30, 2021.

5. Guy Prentiss Waters, *The Lord's Supper as the Sign and Meal of the New Covenant* (Wheaton, IL: Crossway, 2019), 28–29. See further Gentry and Wellum, *Kingdom through Covenant*, 350–53.

fellowship with God. It is here that we witness a marked development with respect to the Abrahamic covenant. To be sure, God had called Abraham and his household to "walk before me, and be blameless" (Gen 17:1), and to "keep the way of the Lord by doing righteousness and justice" (Gen 18:19). These commands are paralleled in the Mosaic covenant, but these commands are not accompanied with the extensive and precise body of legislation that characterizes the Mosaic covenant.[6] The laws of the Mosaic covenant function in just the same way as the commands of the Abrahamic covenant—for the sanctification of the redeemed people of God. The number and precision of those laws, however, reflects the altered condition and circumstances of the people of God in the days of Moses.

In reflecting upon the Mosaic laws in relation to the people of God, it is important to remember that the Old Testament views the people of God in two distinct but compatible respects. On the one hand, Israel stands under these laws "as the chosen, organized, spiritual body under the covenant with Abraham, constituting them Jehovah's peculiar people, and him their God." On the other hand, Israel stands under these laws "as a social and civil organization which is to possess a country guaranteed to them as an inheritance for a special purpose."[7]

The divisions within the Mosaic law reflect this crucial distinction.[8] The Sinaitic legislation opens with the "ten words" (Deut 10:4), that is, ten commandments that constitute the foundation and core of the legislation that follows (Exod 20; Deut 5).[9] What then follows are blocks of laws that govern two spheres of life—Israel's worship of God as a spiritual people,

---

6. It is because of this characteristic that Paul surely terms the Mosaic covenant "law" throughout Galatians 3:15–4:31.

7. Stuart Robinson, *Discourses of Redemption*, 4th ed. (Richmond, VA: Presbyterian Committee of Publication, 1866), 127–28.

8. For a treatment of recent scholarship regarding the divisions of law within the Pentateuch, see John H. Sailhamer, *The Meaning of the Pentateuch: Revelation, Composition and Interpretation* (Downers Grove, IL: InterVarsity Press, 2009), 355–415; and Philip S. Ross, *From the Finger of God: The Biblical and Theological Basis for the Threefold Division of the Law* (Fearn, UK: Mentor, 2010).

9. Note how the Westminster Larger Catechism points to the Ten Commandments as distinct within the Mosaic legislation as a whole—they "were delivered by the voice of God upon Mount Sinai, and written by him in two tables of stone" (Q & A 98). To this we may add that the Ten Commandments were uniquely said to have been written by the "finger of God" (Exod 31:18; Deut 9:10). See the fuller discussion at Bruce K. Waltke, "The Kingdom of God in the Old Testament: The Covenants," in *The Kingdom of God*, ed. Christopher W. Morgan and Robert A. Peterson (Wheaton, IL: Crossway, 2012), 83–84.

and Israel's civil existence as a body politic. We may take the remainder of the book of Exodus and the whole of Leviticus as illustrative examples. The "Book of the Covenant" (Exod 20:22–23:33; compare 24:7) begins (20:22–26) and concludes (23:14–19) with laws regulating Israel's worship. In between are laws that address the treatment of "persons," particularly "the disadvantaged who are more likely to suffer injustice and oppression."[10] Exodus 25:1–31:18 and 35:1–40:38 govern the construction and furniture of the tabernacle, and the priests and Levites who will minister at that tabernacle. The laws of Leviticus address the sacrifices that may be offered at the tabernacle (Lev 1–7), the priests who minister at the tabernacle (Lev 8–10), what may render one unclean and thus unfit to approach the tabernacle (Lev 11–16), and the holiness that God requires in relation both to worship and to one's day-to-day interactions with fellow Israelites (Lev 17–26).[11]

This same pattern holds in the remaining two books of the Pentateuch, Numbers and Deuteronomy.[12] Integrating and underlying these two spheres (worship, civil existence) is the Decalogue itself, the first four commandments governing how human beings are to worship God, and the remaining six commandments governing how human beings are to relate to one another in righteousness. The laws regulating Israel's worship and the laws governing Israel's civil existence are dependent upon the Decalogue. They are given as particular applications of the Decalogue to Israel in her particular circumstances—a people set apart to God, to worship him in holiness; a people set apart from the nations, to serve God and one another in righteousness.[13] And, as we will see below, they point

---

10. John L. MacKay, *Exodus* (Fearn, UK: Mentor, 2001), 364.

11. Following the outline of Gordon Wenham, *The Book of Leviticus*, NICOT (Grand Rapids: Eerdmans, 1979), 4.

12. On which, see Gordon J. Wenham, *Numbers: An Introduction and Commentary*, TOTC (Downers Grove, IL: InterVarsity Press, 1981), 14–18, 54, and Christopher J. H. Wright, *Deuteronomy*, NIBC (Peabody, MA: Hendrickson, 1996), 1–5. Wright argues that the laws of Deuteronomy are sequentially structured by the Decalogue.

13. And yet, Robinson perceptively notes, the civil legislation of the Pentateuch was given to the nation of Israel as "already ha[ving] ... [social] organization and a political constitution," *Discourses of Redemption*, 129. These laws, then, were added to and, in some respects, "modif[ied]" an existing civil polity. The purpose of this addition, Robinson continues, is "to constitute this political commonwealth a type of the great spiritual commonwealth over which [Jehovah] specially rules, as his people, and to be a perpetual prophecy of the coming Messiah," Robinson, *Discourses of Redemption*, 129. For a contemporary treatment of the ways in which the Sinaitic laws typified Christ and his eschatological people, see Vern S. Poythress, *The Shadow of Christ in the Law of Moses* (Phillipsburg, NJ: P&R, 1991).

forward typologically to the person and work of the promised Seed of the Woman.[14]

For what purpose, then, did God give these laws to his people Israel? God gave them to a people that he had expressly redeemed from Egypt and had brought into near relation to himself (Exod 19:4–6). The purpose of these laws was to order the life of an already-redeemed people. Specifically, the law was given not as an instrument for justification, but as an instrument of sanctification. God had called Israel to be holy as he was holy (Lev 11:44; compare 20:7, 26). The way in which Israel was to pursue holiness was by "keep[ing]" God's "statutes" and "do[ing] them" (Lev 20:8a). But it would be "the Lord who sanctifies you" (Lev 20:8b). Thus, the work of holiness was no less a work of sovereign grace than the work of redemption had been.

We may make two further observations. First, the Mosaic laws were calculated to drive sinners to Jesus Christ (Gal 3:21–22). The founding meal of the Mosaic covenant, the Passover, taught Israel that God required the shedding of blood in order to forgive the sins of his people. The sacrificial system of the Pentateuch reinforced this principle on a daily basis—sin merits the penalty of death (compare Gen 2:17), and God is pleased to accept the death of a substitute in making satisfaction to his justice. These Pentateuchal sacrifices, the New Testament emphasizes, had no power or efficacy in themselves to atone. They pointed to the coming sacrifice of the promised Seed of the Woman, by whose blood alone the sins of sinners in any age could be remitted (Heb 9:15; Rom 3:24–25).[15]

The various cleansings and washings required under the Mosaic covenant emphasized the need for each Israelite's purification. No Israelite could approach God in a state of defilement, and God was pleased to provide the washing that was necessary to cleanse the individual and to allow him access into his presence. The association of washing with regeneration in the New Testament (see John 3:3, 5; Titus 3:5; Heb 10:22) highlights the underlying spiritual principle behind these Mosaic ordinances. Sinners

---

14. Edwards, in fact, terms "mostly all those precepts that were given by Moses that did not properly belong to the moral law" as "the typical law." The result was that "the whole nation by this law was as it were constituted in a typical state," *A History of the Work of Redemption*, ed. John F. Wilson, WJE 9 (New Haven: Yale, 1989), 181–82.

15. On which, see Turretin, *Institutes of Elenctic Theology*, trans. George M. Giger, 3 vols. (Phillipsburg, NJ: P&R, 1992–7), 2.247–57 (=L.12 Q.10).

require a change of nature that God alone is able to provide. So made new, they are now able to enter acceptably into the presence of God.

A second observation that we may make about the Mosaic legislation concerns the relationship that it recognizes between its laws and "love." We may look at two passages from the Mosaic law in connection with Jesus's teaching about those passages.

Deuteronomy 6:5, Leviticus 19:18, Matthew 22:34–40

In Deuteronomy 6:5, God commands Israel to "love the Lord your God with all your heart and with all your soul and with all your might." This command follows an affirmation of the unity of the Godhead (Deut 6:4) and precedes a command to set "these words that I command you today" upon "your heart" (Deut 6:6). The call to love the one God in Deuteronomy 6:5 requires that Israel do so with "the powers of heart and soul, but also ... those of the body" and do so through "the zealous keeping of 'these commandments that I give you today.'"[16] The keeping of God's commandments, far from being antithetical to love for God, is in fact the way in which love for God comes to necessary expression.

In Leviticus 19:18, God concludes a series of commands addressing theft, oppression, injustice, and hatred of one's neighbor with the injunction, "you shall love your neighbor as yourself: I am the Lord" (compare 19:34). Jesus (Matt 22:39; Mark 12:31), Paul (Rom 13:9), and James (James 2:8) point to this text as the sum of one's obligations to one's fellow human beings. In similar fashion to the love of God, the love of one's neighbor is not antithetical to observing God's commandments. In fact, it is only by keeping the commands of God with regard to our fellow human beings that we demonstrate love to them. It is for this reason that the apostle Paul says that "the one who loves another has fulfilled the law" (Rom 13:8; compare 13:10).

---

16. Jan Ridderbos, *Deuteronomy*, trans. Ed M. van der Maas, BSC (Grand Rapids: Zondervan, 1984), 115, citing Deuteronomy 6:6. Compare the analysis of Gentry and Wellum, *Kingdom through Covenant*, 405–9.

Jesus cites these two passages (Deut 6:5; Lev 19:18) in answer to the question, "Which is the great commandment in the Law?" (Matt 22:36). After citing them, Jesus states, "On these two commandments depend all the Law and the Prophets" (22:40). Jesus, then, not only conceives the Mosaic legislation in terms of a "single, all-embracing commandment," but also, in summarizing the law in the way that he does, articulates the law's "deepest motives."[17]

The God who had demonstrated love and compassion in redeeming his people from Egypt called his people to live lives of love (Exod 20:1 with 20:2–17). They were to love God sincerely, unreservedly, entirely, and supremely. They were to love fellow Israelites and sojourners—any human being with whom they came into contact—with no less regard than they held toward themselves. In both cases, the totality of God's commandments served as the way in which love would come to expression within Israel. In this way, God would bring his people into moral conformity with himself.

COVENANT SIGN

As we have seen, at the heart of the Mosaic legislation is the system of worship that God instituted for himself. The second commandment (Exod 20:4–6) declares that God is not to be worshiped in any way that he has not authorized. Israel may only worship God in the way that he has commanded them in his law.[18] The worship that God prescribes is centered around the tabernacle, in which he makes himself specially present to his people (Exod 29:43; 40:34–38). Priests and Levites ministered in relation to the tabernacle; sacrifices were to be offered at the tabernacle; the laws regulating ritual purity and cleanliness concerned access to the tabernacle; and the laws concerning Israel's feasts and festivals oriented their observation around the tabernacle.

Preeminent among the feasts and festivals that God appointed for Israel (Lev 23:1–44; Deut 16:1–17) was the Passover. Passover not only inaugurates

---

17. Herman N. Ridderbos, *Matthew*, trans. Ray Togtman, BSC (Grand Rapids: Zondervan, 1987), 417.

18. The judicial deaths of Nadab and Abihu (Lev 10:1–7) are a graphic illustration of this principle. In offering "unauthorized fire before the Lord, which he had not commanded them" (10:1), Nadab and Abihu violated this cardinal principle of the worship of God.

the annual calendar of Israel's worship (Lev 23:4–8; Deut 16:1–8), but it also commemorates the founding events of Israel's existence under the Mosaic covenant, the first Passover and the exodus that soon followed.

Exodus 12

As we observed above, the Passover enacted the principle articulated in Genesis 2:17 that sin merits death. In choosing and sacrificing a lamb according to God's specifications (Exod 12:3–6), each household was to "take some of the blood and put it on the two doorposts and the lintel of the houses in which they eat it" (Exod 12:7). They consumed the lamb that night (Exod 12:8–9). God told Israel that "the blood" would be "a sign for you, on the houses where you are. And when I see the blood, I will pass over you, and no plague will befall you to destroy you, when I strike the land of Egypt" (12:13). Israel, then, was spared the judgment upon the Egyptian firstborn not because of her righteousness but because of God's mercy in providing a substitutionary sacrifice on Israel's behalf. Immediately following the Passover was the seven-day Feast of Unleavened Bread (12:14–20), in which all leaven was to be removed from Israelites' houses. This practice may well have "symbolized leaving behind all Egyptian influences that might work their way through their lives and corrupt them," an identification reflected in Paul's words in 1 Corinthians 5:8.[19] Israel's founding feast, then, highlighted Israel's redemption through the provision of a substitutionary, atoning sacrifice, and the corresponding call to pursue lives dedicated entirely to their Redeemer God. That this feast was to be observed annually was intended to ensure that the meaning of the exodus would not be lost on subsequent generations of Israelites (see Deut 6:20–25).

It is in light of the significance of and purpose for the Passover that we may speak of it as the sign that God appointed to accompany the Mosaic covenant. Just as circumcision functioned as sign and seal of the Abrahamic covenant, so Passover would function under the Mosaic covenant. It represented to Israel the saving work of God for

19. Mackay, *Exodus*, 214, 215.

his people, in particular, God's redemption of Israel from bondage in Egypt. That redemption, in turn, foreshadowed the redemption of sinners by the work of Christ (1 Cor 5:7). Passover, like other sacrificial meals that God appointed in the Pentateuch, was an occasion when "God met with his people and, on the basis of the sacrifice made and accepted, united himself with his people in joy." For this reason, "the feast of Passover occupied an entirely unique place in the cultic life of Israel."[20] This foundational sacrifice and meal signified and sealed to the faith of Israelites the gospel promises that were administered through the Mosaic covenant.

ISRAEL'S MISSION

Closely tied to Israel's laws and her observance of them is the mission with which God tasked Israel in covenant with him. In redeeming Israel from Egypt, God "separated [Israel] as a nation from all other nations to subsist by themselves in their own political and ecclesiastical state."[21] God declared at Sinai that Israel would be his "treasured possession among all peoples ... a kingdom of priests and a holy nation" (Exod 19:5, 6). God stresses later that he did not choose Israel for any merits of her own—she had none (Deut 7:7; 9:6–12). Rather, God has chosen Israel "because the Lord loves you and is keeping the oath that he swore to your fathers (7:8). Israel's calling as a nation set apart from the nations of the earth to be God's treasured possession proceeds from the sovereign, unmerited favor of God toward Israel.

Israel, so chosen and redeemed, is to be "a kingdom of priests." That is to say, Israel was to be "a kingdom which as a whole was to function in a priestly role vis-à-vis the rest of the world."[22] In this respect, Israel, who stood in the presence of God, was to mediate blessing from God to the

20. Bavinck, *Reformed Dogmatics*, 3:541–42, 543.

21. Edwards, *A History of the Work of Redemption*, 177. Edwards observes that Israel had been separated "as strangers and sojourners" from Egypt during her tenure there, but even such limited proximity posed the risk of Israel "los[ing] the true religion" and becoming "overrun with the idolatry of their neighbors," Edward, *A History of the Work of Redemption*, 177. In other words, the judgment of the exodus accomplished the same ends in Moses's day as the judgment of the flood did in Noah's day.

22. Mackay, *Exodus*, 328.

nations around her. She would do so particularly by transmitting "the light of true religion" to the nations.[23]

Israel was to be at one and the same time a "holy nation." As her Redeemer God was holy, so his redeemed people was to image his holiness to the nations around her.[24] The corpus of laws that follow, beginning with the Ten Commandments, supplies the pattern of holiness that God provides Israel to pursue and to implement.

By fulfilling her calling, Israel would glorify the God who had chosen, redeemed, and sanctified her. As God had brought plagues upon Egypt "that my name may be proclaimed in all the earth" (Exod 9:16), so God would redeem and call Israel to the same end. Israel was to be a "kingdom of priests" and a "holy nation" so that the name of God would be magnified among the nations.

This point finds emphasis in Deuteronomy 4:5–8. When Israel takes the land and embraces her calling to "keep" and "do" the "statutes and rules" that God has given her (Deut 4:6, 5), then the nations will take notice: "'Surely this great nation is a wise and understanding people.' For what great nation is there that has a god so near to it as the Lord our God is to us, whenever we call upon him? And what great nation is there, that has statutes and rules so righteous as all this law that I set before you today?" (Deut 4:6b–8). What distinguishes Israel in the sight of the nations, then, is "the nearness of Yahweh to his people" and "the righteousness of the Torah."[25] By living faithfully to the calling that God had assigned her, Israel would mediate blessing to the nations. The spotlight would not fall upon her, but upon the God who had redeemed her and set her apart to himself.

This particular calling should not be understood to exhaust, much less to fulfill, God's promise to Abram in Genesis 12:1–3 that he would be a blessing to the nations. What we are witnessing in Israel's calling, rather, are anticipatory hints and glimpses of the spiritual blessing that God has pledged to bring about for the nations in Christ, namely, redemption applied by the Spirit (Gal 3:13–14).[26] As Israel takes up the work of diffusing

---

23. Mackay, *Exodus*, 328.

24. Israel was "distinct from the rest [of the nations], commissioned with sharing and displaying the divine nature and living in the likeness of God their Saviour (2 Pet 1:2–4)," Motyer, *The Message of Exodus*, 200.

25. Wright, *Deuteronomy*, 47.

26. In the same way, in the life of Abraham, we see how God used Abraham to be a blessing to the nations around him (Gen 14:13–16; 18:22–33; 20:7). These instances of blessing should

the knowledge of Yahweh to the nations, then the nations, alongside and with Israel, can participate in the blessing brought by the saving work of the promised Seed of the Woman.

SHADOWS OF CHRIST

ISRAEL WAS TO POINT TO Christ by pursuing her calling to diffuse the saving knowledge of God to the nations. In addition, Israel herself foreshadows the mission and ministry of Christ. We may explore at least three lines of foreshadowing—the priestly ministry of Christ, the kingly (royal) ministry of Christ, and the prophetic ministry of Christ.[27] As Abraham had foreshadowed the three-fold office of Christ as prophet, priest, and king, so Israel will do the same.

Under the Mosaic covenant, God established a distinct order of priests and Levites with defined and exclusive responsibilities. Those responsibilities by and large converged upon the cultic duties centered around the tabernacle (and, later, the temple). In particular, they functioned as "holy mediators," who brought "the needs of the people to God."[28] But the priests no less served as teachers of God's law to the people: "You are to distinguish between the holy and the common, and between the unclean and the clean, and you are to teach the people of Israel all the statutes that the Lord has spoken to them by Moses" (Lev 10:10–11; compare Mal 2:7; Neh 8:2, 8–9). They would also render judgments according to the law of God (Deut 17:8–13). Furthermore, God appointed the priests to pronounce blessing upon his covenant people (Num 6:24–26). God summarizes this benedictory ministry by saying, "So shall [Aaron and his sons] put my name upon the people of Israel, and I will bless them" (Num 6:27).

---

not be understood as fulfillments of the promise of Genesis 12:1–3 so much as anticipations of God's intention to bless the nations through the work of the promised offspring, Christ.

27. Note the way in which these three offices are brought together in Deuteronomy 16:18–18:22—priest (16:18–17:13, esp. 17:9–13); king (17:14–20); priest (18:1–8); and prophet (18:15–22). For an accessible and fuller discussion of the offices of prophet, priest, and king under the Old Testament, and their relationship to the three-fold office of Christ, see Richard P. Belcher, Jr., *Prophet, Priest, and King: The Roles of Christ in the Bible and Our Roles Today* (Phillipsburg, NJ: P&R, 2016). On Moses himself as a typical mediator, foreshadowing Christ in his three-fold office of prophet, priest, and king, see Gerard Van Groningen, *Messianic Revelation in the Old Testament*, 2 vols. (Grand Rapids: Baker Academic, 1990), 1.205–11.

28. Belcher, *Prophet, Priest, and King*, 60.

Similarly, under the Mosaic covenant, God established the office of king.[29] Although the desire and request for a king is sinfully motivated (Israel wants to be like the nations around her that have human kings), God will grant them the king of his choosing (Deut 17:14–15; compare 1 Sam 8:5, 19–20). Israel's king must himself be an Israelite (Deut 17:15). He must "acquire" neither "many horses for himself," "many wives for himself," nor "excessive silver and gold" (Deut 17:16, 17), lest his heart turn aside from sincere devotion to God. His reign is to be marked by the constant reading, meditation, and practice of God's law (Deut 17:18–20). In these ways, God was emphasizing that the king's power and authority did not reside in himself, but in God. He was to rule not according to his own will, but according to the revealed will of God.[30]

The Mosaic covenant also specified regulations for the office of prophet, in particular the criteria by which the people of God might distinguish a true from a counterfeit prophet (Deut 18:15–22). The prophet is one of whom God says, "I will put my words in his mouth, and he shall speak to them all that I command him" (Deut 18:18b). Whereas a priest stands on behalf of the people before God, the prophet stands on behalf of God before the people. In particular, Moses points to a particular "prophet like me" whom God will "raise up ... from among you, from your brothers" (Deut 18:15).[31] That is to say, although there will be a plurality of prophets in Israel, God will one day raise

---

29. We should note here that, while the office of "king" is a typological and theocratic office under the Mosaic covenant, the Pentateuch points to an office, "elder," that pre-existed the Mosaic covenant, continued under the Mosaic covenant, and existed in the new covenant church after the expiration of the Mosaic covenant, on which see J. A. Alexander, *Essays on the Primitive Church Offices* (New York: Charles Scribner, 1851), 1–28; Stuart Robinson, "The Churchliness of Calvinism: Presbytery *Jure Divino* Its Logical Outcome," in J. Thomson, ed., *Report of Proceedings of the First General Presbyterian Council* (Edinburgh: Thomas and Archibald Constable, 1877), 60–68, esp. 64; Thomas E. Peck, *Notes on Ecclesiology*, 2nd ed. (Richmond, VA: Presbyterian Committee of Publication, 1892), 35; and D. Douglas Bannerman, *The Scripture Doctrine of the Church Historically and Exegetically Considered* (1887; repr., Grand Rapids: Baker Academic, 1976), 97–98, who cites Exodus 3:16–18; 4:29; 12:21; 16:3, 22; 17:5f.; 24:1–11; Ezekiel 14:1–6; 20:1–5, 27f.; Jeremiah 29:1, 4–7. Bannerman concludes that "the eldership ... formed, so to speak, the natural and permanent basis of all other organization in Israel," 98. He points, furthermore, to indications within the Old Testament that the elders functioned in a representative capacity with respect to the people whom they served, 101, esp. 101n1.

30. Peter C. Craigie, *The Book of Deuteronomy*, NICOT (Grand Rapids: Eerdmans, 1976), 253, 257; Wright, *Deuteronomy*, 209.

31. On the complexities of interpretation relating to this verse, see Van Groningen, *Messianic Revelation*, 1.252–53.

up a distinct "Prophet ... like Moses," in that "God will speak face-to-face with this Prophet and will use him to accomplish great signs and wonders."[32]

Although these three offices are designedly distinct, there is one feature that each has in common with the others. Men who were to serve as prophet, priest, or king were to be set apart and installed into office through anointing with oil. Moses installs Aaron as priest through the anointing of oil (Lev 8:12), as priests after him are to be (Lev 21:10, 12). The prophet Samuel set apart Israel's first king, Saul, with the anointing of oil (1 Sam 10:1–8). King David (1 Sam 16:13; compare 2 Sam 2:4) and King Solomon (1 Kgs 1:34, 39) are similarly set apart through the anointing of oil. Similarly, we read of the prophet Elisha being set apart to ministry through the anointing of oil (1 Kgs 19:16).[33]

These three offices (prophet, priest, and king) are not unique to the Mosaic covenant, but they are uniquely established and regulated under the Mosaic covenant. The New Testament underscores how Christ undertakes each office in his mediatorial work and, in this respect, brings fulfillment to these typological Mosaic offices. He is the prophet of whom Moses spoke in Deuteronomy 18 (Acts 3:22; 7:37). Although he is not a Levitical priest, he is a high priest after the order of Melchizedek, superior to and surpassing the Aaronic priesthood (Heb 5:1–7:28). He is a king who is not only descended from King David (Matt 1:1, 17; Acts 2:30), but who also sits upon the "throne of his father David" (Luke 1:32). Uniting these three offices in himself (compare Zech 6:9–14), he is anointed with the Holy Spirit (Isa 61:1; Luke 3:22; Luke 4:18) to undertake his mediatorial work in the power of the Spirit. His very title "Christ" (Messiah) reflects the reality of this anointing and its centrality to the discharge of his labors.

It is as the anointed Prophet, Priest, and King of his church that Jesus brings to fulfillment the promises of Genesis 3:15 and Genesis 12:1–3. Jesus has conquered death and has won eschatological life in his life of obedience, sacrificial death, and resurrection from the dead. The Spirit, whom he, with the Father, has poured out in fulness upon all nations, applies to sinners the salvation that Christ has purchased for them. In this way, the

32. Belcher, *Prophet, Priest, and King*, 25.

33. As Belcher notes in his conclusion to a discussion on the anointing of prophets in the Old Testament, "anointing with oil is closely associated with being a prophet, even if that anointing does not happen to every prophet," *Prophet, Priest, and King*, 30.

offices of the Mosaic covenant comprise so many "shadows" of the "body," that is, "Christ" (Col 2:17, author's translation).

CONCLUSION

The Sinaitic or Mosaic covenant is an extension and expansion of the promises and precepts given under the Abrahamic covenant. The corpus of law delivered in that covenant reflected the two-fold state of Israel, a spiritual people called to trust and obey the God of Abraham, Isaac, and Jacob, and a body politic inhabiting the land that God had given them. Israel received the law as a people redeemed by his saving power. The law was the way in which they were to pursue the calling of holiness. The law was to be the instrument of Israel's sanctification. It was the way in which they would demonstrate love to one another and love to the God who had first loved them.

As God constituted her under the Mosaic covenant, Israel was to point forward to the Lord Jesus Christ, the promised Seed of the Woman. The law typologically looked to Christ. The covenant sign and meal of the new covenant, the Passover, anticipated the sacrificial death of Christ. Israel was called to diffuse the saving knowledge of God to the nations so that they, alongside Israel, might trust in the Redeemer shadowed in the Torah. And the instituted offices of Israel—prophet, priest, and king—anticipated and reflected the three-fold office of the Anointed Mediator to come.

Sadly, Israel failed to discharge her calling. Far from letting this derail his purposes in redemption, God appointed Israel's disobedience, rebellion, and forfeiture of duty as the way in which he would bring Christ into the world and establish a worldwide people in him. The dissolution of Israel under the Mosaic covenant was a prelude to a greater and more permanent work under the new covenant. The prophets of the Old Testament give us important glimpses into both, which we will explore in the next chapter.

FURTHER READING

Belcher, Richard. *Prophet, Priest, and King: The Roles of Christ in the Bible and Our Roles Today.* Phillipsburg, NJ: P&R, 2016. A biblical-theological exploration of the three-fold office of Christ, with particular attention given to the Old Testament's testimony to the office of prophet, the office of priest, and the office of king.

Fairbairn, Patrick. *The Typology of Scripture Viewed in Connection with the Whole Series of the Divine Dispensations.* 2 vols. New York: Funk & Wagnalls, 1900. Fairbairn was a nineteenth-century Scottish Presbyterian, and contemporary with James Bannerman, James Buchanan, William Cunningham, and George Smeaton. This work extensively explores biblical typology, giving particular attention to the tabernacle.

Poythress, Vern S. *The Shadow of Christ in the Law of Moses.* Phillipsburg, NJ: P&R, 1991. An exploration of the Sinaitic legislation in light of these laws' fulfillment in Christ. Poythress engages the claims both of Dispensationalism and Theonomy in such a way as to offer important insights to the constitution of the people of God under the old covenant.

V

THE PROPHETS: JUDGMENT AND HOPE FOR THE CHURCH

To read the Old Testament prophets is to be taken up in two currents.[1] The first current chronicles the decline of Israel from initial Solomonic glory to the division of the kingdom to the ultimate conquest and exile of the Northern and Southern Kingdoms in the eighth and sixth centuries BC. The second current charts God's unfolding purpose to preserve a remnant from the people and to bring them to eschatological blessing. This purpose, the prophets make clear, comes to fruition in the work of the promised Messiah. It is only in light of the fulfillment of God's purposes in Christ that both of these currents are properly understood. They are not mutually canceling but mutually reinforcing. God dismantles the theocratic kingdom of Israel in the interests of erecting an eschatological kingdom that stretches across the globe.

Understanding the people of God at the twilight of the old covenant requires attentiveness to both these currents. The dissolution of the kingdoms and the dispersion of the people is not the end of the people of God.

1. In the English Bible, the Prophets correspond to the portion of the canon extending from Isaiah to Malachi. The Hebrew ordering of the canon, however, identifies Joshua, Judges, Samuel, and Kings as the Former Prophets, and Isaiah, Jeremiah, Ezekiel, and the Twelve as the Latter Prophets. The Former Prophets are prophetic insofar as they tell the history of Israel from the prophetic point of view. In this chapter, we will concentrate on the testimony of the Latter Prophets without neglecting the testimony of the Former Prophets.

It is, in fact, the prelude to that people's reconstitution in light of the coming of the promised Messiah, Jesus Christ. The prophetic promises concerning the remnant and concerning Christ shed light on the dynamic, global future of the eschatological people of God.

Before we consider each of these currents, however, we must explore their headwaters. The covenant that God made with David in 2 Samuel 7 (1 Chr 17) provides needed context for the theocratic kingdom and its dissolution. But it no less prepares us for the restoration announced by the Prophets. In this chapter, then, we will first survey the contours of the Davidic covenant. We will then turn to the history and outcome of the Israelite monarchy. Finally, we will explore the prophetic promises of restoration and renewal. In each section, we will particularly give attention to the implications of these movements and developments in redemptive history for the people of God.

THE DAVIDIC COVENANT

ALTHOUGH THE WORD "COVENANT" DOES not appear in 2 Samuel 7:1–17 or in the parallel text, 1 Chronicles 17:3–15, subsequent revelation denominates this arrangement between God and David a "covenant" (Pss 89:39; 132:11–12; 2 Sam 23:5).[2] The term "offspring" (זֶרַע), describing the recipient and object of the divine promise, in 2 Samuel 7:12 serves to set this covenant in organic continuity with the earlier protoevangelium (Gen 3:15) and the earlier Abrahamic covenant, which had similarly emphasized promises concerning the "offspring" of Abraham.[3] There are at least two ways in which God's covenant with David expands and extends his prior covenantal promises.[4]

---

2. Compare Greg Goswell, "What Makes the Arrangement of God with David in 2 Samuel 7 a Covenant?" *ResQ* 60, no. 2 (2018): 87–98.

3. Van Groningen notes the as-yet-unrealized "covenantal promise concerning the seed of Abraham and the kings to arise from Abraham's seed (Gen 17:7–9) as well as the promise of the continuity of the throne: 'the sceptre shall not depart' (49:10)," *Messianic Revelation in the Old Testament*, 1:297. Richard P. Belcher Jr. has noted that in 2 Samuel 7:25–29, "David uses Adonai Yahweh (Lord GOD) for the name of God," a name that "does not appear anywhere else in Samuel or in the parallel passage in Chronicles," but that "is used in Genesis 15:2 and 8 by Abraham when God spoke to him about the promise of a seed," *The Fulfillment of the Promises of God: An Explanation of Covenant Theology* (Fearn, Rosshire, UK: Christian Focus, 2020), 103, citing Walter C. Kaiser, Jr., "The Blessing of David: The Charter for Humanity," in *The Law and the Prophets*, ed. John H. Skilton (Phillipsburg, NJ: P&R, 1974), 310. This connection indicates, Belcher concludes, David's "aware[ness of] ... the blessing of Abraham [as] continued in the blessing that God has promised to him," Belcher, "The Blessing of David," 310.

4. See a fuller discussion of the ways in which the Davidic covenant brings the Abrahamic and Mosaic promises to fulfillment at Richard P. Belcher, Jr., "The Davidic Covenant," in Guy Prentiss Waters, J. Nicholas Reid, and John R. Muether, *Covenant Theology: Biblical, Theological, and Historical Perspectives* (Wheaton, IL: Crossway, 2020), 183.

The first concerns God's naming the offspring of David his "son" (7:14). The second concerns God's promise to establish the house, or dynasty, and kingdom of David forever (7:16).

2 Samuel 7

God had earlier declared the nation of Israel to be his "son" (Exod 4:22, Deut 1:31; compare Hos 11:1). Now, he declares each descendant in the royal line of David to be his "son." Without nullifying the corporate identification of his people as "son," God now designates a particular individual, the Davidic scion, his "son." This "son" will be subject to the "discipline" of YHWH, but God pledges that his "steadfast love will not depart from him," as it happened with Saul (2 Sam 7:14, 15). As such, the Davidic king plays a mediatorial role between God and the people such that the king's "actions of obedience and disobedience become part of the basis for whether God's people experience His judgment or His blessings."[5] Even so, all such transactions assume the perpetuity and inviolability of the covenant that God is making with David (see Ps 89:28–29, 33–37).[6]

Importantly, nestled in between God's promise to David to "raise up your offspring after you" (7:12) and to "be to him a father, and he ... to me a son" (7:14) is a promise concerning what this offspring will do. God tells David, "He shall build a house for my name, and I will establish the throne of his kingdom forever" (7:13). As Vos has noted, God "generat[es]" the son, and the son, in turn, generates "the house of God."[7] Therefore, the "theocracy is produced and maintained by the son of God and, in the last analysis, by God himself."[8]

God then promises that David's "house" and "kingdom" "shall be made sure forever before me," and that "[his] throne shall be established forever" (7:16). In the parallel text in 1 Chronicles, the "house," "kingdom," and "throne" are said to be *God's* (1 Chr 17:14). Reading these two texts together yields the conclusion that "the kingdom is God's

5. Belcher, *The Fulfillment of the Promises of God*, 113.

6. A point reiterated throughout the narrative of Kings, so rightly, Robertson, *The Christ of the Covenants*, 237–41.

7. Vos, *The Eschatology of the Old Testament*, 128.

8. Vos, *The Eschatology of the Old Testament*, 128.

kingdom, with his rule manifested through the reign of the son of David who sits on the throne," and that "the kingdom of God on earth is established through the Davidic covenant."[9]

David's response to these promises suggests that he understood this covenant to have implications and ramifications beyond the borders of national Israel. In his response to God's promises, David declares, "You have spoken also of your servant's house for a great while to come, and this is instruction for mankind, O Lord God!" (2 Sam 7:19). David not only understands God's promises concerning his "house" to extend well into the future ("for a great while to come") but also across the world ("and this is instruction for mankind"). "Faithfulness on the part of the Davidic son would effect the divine rule in the entire world. ... [T]he covenant that makes the Davidic king son of God is the instrument of bringing Yahweh's Torah to all nations."[10]

The Davidic covenant, then, distinguishes and establishes the line of David as playing a critical role in the forthcoming history of Israel. The descendants of David will be God's "sons," who will serve a mediatorial role between God and Israel. It will be through their rule that God will rule his people. David understood the perpetuity of the promises that God had made to him (7:13, 16) in conjunction with these promises' global reach or scope (7:19). It would be through God's own son, descended from David, that God would realize his rule over all human beings.

THE DISSOLUTION OF ISRAEL

THE REIGN OF KING SOLOMON had a promising beginning in many respects. God not only grants Solomon his request for wisdom (1 Kgs 3:1–15; compare 4:29–31), but unparalleled "riches and honor" besides (1 Kgs 3:13; compare 10:1–29). Solomon builds the "house"—the temple—that David had wanted to build but that God had prevented him from building. In keeping with his covenant with David, God promises to Solomon and his descendants longevity of rule, provided that they continue in obedience to God (1 Kgs 9:1–9; compare 2 Sam 7:13, 16).

9. Belcher, "The Davidic Covenant," 180. Robertson observes how, prior to the Davidic covenant (2 Sam 5:3), David, as king, is represented as "covenant mediator" between Israel and God, *The Christ of the Covenants*, 235.

10. Gentry and Wellum, *Kingdom through Covenant*, 457–58.

Solomon ushers in an era of domestic peace and prosperity—"and [Solomon] had peace on all sides around him. And Judah and Israel lived in safety, from Dan even to Beersheba, every man under his vine and under his fig tree, all the days of Solomon" (1 Kgs 4:25). When the nations do come to Solomon, they come not to wage war but to examine Solomon's reputation for wisdom. The Queen of Sheba, witnessing for herself Solomon's wisdom and prosperity, pronounces a blessing upon Solomon's subjects and upon the Lord himself (1 Kgs 10:6–9). It is difficult not to see in this scene an echo of Moses's words in Deuteronomy 4:6–8, in which the nations of Canaan would express admiration for the wisdom of Israel's statutes and the nearness of God to Israel.

And yet, Solomon's prosperity is not to last. In express violation of the Mosaic covenant, Solomon takes many wives (1 Kgs 11:1–8; compare Deut 17:17). These wives, in turn, lead him after their gods. It is for this act of covenantal treachery that God pledges to divide the kingdom, leaving only a single tribe to the descendants of David (1 Kgs 11:9–13). The ten tribes are ruled by a succession of wicked kings. Their national existence comes to an end with Assyrian conquest and exile. Faithful to his promise, God maintains the line of David in rule over the tribe of Judah. This spiritually checkered line ceases to rule when the Babylonians conquer the Southern Kingdom and carries the Davidic king into captivity in Babylon.

Because the king is the mediator and representative of the people, the people suffer the consequences of their king's actions. The Lord 's displeasure for the king's disobedience is visited upon the people. But the people are not disinterested, much less innocent, bystanders. They take on the character and spiritual priorities of their royal leaders. When God sends his prophets to Israel and to Judah, they indict not only their leaders, but also the people themselves.

Covenant Treachery

We may understand, then, the collapse of the people of God along two lines. The first is the nation's covenant treachery, and the second is the failure of the offices of prophet, priest, and king. When God sent prophets to his people during the period of the divided kingdom, these prophets carried with them the charge that the people of God had committed covenant treachery. God reminds Israel of her unique covenant privilege, a privilege that only accentuates the gravity of Israel's sins (Amos 3:1–2). Consequently, the judgments that befall the people of God are covenantal in nature—the curses that had been threatened under the Mosaic covenant (Lev 26; Deut 28). The prophet Jeremiah makes this connection particularly clear: "Yet they did not obey or incline their ear, but everyone walked in the stubbornness of his evil heart. Therefore I brought upon them all the words of this covenant, which I commanded them to do, but they did not" (Jer 11:8; compare 11:10).[11] Similarly, the prophet Ezekiel surveys the history of God's people, chronicling it in terms of covenant treachery (Ezek 16:59–63; see 16:1–58). The prophets Hosea and Ezekiel describe the conduct of God's people in terms of conjugal infidelity (Hos 2:1–13; Ezek 20; 22). Because marriage is covenantal in nature (Mal 2:14), Israel's spiritual adultery is covenantal treachery.

Israel's breach of covenant is evident in her willful and persistent violation of the stipulations of the covenant, the Mosaic legislation. The prophets emphasize that Israel has corrupted both tables of the law—the laws governing her duties to God, and the laws governing her duties to neighbor. The prophets highlight Israel's sins in relation to the worship of God. On the one hand, Israel has turned her worship to the idols rather than to the God of heaven and earth. Their gods had proliferated—they were "as many as [their] cities" (Jer 11:13), and Israel sought gods from among the surrounding nations to be like the nations (2 Kgs 16:10–20). Israel's practices in worship came to be adopted from the nations as well—the high places and child sacrifice, for example. Israel's idolatry persisted from her sojourn in the wilderness down to her exile in Babylon (Acts 7:42–43; compare Amos 5:25). But on the other hand, Israel has corrupted the worship that God had commanded them to render to him. Israel's confidence lay in the rites and institutions of God's worship, and not in God himself (Jer 7:4). God declared that he would not accept even the ceremonially correct worship of Israel because it was being offered by persons who were committed to a lifestyle of sinning (Jer 7:10–11; Isa 1:10–17). Notwithstanding this

11. The imperfect tense of the verb translated "brought" conveys "a historical resume of the disasters that had come upon the people of the covenant, including the exile of the northern kingdom Israel," a "lesson" that "was not without continuing relevance" to Jeremiah's generation, John L. Mackay, *Jeremiah, Volume 1: Chapters 1–20* (Fearn, UK: Christian Focus, 2004), 400.

attention to cultic formality, the temple would fall into disrepair and the law of God would suffer neglect (see 2 Kgs 20:1–20).

The people of Israel sinned no less against one another. The prophets catalog the injustices that the people commit against one another—violence, oppression, theft, extortion, and sexual immorality, to name simply a few (see, representatively, Jer 7:9).[12] These sinful patterns of behavior mirrored those of the nations around Israel and the nations whom Israel had displaced from Canaan. The people of God even came to exceed the wickedness of Sodom: "Not only did you walk in their ways and do according to their abominations; within a very little time you were more corrupt than they in all your ways" (Ezek 16:47; cf. 16:46, 49). Isaiah therefore addresses Judah's leaders as "rulers of Sodom" and the people as the "people of Gomorrah" (Isa 1:10; compare Jer 23:14). Correspondingly, the punishment that will befall Judah will exceed that which befell Sodom (Lam 4:6).

Failure of Offices

As we have noted, the prophets single out the failures and sins of Israel's and Judah's leadership. Each category of leader—prophet, priest, and king—profoundly failed in their calling and duties as stipulated in the Mosaic covenant. Prophets were to speak only the words of God to the people of God (Deut 18:18b). But false prophets arose whom God had not sent and to whom God had not spoken (Jer 23:21). They spoke "visions of their own minds, not from the mouth of the Lord " (Jer 23:16). Rather than warning God's people of the judgment to come for their sins, they declared, "No disaster shall come upon you" (Jer 23:17; compare 6:14). Ezekiel likens the false prophets to those who whitewash a wall that is in imminent danger of collapse (Ezek 13:8–16). They impeded rather than aided their hearers in reckoning with the sins of the people of God and in repenting of them.[13]

12. As Vos perceptively notes, "The prophetic condemnation of the social sin of Israel does not have its deepest root in humanitarian motives … Oversounding this note of humanitarianism is the note of resentment of social injustice, and with this the whole problem is raised to the religious sphere. For injustice is sin against God, and no consequences, however deplorable from the manward point of view, could equal the terrible significance of the religious fact to the prophetic consciousness. … [W]hat shocks and excites the prophets' resentment is the bearing of the wicked conduct upon Jehovah and His rights," *Biblical Theology*, 274–75.

13. As J. A. Thompson observes in relation to Jer 6:13–15, "The religious leaders treated the people's wound superficially while all the time their rebellious acts and continued

Priests and Levites were to oversee the worship of the taberacle and temple, and priests were to lead and teach the people of God the law of God, particularly as it pertained to holiness (Lev 10:10–11). But as early as the days of the judges, one Levite sold his services to an Ephraimite, Micah, and later to the tribe of Dan (Judg 17:1–13; 18:1–6, 14–20). Later, Jeremiah reports that "both prophet and priest are ungodly, even in my house I have found their evil, declares the Lord " (Jer 23:11; compare 6:13, 8:10). The priests have also failed in their duty to teach the people of God the law of God. Malachi observes that, while "the lips of a priest should guard knowledge, and people should seek instruction from his mouth, for he is the messenger of the Lord of hosts," the priests "have turned aside from the way ... have caused many to stumble by [their] instruction ... [and] have corrupted the covenant of Levi" (Mal 2:7, 8).14 In brief, Ezekiel says, "the law perishes from the priest" (Ezek 7:26).

Kings, for their part, were to rule according to the law of God and in submission to God (Deut 17:14–20). In the Northern Kingdom, each king committed what came to be known as the sin of that kingdom's first king, Jeroboam. Jeroboam's eponymous sin was the establishment and enforcement of an idolatrous system of worship purposefully set up to rival the true worship of God in Jerusalem (1 Kgs 12:25–33). The Southern Kingdom, for its part, witnessed a succession of kings that was spiritually checkered. Godly kings, such as Hezekiah and Josiah, led God's people in the true worship of God and promoted the knowledge of God in the law of God. But wicked kings, such as Ahaz and Manasseh, led Judah in forms of worship drawn from the surrounding nations. In the end, the tide of such wickedness would come to determine the destiny of the royal house of Judah (and of Judah itself).

---

breaches of the covenant only beckoned the forces of judgment to hasten on," *The Book of Jeremiah*, NICOT (Grand Rapids: Eerdmans, 1980), 258.

14. Douglas Stuart has noted that Malachi's words should not be restricted to "a few renegade priests," but rather address "a large and long-established (or reestablished) group, numbering in the thousands, supported by hundreds of Levites and other temple workers, and clearly well-entrenched in terms of their official status," "Malachi," in *The Minor Prophets: An Exegetical and Expository Commentary*, ed. Thomas Edward McComiskey, 3 vols. (Grand Rapids: Baker Academic, 1998), 1322–23.

It is in Ezekiel 34:1–10 that God, in the generation before Judah's exile, offers a synopsis of Judah's kings.[15] Rather than "feed[ing] the sheep" they have been "feeding [them]selves" (34:2). They have exploited the sheep, neglected the sheep, and oppressed the sheep (34:3–4). As a result, the sheep "were scattered, because there was no shepherd" (34:5). God himself stands "against the shepherds" and will hold them to account (34:10). The kings should have taught and exemplified the law of God, as servants, to Judah (and Israel). Instead, their self-centered and self-aggrandizing leadership resulted in the destruction of the people of God.

Whether viewed in light of the people or of the people's prophetic, priestly, and royal leadership, Israel profoundly and fundamentally failed in her calling to be a light to the nations. On the contrary, Israel sought—and found—conformity to the nations (1 Sam 8:5; Ezek 20:32). In keeping with the threatened curses of the Mosaic covenant, God removes his people in judgment from the land "among all peoples, from one end of the earth to the other" (Deut 28:64). God exiled his people to dwell among the nations whom they had emulated, not least in their worship of other gods. Thus, the people of God were scattered, removed from the temple, from Jerusalem, and from their king. How would the covenant of David be maintained and fulfilled?

THE RESTORATION OF ISRAEL

When the canonical prophets anticipate (and chronicle) the dissolution of Israel under her Mosaic constitution, they no less forecast the eschatological reconstitution of God's people. This reconstitution is multidimensional. God will spare a remnant, which will comprise the foundation of the expansion of the people of God to encompass all nations. God will no longer relate to his people under the old covenant but under the new covenant. The new covenant will witness the outpouring of the Spirit of God upon the nations, a new temple, and a new heaven and earth. These expansive blessings all stem from the work of the Davidic servant. Because this prophetic framework of anticipation sets the stage

---

15. On the "shepherds" in Ezekiel 34:1–10 as "a collective term for the kings who had ruled [the Israelites] over the centuries (or possibly just those of recent generations)" rather than "the king, the royal court, and leading figures in the community more generally," see John L. Mackay, *Ezekiel, Volume 2: Chapters 25–48* (Fearn, UK: Christian Focus, 2018), 196–97.

for the ministry of Christ and the church under the new covenant, we may reflect on each of these developments in turn.

In the first place, God will spare a remnant from his people. Through Isaiah's ministry, the people of God will be reduced in number: "And though a tenth remain in it, it will be burned again, like a terebinth or an oak, whose stump remains when it is felled. The holy seed is its stump" (Isa 6:13). It is from this "holy seed" that "a new Israel will sprout."[16] It is likely that this "holy seed" has particular reference to "the shoot out of the stem of Jesse" (11:1).[17] Thus, "the promise of the Messiah is the guarantee of a future people over whom he will reign."[18] Through the prophets, God declares that he will reduce his people to a remnant. But from that remnant both the Messiah and his eschatologically-renewed people will emerge.[19] To be sure, the people of God will be radically transformed, but for all these transformations there is and remains a single people of God tracing its origins to Eve (Gen 3:15) and to Abram (Gen 12:1–3).

Jeremiah 31:31–34

The eschatological people of God will relate to God under what the prophet Jeremiah terms the "new covenant" (Jer 31:31–34). God describes this "new covenant with the house of Israel and the house of Judah" as "not like the covenant that I made with their fathers on the day when I took them by the hand to bring them out of the land of Egypt, my covenant that they broke" (Jer 31:31–32). One important feature of the old covenant is that it was breakable and came to be broken.[20] As Hebrews notes in its commentary on this passage,

16. J. Ridderbos, *Isaiah*, trans. John Vriend, BSC (Grand Rapids: Zondervan, 1985), 79.

17. J. Alec Motyer, *The Prophecy of Isaiah: An Introduction & Commentary* (Downers Grove, IL: InterVarsity Press, 1993), 80. The reason for this identification lies in the "inclusio" that exists between 6:13b and 11:13b, *The Prophecy of Isaiah*, 80.

18. Motyer, *The Prophecy of Isaiah*, 80.

19. Importantly, Isaiah's prophecy closes with God's promise that "your offspring and your name [shall] remain" even as "the new heavens and the new earth that I make shall remain before me" (Isa 66:22). Since the next verse describes "all flesh" coming into the presence of the Lord to worship him, "offspring" here refers to God's global "redeemed humanity," the "single family which is united in the common ancestor Abraham and the common salvation through the Servant (Gen 22:16–18; Is. 53.10; cf. 59:21; 65:9)," Motyer, *The Prophecy of Isaiah*, 543.

20. Mackay observes that "the word rendered 'broke' ... may well ... encompass the idea of rendering the covenant null and void. ... In that case the existing covenant arrangements provided no basis for any further relationship between God and the people. As had been the case in the first place, the subsequent history of the Lord and his people would be rooted

the "first covenant" was not "faultless," but the "fault" lay with the people of God and not with either God or the covenant itself (Heb 8:7, 8). By implication, the new covenant is not susceptible to this kind of breaking. That state of affairs suggests that the new covenant will be a permanent and final covenant that God will establish between himself and his people, a fact confirmed in Jeremiah 31:35–36.

God will make the new covenant "with the house of Israel and the house of Judah." That is to say, for all of the individual soteriological promises encompassed under the new covenant, the "corporate dimension" of God's prior covenantal dealings with his people is not thereby eclipsed or eliminated.[21] God enumerates what the people of God will enjoy under the new covenant—God will "put" his "law within them" and "write it on their hearts. And I will be their God, and they shall be my people" (Jer 31:33). Further, God pledges that "they shall all know me, from the least of them to the greatest." Finally, God promises to "forgive their iniquity, and [to] remember their sin no more" (Jer 31:34).

The promises of the new covenant are not in themselves altogether new or unattested in the experience of God's people under the old covenant. David declared that God's "law is within my heart" (Ps 40:8). David no less rejoiced in the forgiveness of sins (Ps 32:1–2). And Israel knew God and was known by God (Amos 3:2). We may inquire, then, in what respects the new covenant would be new. God's promise to write the law on the hearts of his people was something that the old covenant was of itself incapable of doing, as the apostle Paul graphically emphasizes (2 Cor 3:1–4:6). What is in view in the new covenant is "the greater measure of the Spirit which is to be present to engender spiritual life in the new age."[22] God's promise of the forgiveness of sins would find its historically-realized foundation in the life, death, and resurrection of the Messiah-Servant (Rom 3:21–31). God's promise

in his sovereign and unconditional determination to begin anew with them," *Jeremiah, Volume 2: Chapters 21–52* (Fearn, UK: Christian Focus, 2004), 235. Importantly, only the Mosaic covenant is said to be broken. The conclusion of Jeremiah 30–33 emphasizes that God's new covenant promises are in keeping with his earlier promises to Abraham and to David (Jer 33:26).

21. Robertson, *The Christ of the Covenants*, 287.

22. Mackay, *Jeremiah, Volume 2*, 237.

that "they shall all know me, from the least to the greatest" anticipates a day when the mediatorial offices of the old covenant (prophet, priest, and king), through which God related to his people, would be no more.[23] Henceforth, God's people would have direct access to him, apart from such typological mediation.[24]

The new covenant, then, is not absolutely new with respect to the old covenant, even as it is demonstrably "superior" to it.[25] In fact, as the hallmark promises of the new covenant themselves indicate, what is promised under the new covenant was already experienced in kind by God's people under previous covenants, including the old covenant.[26] What particularly distinguishes the new covenant from previous administrations is both the depth and the scale of the reception of its promised blessings.

This extension and expansion of earlier covenanted blessings is underscored by the new covenant promise of the ministry of the Holy Spirit.[27] The Spirit, of course, had been active covenantally and redemptively under the old covenant (see 1 Cor 10:3–4; Num 11:24–30; Isa 63:11). The new covenant ministry of the Spirit represents, then, a deepening and expansion of his work under the old covenant. Isaiah represents the Spirit's eschatological ministry in terms of the outpouring

---

23. So rightly Robertson, *The Christ of the Covenants*, 293–94.

24. Some interpreters have taken Jeremiah 31:34 to reflect a change in the composition of the covenant community, namely, the exclusion of the children of believers such that only regenerate persons are members of the new covenant community, so Gentry and Wellum, *Kingdom through Covenant*, 554–56. But the phrase "from the least to the greatest" need not exclude children, indeed, it may positively indicate children. The phrase denotes, rather, "from the youngest to the oldest" or "right across the social spectrum," as Mackay, *Jeremiah, Volume 2*, 238 (compare the appearance of this phrase at Jer 6:13 and 44:12). Furthermore, Jeremiah 32:39 envisions children as continuing to participate in this "everlasting covenant." Thus, "like the previous covenants of the Old Testament, there is also a familial aspect to the new covenant," Michael G. McKelvey, "The New Covenant as Promised in the Major Prophets," *Covenant Theology: Biblical, Theological, and Historical Perspectives*, 199. See also Christian Locatell, "Jeremiah 31:34, New Covenant Membership, and Baptism" *Scriptura* 114: no. 1 (2015): 1–14.

25. See the helpful lists of "continuities between the Old and New Covenants" and the "Superiority of the New Covenant to the Old Covenant" at Bruce K. Waltke, "The kingdom of God in the Old Testament: The Covenants" in *The Kingdom of God*, ed. Christopher W. Morgan and Robert A. Peterson (Wheaton, IL: Crossway, 2012), 91–92.

26. For a fuller discussion of the ways in which the new covenant promises of Jeremiah 30–33 stand in organic continuity with prior covenantal administrations, see Belcher, *The Fulfillment of the Promises of God*, 120–26; compare Robertson, *The Christ of the Covenants*, 280–86.

27. Sinclair B. Ferguson, "Infant Baptism View," in *Baptism: Three Views*, ed. David F. Wright (Downers Grove, IL: InterVarsity Press, 2009), 87.

of "water on the thirsty land, and streams on the dry ground" (Isa 44:3) such that the desert shall blossom (Isa 35:1–2, 6–7). God says through the prophet Joel, whom the apostle Peter cites on the day of Pentecost in connection with the Spirit's outpouring by the Father and the Risen Christ, "I will pour out my Spirit on all flesh; your sons and your daughters shall prophesy, your old men shall dream dreams, and your young men shall see visions. Even on the male and female servants in those days I will pour out my Spirit" (Joel 2:28–29). The Spirit's ministry is not only denominated an outpouring but it will reach "all flesh." No sector of humanity, whether reckoned by gender, age, or social station, is exempted from his eschatological activity.[28]

The prophet Ezekiel highlights the Spirit's new covenant ministry in terms of his saving work in the lives of men and women.[29] He will "clean" the people of God "from all [their] uncleannesses," and will give them "a new heart" and a "new spirit" (Ezek 36:25, 26). He will "remove the heart of stone from [their] flesh and give [them] a heart of flesh" (Ezek 36:26). The effect of his indwelling presence in the lives of God's people is a careful observance of the commandments of God (Ezek 36:27), close fellowship with God (36:28), evident covenantal blessing (36:29–30), and humiliation for sin (36:31–32). God will have a people set apart from the nations, consecrated for his worship, service, and glory. Such a work is the sovereign, powerful, irresistible work of God himself. This work of the Spirit, the prophet continues, is nothing short of God bringing the dead to life (37:1–14).

Significantly, this resurrecting work of the Spirit is paired with God's commitment to establish an eschatological temple. Ezekiel devotes nine chapters to detailing the structure of this temple, as well as its officers, sacrifices, and feast days (Ezek 40–48).[30] Its hallmark

28. "But, under the New Testament, the liberty of Christians is further enlarged … in fuller communications of the free Spirit of God, than believers under the law did ordinarily partake of," WCF 20.1.

29. Although the phrase "new covenant" does not appear in Ezekiel's prophecy, Ezekiel does speak of the "covenant of peace" (Ezek 34:25). Furthermore, the prophet in Ezekiel 33–37 discusses many of the same promises and blessings that are featured in Jeremiah in connection with the new covenant, on which see McKelvey, "The New Covenant as Promised in the Major Prophets," 202.

30. For a brief survey of Ezekiel's eschatological Temple, see my "Ezekiel," in *Lexham Context Commentary: Old Testament, Volume 4 (Major Prophets)*, ed. Douglas Mangum and Steven Runge (Bellingham, WA: Lexham, 2020).

characteristic is the abiding presence of God with his people (Ezek 48:35), a people who will undergo eschatological expansion. God promises, through Haggai, that "I will shake all nations, so that the treasures of all nations shall come in, and I will fill this house with glory. … The latter glory of this house shall be greater than the former. … And in this place I will give peace" (Hag 2:7, 9). Zechariah, in Zechariah 6:9–15, envisions "the temple of the Lord" rebuilt by "the Branch," who will "reign in his kingdom as both king and priest."[31] Strikingly, "those who are far off"—the gentiles—"shall come and help to build the temple of the Lord" (Zech 6:15). Malachi anticipates a day of "eschatological messianic universalism," when the nations will offer to God the worship that is acceptable to him and when the "name" of God "will be great among the nations" (Mal 1:11; compare Isa 2:1–5; Mic 4:1–5; Zech 8:23).[32]

The eschatological horizon of the prophets extends to the whole earth. By the saving power of the Spirit, God will gather to himself a people drawn from among the nations. They will offer to him acceptable worship and enjoy covenant fellowship with him. And they will also inhabit the whole earth. According to Paul, God's "promise to Abraham and his offspring" was "that he would be heir of the world" (Rom 4:13; compare Heb 11:9–10, 16). God's covenanted work of renewal, then, extends to "new heavens and new earth," which the prophet Isaiah proceeds to describe in terms of "Jerusalem, the new city" (Isa 65:17–25).33 God himself will be the "glory" of this global, eschatological people, temple, and new creation (Isa 60:19; Zech 14:6, 7; compare Rev 21:23, 22:5).

The prophets make clear that this eschatological renewal, reconstitution, and expansion of the people of God is the work of sovereign, divine power. In particular, this work finds its concentration in the

31. J. Alec Motyer, "Zechariah," in *The Minor Prophets*, 1116.

32. The phrase, "eschatological messianic universalism," is taken from Douglas Stuart, "Malachi," in *The Minor Prophets*, ed. McComiskey, 1306.

33. J. Alec Motyer, *Isaiah*, TOTC (Downers Grove, IL: InterVarsity Press, 1999), 450. For the same relationship of "new creation" and "Jerusalem" in Revelation 21:1, 2, see Beale, *The Temple and the Church's Mission: A Biblical Theology of the Dwelling Place of God*, NSBT 17 (Downers Grove, IL: Intervarsity, 2004), 25. Beale has argued that Paul intentionally alludes to this text in 2 Corinthians 5:17, showing that "Isaiah's promises of 'restoration' from the alienation of exile have begun to be fulfilled by the atonement and forgiveness of sins in Christ," *A New Testament Biblical Theology*, 534, emphasis removed.

offspring of David who will save and reign over this global people. Ezekiel describes this Davidic prince as a "shepherd" who will feed the sheep of Israel (Ezek 34:23, 24). Jeremiah tells us that this "righteous Branch" of David will "execute justice and righteousness in the land" (Jer 33:15), and "will be called, 'The Lord is our righteousness'" (23:6). This Davidic king will be no less the priest of God's people. The king enthroned at God's right hand is "a priest forever after the order of Melchizedek" (Ps 110:4; compare 6:13).

Amid the coming collapse of Judah, Isaiah provides a portrayal of the reign of this Shepherd-King (Isa 9:6–7). He will reign "on the throne of David and over his kingdom ... from this time forth and forevermore," and "of the increase of his government and of peace there will be no end" (9:7). Isaiah points to the fact that this king will be no ordinary man. He will be "born" a "child," even as "his name shall be called Wonderful Counselor, Mighty God, Everlasting Father, Prince of Peace" (9:6; compare Ps 2:6, 7). This "shoot from the stump of Jesse" will reign in the power of the abiding Spirit (11:1–2). His reign will permanently reverse the effects of the fall (11:6–8) and make "the earth ... full of the knowledge of the Lord as the waters cover the sea" (11:9).

It is in Isaiah's "servant" songs that we see the full reach and depth of the redemptive work of this Davidic priest-king. The servant is "chosen" of God (Isa 42:1). With God's "Spirit" abiding upon him (Isa 42:1), he "will bring forth justice to the nations," "justice in the earth" (42:1, 4). He will be a "covenant for the people, a light for the nations," bringing sight to the blind, and liberty to the captive (42:6, 7; compare 49:6). The servant is characterized by complete obedience to God (50:5–6). That obedience will culminate in the servant's humiliation and death, a death that is penal, substitutionary, and atoning for the sins of God's people (52:13–53:12). As a result of the obedience and death of God's servant, "many" will "be accounted righteous" (53:11), even "many nations" (52:15). Looking upon the fruit of the "anguish of his soul," the servant "shall see and be satisfied" (52:11).

Daniel describes the exaltation of the "son of man" (Dan 7:13).[34] Having completed his work of suffering and humiliation, the Son of

34. On the "son of man" as a specifically *messianic* figure, see Robertson, *The Christ of the Prophets*, 335–56.

Man enters into the presence of the "Ancient of Days," and "to him was given dominion and glory and a kingdom, and that all peoples, nations, and languages should serve him" (Dan 7:14). This kingdom is the reward and pledged outcome of his work on earth and finds its realization and manifestation on earth.[35] It will displace all human kingdoms and will be "an everlasting dominion, which shall not pass away ... that shall not be destroyed" (Dan 7:14; compare 7:27, 2:44–45).[36]

CONCLUSION

THE OLD TESTAMENT CHARTS THE failure of Israel to embrace her calling before the nations and, in particular, the failure of Israel's prophets, priests, and kings to discharge their covenanted duties before God. Such failures occasion Israel experiencing the curses of the Sinaitic covenant, resulting in their exile and dispersion among the nations. But the failures of the people of God, the prophets insist, are in no way the failures of God himself. On the contrary, out of the ruins of disobedience, God is already preparing the way for the obedient son of David, the servant, the Son of Man. He will bring light to the nations. He will die a sacrificial death and make priestly intercession for his people. As a shepherd, he will gather his people into an everlasting kingdom, ruling and defending them against all his and their enemies.

This work of the Messiah—prophet, priest, and king—inaugurates the promised new covenant, a covenant that represents the culmination of covenantal promises extending back to the garden of Eden. By the power of the Spirit, and upon the basis of the work of the Messiah, God will gather a people to himself from all nations. God will bring renewal to all creation, a work that finds its focus in Jerusalem and, in particularly, the temple. It is here that God will bring to pass the promise that characterizes all his covenantal dealings with his people and realizes his intentions for humanity at the creation—"I will be your God and you will be my people."

---

35. "The Christ event initiates the reign of God on earth that Daniel 7 promises," John E. Goldingay, *Daniel*, WBC 30 (Dallas: Word, 1989), 192.

36. "In the end, the indestructible kingdom of God prevails, and peoples from all nations are brought in submission comparable to the first Adam ('one like a Son of Man')," Robertson, *The Christ of the Prophets*, 441.

FURTHER READING

Belcher, Richard P. *The Fulfillment of the Promises of God: An Explanation of Covenant Theology*. Fearn, UK: Christian Focus, 2020. A recent biblical theological survey of covenant theology, with particular attention given to the Old Testament appearances of the Davidic covenant and the new covenant.

Robertson, O. Palmer. *The Christ of the Prophets*. Phillipsburg, NJ: P&R, 2004. A Reformed exploration of the prophetic literature of the Old Testament that sets the canonical prophets in the context of both covenant and law.

Swain, Scott. "New Covenant Theologies." In *Covenant Theology: Biblical, Theological, and Historical Perspectives*, ed. Guy Prentiss Waters, J. Nicholas Reid, and John R. Muether. Wheaton, IL: Crossway, 2020. 551–69. This chapter offers a brief and insightful treatment of Jeremiah 31:31–34 in conversation with recent developments in covenant theology.

Vos, Geerhardus. *The Eschatology of the Old Testament*. Edited by James T. Dennison, Jr. Phillipsburg, NJ: P&R, 2001. A collection of Vos's manuscript writings on Old Testament eschatology that begins with the creation account and that explores Old Testament prophecy. An important complement to his *Biblical Theology: Old and New Testaments.*

VI

JESUS: ESCHATOLOGICAL RECONSTITUTION OF THE CHURCH

THE NEW TESTAMENT CHRONICLES THE eschatological fulfillment of God's covenant promises, promises that trace their historical origin to Genesis 3:15, and find their framework within God's creation of the world and the covenant of works. These promises, we have seen, fundamentally concern the redemption of sinners. This project of redemption entails the ingathering of sinners into a people specially created and set apart by God for himself. God calls this people to holiness, worship, and a global mission.

It is in the person and work of Jesus Christ, the last Adam, that "all the promises of God find their Yes" (2 Cor 1:20). The Gospels chronicle and document the incarnation, life, death and resurrection of Christ—the basis upon which these promises achieve their intended fulfillment. Acts, the Epistles, and Revelation serve, by and large, to explicate the meaning of this once-for-all historical foundation laid in the finished and unrepeatable work of God incarnate.[1] And yet, even in the Gospels, not least in the teaching and activity of Jesus Christ himself, we are introduced to the meaning and significance of Christ's person and work.[2]

1. "The relation between Jesus and the Apostolate is in general that between the fact to be interpreted and the subsequent interpretation of this fact. This is none other than the principle under which all revelation proceeds. The New Testament Canon is constructed on it. ... [T]here is embodied in [the Gospels and the Acts of the Apostles] the great actuality of New Testament redemption," Vos, *Biblical Theology*, 303.

2. Note Vos's observations here, which immediately follow the material cited in the previous note, "Still, it ought not to be overlooked, that within the Gospels and the Acts

In this chapter, we are going to consider the testimony to Jesus Christ in the four Gospels. In particular, we will reflect upon what the Gospels have to say about the person and work of Christ in relation to the people of God in their approaching state of eschatological maturity. We will first think about the identity of Christ as it bears upon God's people, and then address the way in which Christ eschatologically reconstitutes the people of God around himself.

THE IDENTITY OF JESUS CHRIST AND THE CHURCH

Prior to the commencement of Jesus's public ministry, the Gospel narratives introduce us to Jesus in three ways. The first is through the birth narratives. In these narratives, Matthew and Luke highlight the Davidic ancestry and royal calling of Jesus of Nazareth. The highly structured Matthean genealogy introduces Jesus as "the son of David, the son of Abraham," periodizing his ancestry "from Abraham to David ... from David to the deportation to Babylon ... from the deportation to Babylon to the Christ" (Matt 1:1, 17). The virginal conception brings to fulfillment Isaiah 7:14 ("'Behold, the virgin shall conceive and bear a son, and they shall call his name Immanuel,' which means God with us'" [Matt 1:23]), a text that, in its larger context (Isa 7:1–9:7), points to "the birth of the divine son of David and also [lays] the foundation for the understanding of the unique nature of his birth."[3] The subsequent visit of the wise men transpires in connection with the prophecy of Micah, "And you, O Bethlehem, in the land of Judah, are by no means least among the rulers of Judah; for from you shall come a ruler who will shepherd my people Israel" (Matt 2:6; Mic 5:2). Additionally, it is difficult not to see in the wise men's worship of the infant Jesus and the presentation to him of gifts (Matt 2:11) a fulfillment of Isaiah's prophecy in Isaiah 60:1–7. The one who will shepherd Israel is the one who will reign over kings and nations.

---

themselves we meet with a certain preformation of this same law. Jesus's task is not confined to furnishing the fact or the facts; He interweaves and accompanies the creation of the facts with a preliminary illumination of them, for by the side of His work stands His teaching. Only the teaching is more sporadic and less comprehensive than that supplied by the Epistles," *Biblical Theology*, 303.

3. Motyer, *The Prophecy of Isaiah*, 86.

In Luke's Gospel, in the annunciation, the angel tells Mary that Jesus "will be great and will be called the Son of the Most High. And the Lord God will give to him the throne of his father David, and he will reign over the house of Jacob forever, and of his kingdom there will be no end" (Luke 1:32–33). Here, as in Matthew, Jesus is presented as one who is both fully divine and fully human.[4] In fulfillment of the promises that God made to David (2 Sam 7), Jesus will reign from the throne of David. In keeping with the vision of Daniel 7:14, Jesus's kingdom will be unbroken and permanent.[5] Prophesying on the occasion of the birth of John the Baptist, Zechariah blesses "the Lord God of Israel, for he has visited and redeemed his people and has raised up a horn of salvation for us in the house of his servant David" (Luke 1:68–69). Zechariah sees in the birth of Jesus's forerunner, John, the fulfillment of God's covenanted promises to David. When Jesus is born, Luke twice reminds us that he is born in "the city of David" (2:4, 11), and that "he is of the house and lineage of David" (2:4). The one born there, the angels tell the shepherds, is "a Savior, who is Christ the Lord" (2:11). The birth narratives of both Matthew's and Luke's Gospels, then, not only highlight Jesus's Davidic ancestry but also frame his person and work in terms of the Davidic promises and the subsequent prophetic amplification and development of those promises.

A second way in which the Gospel narratives introduce us to Jesus is through the preparatory ministry of John the Baptist. John is, Jesus tells his hearers in the middle of his ministry, "a prophet" and "more than a prophet" (Matt 11:9). Not only is he forerunner of the Lord, prophesied by Malachi (Mal 3:1; cited at Matt 11:10), but he is the climax and culmination of the "Prophets and the Law" (Matt 11:13), that is, "the Old Testament as a whole" as it anticipates the coming Messiah.[6] As such, John's voice is not

---

4. "'Most High' is a description of God (1:76; 6:35; 8:28; Acts 7:48; 16:17). This identity is equivalent to 'Son of God' in v. 35, where its meaning is clarified. It is not simply another messianic title but a reference to his divinity. Strauss points out that ... [Jesus is] the Son of God from the point of conception, before he has taken on any of the functions of kingship," David E. Garland, *Luke*, ZECNT (Grand Rapids: Zondervan, 2011), 80, citing Mark L. Strauss, *The Davidic Messiah in Luke-Acts: The Promise and Its Fulfillment in Lukan Christology*, JSNTSS 110 (Sheffield: Sheffield Academic, 1995), 93.

5. Strauss, *The Davidic Messiah*, 93.

6. Herman N. Ridderbos, *Matthew*, trans. Ray Togtman, BSC (Grand Rapids: Zondervan, 1987), 218. John's Gospel vividly illustrates the point in documenting John's directing "two of his disciples" to Jesus (John 1:35). Upon hearing John's witness to Jesus, "they followed Jesus"

only representative of the entirety of the Old Testament's message, but it is also its zenith with respect to clarity and fullness.

John's witness to Jesus is a manifold one. He speaks of Jesus as coming to "baptize ... with the Holy Spirit and fire" (Matt 3:11; Luke 3:16). What John is describing here is the "eschatological judgment" that Christ has come to usher into human history.[7] John no less describes Jesus as the one who has come to bear judgment on behalf of others. He is "the Lamb of God, who takes away the sin of the world" (John 1:29; compare 1:36). Furthermore, the one who will baptize with the Spirit is himself no less baptized with the Spirit (John 1:32). In some of his last recorded words in John's Gospel, John declares Jesus to be the bridegroom "who has the bride" (John 3:29), words that "obliquely" present "to the faithful remnant in Israel ... none other than Israel's King and Messiah," and no less represent that remnant as the bride of Christ.[8] According to John the Baptist, then, Jesus has come in the power of the Spirit as the (Passover) Lamb of God to save his people, as the Spirit baptizer, as the bridegroom of the redeemed, and, ultimately, as the eschatological judge of the world.

A third way in which the Gospel narratives introduce us to Jesus is through the account of Jesus's baptism and temptation. At Jesus's baptism, after the "Holy Spirit descended on him in bodily form, like a dove," a "voice came from heaven, 'You are my beloved Son; with you I am well pleased'" (Luke 3:22). The Father's pronouncement draws from Psalm 2:7 and Isaiah 42:1. In speaking of Jesus in the way that he does, the Father identifies Jesus as both the "Davidic Messiah" and the Isaianic Servant.[9] Jesus will therefore fulfill his mission, assigned to him by the Father, through humiliation and then exaltation.

Immediately following Luke's account of Jesus's baptism is Jesus's genealogy (Luke 3:23–38). The conclusion to that genealogy ("... the son of Adam,

---

(John 1:37). This witness, and its results, provide in miniature what the Old Testament had done for Israel on a much larger scale—point and direct people to the Messiah.

7. Richard B. Gaffin, Jr., *In the Fullness of Time: An Introduction to the Biblical Theology of Acts and Paul* (Wheaton, IL: Crossway, 2022), 100.

8. D. A. Carson, *The Gospel According to John* (Grand Rapids: Eerdmans, 1991), 211, *pace* Herman Ridderbos, *The Gospel of John: A Theological Commentary*, trans. John Vriend (Grand Rapids: Eerdmans, 1997), 147n131.

9. Garland, *Luke*, 169.

the son of God," 3:38) highlights Jesus's descent from Adam.[10] Sharing a common ancestor with every human being, Jesus is therefore qualified to serve as the redeemer of all kinds of people. This point is underscored in the immediately following narrative, the account of Jesus's temptation in the wilderness.[11] The antithetical similarities in this account to the temptation of Adam in Genesis 3 clarify that Jesus undergoes these temptations as the last Adam.[12] Adam, surrounded by plenty and dwelling in paradise, succumbed to Satan's temptation by sinning against God. The last Adam, surrounded by emptiness and dwelling in the wilderness, withstood Satan's temptations and obeyed God's word. Jesus's withstanding of Satan's temptations and Satan's subsequent retreat (Luke 4:13) should be understood as Jesus's royal defeat of Satan.[13] It reflects the beginning of the end of Satan's kingdom.

Jesus's obedience, after having hungered in the wilderness for forty days (Luke 4:1–2), recalls the failure of another party. Israel, having been amply provided in her wilderness sojourn for forty years (Deut 2:7; Neh 9:21), steadfastly disobeyed God (Ps 95:7–11; Heb 3:7–19). Jesus, then, has obeyed God where Israel disobeyed God. He is the proven obedient Son of God (Matt 2:15; Hos 11:1).[14]

Jesus's baptism and temptation, then, set the stage for his public ministry. He is the Spirit-empowered Servant-Son. The contours of his ministry

---

10. Luke's expression at Luke 3:23, "being the son (as was supposed) of Joseph," clarifies that Jesus is not the ordinarily conceived offspring of Joseph and Mary. He was, rather, conceived in the womb of the virgin Mary by the Holy Spirit (Luke 1:31, 35).

11. As Vos rightly notes, we "nam[e] it from the point of view of Satan a 'temptation', from the point of view of the higher purpose of God a 'probation' of Jesus," *Biblical Theology*, 132.

12. On which, see Vos, *Biblical Theology*, 133–42, and, more recently, Brandon D. Crowe, *The Last Adam: A Theology of the Obedient Life of Jesus in the Gospels* (Grand Rapids: Baker Academic, 2017).

13. Benjamin L. Gladd, *From Adam and Israel to the Church: A Biblical Theology of the People of God* (Downers Grove, IL: InterVarsity Press, 2019), 103, 108.

14. As Gaffin observes on Matthew 2:15, "Jesus goes to Egypt, the primeval place of God's people's enslavement and perennial sign of the need for deliverance caused by human sin, so that he may be called out from there to an exodus ordeal of wilderness testing, leading to salvation for sinners, not only in Israel but also in all nations. The immediate duress of the desert events of Matthew 4:1–11 sets the tone for the subsequent course of Jesus's entire ministry. The testing of his messianic faithfulness that culminates in his death and resurrection secures eschatological deliverance from sin and its consequences," "The Redemptive-Historical View" in *Biblical Hermeneutics: Five Views*, ed. Stanley E. Porter and Beth M. Stovell (Downers Grove, IL: InterVarsity Press, 2012), 108. See further Brandon D. Crowe, *The Obedient Son: Deuteronomy and Christology in the Gospel of Matthew*, BZNW 188 (Berlin: De Gruyter, 2012).

will be suffering and glory, humiliation and exaltation. His ministry will be marked by faithfulness and obedience to God, even and especially in the face of satanic assault. He is the last Adam who stood his probation before God. He is the Son who, unlike Israel, obeyed the God who had called him out of Egypt. In his obedience (an obedience that will lead to his death on the cross), he simultaneously dismantles Satan's kingdom and establishes God's kingdom on earth. What Adam failed to secure (confirmed, eschatological life), the last Adam will secure on behalf of his people, a people drawn from across the human race.

The biblical accounts of Jesus's public ministry, in their manifold emphasis upon his authority, provide a necessary foundation for reflecting upon his identity in relationship to the church. We can now survey this emphasis upon his authority throughout his earthly ministry. Matthew summarizes Jesus's Galilean ministry in terms of his "teaching in their synagogues and proclaiming the gospel of the kingdom and healing every disease and every affliction among the people" (Matt 4:23). This statement, and the similar statement at Matthew 9:35, form an *inclusio*, bracketing a block of material addressing Jesus's teaching (Matt 5–7) and a block of material addressing Jesus's miraculous works (Matt 8–9). Taking his seat upon a mountain, Jesus speaks as one greater than Moses (Matt 5:1–2).[15] Jesus affirms that he has "not come to abolish [the Law and the Prophets] but to fulfill them" (Matt 5:17). That is to say, Jesus has come "to ensure that [the law] receives the full obedience that is its due, to bring fully to light its true and deepest meaning."[16] Jesus therefore proceeds authoritatively to teach the true and full original meaning of the law, clearing away the traditions and misinterpretations of his contemporaries.[17] When Jesus concludes this block of teaching, his hearers realize that he "was teaching them as one who had authority, and not as their scribes" (Matt 7:29).

Jesus exhibits his unique authority, then, over the Mosaic law. He neither revokes it nor adds to it, but makes a claim, unparalleled among his

15. See the discussion at R. T. France, *Matthew*, NICNT (Grand Rapids: Eerdmans, 2007), 157, 157n13.

16. Ridderbos, *Matthew*, 99.

17. The phrase in Matthew 5:18, "until all is accomplished" points to a time when the Mosaic law will find eschatological fulfillment in Christ and, consequently, will undergo transformation appropriate to that fulfillment. See further Ridderbos, *The Coming of the Kingdom*, trans. H. de Jongste (Phillipsburg, NJ: P&R, 1962), 305–6.

contemporaries, of authority that only its divine author could make over it. Such authority is exhibited in Jesus's Sabbath controversies with his opponents. In Matthew 12:1–9, Matthew documents an occasion when the Pharisees rebuke Jesus because his "disciples are doing what is not lawful to do on the Sabbath" (Matt 12:2). Importantly, Jesus does not concede the illegality of their actions. On the contrary, he defends their behavior as in keeping with the Sabbath law. Jesus proceeds to tell his enemies not only that "something greater than the temple is here," but also "the Son of Man is lord of the Sabbath" (Matt 12:6, 8). As Immanuel (Matt 1:23; compare 28:20), Jesus surpasses the "holiness and importance" of the Jerusalem temple.[18] Jesus no less claims supremacy over the Sabbath and its proper interpretation and observance. And because the Sabbath is an ordinance of God, only one possessing divine authority could make the kind of claims that "the Son of Man" makes here.

But Jesus did not merely claim to be greater than the temple. He claimed his person and work be that to which the temple looked and in which the temple found its intended fulfillment.[19] Early in John's Gospel, Jesus authoritatively clears the temple of the "money-changers" and their goods (John 2:14). He does this not from spite or disrespect to the temple, but from "zeal" for his "Father's house" (John 2:17–16). Jesus, when he is then asked by the Jewish leaders for a "sign" warranting his actions, tells them, "Destroy this temple, and in three days I will raise it up" (John 2:19). John subsequently clarifies, "He was speaking about the temple of his body," and particularly his resurrection from the dead (John 2:21, 22). Jesus, then, "saw the connection between the temple and his own body to be fundamentally typological."[20] Such a statement lends significance to the presence of Jesus in Jerusalem, later in this Gospel, at the various feasts regulated by the law. Jesus has come into this world to bring these feasts—Passover and Tabernacles, for example—to fulfillment.[21] His discourses on these occasions elucidate the way in which these feasts were pointing typologically to his person and work.

---

18. Ridderbos, *Matthew*, 230.

19. See further here my *The Lord's Supper as the Sign and Seal of the New Covenant*, SSBT (Wheaton, IL: Crossway, 2019), 76–79.

20. Carson, *John*, 182.

21. See the chart at Andreas Köstenberger, *John*, BECNT (Grand Rapids: Baker Academic, 2004), 104.

One of the chief ways in which Jesus exhibits his authority is by his public miracles. His initial miracle, the turning of water into wine at the wedding of Cana (John 2:1–11), demonstrates his authority over the creation. This authority is exhibited in other respects—Jesus, for instance, walks upon water, stills wind and wave with a word, and multiplies loaves and fish to feed multitudes. Jesus, no less, demonstrates authority over life and death. He heals those who are sick and injured, and even raises Jairus's daughter, the son of the widow of Nain, and Lazarus from the dead. Jesus also demonstrates authority over Satan and the demons. The demons obey Jesus, and Jesus exorcises human beings, freeing them from their miserable bondage to the devil. There is no sphere of creation over which Jesus does not exercise immediate and absolute authority.

In the latter half of Jesus's earthly ministry, Jesus begins to speak more explicitly about his impending passion. As Jesus nears the cross, he does not relinquish or lose his messianic authority. On the contrary, the cross (and his subsequent resurrection) will be the supreme exercise and display of messianic authority. Jesus describes his death as the Good Shepherd in precisely these terms: "No one takes [my life] from me, but I lay it down of my own accord. I have authority to lay it down, and I have authority to take it up again. This charge I have received from my Father" (John 10:18).[22] For this reason, the phrase "'lifted up' acquires a double meaning here [in John 3:14] (as also in 8:28; 12:32, 34): the exaltation of the Son of man (=his glorification) is effected by his being raised up on a cross."[23] Thus, the passion narrative in John offers periodic reminders of Jesus's authority as he advances nearer and nearer to the cross. In what is certainly to be taken as the effect of "open self-disclosure [with] the overtones of God's self-disclosure in the prophecy of Isaiah," those arresting Jesus "drew back and fell to the ground" (18:6).[24] John highlights the fact that Jesus is tried, convicted, and executed as one who is king (19:1–16). The inscription upon the cross—"Jesus of Nazareth, the King of the Jews"—was "written in Aramaic, in Latin,

22. Note the observation of Ridderbos, "The expression 'lay down' suggests taking off a garment and seems to correspond, not only verbally but also in substance, with what Jesus does in 13:4,12. There also it is evident how power and love go together: the Lord remains the Lord, but he lays aside everything for his own (cf. 13:6,12). When he is about to be bound, he has all things in his hands, for he allows himself to be bound in order that his own may go free (cf. 18:6–8)," *The Gospel of John*, 366.

23. Ridderbos, *The Gospel of John*, 136.

24. Carson, *The Gospel of John*, 578.

and in Greek," pointing to the multilingual character of the people of God whom Jesus redeems by his death (19:19, 20; compare 12:31–33).

The crowning exhibition of Jesus's authority is his victory over death in his resurrection from the dead. It is a work that he undertakes in his own authority (John 10:17–18). In his risen humanity, he appears to his disciples and, as we shall see, authoritatively commands and commissions them. His concluding act upon earth is to ascend visibly and bodily in a cloud into heaven (Acts 1:9), whence he receives the worship of his disciples (Luke 24:50–53).

Jesus's earthly life and ministry, from his conception to his ascension, is stamped with authority. It is an authority that highlights the many ways in which the Old Testament has come to its intended realization in Christ. It is an authority wielded as the mediator of his people—their faithful, obedient, servant-king. We may now begin to reflect on the ways in which Jesus Christ, possessed of such authority, reconstitutes and transforms the people of God in the days of eschatological fulfillment.

JESUS CHRIST AND THE RECONSTITUTION AND TRANSFORMATION OF THE CHURCH

Transformed Definition

Jesus Christ brings transformation to the people of God in at least five ways. First, Jesus transforms the people of God by defining them in explicit relation to his person and work. Significantly, Jesus calls twelve disciples (Matt 10:2–4; Mark 3:16–19; Luke 6:12–16), naming them "apostles" (Luke 6:13). That the number twelve is significant becomes evident from the events that Luke documents between the ascension of Christ into heaven and the day of Pentecost. The apostolate is incomplete (Judas having "turned aside to go to his own place," Acts 1:25) and is only complete when a twelfth apostle has become formally selected and enrolled.[25] Jesus elucidates the meaning of the number "twelve" when he tells his disciples that they "who have followed me will also sit on twelve thrones, judging the twelve tribes of Israel" (Matt 19:28; compare

25. On which, see Guy Prentiss Waters, *A Study Commentary on the Acts of the Apostles* (Darlington, UK: EP, 2015), 60–63.

Luke 22:30). Jesus's disciples, then, "under the leadership of the Son of Man constitute a 'new Israel' over against the old, failed regime."[26]

The significance of the twelve, of course, is that Jesus has expressly chosen them and called them, having consulted in prayer beforehand with God the Father (Luke 6:12–13). Membership in the eschatological people of God will be in explicit and conscious reference to the incarnate Christ. It is for this reason that Jesus invites sinners to himself, "Come to me, all who labor and are heavy laden, and I will give you rest. Take my yoke upon you, and learn from me, for I am gentle and lowly in heart, and you will find rest for your souls. For my yoke is easy, and my burden is light" (Matt 11:28–30).[27] There is no access to the Father and to eschatological life but by the Son (John 14:6; 10:7–9).

It is precisely these sorts of claims that give offense to the religious establishment of Jesus's day. Telling is what follows Jesus's grant of forgiveness to the paralytic (Mark 2:1–12, esp. 2:5). The scribes are offended ("He is blaspheming! Who can forgive sins but God alone?" 2:7). The offense is not the pronouncement of forgiveness as such, but the pronouncement of forgiveness in Jesus's own name. It is precisely this claim that Jesus both articulates (Mark 2:10) and demonstrates in the healing of the paralytic (Mark 2:11–12). On another occasion, the Pharisees and the scribes are indignant that Jesus "receives sinners and eats with them" (Luke 15:2). The Jewish leadership is offended that Jesus should in his own name pardon and accept people, particularly people on the margins of Judaism (compare Matt 9:9–13). Such offense to the teaching of Jesus is not a reflection of two distinct but legitimately complementary approaches to participation in the people of God—that of the religious leaders and that of Jesus. It is, rather, symptomatic of these leaders' exclusion from the kingdom of God altogether.[28] To reject Jesus in impenitence and unbelief is to forfeit one's place in the people of God.

---

26. France, *The Gospel of Matthew*, NICNT (Grand Rapids: Eerdmans, 2007), 744. France also observes in this connection that "the choice of the Twelve as [Jesus's] task force was already a pointer in that direction, and now the significance of the number as representing the tribes of Israel is made explicit," pointing to Revelation 21:12, 14 as parallel to this passage. *Gospel of Matthew*, 744.

27. This invitation is grounded upon the exclusive and exhaustive knowledge that the Son has of the Father, and the Father of the Son (Matt 11:27); cf. John Nolland, *The Gospel of Matthew*, NIGTC (Grand Rapids: Eerdmans, 2005), 474.

28. Carson, *Matthew*, 225.

Of course, Jesus teaches that this defining characteristic of the people of God had been true even prior to his incarnation. Jesus tells the Jews, "Your father Abraham rejoiced that he would see my day. He saw it and was glad" (John 8:56). Later in the Gospel, John comments in reference to a citation of Isaiah 6:10, "Isaiah said these things because he saw his glory and spoke of him" (12:41). God's people under the Old Testament beheld Christ as he was represented to them under its types and shadows.[29] Therefore, God's people have always been defined in reference to Jesus Christ. It is the eschatological fulfillment brought about in Christ that accounts for what is distinct with respect to Jesus's teaching in his earthly ministry. Membership in the people of God is now determined in reference to the incarnate person and work of Christ, and the claims that he makes upon human beings.

Transformed Response to God

Second and relatedly, the people of God are known in terms of their response to the incarnate Christ and to his claims. That response, Jesus insists at the outset of his ministry, is repentance and faith in the gospel (Mark 1:15). Human beings are to repent before God of their sin (Luke 13:3, 5), and to one another of their sin (Luke 17:4). Failure to repent at the command of Christ renders one liable to eschatological judgment (Matt 11:20). Coupled to repentance is faith. Faith has as its object God and Christ (John 14:1; compare 12:44). Jesus calls the man born blind to believe in the Son of Man (John 9:35), an act that is accompanied with the worship of Christ (John 9:38; compare 11:26–27). John's stated purpose in writing his Gospel is that his readers would "believe that Jesus is the Christ, the Son of God, and that by believing you may have life in his name" (20:31).

Faith and repentance have their point of reference in the person and work of Christ. But Jesus furthermore insists that he is the source of all spiritual life in his people. In John 15:1–8, he tells his disciples that he is the "true vine" and that his disciples are "branches" (15:1, 2, 4). The vine "imagery ... suggests incorporation, mutual indwelling, fruitfulness."[30] Branches must bear fruit, but, Jesus insists, they cannot do so "unless [they] abide in

29. So, rightly, Andreas J. Köstenberger, *John*, BECNT (Grand Rapids: Eerdmans, 2004), 392.
30. Carson, *John*, 514.

the vine," that is, abide in Christ (15:4).[31] There is, furthermore, a horizontal dimension to this image. As the disciples are "branches," they are not only in "personal relationship" to Jesus but also "incorporat[ed] into the great community of the people God has appropriated for himself out of the world (cf. 17:6)."[32] Membership and participation in the eschatological people of God, then, is bound up with the union with Christ of which Christ speaks in these verses.

Transformed People of God

A THIRD WAY IN WHICH Jesus's transformation of the people of God is evident in his public life and ministry is in his teaching on the kingdom of God. Jesus introduces his public ministry by proclaiming the inbreaking into history of the kingdom of God and proceeds to call people to repent and believe in light of its arrival ("The time is fulfilled, and the kingdom of God is at hand; repent and believe in the gospel," Mark 1:15).[33]

The "coming of the kingdom is nothing less than God's final decisive intervention into world history."[34] While "the kingdom" assumes divine sovereignty, it is not synonymous with the sovereignty of God. It is "the actual exercise of the divine supremacy in the interest of the divine glory."[35] In particular, the kingdom is the redemptive rule and reign of God in Christ. The kingdom, then, is dynamic and not static, and concerns human beings as sinners in need of redemption from the guilt, dominion, and power of sin. Human beings enter into the kingdom as they respond in repentance and faith to the gospel proclaimed by Jesus Christ (Luke 16:16).

In Jesus's teaching, the kingdom admits of a "two-sided conception"—"first, the idea of a present, inwardly-spiritual development, and

---

31. Significantly, as "in the Old Testament the vine is a common symbol for Israel, the covenant people of God," Jesus here declares that he is "the one to whom Israel pointed, the one that brings forth good fruit," Carson, *John*, 513. As Ridderbos observes, "[Jesus] thus becomes the one who represents or embodies the people," *The Gospel of John*, 515.

32. Ridderbos, *The Gospel of John*, 516.

33. The paucity of references to the kingdom in John's Gospel (see John 3:3, 5; 18:36) relative to the Synoptics should not be construed as a declaration of disinterest in the kingdom on the part of the Fourth Gospel. On the contrary, what the Synoptics denominate under "kingdom," John typically denominates under "life," so Geerhardus Vos, *The Teaching of Jesus Concerning the Kingdom of God and the Church* (Phillipsburg, NJ: P&R, 1972), 10. This pairing is evident not only in John (see John 3:3, 5 with 3:15, 16) but also in the Synoptics (see Mark 9:43, 45, 47; 10:17, 23). Vos, *The Teaching of Jesus*, 10.

34. Ridderbos, *Matthew*, 76.

35. Vos, *Biblical Theology*, 386.

secondly, that of a catastrophic ending-up."[36] Each of these "phase[s]" or dimensions to the kingdom is equally "supernatural."[37] In whatever form the kingdom presents itself, or in whatever mode it advances in history and in the world, it is entirely the sovereign working of God.

To speak of the kingdom at present as inward and spiritual is not to say that the kingdom has no outward form or structure. On the contrary, the outward form of the kingdom, according to Jesus, is the church, the people of God. This dimension of the kingdom becomes apparent in the two texts in the Gospels in which the term translated "church" (ἐκκλησία) appears, Matthew 16:13–20 and Matthew 18:15–20.

In taking up the question of the relationship between the kingdom and the church in these two passages, a preliminary question presents itself. Does the paucity of references to the "church" in the Gospels mean that the kingdom, in reality, has little or nothing to do with the church?

The answer to this question is a negative one. It must be remembered, in the first place, that the church, in the Gospels, is not a brand new creation. As Herman Ridderbos observes, the church is an existing and established entity.

> The fact that the word *ekklēsia* does not come to the forefront in the Gospels should not deceive us, because from the very first there appears in the kingdom of God preached by Jesus, with increasing clarity of outline, a people. The concept has its preformation in old Israel, in the people of the covenant and of the promises. In the Gospels it can, therefore, without any further announcement or description, be called *ekklēsia*. For *ekklēsia* in the New Testament is not a new word or a new concept. It is, indeed, nothing but the translation of *kahal*, already current in the Septuagint, denoting the Old Testament people of God, the congregation of Israel.[38]

This existing entity, the *ekklēsia*, undergoes profound eschatological transformation in light of the inbreaking of the kingdom of God in the ministry of Jesus Christ.

---

36. Vos, *Biblical Theology*, 381. See further the discussion on pp. 381–85.

37. Vos, *Biblical Theology*, 385.

38. Herman N. Ridderbos, *When the Time Had Fully Come: Studies in New Testament Theology* (Grand Rapids: Eerdmans, 1957), 21. Compare Greg K. Beale, "The New Testament Background of ἐκκλησία Revisited Yet Again," in *Redeeming the Life of the Mind: Essays in Honor of Vern Poythress*, ed. John M. Frame, Wayne A. Grudem, and John J. Hughes (Wheaton: Crossway, 2018), 47–60.

> The new thing is that this *ekklēsia* now comes into the light of the kingdom of God. All earlier qualifications of the *ekklēsia* as the people of the election, of the covenant and of the promises, are sublimated in the kingdom of God, are 'fulfilled' as it says in the New Testament. When the kingdom comes, the proper and *spiritual* sense of the Church comes into the light. But in the *extensive* sense, too, the *ekklēsia* acquires in the kingdom new proportions and new relations. The *ekklēsia* is integrated in the worldwide power of the kingdom: henceforth it is foregathered from all nations. This is the one great line connecting *basileia* and *ekklēsia*.[39]

The *ekklēsia*, then, is not created de novo upon the inbreaking of the kingdom of God. It is the form that the existing people of God assumes upon that people's transformation in light of the presence of the kingdom.

Matthew 16:13–20

With that general framework in view, we may now turn to what Jesus says about the church in Matthew 16 (and Matthew 18). In Matthew 16:18–19, Jesus tells Peter, "And I tell you, you are Peter, and on this rock I will build my church, and the gates of hell shall not prevail against it. I will give you the keys of the kingdom of heaven, and whatever you bind on earth shall be bound in heaven, and whatever you loose on earth shall be loosed in heaven." In these words of Jesus to Peter, the second person pronouns are consistently singular. The Roman Catholic Church has argued that Jesus is therefore speaking to Peter uniquely.[40] The context, however, compels us to understand these words to apply to Peter in company with the other disciples. These words are preceded by a question that Jesus poses to the disciples, "But who do you say that I am?" (16:15). The word translated "you" is the Greek second personal plural pronoun (ὑμεῖς). It is "Simon Peter" who answers, "You are the Christ, the Son of the living God" (Matt 16:16). Simon Peter, here as elsewhere

39. Ridderbos, *When the Time Had Fully Come*, 21–22.

40. See, representatively, *Catechism of the Catholic Church, with Modifications from the Editio Typica* (New York: Doubleday, 1997), §§552–553.

in the Gospels, answers not for himself only but for the Twelve. He is, then, "the spokesman for the Twelve."[41] Jesus's benediction in the following verse, therefore, is directed to Simon but not restricted to Simon: "Blessed are you, Simon Bar-Jonah! For flesh and blood has not revealed this to you, but my Father who is in heaven" (Matt 16:17). The words of Matthew 16:18–19, no less, apply to Peter in company with the other disciples.

What, then, is Jesus saying about the "church" in these verses? First, the church stands upon "this rock," which, in context, refers to the apostles' confession of Jesus as the Christ, the Son of the living God.[42] The church's foundation must be understood, then, in terms of the office of the apostles in their witness to the person and work of the incarnate Son of God. That the church does not rest upon the personal authority or charisma of the apostles is clear from the fact that it is not "flesh and blood" but the "Father who is in heaven" who has revealed these matters to Peter. They are God's appointed agents of new covenant revelation to the people of God. That revelation constitutes the foundation on which the Father has set the people of God in their eschatological maturity.

Second, Jesus gives the apostles "the keys of the kingdom of heaven" (Matt 16:19). With those "keys" they are to bind and loose.[43] The image of "keys" in this chapter concerns the opening of a storehouse to provide for the household.[44] Put negatively, the image does not summon the admission or exclusion of a person from the house. The Puritan Matthew Poole summarizes and elaborates Jesus's meaning:

41. Carson, *Matthew*, 365, citing Matthew 15:15–16; 19:25–28; 26:40; Mark 11:20–22; Luke 12:41; John 6:67–70 as parallel examples from the Gospels.

42. Even so, we recognize that the personal reference to Peter anticipates the fact that "in the early chapters of Acts it is Peter who leads the disciple group in Jerusalem, and it is he who takes the initiative in the key developments which will constitute the church as a new, international body of the people of God through faith in Jesus: note especially his role in the bringing in of Samaritans (Acts 8:14–25) and gentiles (Acts 10:1–11:18; 15:7–11)," France, *Matthew*, 622–23.

43. The material that follows has been adapted from my *How Jesus Runs the Church* (Phillipsburg, NJ: P&R, 2011), 38–39.

44. France, *Matthew*, 625.

> The sense is, Peter, I will betrust thee, and the rest of my apostles, with the whole administration of the gospel; you shall lay the foundation of the Christian church, and administer all the affairs of it, opening the truths of the gospel to the world, and governing those who shall receive the faith of the gospel. ... Our Savior by this promise declared his will, that his apostles should settle the affairs of the gospel church, determining what should be lawful and unlawful, and setting rules, according to which all succeeding ministers and officers in his church should act, which our Lord would confirm in heaven. ... I cannot think that the sense of binding and loosing here is excommunicating and absolving, but a doctrinal or judicial determination of things lawful and unlawful granted to the apostles.[45]

Jesus's words here, then, are important for understanding the government, discipline, and worship of the new covenant people of God. The apostles, as instruments of divine revelation, will lay down a sufficient foundation for the people of God under the new covenant to order their life and service.[46]

Third, Jesus insists that for all the apostolic labors in view in Matthew 16:19 (and the labors of the post-apostolic church built upon that foundation), it is he who will "build my church" (Matt 16:18). Jesus not only reserves the right of possession of the church ("my") but asserts that it is he who builds the church. He will, furthermore, build his church in the face of concerted satanic opposition ("the gates of hell"). Just as Satan opposed Jesus in his earthly ministry (Matt 4:1–11), so Satan will oppose Jesus's church. The futurity of the verb of (Jesus's) building (οἰκοδομήσω) and of the verb of (Satan's not) prevailing (κατισχύσουσιν) point to a period of time subsequent

---

45. Poole, *A Commentary on the Holy Bible*, 3 vols. (repr., Peabody, MA: Hendrickson, n.d.), 3:77.

46. Jesus's similar statement about binding and loosing in Matthew 18:18 addresses the related but narrower concern of the exercise of discipline within the church under the apostles' supervision. Significantly, the personal pronoun in Matthew 18:18 is the plural ὑμῖν, and the verbs in Matthew 18:18 are in the second person plural (δήσητε, λύσητε). This pronominal and verbal plurality confirms that Jesus, in the previous text (Matt 16:15–19), is addressing Peter along with the other disciples.

to Jesus's earthly ministry, likely after he is raised from the dead.[47] It is not simply that Jesus legislates, through his apostles, the life and ministry of his people after his resurrection. It is that Jesus is also present to his people, building his church, and ensuring that Satan will not defeat or destroy what God has purposed for his people.

Transformed Worship

A FOURTH WAY IN WHICH the transformation of the people of God is evident in the life and ministry of Jesus concerns his teaching about the worship of God's people. To be sure, Jesus issues blistering condemnations of the ways in which the leaders of Israel have corrupted the worship of God (Matt 15:1–9; Mark 7:1–13). But far from denigrating the old covenant forms and laws of worship, Jesus upholds them in his teaching and practice. In his dialogue with the Samaritan woman in John 4, Jesus is explicit in his assessment of the worship of the Samaritans and of the Jews, "You worship what you do not know; we worship what we know, for salvation is from the Jews" (John 4:22). After healing a leper early in his Galilean ministry, Jesus instructs the man to "go, show yourself to the priest and offer for your cleansing what Moses commanded, for a proof to them" (Mark 1:44). And Jesus, each Gospel tells us, faithfully observed the Sabbath and the feasts and festivals legislated in the Old Testament for Israel.

John 4:21–24

JESUS, HOWEVER, POINTS TO A coming transformation in the worship of God's people in his dialogue with the Samaritan woman. He tells her, "the hour is coming when neither on this mountain nor in Jerusalem will you worship the Father. … The hour is coming, and is now here, when the true worshippers will worship the Father in spirit and truth, for the Father is seeking such people to worship him. God is spirit, and those who worship him must worship in spirit and truth" (John 4:21, 23–24).

---

47. The following verse ("Then he strictly charged the disciples to tell no one that he was the Christ," 16:20) confirms this conclusion. The silence of the disciples' open proclamation that Jesus of Nazareth was the promised Messiah would come to an end at the resurrection. After he is risen from the dead, Jesus commands his disciples to do precisely what he forbids them from doing at this earlier time—proclaim him openly.

Jesus points to two fundamental changes in the worship of God, changes that will take place after Jesus has died and been raised from the dead.[48] The first concerns "the impending obsolescence of ... the Jerusalem temple."[49] The reason for this obsolescence is that worship will no longer be fixed to a particular geographical location. God may be acceptably worshiped in all sorts of places. The second concerns the nature of the worship offered. It will be "in spirit and truth," in keeping with the fact that "God is spirit." Jesus is not declaring old covenant worship to be false or intrinsically deficient. He is saying, rather, that new covenant worship will reflect and conform to God's self-revelation in a way that old covenant worship will soon be incapable of doing. "'Spirit'—here linked with 'truth' in a hendiadys as with 'grace and truth' in 1:17—refers to the time of salvation that has come with Christ and to the concomitant new way in which God wants to relate to human beings."[50] ["Spirit and truth"] describe worship "that is no longer mediated by all sorts of provisional and symbolic forms, but by the Spirit of God himself."[51] And when Jesus says that "God is spirit," he is saying "that God is invisible, divine as opposed to human (cf. 3:6), life-giving and unknowable to human beings unless he chooses to reveal himself (cf. 1:18)."[52] Only "spirit and truth" worship best suits and expresses what it means that "God is spirit." While Jesus does not unveil the details of this eschatologically-transformed worship until the post-resurrection ministry of the apostles, he here lays the eschatological groundwork for a profound reordering of the worship of God's people.[53]

Transformed Mission

A fifth and final way in which Jesus, in his life and ministry, prepares for the transformation of God's people

48. In John's Gospel, "the hour" refers to Jesus's death and resurrection. In saying (twice), "the hour is coming," Jesus is pointing to an *eschatological* transformation in the worship of God.

49. Carson, *John*, 222.

50. Ridderbos, *John*, 163.

51. Ridderbos, *John*, 164.

52. Carson, *John*, 225.

53. Significantly, the acceptable public worship of God under both dispensations (prior to the new covenant and under the new covenant) shares a common denominator—only that which God expressly authorizes is permitted in worship. Put negatively, that which is not expressly authorized is thereby forbidden.

concerns the mission of God's people. In his earthly ministry, Jesus selects twelve men "(whom he named apostles) so that they might be with him and he might send them out to preach" (Mark 3:14). The apostles, then, become early extensions of Jesus's itinerant ministry. He commissions them to work miracles, to declare the kingdom of God, and to summon people to respond in faith and repentance (see Matt 10:5–15). In short, they are tasked with the very things in which Jesus was himself engaged. Significantly, he commands them, "Go nowhere among the gentiles and enter no town of the Samaritans, but go rather to the lost sheep of the house of Israel" (Matt 10:5–6). As Jesus's earthly mission was largely (although not exclusively) confined to Israel, so must his apostles' mission be.

But there are hints that the apostles will one day extend their ministry beyond Israel. Jesus tells his disciples just a few verses later, "you will be dragged before governors and kings for my sake, to bear witness before them and the Gentiles" (Matt 10:18).[54] Jesus has earlier described "many ... from east and west" as "reclin[ing] at table with Abraham, Isaac, and Jacob in the kingdom of heaven" (8:11), and later declares that he will dispatch "his angels" to "gather his elect from the four winds, from one end of heaven to the other" (Matt 24:31).

Jesus, therefore, prepares us for the ministry of the apostles (and, in important ways, of the church after the apostles) in at least two respects. First, Jesus's own earthly ministry provides the pattern and paradigm for the apostles' ministry. Second, Jesus prepares the apostles for a ministry that will extend to the nations. Jesus is the "Savior of the world" (John 4:42; compare 12:47), that is, the one who alone saves sinners from among all the nations.[55] In due time, his apostles will proclaim him to the nations so that men and women of all ethnicities may come to Jesus Christ in the way of repentance and faith. In this way Jesus will gather his people and build his church, thus bringing about the fulfillment of God's promises to Abraham.

CONCLUSION

As one might expect, Jesus Christ has brought basic transformation to the old covenant, the order and era that God designed to prepare his people for the coming of his Son. The authority that Jesus bears in his teaching and actions extends to every aspect

54. Carson, *Matthew*, 242.

55. On "world" in John, see the illuminating discussion of Benjamin B. Warfield, *The Saviour of the World* (1916; repr., Edinburgh: Banner of Truth, 1991), 103–30, and the more recent treatment of Andreas J. Köstenberger, *A Theology of John's Gospel and Letters*, BTNT (Grand Rapids: Zondervan, 2009), 281–82.

and dimension of that covenant and of the Scriptures that legislated the life, worship, and mission of God's people under that covenant. Although Jesus's earthly ministry transpired entirely under the old covenant, the Gospels give us glimpses of the radical transformation that is soon to come—in his proclamation of the kingdom of God, in calling people to repentance and to faith in himself, in the new form that God's people (the "church") are to assume under the era of eschatological fulfillment, in his teaching about eschatological worship, and in the mission that will belong to the people of God in light of his person and work. In the following chapter, we will trace the lines of the identity, life, government, worship, and mission of the new covenant people of God, pursuing them as far as their consummation at the glorious return of Christ at the end of the age.

FURTHER READING

Ridderbos, Herman N. *The Coming of the Kingdom*. Translated by H. de Jongste. Phillipsburg, NJ: P&R, 1962. A standard and exhaustive Reformed survey of Jesus's teaching about the kingdom of God. Ridderbos gives focused attention to the relationship between the kingdom of God and the people of God.

Ridderbos, Herman N. "The Kingdom of God according to the Witness of the Synoptic Gospels." In *When the Time Had Fully Come: Studies in New Testament Theology*, 9–25. Grand Rapids: Eerdmans, 1957. A brief overview of the testimony of the Synoptic Gospels to the kingdom of God. It serves as a good introduction to Ridderbos's longer *The Coming of the Kingdom*.

Vos, Geerhardus. *The Teaching of Jesus Concerning the Kingdom of God and the Church*. Phillipsburg, NJ: P&R, 1972. A concise and insightful biblical theological treatment of the kingdom in Jesus's teaching and its bearing upon the church.

VII

THE APOSTLES: THE ESCHATOLOGICALLY MATURE CHURCH

The bodily resurrection of Jesus Christ marks the formal commencement of the age of eschatological fulfillment in redemptive history.[1] God in Christ is "making all things new" (Rev 21:5), and Paul writes, "If anyone is in Christ, new creation" (2 Cor 5:17, author's translation). This new work profoundly transforms the people of God.

In this chapter, we will reflect on the testimony of the risen Christ and his apostles to the people of God. In anticipation of our discussion in part 2, we will consider the identity, life, government, worship, and mission of God's people in light of the resurrection of Christ and the dawn of the new covenant. We will also reflect on the perfection and consummation of the people of God at the return of Christ in glory at the end of the age.

THE IDENTITY OF GOD'S PEOPLE

The New Testament writers use a number of metaphors to describe the people of God under the new covenant.[2] These metaphors,

1. On which, see further my *The Sabbath as Rest and Hope for the People of God* (Wheaton, IL: Crossway, 2022), 73–81.

2. On the nature of "metaphor" in relation to these biblical characterizations of the church, see Edmund P. Clowney, "Interpreting the Biblical Models of the Church: A Hermeneutical Deepening of Ecclesiology," in *Biblical Interpretation and the Church: Text and Context*, D. A.

beyond their descriptive character, accomplish two goals. The first is to demonstrate fundamental continuity with the people of God under the old covenant. The new covenant people of God is not a distinct or separate people from old covenant Israel. God, rather, has a single people across redemptive history. The second goal is to reflect the profound transformation this people has undergone in light of the finished work of Jesus Christ. We will trace five such metaphors, noting their roots in old covenant Israel and their meaning in light of the person and work of Christ.

Vine

In John's Gospel, Jesus declares himself "the true vine," and each one of his people a "branch" that is "in" him (John 15:1, 2). To be sure, this description of the relationship between Christ and his people captures Christ's indwelling the believer by his Spirit (John 14:16–18).[3] But, as Jesus develops the image in this chapter, the picture is no less corporate than it is individual. It describes the people of God.

In the Old Testament, and particularly in the prophets, God describes Israel as a vine (see, representatively, Isa 5:1–7; Jer 2:21; Ezek 15:1–8; 17:1–21, Hos 10:1, 2). When the prophets describe Israel as a vine, they do so to underscore Israel's "lack of fruitfulness and spiritual degeneracy."[4] In saying that he is the "true vine," Jesus makes a couple of central claims. He is "the one to whom Israel pointed," and "the one that brings forth good fruit."[5] It is for this reason that Jesus emphasizes the source and necessity of fruitfulness in his teaching in John 15:1–8. In Christ, the eschatological people of God will, by the ministry of the Spirit, bear forth fruit in a way that Israel never did. Tellingly, Paul speaks of the good works done by the Christian as "fruit" (Rom 6:21, 7:4; Col 1:10; Eph 5:9), works that are ultimately the "fruit" of the Spirit (Gal 5:22). As Paul looks to the return of Christ, he envisions

---

Carson, ed. (Grand Rapids: Eerdmans, 1987), 65–75. Note Clowney's caution, taking Jesus's statement, "I am the true vine" (John 15:1), as an example, "The metaphor is not found in one word. ... In the vine and branches example, our interpretation of the metaphor depends not only on the statements quoted [in the text], but on the context of the discourse of Jesus recorded in the gospel, and on the universe of discourse that includes the Old Testament background and the use of metaphor there," 72.

3. Köstenberger, *John*, 450.

4. Köstenberger, *John*, 450.

5. Carson, *John*, 513. Carson notes in this connection the importance of Psalm 80:7–8, 14–17, in which "vine" and "son of man" are brought together, *John*, 513–14.

believers who will be "pure and blameless for the day of Christ, filled with the fruit of righteousness that comes through Jesus Christ, to the glory and praise of God" (Phil 1:10, 11). The people of God at the consummation will be characterized by an abundance of fruit borne in relation to Christ, the Vine.

Sheep IN JOHN'S GOSPEL, JESUS EARLIER describes himself as the "good shepherd" (John 10:11, 14), and his people as his "sheep" (10:3, *et pass.*). Jesus describes his relationship with his sheep in individual and personal terms—he "lays down his life for the sheep" (10:11), "I know my own and my own know me" (10:14), "they will listen to my voice" (10:16). But he no less describes his relationship with his sheep in corporate terms—"one flock, one shepherd" (10:16). Jesus, then, is describing the people of God as the sheep of his pasture.

The Old Testament, as we have seen, describes Israel as the flock over which God presides as shepherd (Pss 23:1; 80:1), and which Israel's leaders serve, under God's authority, as shepherds (Isa 56:11; Jer 23:1–4).[6] As with the image of vine, the image of shepherd in the Old Testament serves to underscore the failings of Israel's leadership with respect to the people of Israel. Ezekiel 34:1–10 offers one of the most blistering and sustained criticisms of the selfish and proprietary behavior of Israel's shepherds. God remedies these circumstances by pledging himself to "be the shepherd of my sheep" (34:15), and to "set up over [the sheep] one shepherd, my servant David, and he shall feed them: he shall feed them and be their shepherd" (34:23). This state of affairs will take place concurrently with God's making with his people "a covenant of peace" (34:25; 37:26), and is accompanied by God's promise to pour out his Spirit and set his Spirit within his people (36:22–32), bringing them to new life from the dead (37:1–14). God's promises in Ezekiel 34, then, are promises of the new covenant that Jesus has come to fulfill.

Jesus claims to be the shepherd of whom Ezekiel spoke. As such he indicts Israel's faithless leaders as thieves and robbers (John 10:1). As sheep, the people of God, by contrast, are characterized by listening to Jesus's

6. Both Moses and David originate as (literal) shepherds. It is difficult not to see their subsequent leadership over God's people in light of their earlier vocational identity and endeavors as shepherds.

voice (10:3–4). Jesus's sheep are drawn not only from within Israel but from outside the "fold" of national Israel (10:16). The image, then, encompasses the eschatological people of God, Jew and gentile, under the new covenant.

As Jesus relates his identity as shepherd to his imminent sacrificial death for the sins of his people (10:11, 15, 17–18), so the author of Hebrews relates Jesus's identity as shepherd to his resurrection from the dead (Heb 13:20). It is the death *and* the resurrection of Christ that saves sinners and establishes them as sheep in relation to the Shepherd, Christ. Peter correspondingly summons believers to look to Christ as the "Shepherd and Overseer of your souls" (1 Pet 2:25). Importantly, Peter tells the church's "elders" to "shepherd the flock of God that is among you, exercising oversight" (5:4).[7] Significantly, the verbs that Peter uses of the elders' duties in 1 Peter 5:2 (ποιμάνατε, ἐπισκοποῦντες) are cognate with the nouns that Peter uses to describe Christ in 1 Peter 2:25 (τὸν ποιμένα καὶ ἐπίσκοπον).[8] The ordinary exercise of the church's government, Peter is saying, is the way in which Christ shepherds his people. Similarly to the old covenant, God employs undershepherds to lead his people. Unlike the shepherds who contributed to Israel's ruin, new covenant shepherds are to exhibit the character and demeanor of Christ to the flock (1 Pet 5:2, 3).[9] Faithful shepherds, Peter reminds them, "will receive the unfading crown of glory … when the chief Shepherd appears" (1 Pet 5:4).

John describes the consummation as the ingathering of the people of God before their "shepherd" (Rev 7:17). Significantly and paradoxically, this shepherd is none other than "the Lamb," to whom the redeemed ascribe "salvation" (7:10), and by whose "blood" the people of God have "washed their robes and made them white" (7:14). The Shepherd-Lamb will provide for and protect them in every way (7:15–17). Throughout eternity, the people of God will be the flock of God in the presence of their Shepherd.

---

7. Note here Christ's three-fold command to "feed my lambs," "tend my sheep," "feed my sheep" (John 21:15, 16, 17). The whole of Peter's apostolic ministry is to be understood in terms of the shepherding of Christ's sheep.

8. Schreiner notes how the verb in 1 Peter 5:2 (*poimainō*) appears in both Acts 20:28 and John 21:16, Thomas R. Schreiner, *1, 2 Peter, Jude*, NAC (Nashville: B&H, 2003), 233.

9. Note the contrast between Peter's description of what the new covenant shepherd is to be and the descriptions of what Israel's undershepherds were at Ezekiel 34:4, 8. Schreiner, *1, 2 Peter, Jude*, 233.

Temple As WE HAVE SEEN, JESUS in his earthly ministry declares himself to be Lord over the Jerusalem temple (John 2:13–22), to be greater than this temple (Matt 12:6), and to be the one to whom the temple points (John 2:21). The Gospels show in particular ways from the Old Testament how the temple (and the tabernacle) anticipated his person and work. In John's Gospel, the prologue links the Old Testament tabernacle with the incarnation of Christ, "And the word became flesh and dwelt among us, and we have seen his glory, glory as of the only Son from the Father, full of grace and truth" (John 1:14).[10] "The outward picture of God's dwelling among his people becomes a reality in the incarnation."[11] Jesus's words in John 1:51 ("Truly, truly, I say to you, you will see heaven opened, and the angels of God ascending and descending on the Son of Man") not only reference Genesis 28:12 but also constitute the "claim that [Jesus], not the Jerusalem temple, is the primary link between heaven and earth."[12]

At the conclusion of his public ministry, Jesus, having been decisively rejected by Israel's leadership, declares himself to be "the stone that the builders rejected." As such, he is the stone that "has become the cornerstone" (Matt 21:42, citing Ps 118:22). Jesus here "portray[s] himself as the beginning of a new sanctuary ... the foundation stone of the new temple."[13]

This identification prepares us for what the apostles make explicit—the church, engrafted into Christ, is God's eschatological temple. Peter speaks of Christ as "a living stone rejected by men but in the sight of God chosen and precious," and of believers as "living stones ... being built up as a spiritual house, to be a holy priesthood, to offer spiritual sacrifices acceptable to God through Jesus Christ" (1 Pet 2:4, 5). That Peter goes on to cite Psalm 118:22 (1 Pet 2:7) indicates that Jesus's self-identification as "the stone that the builders rejected" and "the cornerstone" informs the apostle's reflections on believers as "living stones." Engrafted into Christ, believers are no less indwelt and empowered by the Holy Spirit—the adjective

10. The Greek verb, translated "dwelt," is σκηνόω, which "more literally means 'to pitch one's tent,'" thereby establishing a typological connection between the Old Testament tabernacle and the incarnation of Jesus Christ, Köstenberger, *John*, 41.

11. Edmund P. Clowney, "The Biblical Theology of the Church," in *The Church in the Bible and the World: An International Study*, ed. D. A. Carson (Grand Rapids: Baker Academic, 1987), 27.

12. Beale, *The Temple and the Church's Mission*, 195.

13. Beale, *The Temple and the Church's Mission*, 185, 184. See Beale's argument in support of these claims, *The Temple and the Church's Mission*, 183–87.

"spiritual" describes the presence and ministry of the "Spirit of Christ" (1 Pet 1:11). In Christ, the church is both God's temple and "a holy priesthood" who offer up in the Spirit the kind of "sacrifices" that are fitting for the new covenant people of God.[14] Significantly, according to Peter, what characterizes and constitutes the church is "God's presence"—the "presence of Jesus," the "presence of the Spirit," and the presence of God the Father to whom new covenant believer-priests offer worship.[15]

The apostle Paul says similar things of the church. The church is being "built on the foundation of the apostles and prophets, Christ Jesus himself being the cornerstone, in whom the whole structure, being joined together, grows into a holy temple in the Lord. In him you are also are being built together into a dwelling place for God by the Spirit" (Eph 2:20–22). The Greek word translated "cornerstone" appears in the New Testament only here and in 1 Peter 2:6, where Peter cites LXX Isaiah 28:16 immediately before he cites Psalm 118:22 (LXX Ps 117:21). It is difficult not to conclude that Paul, no less than Peter, has in mind Jesus's teaching in Matthew 21:42. As Peter does, Paul speaks of the church in expressly Trinitarian terms. "Christ Jesus himself [is] the cornerstone of the church," and the church is "being built together into a dwelling place for God by the Spirit" (Eph 2:20, 22).[16] Also in a way similar to Peter, who describes believers as "living stones" (1 Pet 2:5), Paul sees the church as an organic, living, growing building—in Christ, "the whole structure, being joined together, grows into a holy temple in the Lord" (Eph 2:21). Significantly, the church as "temple" is both corporate and individual in orientation. In both 1 Peter and Ephesians, Peter and Paul have primarily in view the church in her corporate, gathered capacity. But Paul, in speaking of the church in this way to the Corinthians in 1 Corinthians 3:16, 17 ("Do you not know that you are God's temple and that God's Spirit dwells in you. ... For God's temple is holy, and you are that

---

14. On the similarities between the description of the church in 1 Peter as "eschatological temple" and the description of the church in Revelation, see Beale, *The Temple and the Church's Mission*, 331–33.

15. Edmund P. Clowney, *The Church* (Downers Grove, IL: InterVarsity Press, 1995), 46.

16. It should be emphasized, in this connection, that Paul is addressing the people of God not in the abstract, but in her present eschatologically mature state. God, in Christ, has "create[d] in himself one new man in place of the two, so making peace" and "you [gentiles] are no longer strangers and aliens, but you are fellow citizens with the saints and members of the household of God" (Eph 2:15, 19). Note the expressly Trinitarian formulation at Ephesians 2:18, "For through [Christ] we both have access in one Spirit to the Father."

temple"), can individualize this characterization.[17] A few chapters later, in dissuading the Corinthians from committing acts of sexual immorality, Paul asks them, "Do you not know that your body is a temple of the Holy Spirit within you, whom you have from God" (1 Cor 6:19). Although Paul is addressing the Corinthians collectively, his reference to the "body" as "a temple of the Holy Spirit within you" necessarily individualizes the metaphor. As they are in Christ and thereby belong to and participate in the eschatological temple, Christians are also to think of themselves individually as a temple in whom the Spirit dwells.[18]

In Revelation, John describes the state of consummation as "the holy city, new Jerusalem, coming down out of heaven from God" (Rev 21:2). As such, Beale observes, this city is "the true temple ... [that] fill[s] the whole creation."[19] City, temple, and cosmos are coextensive in eschatological consummation. John goes on to say that he "saw no temple in the city, for its temple is the Lord God the Almighty and the Lamb" (21:22). What continues to lend to the church its identity is the presence of God in Christ. In this way, the goal of creation—the presence of God with his people in communion and fellowship—is realized.

Body

THAT THE CHURCH IS LIVING, organic, and growing bridges the New Testament's description of the church as "temple" with its description of the church as "body," specifically, the body of Christ.[20] The characterization of the church as "body" is largely, if not exclusively, found in the letters of Paul, particularly Romans, 1 Corinthians, Ephesians, and Colossians. Scholars have long debated the origins of this metaphor, and one need not insist upon a single "fountainhead for the Pauline metaphor."[21] But, as Clowney has argued, an important, even leading, source for this

---

17. As the footnote to the ESV observes, "The Greek for *you* is plural in verses 16 and 17." It is the gathered church to which Paul addresses himself here.

18. Sinclair B. Ferguson, *The Holy Spirit* (Downers Grove, IL: InterVarsity Press, 1996), 176.

19. Beale, *The Temple and the Church's Mission*, 370.

20. Clowney rightly speaks of the "flexibility and interfacing of the metaphors concerning the church" in the New Testament, "Interpreting the Biblical Models of the Church," 77.

21. Thomas R. Schreiner, *Romans*, 2nd ed. (Grand Rapids: Baker Academic, 2018), 635. See the literature cited at Schreiner, *Romans*, 635n10. For a still helpful treatment of Roman Catholic understandings of "the body of Christ" into the mid-twentieth century, see Ridderbos, *Paul*, 362–69.

metaphor surely lies in the body of Christ himself—"the key to Paul's use of the metaphor 'body of Christ' lies in this representative principle as it is applied to the *literal* body of Christ."[22] That is to say, as Christ serves as the representative of his people, and as Christ undertook his mediatorial work for his people in his humanity (living, dying, and rising again), Paul therefore establishes a "close connection ... between the physical body of Christ (who died as our representative) and the church as the body of Christ," particularly in Ephesians 2:13–16.[23] It is, therefore, this representative aspect of believers' union with Christ that provides the background and framework for Paul's depiction of the church as the body of Christ.

When understood in this light, the metaphor, "body of Christ," has background in the Old Testament although it is not used of Old Testament Israel. The principle of mediatorial representation was typologically embedded in the Sinaitic covenant. In particular, the Aaronic high priest represented the nation of Israel when undertaking his official duties. His priestly garments included a "breastpiece of judgment" with "twelve stones [containing the] names of the sons of Israel" (Exod 28:15, 21). When he offered sacrifice on the Day of Atonement, he "confess[ed] over [the live goat] all the iniquities of the people of Israel, and all their transgressions, all their sins" (Lev 16:21). In his priestly vestments and duties, the high priest anticipated the representative office and work of Jesus Christ.[24]

Paul employs the metaphor of the "body of Christ" in two fundamental ways.[25] In Romans and 1 Corinthians, the apostle particularly stresses the "unity" of the church "in and with Christ," that is, "Christ in the redemptive-historical sense, in the inclusion of 'the many' in the one."[26] In Ephesians and Colossians, Paul introduces a new element to the metaphor—Christ as "head" of the body, the church (Col 1:18; 2:19; cf. 2:10;

22. Clowney, "Interpreting the Biblical Models of the Church," 86.

23. Clowney, "Interpreting the Biblical Models of the Church," 86.

24. Ridderbos notes, in this connection, the way in which Paul presents Moses in relation to Israel as typological mediator at 1 Corinthians 10:2 and, as such, "a clear prefiguration of the corporate unity of the church in Christ" *qua* body of Christ, *Paul*, 393.

25. Following the division of Ridderbos, *Paul*, 369–87.

26. Ridderbos, *Paul*, 375. Negatively, Ridderbos rejects the view that "body of Christ" in these two letters "intend[s] in the first place to qualify its mutual unity and diversity," *Paul*, 375. Ridderbos goes on to say that the church's being in Christ "is not restricted to the redemptive-historical aspect, but also works itself out sacramentally and pneumatically," *Paul*, 376.

Eph 4:12, 15–16; cf. 1:20–23). As Ephesians 5:22–33 indicates, by "headship," Paul understands "a position of rulership and authority."[27] The church, then, is under the direct and immediate mediatorial headship of her risen and exalted Lord, Jesus Christ. What integrates the distinct treatments of the "body of Christ" across Paul's letters is the way in which this metaphor affords "christological concentration of [the] 'people of God.'"[28]

Although the church as "body of Christ" is not used explicitly in describing the people of God in their eschatologically consummate state, the underlying concept is very much evident in such biblical descriptions. The church will never cease to be one-in-Christ, and Christ will never cease to exercise rule and authority (with attendant provision and protection) over his people (Rev 7:17; 21:22; 22:1–5). Christ will continue to be to his people in their eschatological heavenly rest what he has been to them in their state of pilgrimage.

Bride

A FINAL METAPHOR THAT CHRIST and the apostles use of the people of God under the new covenant is that of "bride (of Christ)." Part of John the Baptist's witness to Jesus is that Jesus is the "bridegroom ... who has the bride" (John 3:29). In his earthly ministry, Jesus speaks of himself as "bridegroom" (Matt 9:15; Mark 2:19), and no less speaks of the kingdom of God (Matt 22:1–10), and of eschatological consummation (Matt 25:1–10), in terms of a wedding feast.

Such language has deep roots in the Old Testament's testimony to God and his relationship with Israel.[29] In particular, the prophets depict Israel as God's unfaithful bride, and particularly, her idolatry as marital treachery and infidelity (Hos 2:1–13; Jer 3:1–2; Ezek 16:1–52). But the prophets no less describe Israel's restoration in terms of the saving work of God the

---

27. Ridderbos, *Paul*, 381. This rule and authority "is founded in the fact that [Christ] is also the Preserver and Savior of the body," Ridderbos, *Paul*, 381. For a treatment of the lexical evidence, see Wayne Grudem, "The Meaning of *Kephalē* ('Head'): An Evaluation of New Evidence, Real and Alleged," in *Biblical Foundations for Manhood and Womanhood*, ed. Wayne Grudem (Wheaton, IL: Crossway, 2002), 145–202. In this respect, the metaphor is not drawn from "physiological conceptions" relating to "the human body," but from "the structures and connections of the human community," Ridderbos, *Paul*, 382.

28. Ridderbos, *Paul*, 395.

29. For a fuller treatment of the Old Testament's depiction of Israel as God's bride, see Raymond C. Ortlund, Jr., *God's Unfaithful Wife: A Biblical Theology of Spiritual Adultery*, NSBT (Downers Grove, IL: InterVarsity Press, 2003).

bridegroom on behalf of his bride (Hos 2:16–20; Isa 54:4–8; 62:1–5). In identifying himself as bridegroom, Jesus identifies himself as the God of Israel who has come to save his people. In speaking of the kingdom of God along the lines of wedding feast, Jesus underscores the kingdom as the redemptive rule and reign of the bridegroom over his bride, the church.

The apostles maintain this dual identification of Jesus as bridegroom, and the church as his bride. In Ephesians 5:22–33, Paul describes what it means that Christ is the husband of his wife, the church. He is her "head," that is to say, he exercises authority over her (5:23). He is her "Savior," and has saved her from sin and death (5:23; compare 2:1–10). In particular, he has laid down his life for her that he might "sanctify her" and "present the church to himself" in eschatological holiness and glory (5:26, 27). Paul emphasizes, then, the bride's call to spiritual purity and faithfulness to her bridegroom, and the bridegroom's commitment to secure the holiness of his bride. Elsewhere in Paul's letters, this commitment on the part of the bridegroom translates into a duty incumbent upon the bride. Paul reminds the Corinthians, "For I feel a divine jealousy for you, since I betrothed you to one husband, to present you as a pure virgin to Christ" (2 Cor 11:2). The verses that follow explain such purity in terms of absolute and undeviating fidelity to Jesus Christ and his gospel (11:3, 4). Strikingly, Paul identifies himself with God in his marital "jealousy" for his people.[30] It is through such servants as Paul that God will maintain and preserve the spiritual faithfulness of his new covenant people.

The end of the age will be marked by the presentation of the bride to her returning bridegroom. John sees "the holy city, new Jerusalem, coming down out of heaven from God, prepared as a bride adorned for her husband" (Rev 21:2). She is "the Bride, the wife of the Lamb" (21:9; compare 22:17). She is presented to the watching apostle as "having the glory of God" (21:11) and absolutely and impeccably holy (21:27, 22:15).

Summary

EACH OF THESE IMAGES IN its own way underscores the fact that the church—the people of God under the new covenant—is one and the same with Israel, the people of God under the old

30. On which, see Paul Barnett, *The Second Epistle to the Corinthians*, NICNT (Grand Rapids: Eerdmans, 1997), 499–500.

covenant. But each image underscores the degree to which the people of God have undergone radical transformation in light of the person and finished work of Jesus Christ. In particular, the church owes its constitution, form, and identity to its mediator, Christ. Furthermore, the Spirit whom Christ has secured in his death and resurrection and has poured out in full upon his people at Pentecost empowers the church to pursue the divinely-assigned callings reflected in each of these images. More than that, the Spirit ensures that, when Christ returns, he will find his bride to be a fruitful vine, a faithful flock, a holy temple, a mature body, and a pure virgin.

THE LIFE OF GOD'S PEOPLE

God declared to Israel, "You are a people holy to the Lord your God. The Lord your God has chosen you to be a people for his treasured possession, out of all the peoples who are on the face of the earth" (Deut 7:6). With that identity came the calling to be a "kingdom of priests and a holy nation" (Exod 19:6). The Mosaic legislation served as the divinely-provided blueprint for Israel's holiness in all its dimensions—moral, national, and ceremonial. In this way, and by the power of their sanctifying God, Israel would come more and more to resemble the holy God to whom she belonged (Lev 11:44–45; 20:7–8). In living according to the law, Israel would have simultaneously been set apart from the nations and lived in consecration and devotion to her covenant Lord.[31] Israel, however, pursued a course of life in conformity with the nations and in rebellion against God. As a result, God brought upon her the covenant curse of exile, scattering his people among the nations.

In Christ, God has gathered and reconstituted his people. The church under the new covenant is and is called to be a holy people. Peter tells the church, "But you are a chosen race, a royal priesthood, a holy nation, a people for his own possession, that you may proclaim the excellences of him who called you out of darkness into his marvelous light" (1 Pet 2:9; compare Exod 19:4–6). For this reason, the apostles speak of Christians as holy by calling—"saints" (1 Cor 1:2). As with Israel, holiness not only belongs to the church's identity, but is also a calling that the church must

31. On holiness as devotion, see Sinclair B. Ferguson, *Devoted to God: Blueprints for Sanctification* (Edinburgh: Banner of Truth, 2016), 2.

pursue. Paul tells the Thessalonians, "God has not called us for impurity, but in holiness" (1 Thess 4:7; cf. 4:3).

New covenant holiness bears a distinctly christological and pneumatological imprint. The holiness of the believer is bound up in the person and work of Jesus Christ (1 Cor 1:30). It is in union with the risen Christ, Paul reasons, that believers have been delivered from sin's dominion and are now enabled to walk in resurrection life (Rom 6:1–7:6). By definition, every believer possesses the indwelling Spirit of Christ (8:9–11) who is the Spirit of holiness (1:4). There is a "mind" and a "walk" that is in keeping with the Spirit, and antithetical to the flesh (8:1–8).[32] By the power of the indwelling Spirit, the believer is able to do what he is obliged to do—to live in a way that is pleasing to God, and to "put to death the deeds of the body" (8:13). The consummate and spotless holiness of the church is guaranteed by Christ (Eph 5:27; Col 1:22; 1 Thess 3:13; 5:23), and in no way militates against the believer's obligation to pursue holiness through faith in Christ (Col 1:23).

Importantly, Paul understands holiness not simply in individual terms but also in corporate terms. The holiness that Paul enjoins the Thessalonians to pursue consists of such sexual self-control that "no one transgress and wrong his brother in this matter" (1 Thess 4:6). It no less consists of the call to "love one another" as brothers (4:9), and to "walk properly before outsiders and be dependent on no one" (4:12).[33] It is after Paul reminds the Corinthians "we are the temple of the living God" (2 Cor 6:16a; compare 6:16b–18) that he exhorts them, "Since we have these promises, beloved, let us cleanse ourselves from every defilement of body and spirit, bringing holiness to completion in the fear of God" (2 Cor 7:1). The church is and is called to be holy in her life as a community.

THE GOVERNMENT OF GOD'S PEOPLE

As we observed in the last chapter, the Gospels impress upon readers the authority of the incarnate Son of God. Jesus asserts to

---

32. "Spirit" and "flesh" in Paul's writings do not denote an anthropological dualism (mind/body), but an eschatological dualism. In Romans 8, they characterize the priorities, mindset, and lifestyle that mark life in Christ as opposed to life in Adam.

33. James W. Thompson has observed the parallels between Paul's commands in 1 Thessalonians 4:3–8, 9–12 and Leviticus 17–26. Such parallels confirm the way in which Paul "identifies the church with Israel, whom God called to be holy (Lev 19:2)," *The Church According to Paul: Rediscovering the Community Conformed to Christ* (Grand Rapids: Baker Academic, 2014), 39.

his disciples the authority that is his by virtue of his resurrection, "All authority in heaven and on earth has been given to me" (Matt 28:18). The authority in view is not the authority essential to Jesus as the second person of the Godhead. It is an authority that has been "given" to him, that is, by the Father. This grant of authority takes place upon the resurrection of Jesus from the dead. The background to this claim is the prophecy of Daniel 7:14 ("And to him was given dominion and glory and a kingdom, that all peoples, nations, and languages should serve him; his dominion is an everlasting dominion, which shall not pass away, and his kingdom one that shall not be destroyed").[34] The authority in view, then, is his mediatorial authority.[35]

The risen Jesus continues to exercise this royal authority over all things for the sake of his church (Matt 28:20; see also Eph 1:20–23).[36] It would be an authority exercised, in the first instance, through the apostles who would provide form and order for the new covenant people of God (Matt 16:13–20). Jesus pledged the grant of the Spirit to the apostles in order to "declare to [them] the things that are to come. ... He will take what is mine and declare it to you" (John 16:13b–14). Thus, the apostles, by their teaching and by their example, make known the form of government for the new covenant church that the church's king, Jesus, has purposed for his people.

Christ has a couple of leading purposes for the government that he has appointed in the church. One is to provide order within the church. Paul says of the elder that "he must manage his own household well, with all dignity keeping his children submissive, for if someone does not know how to manage his own household, how will he care for God's church?" (1 Tim 3:4, 5).[37] Similarly, deacons must "manag[e] their children and their

---

34. Ridderbos, *Matthew*, 554.

35. Note the pertinent reflections of Ridderbos, "Having followed the path that God had ordained, Christ thus received that which the Devil had once promised to give Him if he forsook God (4:8–9). His assumption of power thus was intimately related to the obedience with which He walked the path to the cross (see Phil. 2:8–9). As the Son of Man, Jesus had already had authority earlier (e.g., 7:29; 9:6; 21:23–27); but at that time it was restricted and hidden in many ways because of the humiliation He had to undergo (see 26:63–64). Now, at last, His claim to all authority (see 11:27) was realized, and He received His place 'at the right hand of the Mighty One' (26:64)," Ridderbos, *Matthew*, 554.

36. For an elaboration of the argument in this paragraph, see my *How Jesus Runs the Church*, 44–48.

37. "The argument moves from the 'lesser' to the 'greater,' in analogous realms, i.e., from the family to the family of God," George W. Knight III, *The Pastoral Epistles*, NIGTC (Grand Rapids: Eerdmans, 1992), 162.

own households well" (3:12). Officers must have proven capabilities of managing their households well so that they may exercise authority in such a way as to promote order within the church. A second purpose of church government is to promote growth and maturity within the church. Paul tells the Ephesians that God has given "the apostles, the prophets, the evangelists, the shepherds and teachers" in order "to equip the saints for the work of ministry, for building up the body of Christ" (Eph 4:11, 12). Each of these four offices, whether extraordinary or ordinary, has in common with the others the ministry of the word of God to the church. As the "saints" receive this word, they are thereby prepared to undertake "the work of ministry," and "the body of Christ" is thereby "buil[t] up." Specifically, as believers "spea[k] the truth in love" they "grow up in every way into him who is the head, into Christ" (4:15).[38] This will continue until "we all attain to the unity of the faith and of the knowledge of the Son of God, to mature manhood, to the measure of the stature of the fullness of Christ" (4:13), that is, until the church achieves eschatological perfection at the consummation. Those who minister the word to the church are therefore a necessary and standing feature of the maturing church.[39] Where Christ reigns, order and growing maturity will be seen in his people.

THE WORSHIP OF GOD'S PEOPLE

The Old Testament prophets envision not only the restoration of God's worship by his people but also its expansion. God will gather the nations to himself and, alongside Israel, they will worship him acceptably (Isa 2:1–5; 19:19–25; 60:10–14; Zech 14:16–18). These promises come to fulfillment in Christ, in and by whom the worship of God's people is

38. Notice how elsewhere Paul distinguishes tongues and prophecy with respect to the latter's capacity for people's "upbuilding and encouragement and consolation" (1 Cor 14:3). This is because tongues are incomprehensible to hearers, while prophecy is understandable to hearers. Therefore, Paul reasons, "The one who speaks in a tongue builds up himself, but the one who prophesies builds up the church" (14:4).

39. Elders edify the church through the ministry of the word not only in their individual capacities as preachers and teachers, but also in their joint capacity as elders meeting in regular assembly. Acts 15:1–35 is an example of an assembly of elders whose deliberations bring renewed clarity to the church's witness to the gospel of grace and its implications in the lives of the people of God.

transformed (John 4:20–24), and who will draw people from all nations to himself (John 12:32).

The New Testament furnishes a portrait of the people of God under the new covenant as a worshiping community.[40] That worship is seen along two complementary but distinct lines. The first is that the whole of the new covenant believer's life is framed in liturgical, even sacerdotal, terms. Paul tells the Roman Christians "to present your bodies as a living sacrifice, holy and acceptable to God, which is your spiritual worship" (Rom 12:1). In this regard, Paul presents himself as an example to believers. He is "a minister of Christ Jesus to the Gentiles in the priestly service of the gospel of God, so that the offering of the Gentiles may be acceptable, sanctified by the Holy Spirit" (Rom 15:16). Paul elsewhere speaks of the Philippians' monetary gifts to him as "a fragrant offering, a sacrifice acceptable and pleasing to God" (Phil 4:18). Similarly, the author of Hebrews urges believers, "through [Christ] then let us continually offer up a sacrifice of praise to God, that is, the fruit of lips that acknowledge his name," speaking of "do[ing] good and … shar[ing] what you have" as "sacrifices … pleasing to God" (Heb 13:15, 16; compare Rom 15:27). Peter speaks, in general terms, of believers as "living stones … being built up as a spiritual house, to be a holy priesthood, to offer spiritual sacrifices acceptable to God through Jesus Christ" (1 Pet 2:5).

The apostles employ this language toward believers in view of the high priestly ministry of Christ who once for all laid down his life an atoning, propitiatory sacrifice for the sins of his people. Given the sufficiency of the atonement for the remission of all the sins of a sinner (Col 1:14; 2:13; Rom 8:1), such priestly language used of believers in no way suggests that believers' services supplement what is lacking in Christ's own sacrifice. On the contrary, as the New Testament writers make clear, such services

40. On the texts pertinent to a biblical-theological survey of New Testament worship, see D. G. Peterson, "Worship," in *New Dictionary of Biblical Theology*, eds. T. Desmond Alexander, Brian S. Rosner, D. A. Carson, and Graeme Goldsworthy (Downers Grove, IL: InterVarsity Press, 2000), 859–63; David Peterson, *Engaging with God: A Biblical Theology of Worship* (Downers Grove, IL: InterVarsity Press, 1992); and David Peterson, "Worship in the New Testament," in *Worship: Adoration and Action*, ed. D. A. Carson (Grand Rapids: Baker Academic, 1993), 51–91. One weakness of Peterson's analysis of New Testament worship is its failure adequately to draw the New Testament's basic distinction between the general service of Christians (characterized by the New Testament in liturgical terms) and the stated, gathered meetings of Christians in Lord's Day worship.

assume the sufficiency of Christ's death on the cross.[41] The significance of this language in the New Testament lies elsewhere. As the priest after the order of Melchizedek, Christ fulfills the typological Levitical priesthood (Heb 5:1–7:28). In Christ, the people of God are constituted priests whose good works, undertaken in the power of the Spirit, are termed spiritual sacrifices. The range of such good works spans the whole of a Christian's life (Col 3:17; Eph 5:20; 1 Cor 10:31).[42]

But there is a distinct and narrow sense in which the New Testament writers speak of the worship of God's people under the new covenant. As with old covenant Israel, the new covenant church gathers weekly, on the day of God's appointment, in stated assembly to worship God according to his revealed will.[43] Such gatherings are especially characterized by the reading and preaching of the word of God, public prayer, the sung or vocal praise of God, and the administration of the sacraments of baptism and the Lord's Supper (Acts 2:42; 20:7–12; 1 Cor 14:26; Eph 5:19).[44] These meetings are not discretionary but obligatory for all new covenant Christians (Heb 10:25). What characterizes these assemblies, more than anything else,

---

41. The exhortation of Romans 12:1 is founded on "the mercies of God," which surely include the death of Christ for sinners' sins (Rom 3:21–26). Peter's exhortation in 1 Peter 2:5 is soon followed by his declaration (referencing Isa 53:5), "by his wounds you have been healed" (1 Pet 2:24). Hebrews' exhortations similarly follow an extensive exposition of the high priestly work of Christ in offering himself once for all as sacrifice for the sins of his people (Heb 9:26, 28; 10:10, 12, 18).

42. So, rightly, Clowney, "Presbyterian Worship," in *Worship: Adoration and Action*, ed. D. A. Carson, 111.

43. On first century worship in New Testament scholarship, see Oscar Cullmann, *Early Christian Worship* (Philadelphia: Westminster, 1953); C. F. D. Moule, *Worship in the New Testament*, 2nd ed. (Bramcote, UK: Grove, 1977–1978); R. P. Martin, *Worship in the Early Church*, 2nd ed. (Grand Rapids: Eerdmans, 1974); Paul F. Bradshaw, *Search for the Origins of Christian Worship*, 2nd ed. (Oxford: Oxford, 2002); and Paul F. Bradshaw, *Reconstructing Early Christian Worship* (London: SPCK, 2009). On the "Lord's Day" (Rev 1:10) or the "first day of the week" (Acts 20:7) as the divinely appointed day for new covenant public worship, see my *The Sabbath as Rest and Hope for the People of God*, SSBT (Wheaton, IL: Crossway, 2022).

44. See the fuller discussion at Clowney, "Presbyterian Worship," 117. On baptism and its relation to old covenant circumcision, see J. V. Fesko, *Word, Water, and Spirit: A Reformed Perspective on Baptism* (Grand Rapids: Reformation Heritage, 2010), esp. 239–42; and David Gibson, "Sacramental Supercessionism Revisited: A Response to Martin Salter on the Relationship between Circumcision and Baptism," *Themelios* 37 no. 2 (2012): 191–208. On the Lord's Supper and its relation to the old covenant Passover, see Andreas J. Köstenberger, "Was the Last Supper a Passover Meal?" in *The Lord's Supper: Remembering and Proclaiming Christ Until He Comes*, ed. Thomas R. Schreiner and Matthew R. Crawford (Nashville: B&H, 2010), 6–30, and I. Howard Marshall, *Last Supper and Lord's Supper* (Grand Rapids: Eerdmans, 1980), 76–80.

is that God is pleased to be present with his people in them, to bless his ordinances for the good of his people (1 Cor 14:25).

Revelation reminds us that presently, in heaven, saints and angels are engaged in ceaseless worship of the Triune God (Rev 4:10; 5:14; 7:11; 11:1, 16; 14:7; 15:4; 19:4, 10; 22:9).[45] Hebrews suggests that, when believers assemble in public worship, they are participating in this heavenly worship (Heb 12:22–24, 28).[46] When Christ returns, there will be "a new heaven and a new earth," "the holy city, New Jerusalem, coming down out of heaven from God" (Rev 21:1, 2). At the consummation, the people of God will engage in continual worship of God and of the Lamb (22:3). God's created purposes for his image bearers will have come to their full realization in Jesus Christ.

THE MISSION OF GOD'S PEOPLE

Under the old covenant, God chose a nation (Israel) for himself, calling them to radiate the light of truth and holiness to the nations around them.[47] In this way, God would make himself known to the world. Israel, however, chose the path of conformity to the nations and ended her old covenant existence in captivity and subjection to the nations. In his earthly ministry, Jesus limited his own missionary activity, and that of his disciples, to Israel. But Jesus's encounters with gentiles as well as his teaching about the extension of the gospel to the gentiles pointed to centrifugally-oriented mission under the new covenant.

Jesus's commissions of his apostles (Matt 28:18–20; Luke 24:44–49; Acts 1:8; John 20:19–23) constitute the foundation of the mission of the people of God between the resurrection and the return of Christ.[48] These commis-

45. D. G. Peterson, "Worship," 863, from which these texts have come.

46. Clowney, "Presbyterian Worship," 112; D. G. Peterson, "Worship," 862, although Peterson does not speak of such a meeting in terms of Lord's Day worship. "The assembly is the earthly counterpart to the heavenly 'congregation' (*ekklēsia*) of God's people (12:23; cf. 2:12)," C. R. Koester, cited at Peter O'Brien, *The Letter to the Hebrews*, PNTC (Grand Rapids: Baker Academic, 2010), 371.

47. For biblical-theological surveys of mission in the New Testament, see especially A. J. Köstenberger, "Mission," in *New Dictionary of Biblical Theology*, 663–68; A. J. Köstenberger and P. T. O'Brien, *Salvation to the Ends of the Earth: A Biblical Theology of Mission* (Downers Grove, IL: InterVarsity Press, 2001); and P. T. O'Brien, *Gospel and Mission in the Writings of Paul: An Exegetical and Theological Analysis* (Grand Rapids: Baker Academic, 1995).

48. One may reliably conclude on textual critical grounds that the commission appearing in the longer ending of Mark (16:9–20) is not part of the original text of Mark's Gospel. Even so, Mark anticipates a sustained ministry of the proclamation of Christ ("And the gospel must

sions coalesce in their defining the mission of the church in terms of witness to Christ to the nations, "you will be my witnesses in Jerusalem and in all Judea and Samaria, and to the end of the earth" (Acts 1:8; compare Luke 24:48). In Matthew's commission, Jesus charges his disciples to "go ... and make disciples of all nations" (Matt 28:19). Luke's commission underscores the fact that Christ has brought the Old Testament to its intended fulfillment, and that "all nations" are to respond to the preaching of Christ in "repentance for the forgiveness of sins" (Luke 24:47; compare John 20:19–23). Both Luke's and John's commissions stress the abiding, empowering presence of the Holy Spirit to make effective the apostolic witness to Christ (Luke 24:49; John 20:22), a reality that Matthew's commission frames in terms of Christ's own presence with his disciples to "the end of the age" (Matt 28:20; compare Acts 1:1, "all that Jesus began to do and teach").

Thus, the apostles are not undertaking a mission that is separate from that which Jesus undertook in his own earthly ministry. As Jesus proclaimed the inbreaking of the kingdom of God in light of his incarnate ministry, so the apostles proclaim the King, Jesus Christ, in light of his finished work of redemption.[49] Underlying this continuity of mission of proclamation is that both Jesus and the apostles are "sent" to undertake their respective missions, "as the Father has sent me, even so I am sending you" (John 20:21). To be sure, one must not collapse these respective missions into one another—Jesus was sent to accomplish the redemption that he also proclaimed, and the apostles are sent strictly to proclaim the redemption that Christ has once-for-all accomplished. But the disciples,

first be proclaimed to all nations," Mark 13:10; "wherever the gospel is proclaimed in the whole world," 14:9a) that will meet with success ("And then [the Son of Man] will send out the angels and gather his elect from the four winds, from the ends of the earth to the ends of heaven," 13:27). Note R. T. France, *The Gospel of Mark*, NIGTC (Grand Rapids: Eerdmans, 2002), 516–17, 555.

49. "However different the modality in Paul's ministry may be as compared with Jesus Christ's, it can be rightly said that Paul does nothing but explain the eschatological reality which in Christ's teachings is called the kingdom. Only, in the case of Paul the emphasis is not especially on the fact, but on the unthought-of *modus quo* of the fact ... Paul as the witness last called stands behind the facts, notably behind the facts of Christ's death and resurrection. It is to these facts that he is to preach and interpret as the culminating point of the kingdom of God which has appeared in Christ, as the deciding acts in the divine, eschatological drama," Herman N. Ridderbos, *When the Time Had Fully Come*, 48–49. Note representatively, in this connection, Acts 20:25; 28:31; Rom 15:7; Col 1:13; 1 Cor 15:24; and 2 Tim 4:18.

in their distinct mission, are thereby "drawn into the unity and mission of Father and Son."[50]

The apostolic miracles serve to credential the apostles as messengers of Christ (Acts 14:3; 2 Cor 12:12; Rom 15:19). Upon the completion of this foundational ministry of the apostles (Eph 2:20), such miracles ceased.[51] Remaining to the post-apostolic church, then, is the proclamation of Christ in the power of the Spirit, calling the nations to repentance and faith. Significantly, essential to (not ancillary to) these dominical commissions is discipleship (Matt 28:19). The church, in proclaiming Christ, is to "make disciples of all nations, baptizing them in the name of the Father and of the Son and of the Holy Spirit, teaching them to observe all that I have commanded you" (Matt 28:19–20). The church's mission does not end when a person professes faith in Christ and is baptized. It is just beginning. The mission of the church encompasses the duration of a professing disciple's growth and maturation in Christ (Col 1:28; Eph 4:12–16).

Revelation presents portraits of the church triumphant, "people from every tribe and nation gathered in heaven to worship God and the Lamb (1:7; 4:10, 11; 5:9; 7:4–17; 14:1–5)."[52] Among the purposes of including these portraits in these scenes of eschatological consummation is impressing the church militant with the certainty of its mission's success. The church may and must persevere in the face of persecution and temptations to idolatry precisely because nothing can thwart that mission and Christ's purposes for his church.[53]

FURTHER READING

Edmund P. Clowney. "The Biblical Theology of the Church." In *The Church in the Bible and the World: An International Study,*

50. Köstenberger, *John*, 573; compare Köstenberger, "Mission," 667. Ridderbos observes, "They represent him, according to the rule that 'Whosoever receives you receives me, and whoever receives me receives the one who sent me' (Mt. 10:40; cf. Jn. 13:20)," *John*, 643.

51. Richard B. Gaffin, Jr., *Perspectives on Pentecost: New Testament Teaching on the Gifts of the Holy Spirit* (Phillipsburg, NJ: P&R, 1979), 101–2; Gaffin, "A Cessationist View," in *Are Miraculous Gifts for Today,* ed. Wayne A. Grudem (Grand Rapids: Zondervan, 1996), 25–64; B. B. Warfield, *Counterfeit Miracles* (New York: Scribner's Sons, 1918), 1–31.

52. Köstenberger, "Mission," 667.

53. Köstenberger, "Mission," 667, referencing Revelation 2:1–3:22, 14:12, representatively.

edited by D. A. Carson. Grand Rapids: Baker Academic, 1987, 13–87. A relatively recent, Reformed, and concise biblical theological treatment of the church. It is especially helpful in its exploration of the metaphors and images used of the people of God throughout Scripture.

Gaffin, Richard B. *In the Fullness of Time: An Introduction to the Biblical Theology of Acts and Paul.* Wheaton, IL: Crossway, 2022. A recent and comprehensive biblical theological survey of the Acts of the Apostles and the Pauline Epistles. Gaffin emphasizes the centrality of the Spirit and of the resurrection of Jesus Christ to the biblical theological framework of this portion of the New Testament canon.

Ridderbos, Herman N. *Paul: An Outline of His Theology.* Translated by John Richard De Witt. Grand Rapids: Eerdmans, 1975. The standard Reformed survey of the theology of the apostle Paul. Ridderbos gives particular attention to Paul's teaching regarding the church and its worship and government.

PART 2

DOCTRINAL CONSTRUCTION

VIII

THE ATTRIBUTES OF THE CHURCH

BUILDING UPON THE TESTIMONY OF the Apostles' Creed, the Nicene Creed prompts the Christian to declare, "I believe in one, holy, catholic, and apostolic church" (*et [credo in] unam, sanctam, catholicam et apostolicam Ecclesiam*).[1] In confessing the church along these four lines, it is important to clarify what precisely one is and is not declaring about the church. Since the Council of Trent, Roman Catholic theologians have denominated these properties, "marks," or identifiers of the church.[2] The effect of this particular denomination is to render the Roman Catholic Church the only true church, and to unchurch all other bodies that would lay claim to the

1. The Apostles' Creed states, "I believe in the holy, catholic Church" (*Credo in sanctam Ecclesiam catholicam*). As Clowney notes, "The Apostles' Creed does not confess that we believe *in* the church in the same way that we believe in God the Father, Jesus Christ and the Holy Spirit. Yet we do *believe* the holy catholic church; the church itself is a matter of Christian faith. Why is this so? Because ... the church is God's creation, not simply a human institution," *The Church*, 71. On the force of the Latin preposition *in*, see John Pearson, *An Exposition of the Creed*, rev. E. Burton, 5th ed. (Oxford: Clarendon, 1864), 591–92n53; Witsius, *The Apostles' Creed*, 2:361–62.

2. Roman Catholic theologians have not been uniform with respect the number of the church's marks. Note the diversity within the seventeenth century, as charted by Turretin, *Institutes*, 18.13.2 (=3:97). Bellarmine, for instance, proposed fifteen marks which, Turretin notes, "nevertheless can in some way be reduced to these four (which are commonly assigned from the Constantinopolitan Creed [A.D. 381]) ... : one, holy, catholic, apostolic," *Institutes*, 18.13.2 (=3:97). Turretin proceeds to refute each of Bellarmine's fifteen marks as genuine marks of the church (*Institutes*, 3:98–120). More recently, see *Catechism of the Catholic Church* §811–870, where "these four characteristics [i.e., unity, holiness, catholicity, and apostolicity]" are said to "indicate essential features of the Church and her mission," §811.

name "church."[3] Protestants have raised a number of objections against defining the church along these lines.[4] First, unity, holiness, catholicity, and apostolicity are not "peculiar" to the church, and do not "distinguish it from all other bodies."[5] Many non-ecclesiastical societies of Christians, for instance, could be said to possess and exhibit unity as a society. Second, as we will see below, Protestants and Roman Catholics are not in agreement with respect to the meaning of each of these terms.[6] Finally, notably absent from Roman Catholic lists of the marks of the church is "truth of doctrine or conformity with the word of God."[7] At best, Rome's marks are "reducible to" or derivative from the truth.[8] At worst, the truth is effectively rendered "no mark of the Christian church at all."[9]

To draw these observations is in no way to set aside unity, holiness, catholicity, and apostolicity from the consideration of the church of Jesus Christ. It is, however, to say that none of these descriptors serves to define the church in such a way as to distinguish it from other human societies or bodies. These four terms, when properly defined, are "properties" or "attributes" of the church.[10] They serve to *describe* the church without at the same time *defining* the church.

---

3. Bannerman, *The Church of Christ*, I:63; compare Bavinck, *Reformed Dogmatics*, 4:320.

4. I am following here the argument of Bannerman, *The Church of Christ*, 1:64–67. For Reformed Protestant engagement of post-Vatican II ecclesiology more generally, see Michael Horton, *The Christian Faith: A Systematic Theology for Pilgrims on the Way* (Grand Rapids: Zondervan, 2011), 741–44; and Gregg R. Allison, *Roman Catholic Theology and Practice: An Evangelical Assessment* (Wheaton, IL: Crossway, 2014), 159–225.

5. Bannerman, *The Church of Christ*, 1:64.

6. See the discussion at Bannerman, *The Church of Christ*, 1:64–65.

7. Turretin, *Institutes*, 18.12.29 (=3:96). Turretin declares this to be "the true and genuine mark of the true church *in thesi*," *Institutes*, 18.12.29 (=3:96).

8. Turretin, *Institutes*, 18.13.4 (=3.97).

9. Bannerman, *The Church of Christ*, 1:65. Bannerman emphasizes that Rome's omission is purposeful. "According to their system, the truth is known through the Church, and not rather the Church through the truth. ... The first and leading idea is the Church, viewed as a system of outward authority and outward ordinances, and known by certain visible and formal marks. ... The first and primary obligation incumbent on all is to recognize the Church, and to submit implicitly to its authority and observances," *The Church of Christ*, 165.

10. The former term is that of Bannerman, *The Church of Christ*, 1:64; the latter term is that of Berkhof, *Systematic Theology*, 572; Vos, *Reformed Dogmatics*, 5:20–23.

It is worth noting that older Reformed theologians have often insisted that these four attributes exclusively describe the *invisible* church.[11] That is to say, they do not properly describe the church visible. This position is understandable, given Rome's insistence that unity, holiness, catholicity, and apostolicity were realized alone in the Roman Catholic Church, understood as "an external institution" or "hierarchical organization."[12] But it must be asked whether some Reformed Protestants have overreacted to Rome's claims. In so distancing the visible and invisible church by predicating these attributes only of the invisible church, one runs the risk of lending credence to Rome's accusation that the visible church / invisible church distinction effectively creates "two churches."[13]

Unity, holiness, catholicity, and apostolicity are attributes of the visible church. This is not to deny that these attributes belong to the invisible church. Nor is it to deny that these attributes are presently imperfectly realized and expressed in the visible church.[14] It is to say that the creed's confession of the church as one, holy, catholic, and apostolic is never less than a confession of the visible church as she now is.

Before exploring these attributes, it is important to state, even briefly, what is meant by "the church," particularly the church visible. Most basically, the church is the people of God.[15] In this respect, the people of God

---

11. "[The attributes of the Church] are peculiar to the invisible church," Vos, *Reformed Dogmatics*, 5:20; Dabney argues that the invisible church possesses in perfection unity and holiness, and that the "visible strives towards" these qualities of the invisible church, which qualities the visible church nevertheless does not properly possess. "The perfection of any one visible church, or the perfection of the great aggregate of visible churches, is to approach as near as may be to the qualities of the invisible church. They cannot possess these qualities, for reasons similar to those which forbid the shell *to be the kernel*, the body *to be the intelligent spirit* within it." "What is Christian Union," in *Discussions*, 2:434, emphasis original. Yet notice the moderation of Witsius, "let us now attend to the *Epithets* and honourable characters given to the Church; which are suitable to it in both forms, yet principally in its internal form. Three of these are mentioned in the Creed: HOLY, CATHOLIC, CHRISTIAN," *Sacred Dissertations on What is Commonly Called the Apostles' Creed*, trans. Donald Fraser, 2 vols. (1823; repr., Escondido, CA: den Dulk, 1993), 2:358.

12. Berkhof, *Systematic Theology*, 572.

13. So Bellarmine, *De Conciliis*, III.2, as cited at G. C. Berkouwer, *The Church*, trans. James E. Davison (Grand Rapids: Eerdmans, 1976), 37.

14. And yet, note even here Berkouwer's caution that the church's awaiting eschatological perfection with respect to unity in no way excuses or mitigates the church with respect to her responsibility to pursue unity in the present, *The Church*, 38–39.

15. See the lexical and historical discussion at Bavinck, *Reformed Dogmatics*, 4:296–301, and John Murray, "The Nature and Unity of the Church," *The Collected Writings of John Murray: Volume Two* (Edinburgh: Banner of Truth, 1977), 321–23.

extends the span of redemptive history, from the constituting *protoevangelium* of Genesis 3:15 to the glorious consummation recorded in Revelation 21:1–22:5. Under the new covenant, the people of God reflects the triunity of the God who creates and preserves the church. In the first place, the church is called by God. This understanding of the church is reflected in the establishment of the church in her new covenant form (Acts 2:39, 47). God calls a people out of the world and to himself, and that people thereby assumes a public and assembled form. In the second place, the church is gathered in Christ. This is true of the church both before and after the death and resurrection of Christ. Prior to the new covenant, Christ and his grace were exhibited to the people of God under the various types, shadows, and ordinances that God had appointed for them. Under the new covenant, through the apostolic preaching of Christ, people are called to Jesus Christ as Savior and risen Lord. Paul tells the Corinthians, "God is faithful, by whom you were called into the fellowship of his Son, Jesus Christ our Lord" (1 Cor 1:9). That the church is "in Christ" underlies her identity as the body of Christ, the bride of Christ, and the temple of God. In the third place, it is by the invincible grace and power of God the Spirit that the church is drawn savingly to Jesus Christ. One "sees" and "enters" the kingdom of God by the new birth, which is the exclusive prerogative of and the sovereign work of God the Spirit (John 3:3, 5). Since the New Testament understands the church as the visible expression of the kingdom, true members of the church have had entrance into the church by the agency and power of the Spirit.

Called by God, gathered in Christ, by the power of the Spirit, the church assembles in local congregations.[16] The New Testament's epistles assume that Christians belong to such congregations, and the Acts of the Apostles portray the apostles' ministry as one of ingathering professing Christians into such local assemblies. These bodies are characterized by no fewer than three distinguishing characteristics. The first is that each congregation is governed by officers appointed to lead that congregation. The establishment of regular government for the churches was a

16. "These persons meet statedly in one place and constitute one *congregation*. It is this fact that makes *ecclesia* their appropriate designation." Thomas Witherow, *The Form of the Christian Temple: Being a Treatise on the Constitution of the New Testament Church* (Edinburgh: T&T Clark, 1889), 58.

priority of the apostles: "And when they had appointed elders for them in every church, with prayer and fasting they committed them to the Lord in whom they had believed" (Acts 14:23). A second characteristic of the local church is that each congregation devotes itself to the worship of God (see Acts 2:42–47). Each church gathers regularly for the public worship of God. A third characteristic of Christian congregations is a shared commitment to holiness. Churches are holy not only in the sense that they are set apart from the world and consecrated to God and his service, but also in the shared pursuit of holy living. These three characteristics find expression in a nineteenth-century Presbyterian denomination's definition of a local congregation, "a particular church consists of a number of professing Christians, with their offspring, associated together for divine worship and godly living, agreeably to the Scriptures, and submitting to the lawful government of Christ's kingdom."[17] What brings coherence and unity to each church's government, worship, and holiness is that each is undertaken in submission to the Scripture, by which the church's King visibly rules her.[18]

ONE CHURCH

WITH THIS DEFINITION OF THE church in place, and with the understanding that unity, holiness, catholicity, and apostolicity are attributes of the church (visible and invisible), we may proceed to consider each of these attributes in turn. In affirming the unity of the church (*unam ecclesiam*), one must also address not fewer than three attendant questions. The first concerns the unity of God's people across redemptive history, namely, that Israel and the church are a single, indivisible people. The second concerns the nature and legitimacy of the visible/invisible church distinction. The third concerns whether the

---

17. *The Book of Church Order of the Presbyterian Church in the United States* (Richmond: Presbyterian Committee of Publication, 1879), II-4-1. See the exposition of this statement at F. P. Ramsay, *An Exposition of the Form of Government and the Rules of Discipline of the Presbyterian Church in the United States* (Richmond: Presbyterian Committee of Publication, 1898), 30–31.

18. "They meet as a Church under divine authority, with the sanction of Christ and in subjection to His revealed will, to do all and everything essential to that which God warrants them to do and nothing more. Without subjecting itself to this authority, a meeting of Christians would not be a Church in the sense that the term is usually applied in the New Testament; it would only be a gathering, a mere voluntary association," Witherow, *The Form of the Christian Temple*, 58.

existence and proliferation of denominations compromises, if not destroys, the profession of the church's unity.

To begin, the Scripture predicates unity of the church. The New Testament writers emphasize the unity of the church in the light of the diversity of the church's members: "There is neither Jew nor Greek, there is neither slave nor free, there is no male and female, for you are all one in Christ Jesus" (Gal 3:28). Christ "has made us both [Jew and gentile] one and has broken down in his flesh the dividing wall of hostility"; he has "create[d] in himself one new man in place of the two, so making peace" (Eph 2:14, 15). The basic unity of the church is reflected in the metaphors used of the church—"the church is the household of God (1 Tim. 3:15), the temple of God (1 Pet. 2:9f.), the one flock of the one Shepherd (John 10:16). All such characterizations make any thought of the plural simply ridiculous."[19] As Calvin furthermore observes, "there could not be two or three churches unless Christ be torn asunder—which cannot happen."[20] A comparable unity obtained of God's people under the old covenant, Israel. As Israel's God was one, so God's Israel was one.[21] Significantly, Israel's pursuit of the gods of the surrounding nations resulted in the covenant curse of division. Even so, the canonical Prophets envision an eschatological future for Israel in which God will savingly unite his divided, scattered people.[22] This prophetic hope comes to realization in the new covenant church.

Although some Reformed theologians predicate unity exclusively of the invisible church, it is difficult to deny that the New Testament writers have the visible church in mind when they speak of the church as one.[23] And yet, the New Testament no less recognizes the threat and presence of division in the visible church (1 Cor 1:10–4:21). Unity is both the present possession of the church and something that the church is obligated to maintain and to bring to expression. Before he enumerates the indicatives underlying the church's unity in Ephesians 4:4–6, Paul exhorts the Ephesians to be "eager to maintain the unity of the Spirit in the bond of peace" (Eph 4:1–3).

---

19. Berkouwer, *The Church*, 42.

20. *Institutes* 4.1.2, cited at Berkouwer, *The Church*, 41.

21. See Berkouwer, *The Church*, 43, referencing Barth, *Church Dogmatics* IV/3, 2, 730f.

22. Berkouwer, *The Church*, 42.

23. See John Murray, "The Nature and Unity of the Church," in *Collected Writings: Volume Two*, 325–26.

Unity is, then, both the indicative and the imperative of the church (see John 17:20–23).[24]

One attendant question broached concerning the unity of the church is the relationship between Israel and the church. Historically, Dispensational interpreters have argued axiomatically for two peoples with two distinct destinies in the course of redemptive history.[25] But the New Testament writers in particular understand a single people of God to span the testaments.[26] Two metaphors used of God's people reflect this understanding. Paul's extended metaphor of an olive tree in Romans 11:16b–25 points to a single people of God. Jews and gentiles, represented by "natural branches" (Rom 11:21) and "wild olive shoot[s]" (11:17) are said to belong, in different times and respects, to the same tree. It is through "unbelief" that a branch is broken off the tree, and it is through "faith" that a branch holds fast to the tree (11:20). Tellingly, God does not have two trees—a Jewish tree and a gentile tree. He has a single tree with a single "root" (11:16b–17). God, therefore, has had a single people across the history of redemption. The Epistle to the Hebrews draws the same conclusions through a different image, that of a house (Heb 3:1–6). Moses is said to have been "faithful in all God's house as a servant" (3:5; compare 3:2), but "Christ is faithful over God's house as a son" (3:6). The writer concludes, "And we are his house if indeed we hold fast our confidence and our boasting in our hope" (3:6). The "house" in this passage represents the people of God—Israel under the old covenant, and the church under the new covenant. God does not have a plurality of houses, but a single house. The people of God is one under both covenants.

The way in which the New Testament handles the text of the Old Testament also points to the unity of God's people across redemptive history. Peter's characterization of the church as "a chosen race, a royal

24. See here the constructive reflections of Bavinck, *Reformed Dogmatics*, 4:321.

25. For a representative classical dispensational statement of the relationship between Israel and the church, see Charles C. Ryrie, *Dispensationalism Today*, revised and expanded (Chicago: Moody, 1995), 123–44. On progressive dispensationalism's understanding of Israel and the church as one people, see Craig R. Blaising and Darrell L. Bock, *Progressive Dispensationalism: An Up-to-Date Handbook of Contemporary Dispensational Thought* (Wheaton, IL: Victor, 1993). For helpful engagements of dispensationalism, see Vern S. Poythress, *Understanding Dispensationalists*, 2nd ed. (Phillipsburg, NJ: P&R, 1993), and Michael J. Glodo, "Dispensationalism," in *Covenant Theology: Biblical, Theological, and Historical Perspectives*, 525–50.

26. What follows is indebted to my *How Jesus Runs the Church*, 2–6.

priesthood, a holy nation, a people for [God's] own possession" gathers language used of Israel (Exod 19:5, 6; see 1 Pet 2:9) and applies it to the new covenant people of God. Such use is predicated upon the unity of Israel and the church. The apostle James understands the prophecy of Amos 9:11–12 (Acts 15:16–17) relating to the restoration of Israel to find its fulfillment in the new covenant church. Such an interpretation posits the underlying unity of Israel and the church as God's people. While there are important differences between Israel and the church, these differences are strictly formal in nature.[27] God has had and continues to have a single people for himself.

A second attendant question touching upon the unity of the church is that of the visible/invisible church distinction. Such a distinction is enshrined in the Westminster Standards (WCF 25.1, 2; WLC 61–65), and "may be traced in the practice of the early church, though it had not then received formal expression."[28] The Reformers formulated the doctrine, occasioned by Rome's identification of the church with the institutional church over which the pope presided.[29] But the doctrine was not a polemical expedient, as Rome alleged.[30] The Reformers argued that the doctrine had incontrovertible biblical support.

Since the doctrine is often subject to misunderstanding, it is important to formulate it properly before turning to the passages in Scripture that teach that doctrine. The doctrine does not predicate two churches, one visible and one invisible. Neither does the doctrine warrant disassociation from the local church or denominations, nor does it absolve members from pursuing unity and demonstrating Christian love to a local body of believers.[31] The doctrine, rather, affirms a single church—not "two separate and

---

27. See Kuyper, *The Work of the Holy Spirit*, 179.

28. John Macpherson, *The Westminster Confession of Faith, with Introduction and Notes* (Edinburgh: T&T Clark, 1911), 142.

29. And yet note Bavinck's caution, in defense of the Reformers, that the invisible/visible church distinction must not be identified with the "distinction between the church as organism and the church as institution," *Reformed Dogmatics*, 4:304.

30. So rightly Turretin, *Institutes*, 18.7.1–2 (=3:32–3). Vos expresses it well, "The doctrine of the invisiblity of the Church is not an aid in the polemic against Rome, but the deepest expression of the antithesis to Rome," *Reformed Dogmatics*, 5:15.

31. Such misuse of the doctrine underlies John Murray's (objectionable) criticisms of the invisible/visible church distinction, "The Church: Its Definition in Terms of 'Visible' and 'Invisible' Invalid," *The Collected Writings of John Murray: Volume One* (Edinburgh: Banner of Truth, 1976), 235.

distinct Churches, but ... the same Church under two different characters"; "two different phases or aspects of what is in substance one and the same"; "one Church that must be defined from the one side as invisible and from the other as visible."[32] With that understanding, we may properly distinguish the church invisible and visible along three distinct lines. First, the invisible church and visible church are "universal," but in different respects.[33] The invisible church is universal across many generations, encompassing all the elect "that have been, are, or shall be gathered into one ..." (WCF 25.1); the visible church (under the new covenant) is universal with respect to a single generation in world today—"all those throughout the world that profess the true religion; and of their children" (WCF 25.2; compare WLC 166). Second, the membership of the invisible church is comprised of the elect only—"the whole number of the elect" (WCF 25.1); the membership of the invisible church is reckoned along two lines, profession and birthright ("all ... that profess the true religion; and of their children," WCF 25.2). Third, the invisible church neither increases nor diminishes, since the number of the elect neither increases nor diminishes (WCF 3.4); the visible church is subject to growth and diminishment as members are born and die, profess faith, and are removed from the church by discipline. Thus, there is "overlap but not identity between the visible and invisible church."[34] A person who is elect, unregenerate, and has no familial connection to the visible church is a member of the invisible church but not (yet) of the visible church. A person who has professed faith in Christ but is reprobate is a member of the visible church but not of the invisible church.

Although the terminology of invisible/visible church is not employed in Scripture, the concept is present. Paul declares, "No one is a Jew who is merely one outwardly, nor is circumcision outward and physical. But a Jew is one inwardly, and circumcision is a matter of the heart, by the Spirit, not by the letter. His praise is not from man but from God" (Rom 2:28–29). These two kinds of Jews describe a member of the visible church

32. Bannerman, *The Church of Christ*, 1:29; William Cunningham, *Historical Theology*, 2 vols. (1862; repr., Edinburgh: Banner of Truth, 1960), 1:14; Vos, *Reformed Dogmatics*, 5:18. Compare the testimony gathered at Heppe, *Reformed Dogmatics*, 665.

33. "The catholic or universal church, which is invisible. ... The visible church, which is also catholic or universal under the gospel" (WCF 25.1, 25.2).

34. Waters, *How Jesus Runs the Church*, 12.

(only) and a member of the invisible church, respectively. Paul articulates the same distinction at the opening of his argument in Romans 9: "For not all who are descended from Israel belong to Israel" (Rom 9:6). The second "Israel" does not "refer to both Jews and gentiles in Christ," but "to a remnant within Israel."[35] This remnant, Paul argues later in the letter, has been "chosen by grace" (Rom 11:5). That is to say, each true Israelite has been sovereignly, eternally, unconditionally elected by God. As Paul goes on to argue in Romans 9:7–13, this discriminating choice of God within Israel did not first emerge in Paul's day. It was already evident in the days of Abraham. Thus, there is one church across redemptive history. This one church admits of a necessary distinction, that between the invisible and visible church.

To conclude our survey of the unity of the church, we must take up a third attendant question and address an objection that is sometimes voiced against the confession of one church, namely, the existence and prevalence of denominations. The question is sometimes asked whether denominations do not give the lie to such a confession. It must be acknowledged that the sheer number of and differences among denominations within the Christian church is profoundly lamentable. The church's unity, as Jesus prays, is designed "so that the world may believe that [the Father has] sent [him]" (John 17:21; compare 17:23). Unity, therefore, is something demonstrable and visible to the unbelieving world, and Jesus's prayer stands as something of a rebuke to the church in her failure to pursue in obedience such unity with more earnestness.[36]

But it is impossible to entertain Jesus's prayers as unfulfilled, frustrated by the sinfulness of his church. We are bound to conclude, then, that the "visible unity of the body of Christ" is "obscured ... not destroyed by its division into different denominations of professing Christians."[37] Even in the church's present fractured condition, the spiritual bonds of unity that obtain among all genuine Christians persist across denominational lines. The existence of denominations is in no way an excuse or pretext to set

35. Schreiner, *Romans*, 482, 483.

36. Berkouwer, *The Church*, 45, 46.

37. *The Book of Church Order of the Presbyterian Church in America* (Lawrenceville, GA: The Office of the Stated Clerk of the General Assembly of the Presbyterian Church in America, 2021), 2-2.

aside the pursuit of visible unity. On the contrary, they are the framework and context, in divine providence, within which Christians, in obedience to Christ, strive to express their already-existing spiritual unity in tangible and demonstrable ways.[38] The church, we will see in the next chapter, is marked or identified by her adherence to the truth. Since this is so, "the Church is *one*, not because those who are members thereof dwell together, or because the rites and ceremonies to which they conform are the same; but on account of their agreement in doctrine, and faith."[39] Truth and unity, then, are not foes. They are friends. Genuine, biblical unity gives visible expression to believers who are united in a common faith in God as he has revealed himself in Scripture. Such unity is never purchased at the expense of the truth, but always maintains and honors the truth.

HOLY CHURCH

As with unity, one must define what one means when one confesses the church as "holy." At the time of the Reformation, Rome understood the holiness of the church largely in terms of the grace sacramentally dispensed by the church.[40] The Reformation tradition has argued that such a conception of the church's holiness runs counter to the testimony of the New Testament. The New Testament, to be sure, speaks of an "objective holiness."[41] Paul addresses the church in Corinth as "those sanctified in Christ Jesus, called to be saints together with all those who in every place call upon the name of our Lord Jesus Christ, both their Lord and ours" (1 Cor 1:2). By virtue of their union with Christ, Christians are "sanctified," and the Father has "called" them to be "saints" in company with believers "in every place." These are objective realities, sourced in the saving work of God alone, and not in the church itself. These objective realities, furthermore, must never be separated from the inner realities denoted by Paul's use of "holiness"

38. On which, see Thomas M'Crie, *Two Discourses on the Unity of the Church, Her Divisions, and Their Removal* (1821; repr., Dallas: Presbyterian Heritage Publications, 1989), and Dabney, "What Is Christian Union?," 2:444–46.

39. Zacharias Ursinus, *Commentary on the Heidelberg Catechism*, trans. G. W. Williard (1852; Phillipsburg, NJ: P&R, n.d.), 289.

40. Berkouwer, *The Church*, 314; Bannerman, *The Church of Christ*, 1:64. Note the testimony of the *Catechism of the Catholic Church*, §828, 829.

41. The phrase is that of Berkouwer, who proceeds to lend critical qualification to it, *The Church*, 315.

terminology throughout his letters. "Believers," Charles Hodge observes, "are saints in both senses of the word; they are inwardly renewed, and outwardly consecrated."[42] Not only must these component ideas of holiness never be separated, but they must be understood in proper relation to one another, "that which God declares holy in Christ is also made holy in Christ."[43] God sets apart and consecrates the church precisely so that, by the power of the Spirit, she may be "conformed to the image of Christ through God's Word."[44]

It is when one appreciates the New Testament writers' insistence that the church's holiness is in Christ alone that the problems with Rome's understanding of holiness come into clearer focus. Rome does not deny, on the contrary it affirms, that, "united with Christ, the Church is sanctified by him." But she continues, "through him and with him she becomes sanctifying. ... It is in the Church that 'the fullness of the means of salvation' has been deposited. It is in her that 'by the grace of God we acquire holiness.'"[45] The Reformation protested this understanding of holiness, which "locate[d] the holiness of the church in its intrinsic character as the bearer of salvation."[46] On the contrary, the Reformation tradition has "maintain[ed] that the Church is absolutely holy in an objective sense, that is, as she is considered in Jesus Christ. In virtue of the mediatorial righteousness of Christ, the Church is accounted holy before God."[47] And to this objective holiness must be united the subjective or inward holiness that is to characterize the visible church.

It is in light of the holiness of the new covenant church that we may appreciate similarities and differences with Old Testament Israel. The cast and form of Israel's holiness was overwhelmingly ceremonial and typological. Such, Paul argues, was reflective of and appropriate to Israel's relative

---

42. Charles Hodge, *An Exposition of the First Epistle to the Corinthians* (New York: Robert Carter & Brothers, 1860), 3–4. Of the participial clause, "sanctified in Christ Jesus," Hodge comments, "the church consists of those whose guilt is expiated, who are inwardly holy, and who are consecrated to God as his peculiar people. ... In the present case, all these ideas may be united," *An Exposition*, 3.

43. Horton, *Christian Faith*, 861.

44. Horton, *Christian Faith*, 861.

45. *Catechism of the Catholic Church*, §824.

46. Horton, *Christian Faith*, 868.

47. Berkhof, *Systematic Theology*, 575, as quoted at Horton, *Christian Faith*, 868.

immaturity as God's people (Gal 4:1–6). When God's people arrive at her maturity in Christ, the Mosaic ordinances peculiar to Israel's national and typological existence are abrogated, having fulfilled their intended purpose. But underlying this difference between "the people of Israel … a church under age" (WCF 19.3) and the new covenant people of God is a more basic similarity. The people of God, in both these stages of their existence, are holy in the sense that they have been set apart from the world and to God. But, in each case, such holiness demands an inward holiness that comes to moral and ethical expression in individual and corporate life.[48] Significantly, when the apostle Peter calls the new covenant people of God to holiness (1 Pet 1:14–16), he does so by quoting Leviticus 11:44 (compare Lev 19:2; 20:7).[49] In each age of redemptive history, the holiness of the people of God carried the same fundamental meaning and laid the same obligations upon its individual members.

CATHOLIC CHURCH

Rome defines catholicity strictly in terms of incorporation into the Roman Catholic Church: "Fully incorporated into the society of the Church are those who, possessing the Spirit of Christ, accept all the means of salvation given to the Church together with her entire organization, and who—by the bonds constituted by the profession of faith, the sacraments, ecclesiastical government, and communion—are joined in the visible structure of the Church of Christ, who rules her through the Supreme Pontiff and the bishops."[50] Many Protestants credit this understanding of catholicity when they allege that to confess "*credo in … catholicam ecclesiam*" is to confess allegiance to the Roman Catholic Church. This state of affairs confirms the timeliness of Turretin's seventeenth-century judgment, "Although all agree that the church is well called catholic, still they do not equally agree concerning the meaning of the word."[51]

---

48. Berkouwer, *The Church*, 319.

49. Clowney, *The Church*, 84.

50. *Lumen Gentium*, as cited by the *Catechism of the Catholic Church*, §837. The Catechism presents this material in answer to the question, "Who belongs to the Catholic Church?" *Catechism*, 241. Note the Catechism's qualifications that follow later in §837 and in §838.

51. Turretin, *Institutes*, 18.6.1 (=3:30).

One must therefore explore the way in which the New Testament defines the church's catholicity. The term "catholic" does not appear in the New Testament, and first appears in the Epistles of Ignatius, "wherever Jesus Christ is, there is the catholic (*katholikē*) church" (*Smyrn.* 8.2).[52] The concept, however, is present throughout the New Testament. Catholicity, or universality, captures what distinguishes, redemptive-historically, the new covenant people of God from the old covenant people of God. Whereas Israel under the old covenant was confined to a particular, geographical location, the church under the new covenant is dispersed and established, by divine command, throughout the whole world (Matt 28:18–20; Mark 13:10; Luke 24:47; Acts 1:8).[53] In this light, the catholicity of the church is bound up with its unity. As Christ has one church and not multiple churches, that one church, comprised of Jew and gentile, is found across the globe. Paul's metaphors of the church as a single body (1 Cor 12:12–31), a single olive tree (Rom 11:16b–24), and a single bride (Eph 5:25–27) both assume and necessitate the catholicity of the church. The fact that Christ, by his "blood," has "ransomed people for God from every tribe and language and people and nation," and has "made them a kingdom and priests to our God," confirms the catholicity of the one people of God (Rev 5:9–10).

Further, one must not detach the church's catholicity from the word of God, which creates and sustains the church. As Berkouwer has noted, "quantitative extension does not necessarily guarantee the truth of what is presented to the world."[54] It is on this ground that the Reformers challenged Rome's claim to catholicity. Rome's widespread geographical extension was insufficient to render her communion "catholic." Genuine catholicity requires that a body adhere to "the faith that was once for all delivered to the saints" (Jude 3).[55] Catholicity, Turretin cautions, "is often a title without the thing."[56] And yet to set to the side Rome's claim to catholicity is

52. *The Apostolic Fathers: Greek Texts and English Translations*, 3rd ed., ed. and trans. Michael W. Holmes (Grand Rapids: Baker Academic, 2007). For a still valuable discussion of the various denotations of the term "catholic" in relation to the church in the writings of the fathers, see Pearson, *An Exposition of the Creed*, 611–17.

53. "She is called *Catholic* because she is diffused over the whole world from the one end of the earth to the other," Cyril of Jerusalem, cited at Witsius, *The Apostles' Creed*, 2:360.

54. Berkouwer, *The Church*, 109.

55. See here Turretin, *Institutes*, 18.6.7 (=3:32).

56. Turretin, *Institutes*, 18.6.9 (=3:32).

not thereby to reject catholicity altogether. It is to affirm that the New Testament inseparably joins the church's catholicity to the word of God upon which she is founded.

APOSTOLIC CHURCH

THE FOURTH PROPERTY OR ATTRIBUTE confessed of the church in the Nicene Creed is the church's apostolicity. Here again, as with the other properties, careful definition is in order. One must ask what an apostle is, and what relationship obtains between the apostles and the church. Early in his ministry, Jesus "called to him those whom he desired ... and he appointed twelve (whom he also named apostles) so that they might be with him and he might send them out to preach and have authority to cast out demons" (Mark 3:13–15). The title "apostles" (ἀποστόλους) is rooted in the work to which Jesus calls them—he "sends" (ἀποστέλλῃ) them to preach. The apostles are, then, an extension of the work of Christ in preaching the kingdom and working miracles as signs of the kingdom. As Christ is the "apostle ... of our confession" (Heb 3:1), so he appoints apostles to minister in his name. Each is "sent"—the Son is sent by the Father into the world to undertake the work of redemption; the apostles are sent by Christ into the world to proclaim salvation in the name of Jesus Christ (John 20:21).

Subsequent to the resurrection, the apostles play a unique role in the establishment of the new covenant church. A *sine qua non* qualification for an apostle is that he has seen the risen Christ (1 Cor 9:1; 15:8; compare 1 John 1:1–4; Acts 1:22). The apostolic office is, therefore, an extraordinary office and, by design, intended to cease early in the life of the post-resurrection church. The apostles, we have observed in chapter 6, are given administrative authority to order the affairs of the church (Matt 16:13–20). Acts and the Epistles afford numerous illustrations of the exercise of that authority in the establishment of the doctrine, government, discipline, and worship of the church. In so acting, they function as "personal plenipotentiaries of the risen Christ."[57] They represent Christ in such a way that "they were His instruments and organs in the continuation of revelation."[58] In the

57. Gaffin, *In the Fullness of Time*, 58.

58. Herman N. Ridderbos, *Redemptive History and the New Testament Scriptures*, trans. H. de Jongste, 2nd rev. ed. (Phillpsburg, NJ: P&R, 1988), 14. "The apostles were not simply witnesses or preachers in a general, ecclesiastical sense. Their word is the revelatory word;

course of an elaborate description of the new covenant church, Paul says the church is "built on the foundation of the apostles and prophets, Christ Jesus himself being the cornerstone" (Eph 2:20). The metaphor requires us to understand the apostles (with the prophets of the new covenant) as establishing the foundation of the church, and the subsequent (post-apostolic) history of the church as the structure built upon that apostolic foundation.

Rome understands the apostolicity of the church in the sense that the church "continues to be taught, sanctified, and guided by the apostles until Christ's return, through their successors in pastoral office: the college of bishops, 'assisted by priests, in union with the successor of Peter, the Church's supreme pastor.'"[59] Affirming the church's once-for-all foundation in the apostles, Rome nevertheless understands the apostles to be succeeded by the church's bishops.[60] According to Rome, Peter's apostolic office was and remains a transmissible one.[61]

In reply, Reformed Protestants have denied both Petrine primacy and the transmissibility of the apostolic office through the episcopacy. The apostolate is not an ordinary office, but one confined to the founding of the new covenant church. This understanding of the apostolic office in no way constitutes a denial of the apostolicity of the church. On the contrary, Protestants affirm that the church is apostolic insofar as the church holds fast to the apostolic word transmitted generationally through the church (2 Tim 1:13–14; 2:2). The Reformation affirmed apostolic succession, but it was defined strictly in terms of *successio Verbi aut doctrinae* (succession of the word or of doctrine).[62]

---

it is the unique, once-for-all witness to Christ to which the church and the world are accountable and by which they will be judged," *Redemptive History*, 15. And yet, to affirm this point is not to affirm the personal infallibility of each apostle. Paul, after all, rebuked Peter publicly when Peter's practice strayed from the gospel that he professed (Gal 2:11–14).

59. *The Catechism of the Catholic Church*, §857, citing *Ad Gentes* 5.

60. *The Catechism of the Catholic Church*, §862, 857.

61. *The Catechism of the Catholic Church*, §862, 857.

62. Berkouwer, *The Church*, 275. Note Berkouwer's important qualification, "The Reformation did not separate the *successio doctrinae* from the *successio personae*, since the former is determined precisely by personal responsibility from generation to generation. The normativity functions in the progression," *The Church*, 275.

CONCLUSION

UNITY, HOLINESS, CATHOLICITY, AND APOSTOLICITY are properties or attributes of the church. None defines the church as the church, but each properly and necessarily describes the church. The next chapter will explore the question of the mark(s) of the church, the implications of the mark(s) of the church for the life and ministry of the church, and the way in which the mark(s) of the church define and structure each of the attributes of the church.

FURTHER READING

Berkouwer, G. C. *The Church*. Translated by James E. Davison. Grand Rapids: Eerdmans, 1976. A contemporary theological treatment of the church by a leading Reformed theologian of the twentieth century. This work emphasizes the church's attributes and thoughtfully engages the claims of the Roman Catholic Church.

Turretin, Francis. *Institutes of Elenctic Theology*. 3 vols. Translated by James T. Dennison, Jr. Phillipsburg, NJ: P&R, 1992–1997. A leading Reformed scholastic theologian of the late seventeenth-century, whose work greatly influenced American Presbyterians in the nineteenth century. Turretin's treatment of the church, in the third volume, is wide ranging and especially helpful in its constructive engagement of non-Reformed doctrine.

Witsius, Herman. *Sacred Dissertations on the Apostles' Creed*. Grand Rapids: Reformation Heritage, 2012. An exposition of the Apostles' Creed by a seventeenth century Continental Reformed theologian. Witsius's treatment of the church explores the nature and attributes of the church.

IX

THE MARKS OF THE CHURCH

THE ATTRIBUTES OF THE CHURCH, confessed in the Nicene Creed, aptly describe the church of Jesus Christ. The church is one, holy, catholic (universal), and apostolic. But to *describe* the church is not necessarily to *define* the church. The task of defining the church as the church and in distinction from other human organizations or assemblies is taken up in the question, "Which are the marks of the church (*notae ecclesiae*)?" This question was a live question at the time of the Protestant Reformation, as Protestant churches sought to justify their existence as churches in the face of Rome's insistence that Protestants had schismatically departed from the one, true church.

In this chapter, we will explore the ways in which Reformed Protestants answered the question, "Which are the marks of the church?" Reformed churches concurred in declaring the pure preaching of the word of God as the mark of a true branch of the church visible. On the basis of that conviction, a conviction shared with the church prior to the Reformation, the church has publicly and formally framed its understanding of the teaching of the word of God in creeds and confessions. This practice raises the question of the warrant or justification for creeds and confessions in the church. Finally, we will see how the marks of the church offer definition and form to the attributes of the church.

THE MARKS OF THE CHURCH

Rome

In the previous chapter, we observed that Roman Catholics identify several marks of the church. Post-Reformation Roman Catholic theologians agreed that there were multiple marks of the church, but did not concur as to those marks' number and identity.[1] Frequently cited are the fifteen marks of Robert Cardinal Bellarmine (1542–1621)—(1) the very name; (2) antiquity; (3) long duration; (4) the multitude and variety of the believers of the Catholic Church; (5) the succession of its bishops; (6) its agreement in doctrine with the ancient church; (7) the unity of its members among themselves and with their head; (8) the holiness of its doctrine; (9) the efficacy of its doctrine; (10) the holiness of life of the early fathers; (11) the glory of its miracles; (12) the light of prophecy; (13) the confession of its adversaries; (14) the unhappy fate of those who oppose the church; (15) temporal happiness.[2] One may detect in this list the four Nicene attributes alongside many other characteristics that are said to define the true church.

The Reformation objected to such lists as these for a few reasons. First, many of these properties are not unique to the church. Organizations and associations other than the church may lay claim to unity, universality, or holiness.[3] Second, many of these properties are "accidental and contingent marks, not necessary and essential: such as the confession of opponents, temporal happiness, unhappy end of persecutors."[4] As such, these properties are insufficient as marks of the church. Third, it is notable what is *absent* from Bellarmine's list and, in fact, each of the post-Reformation Roman Catholic lists. No list mentions the word of God as a/the mark of the church. This omission is not accidental but is the necessary consequence of Rome's ecclesiology, as James Bannerman explains.

> According to [Rome's] system, the truth is known through the Church, and not rather the Church through the truth. ... The first and leading idea is the Church, viewed as a system of outward

1. See Turretin, *Institutes*, 18.13.2 (=3:97).
2. Bellarmine, *De ecclesia militante*, 4.4–18, as cited by Bavinck, *Reformed Dogmatics*, 4:307.
3. Turretin, *Institutes*, 18.13.4 (=3:97).
4. Turretin, *Institutes*, 18.13.4 (=3:97).

> authority and outward ordinances, and known by certain visible and formal marks. [T]he first and primary obligation incumbent on all is to recognize the Church, and to submit implicitly to its authority and observances. Second merely to the Church, and subordinate to it, is the idea of the truth of Christ, which can be known only through the teaching of the Church; and the inferior obligation, and not the principal, is the obligation of embracing the truth of Christ on the authority of the Church.[5]

This understanding of the marks of the church places Rome in an untenable position. Because, on this doctrine, Scripture is subordinate to the church, the marks cannot therefore be derived from the Scripture. The marks simply subsist in the church itself. In light of the indisputable fact that the identification of the church as the church is not "absolutely demonstrable to everyone," one must conclude that there is no logical, objective path to ascertaining whether or if Rome is a true church.[6]

In the context of the Reformation, Rome's understanding of the marks of the church possessed evident polemical value against the churches of the Reformation. Whether one employs the briefer or more expansive lists advanced by Roman Catholic theologians, each had in common that the Roman Catholic Church was the only body that had legitimate claim to be the true church. The necessary implication of such a doctrine is to "unchurch every denomination but its own."[7] That is to say, the Protestant assemblies—whether Lutheran or Reformed—were by definition deprived of any recognizable claim to be part of the true church.

5. Bannerman, *The Church of Christ*, 1:65–66.

6. Bavinck observes that Vatican I asserts that "to this testimony the efficacious help coming from the power above is added," *Dei Filius* 3 (Denzinger, *Enchiridion*, §3014), *Reformed Dogmatics*, 4:308. That is to say, Rome's position, for all its appearances of objectivity, is ultimately profoundly subjective. To accept the testimony of the church to her identity as the church requires a suprarational work of the Spirit, *Reformed Dogmatics*, 4:308. But the Scripture does not promise human beings such a work of the Spirit, and, on Rome's own terms, one may not legitimately appeal to the Scripture to ascertain such a work (after all, the Scripture is subordinate to the church). One is left with the authority of the church to warrant such a work of the Spirit—the very church whose identity as true church the inquiring or seeking individual has yet to ascertain!

7. Bannerman, *The Church of Christ*, 1:66.

The Reformation

The Reformers were convinced that Scripture is the sufficient rule of faith and practice (WCF 1.6), and that "the Holy Spirit speaking in the Scripture" is the "supreme judge" of all human doctrines, opinions, and disagreements (WCF 1.10). They therefore appealed outside the church to the Scripture alone in order to ascertain the marks of the church. They furthermore argued that the Scripture does in fact afford objective marks of the church against which the claims of any assembly of persons to be the church could be adjudged. The churches of the Reformation were therefore able to advance a case for their ecclesiastical legitimacy in the face of Roman Catholic claims to the contrary.

But it is here that one encounters a difference, even an apparent contradiction, among the Protestant theologians and confessions of the sixteenth and seventeenth centuries. Some affirmed *one* mark of the church. The Westminster Confession of Faith declares, "The visible church ... consists of all those throughout the world that possess the true religion; and of their children" (25.2). Thus, to possess and to profess the truth of the word of God is the one mark of the church. Others affirmed *two* marks of the church. The Augsburg Confession defines the church as "the congregation of saints, in which the Gospel is rightly taught and the sacraments are rightly administered" (Art. 7; compare Art. 8). The Thirty-Nine Articles makes a similar declaration, "The visible Church of Christ is a congregation of faithful men, in which the pure word of God is preached, and the sacraments be duly administered, according to Christ's ordinance, in all those things that of necessity are requisite to the same" (Art. 19). Calvin affirms the same position:

> From this the face of the church comes forth and becomes visible to our eyes. Wherever we see the word of God purely preached and heard, and the sacraments administered according to Christ's institution, there, it is not to be doubted, a church of God exists. ... The pure ministry of the Word and pure mode of celebrating the sacraments are, as we say, sufficient pledge and guarantee that we may safely embrace as church any society in which both these marks exist. The principle extends to the point that we must not

> reject it as long as it retains them, even if it otherwise swarms with many faults.[8]

Still others affirmed *three* marks of the church. The Belgic Confession declared, "If the pure doctrine of the Gospel is preached [in the Church]; if it maintains the pure administration of the sacraments as instituted by Christ; if Church discipline is exercised in punishing sin; in short if all things are managed according to the word of God; all things contrary thereto rejected, and Jesus Christ acknowledged as the only Head of the Church. Hereby the true Church may certainly be known, from which no man has a right to separate himself" (Art. 29). In the British Isles, the First Scots Confession similarly defined the marks of the church: "The notes of the true Kirk, therefore, we believe, confess, and avow to be: first, the true preaching of the word of God, in which God has revealed Himself to us, as the writings of the prophets and apostles declare; secondly, the right administration of the sacraments of Christ Jesus, with which must be associated the word and promise of God to seal and confirm them in our hearts; and lastly, ecclesiastical discipline uprightly ministered, as God's word prescribes, whereby vice is repressed and virtue nourished" (Art. 18).

We have, then, statements from Reformation and post-Reformation sources affirming one, two, and three marks of the church.[9] At first glance, it could appear that the Reformation never achieved consensus in its attempts to lend biblical definition to the church. On closer inspection, however, it becomes evident that the disagreement is merely apparent. Surveying the discussion at the close of the seventeenth century, Turretin notes "a certain diversity in words among the orthodox" while "still they agree in the thing itself. For whether it is called one alone ... or many ... it is all the same thing."[10] The verbal differences notwithstanding, the Reformation stood united in their understanding of the marks of the true church.

---

8. Calvin, *Institutes*, IV.1.9, 12. Battles notes that Bucer agreed with this formulation of Calvin's, *Institutes*, 1023n18.

9. For a fuller list of theologians and confessions affirming one, two, or three marks of the church, see Bavinck, *Reformed Dogmatics*, 4:312. Note further the seventeenth century testimonies at Heppe, *Reformed Dogmatics*, 669–70.

10. Turretin, *Institutes*, 18.12.6 (=3:87).

This agreement may be seen from the fact that the pure preaching of the word of God is common to sixteenth- and seventeenth-century Protestant theologians' and confessions' affirmation of the marks of the church. Furthermore, where more than one mark is provided, the pure preaching of the word is consistently placed first. Protestants understood that the administration of the sacraments and the exercise of biblical discipline not only required the word of God but were themselves ways in which the word was necessarily brought to bear upon the life of the church.[11] Priority fell, then, upon the word as mark of the church. Calvin, for instance, after identifying two marks of the church (word and sacrament), emphasizes the embrace of the word in ascertaining the presence of a true church: "But that we may clearly grasp the sum of this matter, we must proceed by the following steps: the church universal is a multitude gathered from all nations; it is divided and dispersed in separate places, but agrees on the one truth of divine doctrine and is bound by the bond of the same religion."[12] Moreover, a commitment to the pure preaching of the word necessarily entails the right administration of the sacraments and the proper exercise of discipline. Put negatively, it is impossible to maintain the sacraments and discipline in their fundamental integrity where a commitment to the word of God is absent. In summary, "submission to the word is thus in the deepest sense the sole mark. But of itself, this one mark divides into three when one recalls that each visible church must be the gathering and the mother of believers at the same time."[13]

The Scripture confirms the Reformation's identification of the pure preaching of the word, the possession and profession of the truth, as the mark of the church. On the day of Pentecost, Peter preaches the first new covenant sermon, proclaiming the death and resurrection of Christ and calling upon his hearers to repent and believe in Christ (Acts 2:14–41). Multitudes "received his word," "were baptized," and, Luke adds, "there were added that day about three thousand souls" (2:41). Luke then gives

---

11. "For where the truth obtains publicly, there also love and holiness flourish in their own way; nor can the pure word of God be preached anywhere without the sacraments being also administered lawfully in the same place and the discipline prescribed in the word of God being observed and thriving, since these two flow from the word of God and are appendages of it," Turretin, *Institutes*, 18.12.6 (=3:87).

12. Calvin, *Institutes*, IV.1.9.

13. Vos, *Reformed Dogmatics*, 5:24.

a description of the people of God under the new covenant, "And they devoted themselves to the apostles' teaching and the fellowship, to the breaking of bread and the prayers" (2:42). The word of God was the means by which sinners had been called to Christ and placed among the people of God. The word of God would no less define the people of God in their corporate existence. The church is brought into being in connection with the word and is defined and identified by that same word.

The metaphors Scripture employs in connection with the church confirm the word as defining of the church. Jesus builds his church "on this rock," that is, the apostolic confession that Jesus is the promised Messiah (Matt 16:18). Paul declares that the church is "built on the foundation of the apostles and prophets," that is, the extraordinary officers by whom Christ revealed his will to his people under the new covenant (Eph 2:20; compare Rev 21:14). At the close of his ministry, Paul tells Timothy that "the church of the living God" is "a pillar and buttress of the truth" (1 Tim 3:15), before proceeding to summarize that truth (the "mystery of godliness," 3:16). The image employed does not communicate that the church supports the truth. Rather, the church, like an ancient pillar, holds forth the word to the world.[14] In light of these metaphors, it is inconceivable that the church could exist apart from the word. The word, moreover, must serve to identify and mark the true church.

When adherence to the word in its fundamental integrity is jeopardized, the church forfeits the right to bear that name. Paul pronounces a curse upon any who "should preach to you a gospel contrary to the one we preached to you ... contrary to the one you received" (Gal 1:8, 9). The "curse" pronounced is not a mere statement of disapproval. It is the very term employed in the Septuagint to denote placement outside the covenant community and dedication to destruction.[15] If such a curse applies to angels or church officers, it applies no less to communities that renounce the gospel of grace. Similarly, the apostle John declares, "everyone who goes on ahead and does not abide in the teaching of Christ, does not have God" (2 John 9). Therefore, he continues, "If anyone comes to you and does

14. See I. Howard Marshall, *The Pastoral Epistles*, ICC (London: T&T Clark, 1999), 510–12, and George W. Knight, *The Pastoral Epistles: A Commentary on the Greek Text*, NIGTC (Grand Rapids: Eerdmans, 1992), 180.

15. Richard N. Longenecker, *Galatians*, WBC 41 (Nashville: Thomas Nelson, 1990), 17.

not bring this teaching, do not receive him into your house or give him any greeting, for whoever greets him takes part in his wicked works" (2 John 10–11).[16] The "teaching of Christ," delivered by the apostles to the church (see 1 John 1:1–4; 4:1–3), so defines the church that churches must give no place in their ministry and fellowship to any teacher who does not bear this teaching.

The sacraments and discipline define the church so far as they are extensions of the word of God. The sacrament of baptism signifies and seals the word of God to human beings. Paul's appeal to baptism in Romans 6:1–4 serves to press upon believers the gospel promises of the death and resurrection of Christ. When he tells the Galatians, "for as many of you as were baptized into Christ have put on Christ" (Gal 3:27), he is reminding them that baptism is sign and seal of union with Christ. Baptism, in other words, represents the truths contained in the word. The Lord's Supper operates in a similar way. In Acts 2:42, Luke appends "the breaking of bread" to "the apostles' teaching" as defining of the church in the days after Pentecost.[17] By Christ's appointment, the Lord's Supper is an ordinance of the "remembrance" of the person and work of Christ (Luke 22:19; 1 Cor 11:24, 25). In particular, it emphasizes the death of Christ, which stands at the heart of the Christian gospel (1 Cor 2:1–5). The sacrament of the Lord's Supper administers the word of God to the people of God. Formal discipline in the church, according to Jesus, is triggered by some "sin" (Matt 18:15). Since it is the word that identifies and defines sin, the exercise of discipline is necessarily dependent upon the word. Conversely, discipline is a required implication of Jesus's subsequent command that his disciples "observe all that I commanded you" (Matt 28:20). When a professing disciple steadfastly fails to observe Jesus's word, discipline is the requisite remedy. This dynamic is apparent from the exhortations of the apostle Paul to the churches in Thessalonica. Paul tells the Thessalonians, "Now we command you, brothers, in the name of our Lord Jesus Christ, that you keep away from any brother who is walking in idleness and not in accord with the

---

16. Turretin, *Institutes*, 18.12.12 (=3:90).

17. Luke's expression, τῇ κλάσει τοῦ ἄρτου, is debated among New Testament scholars. Some understand the phrase to denote fellowship meals among Christians. Others understand it to refer to the observance of the Lord's Supper in the context of public worship. The appearance of nearly the same phrase later in Acts, κλάσας τὸν ἄρτον (Acts 20:11), in a Lord's Day service of worship over which the apostle Paul presided, points to the latter definition as that which is in view in Acts 2:42.

tradition that you received from us" (2 Thess 3:6); "If anyone does not obey what we say in this letter, take note of that person, and have nothing to do with him, that he may be ashamed" (2 Thess 3:14). Discipline is therefore necessary to the enforcement of the word in the church. The administration of the sacraments and the exercise of discipline, each according to the word, may be said in this sense to be marks of the church.

THE CONFESSION OF THE CHURCH

THE WORD CREATES THE CHURCH and gives definition to the church. Proclaiming the word is the church's mission. These considerations explain why the church has framed and employed creeds and confessions throughout her history. Because a number of important questions arise from the church's creeds and confessions, addressing these questions merits attention in connection with a study of the marks of the church. First, we will consider what creeds and confessions are. Second, we will offer a biblical justification for creeds and confessions. Finally, we will respond to certain objections that have been raised against creeds and confessions.

Definition

THE TERMS "CREED" AND "CONFESSION" are often used interchangeably. Each term, however, carries a precise meaning distinct from the other. Creeds refer to the earliest, ecumenical statements of Christian faith. Such statements include the Apostles' Creed and the Nicene (Nicene-Constantinopolitan) Creed. Confessions span the history of the church and typically do not enjoy ecumenical support. They serve as "fuller explanations of the creeds themselves."[18] Frequently, confessions are associated with the denominations that have characterized the landscape of Western Christianity since the Reformation. As such, confessions not only affirm doctrine in positive form, but also deny what are thought to be errors and defections from the word of God. Confessions,

18. Turretin, *Institutes*, 18.30.7 (=3:283). Viewed across the landscape of church history, creeds and confessions evidence a tendency to greater length and doctrinal precision. This tendency was occasioned by the rise of error within the church in successive generations, on which see J. Gresham Machen, "The Creeds and Doctrinal Advance," in *God Transcendent and Other Selected Sermons*, ed. Ned B. Stonehouse (1949; repr., Edinburgh: Banner of Truth, 1982), 157–67.

then, affirm the doctrines and morals of the ecumenical creeds, while developing those creeds and responding to errors (ancient and contemporary).

The early nineteenth-century American Presbyterian, Samuel Miller, proposed a definition of a confession that remains serviceable today.

> An exhibition, in human language, of those great doctrines which are believed by the framers of it to be taught in the Holy Scriptures; and which are drawn out in regular order, for the purpose of ascertaining how far those who wish to unite in church fellowship are really agreed in the fundamental principles of Christianity.[19]

We may note several important aspects of this definition. First, confessions are, in form, human documents that are to contain, for substance, only what is revealed in the Bible. They are summaries, in uninspired language, of the truths of inspired Scripture.[20] As such, confessions are declarative and subordinate to the authority of Scripture. They do not legislate truth upon their own (or the church's) authority. Second, confessions are public and ecclesiastical statements. They do not reflect the private sentiments of one or a few Christians. They are the declaration of what a branch of the visible church understands the Bible to teach. Third, confessions do not say everything that may be said from the Bible. They "only profess to be summaries, extracted from the Scriptures, of a few of those great gospel doctrines which are taught by Christ himself; and which those who make the summary in each case concur in deeming important."[21] Fourth, a criterion of what biblical teaching is to be included in a particular confession is not only its intrinsic importance with respect to Bible's system

---

19. Samuel Miller, *The Utility and Importance of Creeds and Confessions* (1839; repr., Dallas: Presbyterian Heritage Publications, 1989), 5. Miller uses "creed" and "confession" interchangeably throughout this work.

20. A principle that the best and most thorough confessions will enshrine in explicit terms, as, for instance, WCF 1.10, "The supreme judge by which all controversies of religion are to be determined, and all decrees of councils, opinions of ancient writers, doctrines of men, and private spirits, are to be examined, and in whose sentence we are to rest, can be no other but the Holy Spirit speaking in the Scripture." See also the helpful formulations at Turretin, *Institutes*, 18.30.9 (=3.284).

21. Miller, *Utility of Creeds and Confessions*, 5–6.

of doctrine, but also its service as a term of ecclesiastical unity and fellowship.[22] Importantly, creeds, which are often faulted for dividing the church, are designed to foster unity in the church. Fifth, the doctrines presented in a confession are to be presented in the logical and theological order in which they appear in biblical teaching. Confessions, like the creeds on which they are founded, do not only declare biblical truths and declare them in biblical proportion, but they declare them in the dogmatic sequence in which the Bible presents them.

Justification IN LIGHT OF WHAT CONFESSIONS are, the question arises as to their warrant. For at least five reasons, confessions (and creeds) are not only permissible, but also required in the contemporary church.[23] First, although the Scripture does not contain an example of a formal creed or confession, the biblical materials provide creedal affirmations that explain and account for the subsequent rise of ecclesiastical creeds and confessions. The apostle Paul offers a number of examples of summarizing the person and work of Christ in pithy and memorable form (e.g., 1 Cor 15:3–4; Phil 2:5–11; Col 1:15–20; and 1 Tim 3:16).[24] This is not to say that Paul was either consciously crafting new confessions or adapting existing confessions for use in the early church. It is to say, however, that these passages afford examples of brief and digested statements of what Paul recognized to be central teachings in his gospel theology. Similarly, the "faithful sayings" of the Pastoral Epistles (1 Tim 1:15; 3:1; 4:7–9; 2 Tim 2:11–13; Titus 3:4–8) are pithy formulations of crucial doctrines within Paul's theology, addressing "redemption, church order, and ethical

---

22. It is for this reason, then, that confessions often properly include biblical teachings that are not "strictly fundamental." This necessity stems from the fact that "the members, and especially the ministers, of every church should be harmonious in their views and practices," particularly given the present "divi[sion]" of "the visible Church of Christ ... into different sections or denominations," Miller, *Utility*, 54. Thus, the Westminster Standards (and the Second London Baptist Confession) include statements about the mode and recipients of baptism, not because each judges those matters to be fundamental to biblical teaching, but because each judges confessing such matters to be requisite to the peace and purity of the respective confessing branches of the visible Church, so Miller, *Utility*, 56.

23. That is, given the denominational divisions noted above and the prevalence of error and heresy, creeds assume a "hypothetical" (not an "absolute") necessity for the church, so Turretin, *Institutes*, 18.30.8 (=3:284).

24. On the intricate literary structure of 1 Timothy 3:16, see Knight, *The Pastoral Epistles*, 183–86.

conduct."[25] Whatever their provenance or ecclesiastical use may have been, the "faithful sayings" illustrate the creedal impulse of Paul's letters generally. That the Pastoral Epistles, relative to the earlier epistles of Paul, contain a proportionately high number of such statements suggests that the apostle was preparing the post-apostolic church for the digesting and widespread transmission of new covenant revelation.

Paul signals such an intent in a statement to Timothy in his final epistle, "and what you have heard from me in the presence of many witnesses entrust to faithful men who will be able to teach others also" (2 Tim 2:2). Envisioned in this statement are four distinct bodies of persons—Paul, Timothy (amidst "many witnesses"), "faithful men," "others." Paul charges Timothy to transmit his apostolic teaching to men who are both equipped ("able to teach") and trustworthy ("faithful") to transmit that teaching to other people. This transmission is spatial in the sense that Paul's teaching is to expand to ever-widening concentric circles of recipients. But it is no less temporal—Paul provides for a *generational* transmission of apostolic teaching in this command. For Timothy to fulfill this obligation, he necessarily must summarize and digest the teaching of Paul in brief, concise form. We have, then, by implication a charge to formulate and transmit confessional summaries of biblical teaching to the church. Jude's expression at the outset of his epistle, "contend for the faith that was once for all delivered to the saints" (Jude 3), suggests that what we encounter in Paul's letters, particularly the Pastoral Epistles, was characteristic of apostolic Christianity generally.

Such summaries of apostolic teaching not only were disseminated to instruct and edify the faithful, but they were also designed to refute doctrinal and moral errors threatening the church.[26] John's Epistles, for instance, frame the Gospel's teaching about the incarnation of Christ in such a way

25. John V. Fesko, *The Need for Creeds Today: Confessional Faith in a Faithless Age* (Grand Rapids: Baker Academic, 2020), 10. Fesko addresses these Pauline "faithful sayings" in connection with ecclesiastical creeds and confessions. On the "faithful sayings," see Marshall, *The Pastoral Epistles*, 326–30, and George W. Knight, *The Faithful Sayings in the Pastoral Letters* (Grand Rapids: Baker Academic, 1979).

26. For a constructive response to the claim that creeds were produced primarily to refute error in the early church, see Paul Wooley, "What Is a Creed For? Some Answers from Church History," in *Scripture and Confession: A Book About Confessions Old and New*, ed. John H. Skilton (Phillipsburg, NJ: P&R, 1973), 98–100.

as to refute individuals who are denying the incarnation. John's affirmation, "the word became flesh and dwelt among us" (John 1:14), is stated polemically in the letters, both positively ("By this you know the Spirit of God: every spirit that confesses that Jesus Christ has come in the flesh is from God," 1 John 4:2) and negatively ("Every spirit that does not confess Jesus is not from God. This is the spirit of the antichrist, which you heard was coming and now is in the world already," 1 John 4:3).[27] Similarly, Paul's admonishment of Hymenaeus and Philetus, "who have swerved from the truth, saying that the resurrection has already happened" (2 Tim 2:18), assumes the prior confession of the future resurrection of the body, encompassed in what Paul terms "the word of truth" (2:15).[28]

A second reason for the necessity of creeds and confessions in the church concerns the church's mission. That mission, as set forth in Matthew 28:18–20 and that we will discuss in a later chapter, is to "gather and perfect the saints" (see WCF 25.3). Creeds and confessions answer each of these two ends. The church holds Christ out to the world (1 Tim 3:15). For the church to bear witness to Christ, proclaiming him and pressing his claims upon human beings, the church must be able to communicate the gospel precisely, clearly, concisely, and consistently. Creeds and confessions enable the church to accomplish that end. The church must furthermore instruct its disciples in all that Christ has commanded them. Creeds and confessions offer both teacher and taught systematic and accessible presentations of the "faith that was once for all delivered to the saints" (Jude 3). In this way, the church observes Paul's commands to "follow the pattern of the sound words that you have heard from me" (2 Tim 1:13), and "with one mind striv[e] side by side for the faith of the gospel" (Phil 1:27).[29]

A third reason for the necessity of creeds and confessions in the church concerns the exigencies of unity within a particular denomination or church, and of fellowship among multiple denominations or churches. As Miller has noted, "without a creed explicitly adopted, it is not easy to see how the ministers and members of any particular church, and more

---

27. Bannerman, *The Church of Christ*, 1:292

28. Norman Shepherd, "Scripture and Confession," in *Scripture and Confession*, 16; compare Bannerman, *The Church of Christ*, 1:292–93.

29. Miller, *The Utility of Creeds and Confessions*, 11.

especially a large denomination of Christians, can maintain unity among themselves."[30] The biblical commands that require unity of mind (Phil 1:27; 1 Cor 1:10) lay upon the church the practical necessity of adopting some standard around which the church may unite and against which error may be defined and rejected.[31] Similarly, for churches or denominations to enter into fraternal relations with one another, or to pursue organic unity with one another, they must first ascertain the degree to which they are united in their understanding of biblical doctrine. Absent comparison of the confessions of each body, it is difficult to conceive how either body could meaningfully entertain some form of unity with the other. A necessary condition for biblically faithful unity within and across churches, then, is a creed or confession.

A fourth reason for the necessity of creeds and confessions in the church is the preservation of Christian liberty.[32] "God alone is Lord of the conscience, and has left it free from the doctrines and commandments of men, which are, in anything, contrary to his Word; or beside it, if matters of faith, or worship" (WCF 20.2). Therefore, the church has no power to require assent to any doctrinal teaching unless that teaching is expressly taught in Scripture. Creeds and confessions, accordingly, constitute a necessary safeguard to the liberty of the Christian. They declare what a particular church or denomination will and will not teach, and individuals may decide on the basis of that declaration whether or not to become

30. Miller, *The Utility of Creeds and Confessions*, 6. In this connection it is important to underscore the fact that creeds and confessions, by design, do not offer an exhaustive summary of biblical doctrine. That is to say, they do not contain everything that is taught in Scripture. Neither do they speak with equal precision or emphasis upon all matters that they do confess. Both of these dynamics reflect confessions as consensus documents that are designed to permit legitimate diversity within the bounds of confessional orthodoxy. See further Robert L. Dabney, "The Doctrinal Contents of the Confession," in *Memorial Volume of the Westminster Assembly, 1647–1897* (Richmond, VA: Presbyterian Committee of Publication, 1897), 87–114, esp. 95–102, for a discussion of what Dabney terms the "doctrinal moderation" of the Westminster Confession of Faith; and Fesko, *The Need for Creeds Today*, 82–89. Fesko helpfully observes that the existence and employment of a confession in a particular ecclesiastical context invaluably distinguishes "confessional," "contra-confessional," and "extra-confessional" claims from one another, 88.

31. Miller, *The Utility of Creeds and Confessions*, 7–11. Miller concludes that, absent the adoption of some confessional standard by a church or denomination, "I see not how she can be expected, without a miracle, to escape all the evils of discord and corruption," 11.

32. See the valuable discussion of Carl R. Trueman, *The Creedal Imperative* (Wheaton, IL: Crossway, 2012), 163–67.

members of that particular church. Conversely, creeds and confessions provide wholesome parameters for the governing officers of the church of which they are part. In framing doctrinal declarations or in the exercise of church discipline, church courts must operate within the doctrinal boundaries established by their church's confession. Were an elder or a court of the church, in the course of their official labors, to transgress or to step outside of their church's confession, members of the church would be within their rights to express their disagreement in keeping with the rules and procedures of their church or denomination. Simply the awareness that confessions function in this fashion encourages biblical knowledge and theological vigilance on the part of members, and an encouragement to church officers "not to go beyond what is written" (1 Cor 4:6).

A fifth reason for the necessity of creeds and confessions in the church is the inevitability of creeds and confessions. It is impossible for a church *not* to have some kind of confession, albeit an unwritten one.[33] Congregations or denominations that decry creeds and confessions, therefore, are unable to escape them. Given that state of affairs, written confessions are preferable to unwritten confessions in several respects. Written confessions reflect the contributions of many people who have collaborated to produce a carefully drafted statement. Often these confessions have been transmitted and, in some cases, refined across several generations. Written confessions are public documents, accessible to officers, members, and outsiders. Written confessions, as we have noted above, establish bonds of mutual accountability between church members and the teaching officers of the church. None of these may be reliably affirmed of an unwritten confession. Unwritten confessions, moreover, are subject to change and shifting without the settled procedures of amendment that ordinarily attend the revision of confessional documents.

Objections

Creeds and confessions are, therefore, not only beneficial but also necessary to the church in its present

33. Miller offers the example of the impossibility of "a Unitarian congregation engaging as their pastor a preacher of Calvinism, knowing him to be such," because that congregation will inquire "how he interprets the Bible: in other words, what is his particular creed; whether it is substantially the same with their own or not." *The Utility of Creeds and Confessions*, 26. In short, "the enemies of creeds themselves cannot get along a day without them," 27.

existence. Even so, objections have surfaced within the church to creeds and confessions. Three objections in particular merit articulation and response.

First, it is sometimes alleged that creeds and confessions violate the Protestant principle of *sola scriptura* (Scripture alone). Creeds and confessions are said to elevate a fallible, human standard over the infallible word of God, thereby subordinating Scripture to the teaching of the church.[34] Were this allegation true, of course it would be a fatal argument against the use of creeds and confessions in the church. We may respond to this objection along two lines. First, creeds and confessions do not present themselves as standing over Scripture. To the contrary, Protestant confessions and theologians forthrightly acknowledge that such statements are subordinate standards in the church.[35] The objection may reflect misuse of confessions within the church, but not their proper and intended use. Second, the objection calls into question the legitimacy of framing inspired truths in uninspired words and sentences.[36] Ought not rather the church, the objection reasons, simply to content itself with expressing Scripture truths in the very words with which the Scripture expresses those truths? The problem with such a position is that, frequently in the history of the church, heresy and error has expressed itself in the words of Scripture, misconstruing and twisting the meaning of Scripture (see 2 Pet 3:16).[37] The biblical confession that Jesus is "the Christ, the Son of the living God" (Matt 16:16) is one that those who deny the full deity of Jesus Christ would

---

34. For a recent discussion of objections to creeds and confessions, see Robert D. Cornwall, "Disciples of Christ: Confessing Faith as a Non-Creedal Community," *Journal of Discipliana* 74 (2021): 1–17.

35. See WCF 1.10, cited at footnote 21 above; Turretin, *Institutes*, 18.30.9 (=3:284). Turretin recognizes that confessions' "authority ought indeed to be great with the pious in the churches, but still sinking below the authority of the Scripture. For the latter is a rule, they the thing ruled. It alone is self-credible (*autopistos*) with respect to words as well as to things, divine and infallible; they, as divine in things, still in words and manner of treatment are human writings," *Institutes*, 18.30.9 (=3:284).

36. "So that the precise thing to be considered is, Whether Creeds may be drawn up in other words and phrases than those precise ones which are to be found in Scripture—not as rules of faith, but as declarations of our own sentiments, and means of discovering the opinions of others concerning religious controversies?" William Dunlop, *The Use of Creeds and Confessions of Faith* (London: Hamilton, Adams, & Co., 1867), 109.

37. Dunlop, *The Use of Creeds*, 110.

happily affirm.[38] But such persons can affirm these words only because they have misinterpreted Peter's confession. Thus, "since the death of the inspired men, the Scriptures alone are no longer a sufficient test of fidelity to divine truth. ... The necessity of a further test in form of a subsequent creed results not from any lack of proper selection or infallible accuracy in the words of the languages of inspiration, but from the human nature and infirmity of mankind in their use of language."[39] We may furthermore observe that objectors to creeds do not object to reading the Scripture in translation. Neither do they object to the preaching of Scripture, that is, its interpretation and application of a text of the Bible. But both the translation and preaching of the Scripture operate on the same principle as creeds and confessions—to render the text of Scripture understandable to audiences through uninspired words.[40] The objection, therefore, proves too much. If the translation and preaching of the Scriptures are lawful, then creeds and confessions are no less lawful.

A second objection to creeds and confessions is that they bind the conscience to a standard that is other than the Scripture. Creeds and confessions, therefore, are said to violate the Protestant doctrine of the liberty of the conscience of every believer. In reply, it is important first to note that creeds and confessions only have authority to the degree that they summarize biblical truths. Furthermore, Protestants recognize creeds and confessions to be subordinate to the Scripture. When properly used, then, creeds and confessions do not bind the conscience of any believer. In the next place, it must be remembered that the church (unlike the state) is a voluntary organization.[41] Voluntary organizations have the right and obli-

---

38. Compare Dunlop, *The Use of Creeds*, 115.

39. Dabney, "The Doctrinal Contents of the Confession," 109.

40. "It cannot be said that the words of any translation of the Bible are the very words of the Holy Spirit. They are only the words which uninspired men have chosen, in which to express, as nearly as they were able, the sense of the original. ... If admitted, [the objection] would prove that all preaching of the gospel is presumptuous and criminal; because preaching always consisted in explaining and enforcing Scripture, and that, for the most part, in the words of the preacher himself," Miller, *The Utility of Creeds and Confessions*, 32, 33. Consistency with the objection requires, Miller urges, that the preacher do no more than read the Hebrew and Greek text of the Scripture *verbatim* to the congregation! *The Utility of Creeds and Confessions*, 33, 32. Compare the identical argument of Dabney, "The Doctrinal Contents of the Confession," 106–7.

41. See here the perceptive remarks of Miller, *The Utility of Creeds and Confessions*, 34–42, to which the argument of this paragraph is indebted.

gation to set their own terms for membership and for holding office within them.[42] No one is compelled to join the church or any particular branch of the church. No one is compelled to become an officer in the church. If persons find the requirements for entrance into membership or office in a particular church to be unacceptable, they may opt to look elsewhere. If they opt to become members or officers of a particular church, they thereby consent to those terms of membership or office. In no case has the church invited or compelled them to violate their consciences.[43]

A third objection to creeds and confessions is that they sow division and discord within the church. In light of those alleged effects, unity and peace demand, it is reasoned, that the church refrain from the use of creeds and confessions. In reply, it must be stressed that the objection is premised on an observation that is false. According to the Scripture, only error yields division and discord, never the truth. The truth alone, rather, promotes unity and peace.[44] Creeds and confessions, as summary expressions of biblical truth, are not productive of division but of unity. Because error

---

42. See the way that the Presbyterian Church in America, in company with other American Presbyterian churches, has articulated this doctrine in its Second Preliminary Principle, "[E]very Christian Church, or union or association of particular churches, is entitled to declare the terms of admission into its communion and the qualifications of its ministers and members, as well as the whole system of its internal government which Christ has appointed. In the exercise of this right it may, notwithstanding, err in making the terms of communion either too lax or too narrow; yet even in this case, it does not infringe upon the liberty or the rights of others, but only makes an improper use of its own." Historically, Presbyterians have required nothing more of members than to assent to a set of questions that summarize the faith and practice of any and every professing Christian, on which see *BCO* 57-5. Officers, however, are expected to affirm *ex animo* the church's subordinate standards. On the history and theology of subscription to subordinate standards in Presbyterianism, see David W. Hall, ed., *The Practice of Confessional Subscription* (Oak Ridge, TN: Covenant Foundation, 1997); David F. Coffin, Jr., "The Justification of Confessions and the Logic of Confessional Subscription," in *The Practical Calvinist: An Introduction to the Presbyterian and Reformed Heritage, In Honor of Dr. D. Clair Davis on the Occasion of His Seventieth Birthday*, ed. Peter A. Lillback (Fearn, UK: Christian Focus, 2002), 329–55; Guy Prentiss Waters, "Taking Exception," *Reformation21* (2018), https://www.reformation21.org/blogs/taking-exceptions.php, accessed June 09, 2022.

43. To the contrary, Miller notes, for the church to "give up its own testimony to the truth and order of God's house ... for the sake of complying with the unreasonable demands of a corrupt individual, would be to subject itself to the worst of slavery. What is the subjugation of the many, with all their interests, rights, and happiness to the dictation of one, or a few, but the essence of tyranny?" *The Utility of Creeds and Confessions*, 42.

44. These twin observations powerfully illustrated by Luke's account of the Jerusalem Council (Acts 15:1–35). False teaching promotes division and discord. The church's reaffirmation of the truth of the gospel (and its implications for the fellowship of believers) yields unity, peace, and a renewed commitment to the mission of the church.

persists within the visible church in her militancy, those who hold to the truth must contend on behalf of the truth. But, Miller observes, "in this case, a creed, supposing it to be a sound and scriptural one, is no more the cause of conflict and division, than a wholesome medicine is the cause of that disease which it is intended to cure."[45] Moreover, the alternative to truth's engagement of error within the church is unthinkable—"indifference to the purity of faith."[46] Any such peace would be purchased at the expense of the truth, and is far removed from the peace that Scripture joins to pure doctrine (see James 3:17).

THE MARKS OF THE CHURCH AND THE ATTRIBUTES OF THE CHURCH

To conclude this study of the marks of the church, it is helpful to reflect briefly on the church's four attributes, considered in the previous chapter, in light of the church's mark(s). Each of the four attributes (unity, holiness, catholicity, and apostolicity) must be framed in terms of this defining mark of the church. The church's unity must be understood in light of the fact that the mark of the church is the word of God (and, alongside it, the sacraments and discipline). Unity may not be conceived, in the first instance, along governmental or sacramental lines. Unity exists no further than a commitment to the "faith that was once for all delivered to the saints" (Jude 3) exists within a particular church or across particular churches. This is not to relegate unity to an invisible sphere of doctrinal concurrence. On the contrary, unity that is built around the truth must come to visible expression. But it is to say that unity must never be pursued at the expense of the truth of Scripture.

The church's holiness is likewise rooted in the church's commitment to the truth. The pattern for and standard of holiness is the character of God himself (1 Pet 1:15; 2:9), who has revealed himself fully and finally in Scripture. Individually and in shared life with one another, believers pursue and exhibit such biblical holiness in life, service, and worship. It was for this understanding of holiness, rooted in the truth, that the

45. Miller, *The Utility of Creeds and Confessions*, 52.
46. Miller, *The Utility of Creeds and Confessions*, 53.

Reformation contended against Rome's prevailingly "liturgical," sacramental, and institutional understanding of holiness.[47]

The church's catholicity must be conceived in light of the church's relationship to the truth of God. Universality must not be measured merely by geographical extension ("quantitative catholicity") but by the reality that the church under the new covenant is the repository of "the salvation that is preached to all" ("qualitative catholicity").[48] The people of God are no longer confined to a limited territory or to primarily one people. The church is comprised of persons from among the nations. To the degree that this transnational people of God embraces the truth that the Lord Jesus Christ has given her, this people is properly catholic, or universal.

The church's apostolicity is linked strictly to the doctrine that the apostles transmitted to the church. True apostolic succession, then, is not a measure of an "unbroken line" linking contemporary "office-bearers ... [with those who] received their power and authority from those who themselves in turn received it in lawful succession from the apostles."[49] It is measured by fidelity to the apostolic doctrine transmitted in successive generations (2 Tim 2:2). One may never detach apostolicity from the persons of the apostles, but one may never define apostolicity strictly in terms of their persons either. It is apostolic *doctrine* that not only renders the church "apostolic," but also defines and identifies the church as the church.

The church's attributes, then, derive their meaning and definition from the church's mark(s). We understand and confess the church as one, holy, catholic, and apostolic in light of the word of God that creates, sustains, and defines the church. With such a definition and understanding of the church, we will consider in the following chapters four distinct dimensions of the life and ministry of this church—her government, worship, life, and mission.

---

47. Bavinck, *Reformed Dogmatics*, 4:321.

48. Berkouwer, *The Church*, 108.

49. Bavinck, *Reformed Dogmatics*, 4:323. In Roman Catholicism, Bavinck notes, apostolic succession "is totally determined by [office-bearers'] fellowship with the pope," *Reformed Dogmatics*, 4:323.

FURTHER READING

Bannerman, James. *The Church of Christ: A Treatise on the Nature, Powers, Ordinances, Discipline, and Government of the Christian Church.* 2 vols. Edinburgh: T&T Clark, 1868. A magisterial and comprehensive treatment of the doctrine of the church by a nineteenth-century Scottish theologian. Bannerman primarily addresses the nature, government, and worship of the church.

Fesko, John V. *The Need for Creeds Today: Confessional Faith in a Faithless Age.* Grand Rapids: Baker Academic, 2020. A contemporary Reformed statement of the necessity of confessions for the church. Fesko's work is especially helpful in exploring the historical background to the confessions of the Reformed church.

Miller, Samuel. *The Utility and Importance of Creeds and Confessions.* 1839. Reprint, Dallas: Presbyterian Heritage Publications, 1989. A classic exposition of the nature and necessity of creeds and confessions. Miller excels in succinctly presenting the biblical and theological arguments for confessions, and in handling common objections to confessions.

X

THE GOVERNMENT OF THE CHURCH

IT IS INCONCEIVABLE THAT THE church should be without government. As Samuel Miller noted in the nineteenth century, "The Church, being a social body, called out of the world, and constituted by the authority of Jesus Christ, indispensably needs a form of government. No Society can exist in purity and peace without order. And no order can be maintained without authority, laws, and a set of officers to apply the laws, and administer the form of order which may have been adopted."[1] Historically speaking, most Christians have concurred with that assessment, differences about the particular details of the church's government notwithstanding.[2] In this chapter, we will argue that the Bible provides a form of government for the church, and we will explore the contours of that government. We will make the case that Presbyterianism is biblical, and acknowledge at the outset that Christians of good will differ about what the Bible reveals regarding the church's government.[3]

---

1. Samuel Miller, *Presbyterianism the Truly Primitive and Apostolical Constitution of the Church of Christ* (Philadelphia: Presbyterian Board of Publication, 1835), 44–45.

2. Within the Protestant tradition, one notable outlier in this respect has been the Society of Friends (Quakers). See Robert Barclay, *An Apology for the True Christian Divinity: Being an Explanation and Vindication of the Principles and Doctrines of the People Called Quakers*, 9th ed. (London: Thomas Tegg, 1825), 10, 258–326.

3. Throughout this chapter we will be quoting from the Presbyterian Church in America's *Book of Church Order* (*BCO*). The PCA's *BCO* was adopted in 1973, and traces its descent, through the 1933 *Book of Church Order* of the Presbyterian Church in the United States (PCUS) and the 1879 *Book of Church Order* of the PCUS, to the Form of Government and Discipline adopted by the Presbyterian Church in the United States of America in 1789. The polity

The starting point of biblical polity is biblical Christology. The Westminster Assembly, in its preface to its "Form of Presbyterial Church Government," makes this connection explicit.

> JESUS CHRIST, upon whose shoulders the government is, whose name is called Wonderful, Counsellor, The mighty God, The everlasting Father, The Prince of Peace; of the increase of whose government and peace there shall be no end; who sits upon the throne of David, and upon his kingdom, to order it, and to establish it with judgment and justice, from henceforth, even for ever; having all power given unto him in heaven and in earth by the Father, who raised him from the dead, and set him at his own right hand, far above all principalities and power, and might, and dominion, and every name that is named, not only in this world, but also in that which is to come, and put all things under his feet, and gave him to be the head over all things to the church, which is his body, the fulness of him that filleth all in all: he being ascended up far above all heavens, that he might fill all things, received gifts for his church, and gave officers necessary for the edification of his church, and perfecting of his saints.[4]

Government in the church, then, originates from the mediatorial kingship of Jesus Christ over all things for the sake of his church. This chapter will explore the ways in which Christ's kingship provides the framework within which reflection on the church's polity must take place. It will then address three related but distinct dimensions of that government—power and authority in the church; office in the church; and the courts of the church.

---

adopted by Presbyterians at the PCUSA's founding in 1789 is, in turn, indebted to Scottish Presbyterianism. The PCA's *BCO*, therefore, draws from centuries of reflection upon biblical church government by multiple Presbyterian denominations. On the literary history of each chapter and paragraph of the PCA's *BCO*, see https://www.pcahistory.org/bco/index.html.

4. "The Form of Presbyterian Church Government ... Agreed Upon by the Assembly of Divines at Westminster," in *The Westminster Confession* (Edinburgh: Banner of Truth, 2018), 587. Compare Benjamin M. Palmer's sermon on Ephesians 1:22–23, delivered in 1861 at the first General Assembly of what would become the Presbyterian Church in the United States, in Thomas Cary Johnson, ed., *The Life and Letters of Benjamin Morgan Palmer* (Richmond: Presbyterian Committee of Publication, 1906), 247–62.

THE LORD JESUS, KING AND HEAD OF THE CHURCH

Both Old Testament prophecy and the New Testament's witness to the person and work of Christ underscore the mediatorial kingship of Jesus Christ. Both testaments distinguish the kingship of Jesus Christ with respect to his mediatorial work from the kingship that God the Son shares with God the Father and God the Spirit—the *mediatorial* reign of Christ in distinction from the essential reign of God. To speak of the mediatorial reign of Jesus Christ, then, brings into view the universal reign of the risen Christ over all things for the sake and benefit of his church, which is his visible "mediatorial and economical kingdom."[5]

Paul testifies that, upon the resurrection and ascension of Christ, the Father "seated him at his right hand in the heavenly places far above all rule and authority and power and dominion, and above every name that is named, not only in this age but also in the one to come. And he put all things under his feet and gave him as head over all things to the church, which is his body, the fullness of him who fills all in all" (Eph 1:20–23). Here Paul underscores the way in which such prophecies as Daniel 7:13–14, Psalm 2, and Psalm 110 have found their intended fulfillment in the exaltation of Christ. The reward for the Servant's obedience is nothing less than universal, eschatological dominion. While this dominion is without limit, it finds its center and focus in the church.[6]

The Protestant Reformation, and especially its Reformed wing, has emphasized that the nature of Christ's kingship over his church was such as to exclude any other or additional heads over the church (WCF 25.6).[7] In particular, the Reformers rejected claims of the Roman pontiff to

---

5. Turretin, *Institutes*, 14.16.2 (=2:486); James Fisher, *The Westminster Assembly's Shorter Catechism Explained by Way of Question and Answer*, 3rd ed (repr., Philadelphia: Presbyterian Board of Christian Education, 1925), 138. Note the important qualification of A. A. Hodge, "while Christ has been virtually mediatorial King as well as Prophet and Priest from the fall of Adam, yet his public and formal assumption of his throne and inauguration of his spiritual kingdom dates from his ascension and session at the right hand of his Father," *Outlines of Theology* (1879; repr., Edinburgh: Banner of Truth, 1972), 429.

6. "The Church is [Jesus's] immediate domain: its members are His citizens; and for their benefit His powers are all wielded. But His power extends over all the human race, the angelic ranks, good and bad, and the powers of nature," Dabney, *Systematic Theology*, 550. Compare R. B. Kuiper, *The Glorious Body of Christ* (Grand Rapids: Eerdmans, 1967), 95.

7. Thomas Witherow, *The Form of the Christian Temple*, 216–21.

exercise dominion or monarchical rule over the church. The church has a single Head, not multiple heads. As Turretin memorably expresses the point, "it is monstrous to ascribe a double head to one body."[8] Nor could one properly conceive the pope as the vicar of Christ, since Christ's active and personal reign over his church necessarily excludes the reign of a "substitute" in his place.[9]

That Jesus Christ alone is king and head of his church has immediate implications for the very nature and shape of the church's government. As the church's king, he has "therein appointed a government, in the hand of church officers, distinct from the civil magistrate" (WCF 30.1). The prophet Isaiah says of the "Prince of Peace"—the one who sits "on the throne of David"—that "the government shall be upon his shoulder" (Isa 9:6, 7). That is to say, the exalted Christ, as King, personally governs his people. After declaring that Christ is "head" with respect to "his body ... the Church," Paul stresses that this body "grow[s] up in every way into him who is the head, into Christ" through the government that the ascended Christ provides his church (Eph 1:22, 23; 4:15).

The church's government, then, not only derives from the will of the church's reigning Monarch, but derives alone from the will of the church's reigning Monarch.[10] This will has been revealed exclusively in the pages of Scripture through the teachings and example of Christ's apostles.[11] The church's government is therefore *jure divino* (by divine right) and not *jure humano* (by human right).[12] Few in the church have disputed that the Scriptures of the New Testament guide the church in framing her polity. But jure divino church government claims that the Bible alone affords

8. Turretin, *Institutes*, 3.16.10 (=3:150); see his argument at 3.16.12 (=3:151).

9. Turretin, *Institutes*, 3.16.13 (=3:151). Turretin here critically distinguishes the biblically forbidden category of vicarage in church governance from the biblical sanctioned category of servant—"Whoever dispenses to others the word and sacraments ought to do it as a minister of Christ and in his name alone, not as the substitute for another man," *Institutes*, 3.16.13 (=3:151).

10. Alexander T. McGill, *Church Government: A Treatise Compiled from His Lectures in Theological Seminaries* (Philadelphia: Presbyterian Board of Publication and Sabbath-School Work, 1888), 28–29.

11. On which, see my *How Jesus Runs the Church*, 45–48.

12. For the classical statement and defense of this doctrine, see *Jus Divinum Regiminis Ecclesiastici* or *The Divine Right of Church-Government*, rev. and ed. David W. Hall (1646; repr., Dallas: Naphtali Press, 1995). On the definition of *jus divinum*, see particularly *Jus Divinum Regiminis Ecclesiastici*, 7–8.

the church its elements of polity, thereby excluding any human additions whether deriving from custom, tradition, human authority, expediency, or any other consideration. In this respect, what the regulative principle is to worship, jure divino polity is to church government.[13] Each doctrine frames the sufficiency of Scripture with respect to the worship and government of the church.

It needs to be stressed that proponents of jure divino church government do not claim that every detail of the church's government is set forth, either explicitly or by necessary implication, in the text of Scripture. The claim, rather, is that church government "in its fundamental principles and leading features is sanctioned by Scripture and apostolic practice ... and that this can not be predicated of any other form of church government, such as Prelacy and Congregationalism."[14] Furthermore, these principles "are legitimately applied in the circumstances and under the conditions which are peculiar to our own age and country."[15] Thus, while the polities of Presbyterian churches across time and space will necessarily possess a common set of biblical principles, jure divino church government does not require uniformity in the implementation of these principles in local circumstances. Rather, as to its "substance of fundamental principles," Presbyterianism "is binding jure divino as the form of government by which the church of Christ ought permanently and everywhere to be regulated."[16]

Two further comments are necessary to preclude misconstrual of the claims of jure divino church government. First, these fundamental principles are accessed not only through the direct commands of the New Testament but also through apostolic example.[17] The latter carries equal weight and authority with the former, and that for the same

13. On the Regulative Principle of Worship, see the discussion in chapter 11.

14. Cunningham, *Historical Theology*, 1:74, emphasis removed.

15. MacPherson, *Presbyterianism*, 9.

16. Cunningham, *Historical Theology*, 1:77.

17. On which, see the magisterial discussion of Bannerman, "Relative Obligation of Scripture Precept, Example, and Principle," in *The Church of Christ*, 2:404–8, summarized in my *How Jesus Runs the Church*, 52–4. Compare *Jus Divinum Regiminis Ecclesiastici*, 9–35. "Apostolic example" does not encompass everything that the apostles say and do in the New Testament. A particular instance of apostolic example with respect to church government only binds the church in every age "provided we be in like circumstances" as the apostolic church. Bannerman, *The Church of Christ*, 2:406, emphasis removed.

reason—"both alike embody the will of Christ to His Church."[18] Second, jure divino recognizes and makes provision for circumstances in the government of the church—"there are some circumstances concerning the worship of God and government of the church, common to human actions and societies, which are to be ordered by the light of nature, and Christian prudence, according to the general rules of the Word, which are always to be observed" (WCF 1.6). A circumstance is "a concomitant of an action, without which it can either not be done at all, or cannot be done with decency and decorum."[19] By definition, then, circumstances "do not belong to the substance of an act."[20] Legitimate circumstances in the church's government, according to the Westminster Confession of Faith, must be "common to human actions and societies." Put negatively, they may not be unique or peculiar to the church. Circumstances must also be "ordered by the light of nature, and Christian prudence, according to the general rules of the Word, which are always to be observed." Thus, the church's ordering of circumstances is always in submission to divine revelation, whether natural or special, and in accordance with the dictates of the virtue of prudence. The church therefore does not claim the power to make law, but only to "arrang[e] and order under the law."[21] Examples of legitimate circumstances in the government of the church include rules of parliamentary procedure and rules for discipline. Without such rules, implemented of course according to the standards set forth in WCF 1.6, the church would be unable to perform the work that Christ has called the church to undertake.

THE POWER OF THE CHURCH

The church receives her government from her king, the Lord Jesus Christ, and from him alone. Christ is no absentee ruler. He is actively extending, maturing, preserving, and defending his people. He is pleased to accomplish these ends through means—the "ministry, oracles, and ordinances of God" (WCF 25.3). This manner of Christ's governing his church

18. Bannerman, *The Church of Christ*, 2:408.

19. Thomas E. Peck, *Notes on Ecclesiology* (Richmond: Presbyterian Committee of Publication, 1892), 117.

20. Peck, *Notes on Ecclesiology*, 118, noting the etymology of the word "circumstance" (Lat., *circum stare*—"to stand around").

21. Peck, *Notes on Ecclesiology*, 116.

raises the question of power in the church. We may reflect on church power along two lines—its origins and outworking; its nature and character.

Origins and Outworking of Church Power

ALL CHURCH POWER ORIGINATES IN Christ as the head and king of his church. This is Christ's own claim in his preface to the commission that concludes Matthew's Gospel, "all authority in heaven and on earth has been given to me" (Matt 28:18).[22] The church therefore possesses no power in her own name or right. Power is derived entirely from the risen Christ.

Christ delegates power to the church. "The power which Christ has committed to His Church vests in the whole body, the rulers and the ruled, constituting it a spiritual commonwealth. This power, as exercised by the people, extends to the choice of those officers whom He has appointed in His church."[23] Power, therefore, "resides with the church as a whole."[24] In considering the exercise of church power, one must consider the respective roles of the congregation and of the elected officers of the congregation.[25] Neither the congregation nor the officers derive power from the other.[26] Power derives from Christ. The "exercise of [church] power cannot occur other than by the office-bearers in the church connected with the congregation."[27] With one exception, the exercise of church power is limited to the officers of the church. That single exception is the congregation's exercise of its inalienable right to choose its own officers, as the apostles instruct the church in Jerusalem to do when the apostles establish the office

22. Stuart Robinson, *The Church of God as an Essential Element of the Gospel* (1858; repr., Willow Grove, PA: The Committee on Christian Education of the Orthodox Presbyterian Church, 2009), 61.

23. *BCO* 3-1.

24. Vos, *Reformed Dogmatics*, 5:39. Vos is, here and in the discussion that follows, summarizing the position of Gisbertus Voetius (1589-1676).

25. Note Bannerman's observation regarding this question, "Perhaps, in the whole range of ecclesiastical theology, there is no question in regard to which a greater diversity of judgment among competent divines has prevailed; and none, probably, in regard to which it is more necessary to speak with caution and diffidence," *The Church of Christ*, 1:263.

26. Bannerman, *The Church of Christ*, 1:263. Vos cites Voetius, "[Power] is not passed from the body of the people to the church council and also not the reverse—no more than my right eye is the real, first, immediate and nearest subject of my sight and this sight passes over to my left eye, nor the reverse," *Reformed Dogmatics*, 5:38-39.

27. Vos, *Reformed Dogmatics*, 5:39.

of deacon in the church (Acts 6:1–6).[28] In all other respects, however, only church officers exercise power in the church.[29]

This understanding of church power must be distinguished from two alternatives. The first is Episcopacy's insistence that power resides exclusively in the clergy of the church, as distinguished from the laity.[30] The second is Independency's insistence that power not only resides in the church, but is also exercised by the congregation.[31] Episcopacy removes power from the church, while Independency deprives officers of the exercise of that power that Scripture has committed to church officers. The Presbyterian doctrine, sketched above, sustains the duty of church officers to exercise power in the church without abridging the rights of the congregation.[32]

The Mode of Church Power

CHURCH POWER, RESIDING IN THE church as a whole, is in most instances to be exercised by church officers. The fact that all power in the church derives from Jesus Christ, the king of the church, guides and determines the ways in which the church exercises her power. We may now reflect on the mode of that power in ecclesiastical exercise along two lines.[33] First, all church power

---

28. See further Witherow, *The Form of the Christian Temple*, 109–19.

29. On the relationship between the congregation and its officers in relation to the exercise of church power, see further Peck, *Notes on Ecclesiology*, 85, 170.

30. Episcopacy is a form of church government distinguished by the rule of monarchical bishops. Independency, discussed below, is a form of church government distinguished by the governmental autonomy of local and independent congregations.

31. Not all Independents maintain this position. The English Puritan, John Owen, argued for an Independent polity that concurred with Presbyterians' understanding of church power, namely, that power resides in the church, but (apart from the congregation's choice of its officers) is only to be exercised by the church's officers, "The True Nature of a Gospel Church," in *The Works of John Owen*, 16:1–208, esp. 42. By and large, however, Independents, argue that church power resides in and is to be exercised by the congregation. See, for instance, J. L. Dagg, *Manual of Theology, Second Part: A Treatise on Church Order* (1858; repr., Harrisonburg, VA: Gano, 1990), 268–74; Gregg R. Allison, *Sojourners and Strangers: The Doctrine of the Church* (Wheaton, IL: Crossway, 2012), 277–83.

32. See further Peck, *Notes on Ecclesiology*, 170–78. "Power, then, is *in primo actu*, in the church as a body, an organic whole; the people and the rulers are the organ of election. The officers elected are the organs by which the functions of teaching, government, and distribution of revenues are exercised. ... Power *in actu secondo*, or as to its exercise, is in the officers of the church," Peck, *Notes on Ecclesiology*, 175. Compare Peck's discussion at *Notes on Ecclesiology*, 85–86.

33. Following the outline of my *How Jesus Runs the Church*, 63–76.

is spiritual in nature, "so purely, properly, and merely spiritual is this power that it really, essentially, and specifically differs and is contradistinct from that power which is properly civil, worldly, and political, in the hand of the Civil Magistrate."[34] One necessary implication of the spirituality of the church's power is that "All church power, whether exercised by the body in general, or by representation, is only ministerial and declarative."[35] The qualifiers "ministerial and declarative" serve to distinguish a Protestant and Reformed understanding of church power from that of Rome. Rome claims power that is magisterial and legislative. Protestants have argued that "the Bible, and the Bible only, is the rule of Church power" and, therefore, church officers "are ministerial and subordinate, having no authority or discretion of their own, and being merely ministers or servants to carry out the will and execute the appointments of Christ."[36] In both the Old and the New Testaments, word-ministers (whether prophets, apostles, or elders) are tasked with declaring the revealed will of God and are forbidden from adding to that will (Deut 12:32; Isa 29:13; Matt 15:9; 28:18–20; 2 Tim 2:2; Jas 4:12).[37] Writing the church in Corinth, the apostle Paul expressly disavows that he should "lord it over your faith" (2 Cor 1:24), affirms the right of private judgment (1 Cor 11:13), stresses that what he writes to them is "a command of the Lord" (1 Cor 14:37), and points to his own example as a model to imitate only so far as Paul is an imitator of Christ (1 Cor 11:1). Paul presents himself and his fellow ministers to the church in Corinth as "servants of Christ and stewards of the mysteries of

---

34. *Jus Divinum Regiminis Ecclesiastici*, 57, emphasis removed. The authors proceed to specify the spirituality of the church's power along several distinct lines—the rule, fountain, matter, form, subject, object, and end of church power, 57–60. Compare the concurring testimony of *BCO* 3-4, "The power of the Church is exclusively spiritual; that of the State includes the exercise of force." See further Turretin, *Institutes*, 18.29.1–25 (=3:274–81); Heidegger, *Medulla Theologiae Christianiae* (1696): 27.22, cited at Heppe, *Reformed Dogmatics*, 682; Bannerman, *The Church of Christ*, 1:223–5; Bavinck, *Reformed Dogmatics*, 4:395.

35. Preliminary Principle 7, *BCO*. The eight prefatory Preliminary Principles date to immediately prior to the founding of the Presbyterian Church in the United States in America, J. Aspenwall Hodge, *What Is Presbyterian as Defined by the Church Courts?* 7th ed. (Philadelphia: Presbyterian Board of Publication and Sabbath-School Work, 1894), 21. The Preliminary Principles are thought to have been principally drafted by the Scottish-American Presbyterian, John Witherspoon.

36. Bannerman, *The Church of Christ*, 1:219.

37. Most of texts are both cited and explained at Turretin, *Institutes*, 18.31.5–10 (=3:287–8).

God" (1 Cor 4:1). They "proclaim ... not ourselves, but Jesus Christ as Lord, with ourselves as your servants for Jesus's sake" (2 Cor 4:5). No minister (or assembly of ministers) has the power to make laws or otherwise to bind the conscience of the believer. Because "God alone is Lord of the conscience," people are "free from the doctrines and commandments of men, which are, in any thing, contrary to His Word; or beside it, if matters of faith or worship" (WCF 20.2). Church power is, therefore, exclusively and entirely ministerial and declarative.

A second way to conceive of the mode of church power builds on the first. Church power is "of three sorts, according to the three different and separate classes of things with which it is conversant."[38] These three classes of church power relate to doctrine (dogmatic power), order (diatactic power), and discipline (diacritical power).[39] The church's dogmatic power concerns her teaching the "whole counsel of God" (Acts 20:27) to "those that are without [and] those that are within."[40] This power extends, we have seen earlier, to the framing of creeds and confessions. In such statements, the church declares the truth and refutes error, thereby instructing the faithful, correcting the errant, and testifying to unbelief. This power, we have also seen, is not legislative but declarative. The church does not propound new doctrines or laws, but only declares what God has already said in the Bible. Neither does the church declare the truth of Scripture in her own authority, but only by the authority of Jesus Christ.

The church's power of order is the "arranging, ordering power of the church."[41] This power is not legislative in nature. Rather, this dimension of the church's power orders the affairs of the church under the law of God. The "laws" of God and the (diatactical) "regulations" of the church differ in crucial respects. The former "bind the conscience *per se* or *simpliciter*"; the latter "bind it *secundum quid, i.e.*, indirectly and mediately in case of scandal and contempt." In the former, "we regard the authority of God

38. Bannerman, *The Church of Christ*, 1:225.

39. On the various distinctions employed with respect to the church's power in the sixteenth and seventeenth centuries, see the discussion at Peck, *Notes on Ecclesiology*, 119–20.

40. Peck, *Notes on Ecclesiology*, 119–20.

41. Peck, *Notes on Ecclesiology*, 121.

alone; in the [latter], we regard the good of our neighbors."[42] The church's diatactical regulations, furthermore, concern the "circumstances" of WCF 1.6.[43] As such they concern the "worship of God" and "the government of the Church" (WCF 1.6).

The church's power of discipline concerns the church's enforcing the law of God among the membership of the church.[44] The church's discipline may extend to the administering of censures leading up to the removal of an offender from the church's membership (Matt 18:15–20; 1 Cor 5:1–13). These censures, and the whole of the church's discipline, is entirely spiritual and non-temporal in character. As we will explore further in a later chapter, formal ecclesiastical discipline is not designed to inflict punishment upon wrongdoers but to bring the impenitent to such a sense of their sin as that, by the grace of God, they repent of their sin and return to fellowship with Christ and his people.

All ecclesiastical power is spiritual and may be understood along the three distinct lines of doctrine, order, and discipline. There is a final distinction that is critical to understanding the exercise of power within the church. Power may be exercised "severally," that is, by elders acting individually; and power may be exercised "jointly," that is, by elders acting together in regular assembly. The power of doctrine may be several or joint. It is several when a minister proclaims the word of God from the pulpit. It is joint when a court of the church drafts a confession or bears witness against some particular error.[45] The power of order and discipline is joint. Were individual elders to issue diatactical regulations, the result would be chaos and confusion, contrary to the ends for which Christ has committed power to the church. Discipline, in the New Testament, is administered either by individual apostles (1 Cor 5:2, 3, 13; 1 Tim 1:20; compare Acts 5:1–11) or by the church (Matt 18:15–20; Rom 16:17; 2 Thess 3:6, 14; 2 John 10; Rev 2:2).[46] Elders acting individually are never said to administer formal disci-

42. Peck, *Notes on Ecclesiology*, 124. Compare the discussion of Bannerman, *The Church of Christ*, 1:226–27.

43. Peck, *Notes on Ecclesiology*, 122.

44. The Church does not discipline those who are outside her membership, but only those who are counted her members (1 Cor 5:12).

45. These illustrations come from Peck, *Notes on Ecclesiology*, 120.

46. Bavinck, *Reformed Dogmatics*, 4:425.

pline within the church. This fact indicates that, when apostles individually administered discipline, such actions are reflective of their extraordinary office. In the post-apostolic life of the church, discipline is to be administered in an exclusively joint manner. When the New Testament says that the "church" administers discipline, what is meant is that the church administers discipline through the elders gathered in regular assembly.[47] In this respect, the church continues the pattern reflected in the synagogue, where it is the synagogue's elders that administer discipline (see John 9:13–34). Thus, the power of doctrine may be administered either severally or jointly, but the power of order and discipline must be administered jointly.

OFFICE IN THE CHURCH

Considerations of church power lead directly to the subject of office in the church. Although the word "office" does not appear in the New Testament, the concept is present.[48] By definition, office entails the exercise of authority within the church.[49] Church officers possess gifts for ministry within the church, although not every gift warrants entrance into office.[50] Certain

47. See Samuel Miller, *An Essay on the Warrant, Nature, and Duties of the Office of The Ruling Elder in the Presbyterian Church* (Philadelphia: Presbyterian Board of Publication, 1832), 65–66, and the historical sources cited there. Compare Calvin, *Institutes* IV.8.15.

48. Murray, "Office in the Church," in *Collected Writings: Volume Two*, 357. Note, for instance, the testimony of such passages as Acts 1:20 and 1 Timothy 3:1.

49. Some theologians have argued for and pressed the distinction between what is called "general office" and "special office," Kuyper, *The Work of the Holy Spirit*, 183; Kuiper, *The Glorious Body of Christ*, 126–31; Clowney, *The Church*, 207–10. The former is said to belong to every believer by virtue of his or her union with Christ. As "Christ, the Head of the church, [is] prophet ... priest, and ... king," so "every single church member is at once a prophet, a priest and a king," Kuiper, *The Glorious Body of Christ*, 126. Functionally, this entails participation in the "worship, nurture, and witness" of the church, through the "means of ministry," namely, word, mercy, and order, Clowney, *The Church*, 209. Such a conception of "office" in the Church laudably strives to root itself in Luther's doctrine of the priesthood of all believers, and to stand against the clericalism that characterizes Roman Catholicism. The problem, however, is the confusion that is generated when the concept of office is applied to every member of the church. Not only is the same term ("office") employed to describe two distinct ideas, but "general office" risks self-contradiction. Office necessarily entails the exercise of authority, and, by definition, only some members of a society may exercise authority. One, however, need not resort to a doctrine of "general office" either to preclude clericalism or to ennoble the services of non-officers within the church. And, of course, none of these reflections is to deny the reality that believers, in Christ, are denominated "a royal priesthood" (1 Pet 2:9), "a kingdom, priests to his God and Father" (Rev 1:6; compare 5:10). It is to say, however, that what is termed the "general office" of each believer does not follow from such denominations as these.

50. Macpherson, *Presbyterianism*, 20–21.

men, possessing requisite gifts, are called into office to exercise those gifts "in virtue of which they are set apart and distinguished from others by certain designations indicative of the specific functions performed."[51]

The apostles are the original officers of the New Testament church. They are Christ's representatives tasked with the unique call to bear witness to the risen Christ whom they have seen (Acts 1:8; 1 Cor 9:1; 1 John 1:1–4). The miracles that they perform are the way in which Christ himself witnesses to their apostolic witness as his own (Acts 14:3). The apostles exercise the power of doctrine, order, and discipline (Matt 16:19; 1 Cor 5:1–13), and do so severally or individually. Of necessity, the apostolic office is an extraordinary one. Once these unique witnesses die, none succeeds them. The church, rather, is built upon the foundation of the apostles. Thus, the church holds forth the deposit of truth that the apostles have committed to her (1 Tim 3:15; 2 Tim 2:2). Elders in particular continue the word-proclamation function undertaken by the apostles. This overlap between the work of the apostle and the work of the elder is the reason that Peter can declare himself both "a fellow elder" and "a witness of the sufferings of Christ" (1 Pet 5:1). Apostles and elders function together as elders at the Jerusalem Council (Acts 15:1–35). Furthermore, the task of service is, in origin, performed by the apostles. In time, however, the office of deacon emerges from the apostolic office so that the apostles may not be hindered in "prayer" and "the ministry of the word" (Acts 6:4; see 6:1–6).[52] The standing offices of elder and deacon, then, succeed the office of apostle. Elders existed in the Old Testament people of God and in the Jewish synagogue at the

---

51. Murray, "Office in the Church," in *Collected Writings: Volume Two*, 357. In this book, the gendered word "man" is used intentionally in relation to officeholders in the church. Elders and deacons, according to the testimony of the New Testament, are men only, on which see my *How Jesus Runs the Church*, 108–16. To affirm this in no way necessitates affirming women as the ontological inferiors of men, denying that women possess and exercise gifts within the church, or that women may properly exercise gifts of teaching in various spheres within the church (as with children, 2 Tim 3:14–15; other women, Titus 2:2; and even ministers in private settings, Acts 18:26), or gifts of service within the church (Acts 9:36; 1 Tim 2:10; 5:10). It is simply to say that the order set forth in Scripture, an order rooted in creation (1 Tim 2:11–15), admits only men to office in the church.

52. On Acts 6:1–6 as the apostolic establishment of the diaconate, see the literature cited at C. N. Willborn, "The Deacon: A Divine Right Office with Divine Uses," *Confessional Presbyterian* 5 (2009): 185–86.

time of the New Testament, and continue in the New Testament church.[53] Deacons, however, are unattested in the Old Testament or in Second Temple Judaism. This office appears to be unique to the polity of the apostolic church. However the origins of the eldership and the diaconate may differ, each office is anchored in the apostolic office.

To draw these observations is to register the distinction between "extraordinary" and "ordinary" office. "Extraordinary officers" are those "who received extraordinary gifts of the Spirit and who were agents by whom God completed His revelation to His Church. Such officers and gifts related to new revelation have no successors since God completed His revelation at the conclusion of the Apostolic Age."[54] The apostles were commissioned to convey new revelation to the church under the new covenant (John 14:26; 16:12–14).[55] Their foundational ministry having been completed (Eph 2:20), the office of apostle has thereby ceased. As we will see in a later chapter, the same may be said of the revelatory office of prophet (Eph 2:20).

The "ordinary and perpetual classes of office in the church," however, "are elders and deacons."[56] In his first epistle to Timothy, Paul sets forth the qualifications for elders (1 Tim 3:1–7) and deacons (3:8–13), and then stipulates the duties of the elder (4:8–16; 5:17–25) and of the deacon (5:1–16). Neither in this epistle nor elsewhere does Paul legislate or anticipate additional offices in the church between the apostolic age and the return of Christ. In the work of the elder and of the deacon, therefore, are

53. This observation is frequently drawn in discussions of Reformed polity. For an early and influential witness, see Campegius Vitringa, *Ancient Roots for Reformed Polity: De Synagoga Vetere and the Ecclesiology of the Early Church—An Annotated Compendium*, trans. Joshua L. Bernard (1685, 1696; n.p.: North Star Ministry Press, 2020).

54. *BCO* 7-1. Forms of this provision have appeared in American Presbyterian Books of Order since the PC(USA)'s founding in 1789. As Ramsay notes, "And since the miraculous gifts have ceased, all classes of officers having functions that require miraculous gifts have also ceased," *An Exposition of the Form of Government*, 44; compare Bannerman, *The Church of Christ*, 2:214–44.

55. See further *How Jesus Runs the Church*, 44–46; Clowney, *The Church*, 75–76; Sinclair B. Ferguson, *The Holy Spirit* (Downers Grove, IL: InterVarsity Press, 1996), 209–10. It is important to note that the New Testament occasionally uses the term "apostle" in a broader and non-technical sense to denote "messengers of the churches rather than eye-witnesses of the risen Christ" (Acts 14:14), Ferguson, *The Holy Spirit*, 210.

56. *BCO* 7-2.

comprehended the "whole polity of the Church, [namely,] doctrine, government, and distribution."[57]

The work of the elder is to govern or rule in the church (1 Tim 3:4; 5:12; Heb 13:17; 1 Pet 5:5a). Elders are "overseers" (1 Tim 3:1, 2; Acts 20:28; 1 Pet 5:2). Within the Reformed tradition, it has been debated whether the "minister" and the "elder" are two offices, or whether they are two orders of the same office of elder.[58] In light of what Paul tells Timothy in 1 Timothy 5:17, the latter option is likelier. Some elders, in addition to the work of rule in the church, take on the work of teaching, and are compensated by the church for their labors (1 Tim 5:17).[59] While all elders must be "able to teach" (1 Tim 3:2), some elders—such as Timothy—also take up the work of proclaiming the word of God as a full-time vocation from God (2 Tim 4:1–5).

The work of the deacon is to serve in the church.[60] Deacons do not serve *in the place of* all believers in the church. Rather, deacons mobilize the church's members to serve one another.[61] The office requires men who possess spiritual qualifications (1 Tim 3:8–13; Acts 6:1–6), and who are able to engage and coordinate believers to give visible expression to the communion of the saints (WCF 26.2).[62] As such, while the office of the deacon is

---

57. *Form of Government of the Presbyterian Church in the United States* (1879), IV–1,2. Note Ramsay's observation, "By polity is meant activity as an organization. This whole activity consists in, or the sole work of the organized Church is limited to, doctrine, which is teaching or proclaiming the law of Christ revealed in the Scriptures; government, which is administering and enforcing this law; and distribution, which is the application of the material offerings presented in the worship that the Church maintains in obedience to this law. And as the Church has nothing else to do but these three things, so it needs only the three classes of officers corresponding to these three functions," *An Exposition of the Form of Government*, 45.

58. See the literature cited at *How Jesus Runs the Church*, 87nn3–15.

59. See George W. Knight III, "Two Offices and Two Orders of Elders," in *Pressing Toward the Mark: Essays Commemorating Fifty Years of the Orthodox Presbyterian Church*, ed. C. G. Dennison and R. C. Gamble (Philadelphia: The Committee for the Historian of the Orthodox Presbyterian Church, 1986), 22–32. See further Knight's treatment of 1 Timothy 5:17 in Knight, *The Pastoral Epistles*, 231–33.

60. On the office and work of the deacon within American Presbyterianism, see C. N. Willborn, "The Deacon: A Divine Right Office With Divine Uses," *Confessional Presbyterian* 5 (2009): 185–99, and "The Gospel Work in the Diaconate: 'A Ministry 'Proportioned in Number' " *Confessional Presbyterian* 10 (2014): 23–32. See also Cornelis Van Dam, *The Deacon: Biblical Foundations for Today's Ministry of Mercy* (Grand Rapids: Reformation Heritage, 2016).

61. While the work of the deacon in the New Testament is set forth and exemplified largely in terms of the relief of the temporal need and wants of believers, deacons are also tasked with tending generally to the this-worldly needs of the church. It is for this reason that deacons often "care [for] the property of the congregation," *BCO* 9–2.

62. Peck, *Notes on Ecclesiology*, 207.

an office of *service*, it is nevertheless an *office* of service. Deacons possess authority from Christ to undertake the work to which they are called. This point is vividly illustrated in Paul's instructions, through Timothy, to the deacons in 1 Timothy 5:1–16.[63] The deacons, acting together as a board, are authoritatively to make decisions, based upon apostolic criteria, with respect to which widows are eligible to receive the church's benevolences.

Elders and deacons enter into office through ordination. Candidates for these two offices must desire to enter into the office (1 Tim 3:1; 1 Pet 5:2), must possess biblical qualifications for that office and be tested as to those qualifications (1 Tim 3:10; 5:22), and must be elected by the church to serve in that office. But a final step is required before a man may exercise that office to which he is called—ordination.[64] Ordination "is the authoritative admission of one duly called to an office in the church of God, accompanied with prayer and the laying on of hands, to which it is proper to add the giving of the right hand of fellowship."[65] Ordination, in the New Testament, is the work of a court of the church. Elders gather in regular assembly to set apart a gifted and approved man to sacred office by the laying on of hands. Examples of this action appear at Acts 6:6 and 13:1–3, and 1 Timothy 4:14, but Moses's setting Joshua apart by the laying on of hands is an important Old Testament precedent (Num 27:12–23; Deut 34:9; compare Num 8:10).[66] The New Testament appoints ordination only for deacons and elders. It is therefore not authorized for others in the church.

One must make neither too much nor too little of ordination. It is not a sacrament, as the Roman Catholic Church since Trent has maintained.[67] In it, Rome contends, "the Holy Spirit is ... given," and "grace is conferred," such that "a character is imprinted that can be neither erased nor taken

63. The work that Paul describes in these verses is the church's care of qualified widows within the church. Since this work is expressly said to be the task of deacons in Acts 6:1–6, we should take the work envisioned in 1 Timothy 5:3–16 as the work of the diaconate. Taking the tasks of these verses as specifically diaconal tasks, furthermore, helps us to see the progression of Paul's argument in these chapters of the letter—qualifications for elders (3:1–7); qualifications for deacons (3:8–13); the tasks of elders (4:6–16); the tasks of deacons (5:3–16).

64. Bannerman, *The Church of Christ*, 1:428, 430.

65. *BCO* 17-2.

66. For some of the exegetical questions attending these passages, see Witherow, *The Form of the Christian Temple*, 124–35.

67. "Session 23, July 15, 1563. Doctrine and Canons on the Sacrament of Orders," Denzinger, §1763–78.

away."[68] But the New Testament's examples point, rather, to the recognition of gifts already possessed, recognized, and examined within the church. Ordination, therefore, does not confer a grace not yet possessed by the recipient. Neither, however, is ordination to be slighted or dismissed. By apostolic example, it is a perpetual rite, enduring so long as there are elders and deacons in the church. It is not a *mere* rite, but an act whereby the church through its officers admits a man to the exercise of office. It "gives him full ecclesiastical authority to discharge its functions."[69] Even so, the office and authority "invest[ed]" in ordination "are things which, if forfeited by misconduct, can be withdrawn by the same power by which they were bestowed."[70] In summary, therefore, "ordination is less than a charm, but it is more than a form."[71]

Many in the history of the church have pled for the office of monarchical bishops.[72] Such bishops preside and exercise authority over the pastors and congregations in a given diocese. This authority includes the exercise of discipline and the administration of the sacraments. The strength of certain Anglicans' claims to episcopacy in the nineteenth century particularly were met by no less vigorous Presbyterian and Reformed responses.[73] Many proponents of the office of bishop recognize that the office has either slim or no warrant in Scripture.[74] They plead, however, for the church's

---

68. Denzinger, §§1774, 1766, 1767.

69. Witherow, *The Form of the Christian Temple*, 141. Witherow cites the seventeenth-century Scottish Presbyterian, George Gillespie, "It is ordination that *maketh men ministers*," *The Form of the Christian Temple*, 141, emphasis original.

70. Witherow, *The Form of the Christian Temple*, 142.

71. Bannerman, *The Church of Christ*, 1:470. See further Bannerman's valuable discussion of ordination at *The Church of Christ*, 1:467–80.

72. The phrase "monarchical bishop" distinguishes the office of bishop, for which Episcopalian forms of church government plead, from the title, "bishop" or "overseer" (ἐπίσκοπος). This title ("bishop," "overseer") is used of and interchangeably with "elder" in the New Testament (Acts 20:17, 28; Titus 1:5, 7). Thus "bishop" in the New Testament does not denote an office other than the office of elder, but a title belonging to the office of elder.

73. Thomas Smyth, *Ecclesiastical Republicanism, or the Republicanism, Liberality, and Catholicity of Presbytery, in Contrast with Prelacy and Popery* in *Complete Works of Thomas Smyth, Volume Three*, ed. J. William Flynn (Columbia, SC: R. L. Bryan, 1908); Witherow, *The Form of the Christian Temple*, 273–390; Bannerman, *The Church of Christ*, 2:260–95; Bavinck, *Reformed Dogmatics*, 4:348–68.

74. "It is a fact now generally recognized by theologians of all shades of opinion, that in the language of the New Testament the same officer in the Church is called indifferently 'bishop' (*episkopos*) and 'elder' or 'presbyter' (*presbyteros*)," J. B. Lightfoot, *St. Paul's Epistle to the Philippians* (1868; repr., Peabody, MA: Hendrickson, 1995), 95. Compare Edward Arthur

"power of discretion" to adapt her polity "so as to meet the exigencies of the age."[75] But if the church's government is *jure divino*, then the Scriptures alone warrant the establishment of an office in the church. The absence of the office of monarchical bishop from the New Testament, notwithstanding its antiquity, widespread use, and perceived expedience, suffices to bar it from the church's government.

THE COURTS OF THE CHURCH

But even though there is no particular office higher than the elder that presides over multiple pastors and congregations, church government nevertheless extends higher than the congregational level. As the local church is governed by an assembly of elders, so the church at the regional and universal levels is governed by representative assemblies of elders.[76] In contrast to episcopacy, Presbyterianism insists that such government is undertaken by a plurality of elders meeting in regularly constituted assemblies. The power of elders to govern at levels higher than the congregation is joint and not several. In contrast to Independency, Presbyterianism argues that such assemblies above the level of the congregation have biblical warrant, reflecting the form of government that Christ delivered to the church through his apostles.

The argument for representative assemblies of elders at levels higher than the congregation proceeds along two basic lines. The first is that the unity of the visible church lends presumptive weight for such a form of government. Christians universally acknowledge the visible church to be one, and the church to be governed at the local level (John 17:22–23;

Litton, *The Church of Christ in Its Idea, Attributes, and Ministry*, 3rd rev. ed. (Philadelphia: Smith & English, 1863), 275–311; Roger Beckwith, *Elders in Every City: The Origin and Role of the Ordained Ministry* (Carlisle, UK: Paternoster, 2003), 11–14; and Gerald Bray, *The Church: A Theological and Historical Account* (Grand Rapids: Baker Academic, 2016), 47–48.

75. Litton, *The Church of Christ*, 308. Litton argues that the events of AD 70 marked the occasion for the church's "extension of its polity" beyond the two offices of elder and deacon to encompass the office of bishop, *The Church of Christ*, 298. The office is apostolic in origin, he asserts, but the materials by which we come to this conclusion are "uninspired" ones, *The Church of Christ*, 302.

76. These assemblies have gone under a number of names. In the Dutch Reformed tradition, "consistory" describes the local or congregational assembly of elders, and "classis" and "synod," the regional and universal assemblies of elders, respectively. In Presbyterianism, "session" describes the local or congregational assembly of elders; "presbytery," "synod," or "general assembly," regional or universal assemblies of elders.

Eph 4:4–6; 1 Cor 10:17; 12:12).[77] Since that is the case, our expectation is that the church would likewise be governed at every level (local, regional, universal) by assemblies of elders. If government is an expression of the church's unity, then that expression ought to characterize the church at every level of her existence.[78]

Second, the Scripture shows that multiple congregations were governmentally united.[79] The church in Jerusalem serves as a telling example.[80] On the one hand, Acts documents the existence of thousands of Christians in the church in Jerusalem (Acts 2:41, 47; 4:4; 5:14; 6:7; 21:20). Since there was no single building to accommodate all these believers, the church in Jerusalem necessarily consisted of multiple congregations meeting in multiple locations throughout that city.[81] On the other hand, Acts speaks of the church in Jerusalem in the singular (8:1; 11:22; 15:4). The plurality of congregations in Jerusalem were therefore united as one church in that city. Furthermore, the church in Jerusalem was served by elders (15:2) and deacons (6:1–6). Certainly, these officers concentrated their labors in particular congregations. But they also served the church in Jerusalem beyond the

---

77. John Mitchell Mason, *Essays on the Church of God: In Which the Doctrines of Church Membership and Infant Baptism Are Fully Discussed* (1843; repr., Taylors, SC: Presbyterian Press, 2005), as cited at Peck, *Notes on Ecclesiology*, 195.

78. Peck, *Notes on Ecclesiology*, 195. See an elaboration of this argument at McGill, *Church Government*, 457–62. Note as well McGill's argument from the purity of the church for church government at levels higher than the congregation, *Church Government*, 462–66.

79. Proponents of Independency argue that churches have bonds of association and fellowship, up to and including "the duty of special consultation with regard to matters affecting the common interest," Augustus H. Strong, *Systematic Theology* (Philadelphia: Judson, 1907), 927. But such consultation is non-governmental and, therefore, non-binding in nature. Should a congregation in fellowship with another congregation "manifest[ly] depart from the faith or practice of the Scriptures," then all that a concerned congregation may do is "withdraw their fellowship" from the offending congregation," 928. Compare Stephen J. Wellum and Kirk Wellum, "The Biblical and Theological Case for Congregationalism," in *Baptist Foundations: Government for an Anti-Institutional Age*, ed. Mark Dever and Jonathan Leeman (Nashville: B&H, 2015), 64–69; Gregg R. Allison, *Sojourners and Strangers: The Doctrine of the Church* (Wheaton, IL: Crossway, 2012), 283–87. Presbyterians readily acknowledge and affirm associational bonds and connections as present among churches in the New Testament, on which see Witherow, *The Form of the Christian Temple*, 182–88. But Presbyterians go on to say that the New Testament no less testifies to the governmental character of those bonds.

80. For what follows, see my *How Jesus Runs the Church*, 121–24, which depends, in turn, on Peck, *Notes on Ecclesiology*, 200–201.

81. *Jus Divinum*, 211. See also Witherow, *The Form of the Christian Temple*, 176–82.

congregational level.[82] The elders of the church in Jerusalem, for instance, are said to act together on more than one occasion (see Acts 11:22, 30; 15:2).[83] These actions—the disbursement of funds and the settling of a doctrinal dispute—are acts of government. The elders, therefore, met as a regional assembly to deliberate upon and conclude matters affecting the churches in that region.

The assembly of elders that met in Jerusalem to address a doctrinal question brought up to it by the church in Antioch (Acts 15:2) confirms that the work of the elders in assembly at levels above the congregation is governmental in nature.[84] Elders from local congregations gathered, as a representative assembly, to deliberate matters that are properly before that body (15:6–22). Through deliberation, they concluded those matters, and communicated their decision to the churches under their authority (Acts 15:23–29).[85] Those churches received that decision for what it was—a decision that was binding upon them (Acts 15:30–35; 16:1–5).[86] The outcome of that decision was not only the maturation of the church according to the gospel that had since been reaffirmed by that council, but also a renewal of missionary zeal and endeavor on the part of the church (16:4, 5). This assembly, in other words, is the means of building the church outward and upward.

---

82. "The visible Church is one body consisting of many members; and as the motions of the hand, the head, the foot, are the motions of the man, so the healthful and regular action of any single congregation is the action of the universal Church. ... He who is called by a single congregation is called by the entire Church; he who is supported by a single congregation is supported by the entire Church. ... Every pastor is a Minister of the whole," James H. Thornwell, *The Collected Writings of James Henley Thornwell*, 4 vols. (1875; repr., Edinburgh: Banner of Truth, 1974), 4.39.

83. *Jus Divinum*, 217–18.

84. For a fuller discussion of Acts 15 in relation to the courts of the church, see my *How Jesus Runs the Church*, 126–35, *Jus Divinum*, 225–36, and Cunningham, *Historical Theology*, 1:43–78.

85. That the assembly's deliverance was sent down to "the brothers who are of the Gentiles in Antioch and Syria and Cilicia" (Acts 15:23) suggests that churches other than Antioch were under the jurisdiction of this assembly, whether this assembly was regional or universal in its scope.

86. One virtue of this biblical form of government is that it allows higher courts to redress the errors of lower courts, including errors relating to the trial and conviction of accused members and elders. Independency requires that the decisions of the congregation be final and beyond appeal, on which see Miller, *Presbyterianism*, 61–63, Macpherson, *Presbyterianism*, 127–31, and McGill, *Church Government*, 492.

As courts of the visible church, regional and universal assemblies of elders exercise the same kinds of power that congregational assemblies undertake—doctrine, order, and discipline. That each church court is "one in nature, constituted of the same elements, possessed inherently of the same kinds of rights and powers," raises the question of their relationship with one another.[87] Negatively, no church court derives its existence, rights, or powers from another church court, whether higher or lower.[88] It is the church's written and adopted constitution that determines their mutual interrelation.[89] Thus, in Thomas E. Peck's formulation, "the power of the whole is in every part, and the power of the whole is over the *power* of every part."[90] Every church court is equal in nature to every other church court. But "the lower courts are subject to the review and control of the higher courts, in regular gradation," and Presbyterian constitutions furnish explicit provisions of such review and control.[91] In this way, the church realizes her unity without compromising the biblical integrity of the duties and responsibilities of local assemblies of elders.

CONCLUSION

THE CHURCH'S GOVERNMENT HELPS TO actualize the church's unity. It no less provides visible expression to the reign of the church's only head and king, Jesus Christ. God has not only set down a form of government for his people in the Scripture, but he has also established the way in which his people are to worship him. The way in which God would have his people to worship him is the concern of the next chapter.

87. *BCO* 11-3.

88. Peck, *Notes on Ecclesiology*, 205.

89. "The Session exercises jurisdiction over a single church, the Presbytery over what is common to the ministers, Sessions, and churches within a prescribed district, and the General Assembly over such matters as concern the whole Church. The jurisdiction of these courts is limited by the express provisions of the Constitution," *BCO* 11-4.

90. Peck, *Notes on Ecclesiology*, 205, emphasis original. Compare Peck, "The Action of the Assembly of 1879 on Worldly Amusements, or the Powers of Our Several Church Courts," in *Miscellanies of Rev. Thomas E. Peck*, ed. Thomas Cary Johnson, 3 vols. (Richmond, VA: Presbyterian Committee of Publication, 1895–1897), 2.335.

91. *BCO* 11-4.

FURTHER READING

Jus Divinum Regiminis Ecclesiastici or *The Divine Right of Church-Government.* Revised and edited by David W. Hall. 1646. Reprint, Dallas: Naphtali Press, 1995. Drafted by members of the Westminster Assembly, this work is a clear and forceful exposition of the doctrine of church government by divine right. Noteworthy is its exegetical defense of higher courts as part of the divinely revealed pattern of church government in Scripture.

Miller, Samuel. *Presbyterianism the Truly Primitive and Apostolical Constitution of the Church of Christ.* Philadelphia: Presbyterian Board of Publication, 1835. An early nineteenth-century survey and defense of Presbyterian doctrine, government, and worship. Miller gives particular attention to Presbyterianism's growth and development across the history of the church.

Thomas E. Peck. *Notes on Ecclesiology*. Richmond: Presbyterian Committee of Publication, 1892. A published form of Peck's lecture notes at Union Theological Seminary (Virginia). This work is a mature expression of American Presbyterian polity at the close of the nineteenth century.

Witherow, Thomas. *The Form of the Christian Temple: Being a Treatise on the Constitution of the New Testament Church.* Edinburgh: T&T Clark, 1889. Witherow, a nineteenth-century Irish Presbyterian theologian, authored an extensive work on the church, with particular attention to the church's government. Readers should also note his briefer, more accessible, and often reprinted defense of Presbyterian church government, *The Apostolic Church, Which Is It?*

Waters, Guy Prentiss. *How Jesus Runs the Church.* Phillipsburg, NJ: P&R, 2011. A contemporary articulation and biblical defense of Presbyterian church government.

XI

THE WORSHIP OF THE CHURCH

WORSHIP IS CENTRAL TO THE life of the people of God. God created Adam and Eve to enjoy fellowship with him in Eden (Gen 3:8a). The covenant of works was designed for Adam to lead himself and his posterity into confirmed and heightened eschatological life with God (Gen 2:15–17). After the fall of humanity into sin, God gathered a people who "call[ed] upon the name of the Lord" (Gen 4:26). Noah, Abraham, and Jacob offered sacrifices in worship to the God who had entered into covenant with them. At Sinai, God appointed for his redeemed people a system of worship by which they were to enter into his presence. The prophets condemned Israel for their idolatry and abandonment of the true worship of the living and true God. They also pointed to a day when God would gather the remnant of his people and people from among the nations to worship him on his holy mountain. Jesus's ministry not only reformed but transformed worship. His redemptive work reflected the purpose of his Father who was seeking "true worshipers [to] worship the Father in spirit and truth" (John 4:23). The church under the supervision of the apostles is a church fervently engaged in the worship of God (Acts 2:42–47). The church at the consummation ceaselessly worships God in Christ (Rev 7:9–17). The ultimate purpose of the church, the end for which the gathering and perfecting of the saints (WCF 25.3) takes place, is worship.

In this chapter, we will explore the Scripture's testimony to the church's worship of God along several lines. First, we will consider the way in which the Scripture defines and describes worship. Second, we will explore the primary elements of public worship—the reading and preaching of the word of God; the sacraments of baptism and of the Lord's Supper; and, briefly, prayer. Third, we will reflect on the way in which God appoints one day each week—the Sabbath—for God's people to rest from their daily employments and to devote themselves to his worship.

THE BIBLICAL DEFINITION AND DESCRIPTIONS OF WORSHIP

Worship is the attribution of glory ("worth") to God, preeminently in the context of the "meeting of the Triune God with his chosen people," and exclusively upon "the terms that he proposes."[1] The New Testament metaphorically and comprehensively applies the liturgical language and imagery of the Old Testament to believers under the new covenant. Paul tells the church in Rome to "present your bodies as a living sacrifice, holy and acceptable to God, which is your spiritual worship" (Rom 12:1). Hebrews enjoins believers to "continually offer up a sacrifice of praise to God, that is, the fruit of lips that acknowledge his name," and speaks of "do[ing] good" and "shar[ing] what you have" as "sacrifices ... pleasing to God" (Heb 13:15–16). Picking up the language of Exodus 19:6, Peter speaks of the church as "a holy priesthood" who "offer spiritual sacrifices acceptable to God through Jesus Christ" (1 Pet 2:5; see 2:9).

One may speak, then, of the entirety of the Christian life in terms of worship. God lays claim to every thought, choice, action, or relationship of the Christian, and Christians must embrace and nurture a suitable self-consciousness in every department and aspect of their lives. But it does not thereby follow that there is no other sense in which the New Testament speaks of worship.[2] As Clowney has noted, not only does the New Testament document both Jesus and Paul in attendance at weekly

---

1. *BCO* 47–2; David Peterson, *Engaging with God: A Biblical Theology of Worship* (Downers Grove, IL: InterVarsity Press, 1992), 55. Note Peterson's own definition of worship, from which the cited clause is drawn, "The worship of the living and true God is essentially an engagement with him on the terms that he proposes and in the way that he alone makes possible," Peterson, *Engaging with God*, 55.

2. *Pace* Peterson, "There is no divinely ordained ritual of approach to God for believers under the new covenant. Nevertheless, several texts suggest that God presences himself in a distinctive way in the Christian meeting through his word and the operation of his Spirit," *Engaging with God*, 287. Compare Peterson, "Worship in the New Testament," in *Worship:*

synagogue services, but Paul, "when rejected in the synagogue ... continued similar gatherings for believing Jews and Gentiles."[3] Furthermore, Paul explicitly distinguished the gathering of the Corinthians in public worship "from gatherings at homes"—"when you come together as a church (ἐν ἐκκλησίᾳ)" (1 Cor 11:18).[4] The Old Testament pattern of stated, public gatherings of God's people to meet with him in the manner of his appointment continues under the new covenant.

One may certainly characterize the worship of the New Testament church descriptively. That is to say, one may enumerate the activities that characterize the church's public worship on the pages of the New Testament. Prior to such an exercise, however, is the more basic question of what principle guides the inclusion of those activities (and the exclusion of other activities) from public worship.

This principle has come to be known as the "Regulative Principle of Worship," and finds succinct expression in the Westminster Confession of Faith: "But the acceptable way of worshipping the true God is instituted by Himself, and so limited by His own revealed will, that He may not be worshipped according to the imaginations and devices of men, or the suggestions or Satan, under any visible representation, or any other way not prescribed in the Holy Scripture" (WCF 21.1).[5] Calvin pithily articulated the doctrine, "God disapproves of all modes of worship not expressly sanctioned by his Word."[6] That which God has not expressly authorized in his word for public worship is thereby forbidden. Scripture is a sufficient guide and rule for God's worship. Such a formulation stands in marked contrast

---

Adoration and Action, ed. D. A. Carson (Grand Rapids: Baker Academic, 1993), 51–91, esp. 82, 90–91.

3. Edmund P. Clowney, "Presbyterian Worship," in *Worship: Adoration and Action*, 112.

4. Edmund P. Clowney, "Corporate Worship: A Means of Grace," in *Give Praise to God: A Vision for Reforming Worship*, ed. Philip Graham Ryken, Derek W. H. Thomas, and J. Ligon Duncan III (Phillipsburg, NJ: P&R, 2003), 98.

5. The phrase, "Regulative Principle of Worship," is of uncertain origin and may have originated as late as the nineteenth or twentieth centuries. What it expresses finds much deeper roots in Reformed theology and, more importantly, in the testimony of Scripture.

6. Calvin, "On the Necessity of Reforming the Church," in *John Calvin: Tracts and Letters*, 7 vols. (repr., Edinburgh: Banner of Truth, 2009), 1:128. On Calvin and the Regulative Principle, see further the discussion at William Young, "The Puritan Principle of Worship," in *Reformed Thought: Selected Writings of William Young*, ed. Joel R. Beeke and Ray B. Lanning (Grand Rapids: Reformation Heritage, 2011), 143–51. Compare the *Annotations* of the Westminster Assembly, on Leviticus 10:1, "In Gods worship Gods command, not man's wit, or will, must be our rule," as cited at Fesko, *The Theology of the Westminster Standards*, 341.

to the Thirty-Nine Articles of the Church of England, "The Church hath power to decree Rites and Ceremonies. ... And yet it is not lawful for the Church to ordain any thing that is contrary to God's Word written" (Art. 20). This doctrine declares, in the arena of public worship, that that which is not forbidden in the word of God is thereby permitted. Scripture guides and norms public worship, but it is not designedly a sufficient guide or norm in that respect. The principle formulated in the Thirty-Nine Articles is permissive in nature. The Regulative Principle "is purely negative and prohibitory."[7] It categorically excludes from the public worship of God that which Scripture has not authorized.

The Reformed tradition has tied the Regulative Principle to the second commandment. According to the Heidelberg Catechism, the second commandment requires "that we in nowise make any image of God, nor worship him in any other way than he has commanded in his word" (Q&A 96). The Westminster Shorter Catechism affirms that "the second commandment forbiddeth the worshipping of God by images, or by any other way not appointed in his Word" (Q&A 51). If the first commandment stipulates the *object* of worship (God alone), the second commandment stipulates the *way* in which God is to be worshiped (only according to God's revealed will).[8]

Theologically, the Regulative Principle must be understood in terms of the power that Christ has committed to the church. The church, William Cunningham writes, "has no power to decree rites and ceremonies, or to introduce into her worship and government anything which the word of God has not positively sanctioned or authorized."[9] For the church, or any church officer, to do so is an "exercise of ... unlawful authority" and "exercis[es] a tyranny" over the consciences of human beings.[10] Thus, to intro-

---

7. William Cunningham, *The Reformers and the Theology of the Reformation* (Edinburgh: T&T Clark, 1862), 36.

8. Ursinus, *Commentary on the Heidelberg Catechism*, 518; William Cunningham, *Historical Theology*, 1:373–74; Nahum M. Sarna, *The JPS Torah Commentary: Exodus* (Philadelphia: Jewish Publication Society, 1991), 110. Compare Calvin, *Institutes*, 2.8.17 (=1:383–84).

9. William Cunningham, "Church Power," in *Discussions of Church Principles: Popish, Erastian, and Presbyterian* (Edinburgh: T&T Clark, 1863), 254.

10. Cunningham, "Church Power," 254. Compare Thomas E. Peck, "The liberty, on the part of the rulers of the church, to make laws which Christ has not made is simply and really the liberty to put an intolerable yoke upon the necks of the people," "The Wisdom of Man vs. the Power of God," in *Miscellanies of Rev. Thomas E. Peck*, ed. Thomas C. Johnson, 3 vols. (Richmond: Presbyterian Committee of Publication, 1895), 1:111.

duce unauthorized worship into the church not only is an offense against God but also strikes at the liberty of the consciences of worshipers.[11]

The Regulative Principle is also designed to preserve the church's peace and unity. The Regulative Principle restricts elements in public worship to what God has authorized in his word. Therefore, its "supporters never devise innovations and press them upon the church. The principle itself precludes this. It is the deniers of this principle, and they alone, who invent and obtrude innovations, and they are responsible for all the mischiefs that ensue from the discussions and contentions to which these things have given rise."[12] In insisting only upon what Scripture authorizes for the church's worship, the church's unity is thereby maintained.

To understand what the Regulative Principle is and is not saying about the church's worship, it is important to review some terms and distinctions—"element," "form," and "circumstance." The constituent ordinances of public worship are the "elements" of worship. Elements include the reading and preaching of the word of God, prayer, the singing of psalms and hymns, and the administration of the sacraments of baptism and the Lord's Supper. "Form" describes the particular shape or "content" of a given element.[13] The Lord's Prayer, for example, is a particular form of prayer that may be offered in public worship. Presbyterians have not been opposed to the use of forms in public worship. They also readily acknowledge the need for liturgical order in the church's worship. Their opposition to forms has extended only to the *imposition* of forms and liturgies within the church. That is to say, it is an unwarranted exercise of ecclesiastical power to compel a minister to employ a set form or liturgy in congregational worship.[14] "Circumstances," discussed in the previous chapter, relate to both

11. "The very issue [that] the regulative principle was *designed* to address [is] the limits of church power and the liberty of conscience," T. David Gordon, "Some Answers About the Regulative Principle," *WTJ* 55 (1993): 323, emphasis original.

12. Cunningham, *The Reformers and the Theology of the Reformation*, 36, as cited at Gordon, "Some Answers," 325.

13. Gordon, "Some Answers," 326, referencing WLC 186 and WSC 99, which speak of the Lord's Prayer in terms of a "form of prayer."

14. On the unlawfulness of the imposition of forms and liturgies, see George Gillespie, *A Dispute Against the English-Popish Ceremonies Obtruded on the Church of Scotland* (1662; repr, Edinburgh: Ogle, Oliver, and Boyd, 1844); John Owen, "A Discourse Concerning Liturgies and Their Imposition," in *The Works of John Owen, Volume 15*, 1–55; Bannerman, *The Church of Christ*, 1:335–91; and Miller, *Presbyterianism*, 66–73.

the church's government and worship (WCF 1.6). They are not elements in worship but "concomitants" thereof, "without which [an action] can either not be done at all, or cannot be done with decency and decorum."[15] It falls within the legitimate exercise of the church's diatactical power to order circumstances in the worship of God.[16] In this way, worship may be conducted "decently and in order" and in such a way as to reflect the character of God as "a God ... of peace," not "of confusion" (1 Cor 14:33, 40).

It is important to express clearly the distinction between "elements" and "circumstances" in the worship of God. The former concern "matters *in sacris* [in sacred things]"; the latter, "matters *circa sacra* [around or about sacred things]."[17] Bannerman explains the distinction.

> The *ceremonies* and institutions of Church worship are properly and distinctively matters *in sacris*; the *circumstances* of Church worship, or those that belong to it in common with the ordinary proceedings or peculiar solemnities of men, are properly and distinctly matters *circa sacra*. The ceremonies and institutions of worship are matters *in* the public worship of God; the circumstances of worship common to it with civil solemnities are matters *about* the public worship of God.[18]

An element, then, may be a reading of Scripture, a sermon, a prayer, or hymn of praise. Examples of circumstances include the length of the Scripture reading, sermon, or prayer, and the number of prayers and hymns to be included in a particular service.[19] The distinction between elements and circumstances illustrates why and how it is that the church has no discretionary power with respect to the former, but is afforded limited discretion with respect to the latter.

---

15. Peck, *Notes on Ecclesiology*, 122.

16. "It belongeth to synods and councils ... to set down rules and directions for the better ordering of the public worship of God, and government of His church" (WCF 31.2).

17. Bannerman, *The Church of Christ*, 1:349; compare Heppe, *Reformed Dogmatics*, 693.

18. Bannerman, *The Church of Christ*, 1:349, emphasis removed.

19. Gordon, "Some Answers," 324, 326.

THE ELEMENTS OF WORSHIP

With this framework of biblical public worship in place, we may now consider the elements of public worship. Since the reading and preaching of the word of God, the sacraments of baptism and the Lord's Supper, and prayer are "means of grace" (*media gratiae*), we must first reflect upon the nature, function, and purpose of these means in public worship before giving particular consideration to the elements of the word and the sacraments.[20]

By "means of grace" are meant "objective channels which Christ has instituted in the church, and to which he ordinarily binds himself in the communication of His grace."[21] Saving grace, in other words, is ordinarily communicated through means or instruments of God's own choosing. It is important to stress that these are *means* of grace. The Spirit is the efficient cause in each and every case where saving grace is effectively communicated to a recipient. While God is free to communicate grace in any manner that he pleases, he ordinarily does so through his preferred means.[22] Those who seek grace must do so employing these divinely-appointed instruments. And yet, the grace of regeneration is not communicated through any means of grace. It is, rather, immediate.[23]

God has not established each of these means to function identically. "The grace of faith ... is ordinarily wrought by the ministry of the Word," but not by the sacraments (WCF 14.1). The ministry of the word joins the sacraments and prayer as means fitted to "increase" and "strengthen" saving faith. The sacraments, then, are not converting ordinances. They are, rather, ordinances ordered to the sanctification of the believer. In light of this

---

20. Following the identification of word, sacrament, and prayer as means of grace in WLC 153, 154; WCF 14.1. Note that the Westminster Standards do not exhaustively identify the means of grace as these three particular means ("*especially* the Word, sacraments, and prayer," WLC 154, emphasis added). For a survey of historical discussion and differences among Reformed theologians in identifying which are the means of grace, see Berkhof, *Systematic Theology*, 604–5.

21. Berkhof, *Systematic Theology*, 605.

22. Note Vos's qualification, "Even when [effectual grace] works mediately, it is not bound up entirely with the means but accompanies them and causes the soul to be receptive to them, so that there is a concurrence of two factors, each of which does its particular work; and they belong with each other," *Reformed Dogmatics*, 5:82.

23. Vos, *Reformed Dogmatics*, 5:82. The ministry of the word of God, however, may be and often is the *occasion*—though not the *cause*—of the gift of the grace of regeneration.

pattern, we may speak of the primacy of the word of God with respect to the means of grace, "The Word is the beginning, middle, and end. If necessary, we can think of Word as a means of grace without sacrament, but it is impossible to think of sacrament as a means of grace without Word. The sacraments depend on Scripture, and the truth of Scripture speaks in and through them."[24]

It bears emphasizing that each of these means is an ecclesiastical ordinance. That is to say, these are means that are committed to the church and to be dispensed by the church.[25] To observe this is in no way to credit Rome's teaching that the church is a repository of grace and is tasked with dispensing that grace through the church's ordinances.[26] After all, "the church is not a means of grace alongside of the Word and sacraments, for all the power entrusted to it consists in nothing other than the administration of these two. The church and its offices as such do not impart grace; this only occurs *through* the Word and the sacraments."[27] Even so, understanding the means of grace as *ecclesiastical* ordinances affords definition to the mission and purpose of the church. As the means of grace are suited for the ingathering and perfecting of God's elect, so the church's mission and purpose must be understood along those very lines—"the gathering and perfecting of the saints" (WCF 25.3).[28]

The Word of God

The Westminster Confession of Faith enumerates the elements of public worship.

> The reading of the Scriptures with godly fear, the sound preaching and conscionable hearing of the Word, in obedience unto God, with understanding, faith and reverence, singing of psalms with grace in the heart; as also, the due administration and worthy receiving of the sacraments instituted by Christ, are all parts of the ordinary religious worship of God: beside religious oaths, vows, solemn

24. Vos, *Reformed Dogmatics*, 5:81. "The Word of God is never separated from the sacrament—not only because the sacrament is a word, conveyed in an image and intended for the eye, but also because a spoken word always accompanies the sacrament," *Reformed Dogmatics*, 5:81.

25. Berkhof, *Systematic Theology*, 605.

26. *CCC* §947.

27. Bavinck, *Reformed Dogmatics*, 4:447.

28. Bavinck, *Reformed Dogmatics*, 4:447.

> fastings, and thanksgivings upon special occasions, which are, in their several times and seasons, to be used in an holy and religious manner. (WCF 21.5)

The primacy of the "reading" and the "preaching" of the word of God in the Westminster Confession's list reflects its primacy in the New Testament. The church under the new covenant is birthed and given form through the apostolic preaching of the word. Peter's sermon on the day of Pentecost highlights the person and work of Christ, and proceeds to press the claims of Christ upon his audience. Those who "repent[ed]" and "received his word" are "added" to the church (Acts 2:38, 41). The church is described as "devoted ... to the apostles' teaching and the fellowship, to the breaking of bread and the prayers" (Acts 2:42). The same apostolic word that had gathered sinners serves to edify and mature the saints.

This pattern is repeated throughout Acts, in the ministries of Peter and Paul. The apostles preach Christ to wide and indiscriminate audiences. It is the Spirit's ministry by and with the word that accounts for sinners repenting and believing in Christ as he is offered to them in the preached gospel (Acts 16:14; compare Luke 24:45; 1 Thess 1:5; 2:13; 2 Thess 2:13).[29] The apostles then proceed to instruct these young believers in the context of the local congregation.[30] The apostle Paul characterizes his own three-year teaching and preaching ministry in Ephesus along several lines—"repentance toward God and ... faith in our Lord Jesus Christ" (Acts 20:21); "the gospel of the grace of God" (20:24); "the kingdom" (20:25); "the whole counsel of God" (20:27); "the word of his grace" (20:32). Each of these expressions captures an aspect of the preaching and teaching ministry that Paul conducted towards "Jews" and "Greeks," both believers and unbelievers, in Ephesus (Acts 20:21). Luke surely intends for his readers to take Paul's self-description of his Ephesian ministry as characteristic of the entirety not only of his whole ministry, but also of the ministry of his apostolic colleagues.

---

29. Ultimately, Luke insists, it is the Father's eternal decree that accounts for the saving of sinners through the work of Christ, applied to them by the Holy Spirit (Acts 13:48).

30. Critically, Paul preaches the same message ("gospel") to unbelieving and believing audiences. He "remind[s]" the Corinthians "of the gospel I preached to you, which you received, in which you stand, and by which you are being saved, if you hold fast to the word I preached to you" (1 Cor 15:1–2). He tells the church in Rome that he is "eager to preach the gospel to you also who are in Rome" (Rom 1:15).

This preaching ministry takes place in stated assemblies of believers, gathered to worship God. Luke gives a glimpse of one such service in Troas, over which the apostle Paul presides (Acts 20:7–12). Here, Paul preaches an extended sermon (20:7), after which he administers the Lord's Supper (20:11). We are to understand Paul's preaching in the synagogue, then, to have been carried over into the church. Ministers are to follow Paul's example. The apostle tells Timothy to "devote" himself "to the public reading of Scripture, to exhortation, to teaching" (1 Tim 4:13). It is in this context that Paul tells Timothy to "keep a close watch on yourself and on the teaching. Persist in this, for by so doing you will save both yourself and your hearers" (1 Tim 4:16; compare 2 Tim 3:16–17). The word, read and preached by Timothy (4:13), is the means by which the Spirit administers saving grace to the congregation (4:16). When the New Testament conjoins the saving activity of the Spirit to the word of God, we are particularly to understand the word of God as it is publicly read and proclaimed to the congregation in public worship.[31]

The Sacraments THE BIBLICAL FRAMEWORK FOR UNDERSTANDING the sacraments of baptism and the Lord's Supper is the gracious covenant that God has made with his people in Christ.[32] Across redemptive history, God institutes covenant signs in order to display and confirm the covenantal promises that he has made to them. The rainbow serves to confirm God's promise never again to destroy the world with a flood of water (Gen 9:11, 12). Circumcision signifies and confirms to Abraham and his offspring the promises that God had earlier made to Abraham (see Gen 12:1–3; 15:1–6, 17–20; cf. 17:10–14). Passover annually commemorates Israel's redemption from bondage in Egypt (Deut 16:1–8).

Under the new covenant, "when Christ the substance was exhibited" (WLC 35), Christ appoints two covenant signs, baptism (Matt 28:19) and the Lord's Supper (Luke 22:14–23). These two signs stand in continuity with signs of previous covenants, circumcision and the Passover (Col 2:11–12;

---

31. For a survey of New Testament passages addressing the Spirit's saving working by and with the word in the lives of men and women, see Bavinck, *Reformed Dogmatics*, 4:458.

32. See further here my *The Lord's Supper as the Sign and Meal of the New Covenant*, SSBT (Wheaton, IL: Crossway, 2017), esp. 19–58.

1 Cor 11:23–26 with 5:7).[33] And yet each new covenant sign supplants its old covenant counterpart, serving to represent the finished work of Christ to the people of God just as this old covenant counterpart represented to God's people in shadows the work of Christ yet to come.

Before addressing the particular dimensions of the sacraments of the new covenant, it is necessary to define what a sacrament is.[34] First, sacraments are "holy signs and seals of the covenant of grace" (WCF 27.1). The two terms, "sign" and "seal," appear in connection with circumcision at Romans 4:11. The term "sign" underscores the way in which a sacrament points to some reality external to itself.[35] In particular, sacraments signify the promises and benefits of the covenant of grace. A sacrament, in the oft quoted formulation of Augustine, is the "visible sign of an invisible grace." Importantly, that "invisible grace" is located neither in the sign nor within the recipient. It stands in relation to the covenant promises that God makes to his people, promises that they are to receive through faith in Jesus Christ.

The term "seal" has proven more susceptible to misunderstanding. At the heart of the idea of sealing is confirmation—God confirms the truth of his promises.[36] Those to whom those promises belong respond appropriately in renewed exercises of faith in those promises. What Mark Ross says of circumcision in the context of Paul's argument in Romans 4 is true

33. A point raised and developed already in the first generation of the Reformation, so Calvin, *Institutes*, 4.16.1–16 (2:1324–39). Proponents of believers' baptism sometimes question or deny that a continuous relationship exists between baptism and circumcision as signs of their respective covenants, Martin Salter, "Does Baptism Replace Circumcision? An Examination of the Relationship between Circumcision and Baptism in Colossians 2:11–12," *Themelios* 35, no. 1 (2010):15–29. For a paedobaptist response, see David Gibson, "Sacramental Supercessionism Revisited: A Response to Martin Salter on the Relationship Between Circumcision and Baptism" *Themelios* 37, no. 2 (2012): 191–208.

34. Baptist theologians have often expressed reserve about the term "sacrament," on which see, for instance, Shawn D. Wright, "Five Preliminary Issues for Understanding the Ordinances," in *Baptist Foundations*, 88–89. Into the seventeenth and eighteenth centuries, at least, Particular Baptist pastors and theologians were comfortable using the terms "sacrament" and "ordinance" interchangeably, on which see Michael A. G. Haykin, *Amidst Us Our Belovèd Stands: Recovering Sacrament in the Baptist Tradition* (Bellingham, WA: Lexham, 2022). Note Calvin's assessment, "in using the word 'sacraments,' the ancients had no other intention than to signify that they are signs of holy and spiritual things," *Institutes* 4.14.13 (=2:1288).

35. Acknowledging that "while all sacraments are signs, not all signs are sacraments," J. V. Fesko, *Word, Water, and Spirit: A Reformed Perspective on Baptism* (Grand Rapids: Reformation Heritage, 2010), 296.

36. Calvin notes the purpose of a "seal"—"not to confer efficacy upon God's promise as if it were invalid of itself, but only to confirm it to us," *Institutes* 4.15.22 (=2:1323).

of each sacrament *qua* seal, "circumcision is the authenticating mark that certifies the truth of God's promise, that he will give righteousness to the one who has faith."[37] As signs *and* seals, then, sacraments point beyond themselves to the truth of God's word, confirming particularly the truth of his promises. They do not effect a change in the individual *ex opere operato* ("by the work having been worked")—grace is not so conjoined to the sacraments that the sacraments thus administer grace to recipients. Nor do the sacraments function to reflect an existing work of grace within the individual.[38] Sacraments are, in the first instance, objective in their orientation. They point to the promises of God, calling observers to respond subjectively in faith in the truth of God so displayed and confirmed.

The sacraments exist, then, as signs and seals within the covenant of grace. They are "immediately instituted by God" himself (WCF 27.1). They therefore belong to the covenant community and serve to administer covenant promises to God's covenant people.[39] Within that covenantal framework, they serve three complementary purposes as the "benefits of the new covenant are represented, sealed, and applied to believers" (WSC 92). First, they "strengthen and increase [the] faith" of "those that are within the covenant of grace" (WLC 162). The sacraments are not designed to create a faith that does not presently exist, but to nurture and grow existing faith (Rom 4:11). Second, they "oblige them to obedience" (WLC 162). As Paul explains the meaning of baptism in Romans 6:1–23, he reasons from what baptism signifies and seals to the duties of believers to put off sin and to pursue righteousness. Third, they "testify and cherish their love and

37. Mark E. Ross, "Baptism and Circumcision as Signs and Seals," in *The Case for Covenantal Infant Baptism*, ed. Gregg Strawbridge (Phillipsburg, NJ: P&R, 2003), 94.

38. Note in this connection the doctrine of the "sacramental union," in which there is "a spiritual relation ... between the sign and the thing signified," WCF 27.2 The "union" between the "sign and the thing signified" is neither "physical," "local," nor "spiritual" [i.e., "so that by the signs the power of justifying and regenerating is immediately instilled"—a different sense from the way in which this term is used in WCF 27.2] but "relative" and "moral," on which see Turretin, *Institutes*, 19.4.1–4 (=3:348–49).

39. It is this characteristic of the sacraments that has prompted Reformed Protestants to reject the Roman Catholic ordinances of marriage and ordination as sacraments. Marriage is an ordinance of the creation, not peculiar to the covenant community. Ordination is reserved for only some within the church, but sacraments are intended for the covenant community at large. Further, as Dabney has observed, ordination "confers no grace," and "in matrimony there is no sacramental element at all, no divine warrant for sacramental institution, no grace of redemption signed and sealed to the recipients," *Lectures in Theology*, 734.

communion with one another [and] distinguish them from those that are without" (WLC 162). Sacraments have a necessarily corporate dimension to them. They express and solidify the bonds of fellowship within the body of Christ (1 Cor 10:16–18; compare 11:17–22). They also give visible expression to the covenant community in distinction from the world (1 Cor 10:21).

The sacraments do "become effectual means of salvation," but "not by any power in themselves, or any virtue derived from the piety or intention of him by whom they are administered" (WLC 161). They become effectual "only by the working of the Holy Ghost, and the blessing of Christ, by whom they are administered" (WLC 161).[40] In this respect, sacramental efficacy must be understood along the same lines as the efficacy of the preached word (see WLC 154, 155).[41] The sacraments present the word in tangible form to the senses of those present at their administration. To the degree that a person, by the operation of the Spirit, responds in faith to Christ and his benefits so represented in a sacrament, to that degree that person may acknowledge in this instance that sacrament's administration of grace in his or her life.[42]

The two sacraments in the church—baptism and the Lord's Supper—both function as signs and seals of the covenant of grace. Yet they differ from one another in some important ways. We will now explore some of the characteristic features of each sacrament. Corresponding to circumcision under the old covenant, baptism is the initiatory sacrament of the new covenant. Baptism is sign and seal of union with Christ (Gal 3:27); the forgiveness of sins in Christ (Rev 1:5); regeneration by the Spirit of Christ (Titus 3:5); adoption as sons in Christ (Gal 3:26–27); and resurrection in

---

40. "But the sacraments properly fulfill their office only when the Spirit, that inward teacher, comes to them, by whose power alone hearts are penetrated and affections moved and our souls opened for the sacraments to enter in. If the Spirit be lacking, the sacraments can accomplish nothing more in our minds than the splendor of the sun shining upon blind eyes, or a voice sounding in deaf ears," Calvin, *Institutes*, 4.14.9 (=2:1284).

41. "But we are not so raw as to know that the sacraments, inasmuch as they are the helps of faith, also offer us righteousness in Christ. Nay, as we are perfectly agreed that the sacraments are to be ranked in the same place as the word, so while the gospel is called the power of God unto salvation to everyone that believeth, we hesitate not to transfer the same title to the sacraments," Calvin, *Tracts and Letters*, 2:400.

42. See the valuable and concise discussion, contrasting Roman Catholic, Memorialist, and Reformed doctrines of sacramental efficacy, at A. A. Hodge, *Outlines of Theology* (1879: repr, Edinburgh: Banner of Truth, 1972), 591–92.

Christ (Rom 6:5).[43] In brief, baptism points to Christ, and the fullness of redemptive blessings that belong to each person who is savingly united to him. Christ, furthermore, underwent baptism at the commencement of his public ministry as an indicator of his identification with his people as their representative sin-bearer.[44] Upon his exaltation, Christ baptized his people on the day of Pentecost, pouring out the Spirit in fullness to bring blessing to the nations.[45] Baptism, then, points both to the blessings that Christ has secured for his people, and to Christ as the bestower of those blessings.

As the initiatory sacrament of the new covenant, baptism is to be administered to every member of the new covenant. That includes the children of at least one professing believer.[46] Baptism does not save such a child, since, as we have seen, it saves no person.[47] Neither does baptism make a child a member of the church. On the contrary, the grounds for the administration of baptism to the child of at least one believer is that they are, by birthright, a member of the visible church and therefore entitled to baptism.[48] Prior to the new covenant, the children of a covenant member were counted members of God's covenant (Gen 17:7). The new covenant does not revoke but reaffirms this principle.[49] Children of at least one believer are said to be covenantally "holy" (1 Cor 7:14). Paul addresses the children of the Ephesian church as among the members of that church, with Christian

---

43. This outline and Scripture proofs have been drawn from WLC 165.

44. Sinclair Ferguson, "Infant Baptism View," in *Baptism: Three Views*, ed. David F. Wright (Downers Grove, IL: InterVarsity Press, 2009), 91. Ferguson observes, compellingly, that circumcision and baptism bear the same signification in relation to Christ, "Infant Baptism View," 87–89.

45. Ferguson, "Infant Baptism View," 89.

46. For a recent rehearsal of the arguments for infant baptism and an engagement of credobaptist arguments against infant baptism, see now Fesko, *Word, Water, Spirit*, 337–67.

47. "Every time we baptize an infant we bear witness that salvation is from God, that we cannot do any good thing to secure it, that we receive it from his hands as a sheer gift of his grace, and that we all enter the kingdom of heaven therefore as little children, who do not do, but are done for," B. B. Warfield, "Christian Baptism," in *Selected Shorter Writings*, ed. John E. Meeter, 2 vols. (Philipsburg: P&R, 1970–1973), 1:329.

48. John Mitchell Mason, *Essays on the Church of God*, 85.

49. Note Warfield's often quoted summary of the argument for infant baptism, "The argument in a nutshell is simply this: God established His Church in the days of Abraham and put children into it. They must remain there until he puts them out. He has nowhere put them out. They are still then members of His Church and as such entitled to its ordinances. Among these ordinances is baptism, which standing in similar place in the New Dispensation to circumcision in the Old, is like it to be given to children," *Studies in Theology* (1932; repr., Grand Rapids: Baker Academic, 2000), 408.

duties and obligations (Eph 6:1–3). The apostles administered baptism to the households of at least one professing believer, indicating their acknowledgment of the continuing ecclesiastical membership of the children of these households. When one compares the new covenant with the old covenant—each an administration of a single gracious covenant—one finds in general that "expansion, not contraction, is in view."[50] This principle holds no less for the composition of the membership of each covenant.

If baptism is the initiatory sacrament of the new covenant, then the Lord's Supper, like Passover before it, is the nourishing sacrament of the new covenant. Both the Passover and the Lord's Supper bring together "the two ideas of expiation and communion."[51] Each ordinance looks at the death of Christ and fellowship with Christ from their respective covenantal vantage points—anticipation and fulfillment, respectively. The Lord's Supper, in particular, is an ordinance of remembrance of Christ, the Passover Lamb (1 Cor 11:24, 25; 5:7). But the Supper may not be reduced to mere re-presentation of Christ's death through the distributed elements of bread and wine. Neither is the humanity of Christ to be locally or physically identified with or united to the elements in the Supper. The Supper, Paul reasons, is communion or participation in Christ (1 Cor 10:16–17, 21). Believers commune with Christ in the Supper in precisely the same way that they commune with Christ on any other occasion—by the ministry of the Spirit of Christ.

> Q. 170. How do they that worthily communicate in the Lord's Supper feed upon the body and blood of Christ therein?
>
> A. As the body and blood of Christ are not corporally or carnally present in, with, or under the bread and wine in the Lord's Supper, and yet are spiritually present to the faith of the receiver, no less truly and really than the elements themselves are to their outward senses; so they that worthily communicate in the sacrament of the Lord's supper, do therein feed upon the body and blood of Christ,

50. Ferguson, "Infant Baptism View," 103. Ferguson writes these words to conclude a discussion of Peter's words in Acts 2:39, "For the promise is for you and for your children and for all who are far off, everyone whom the Lord our God calls to himself."

51. Warfield, "The Significance of the Lord's Supper," *Selected Shorter Writings*, 1:335.

> not after a corporal and carnal, but in a spiritual manner; yet truly and really, while by faith they receive and apply unto themselves Christ crucified, and all the benefits of his death. (WLC 170)

The Supper, then, is a covenant meal, in which believers come to the "table of the Lord" to meet with their living Savior (1 Cor 10:21). Feeding upon Christ by faith, they are nourished by him and all his benefits.

Unlike baptism, the Lord's Supper is not for every member of the covenant community. Paul establishes spiritual qualifications that are requisite to approaching the Lord's Table (1 Cor 11:27–32).[52] Only when covenant children are "of years and ability to examine themselves" may they be admitted by the church's elders to the Lord's Table (WLC 177).[53] To approach the Table when one lacks the requisite qualifications, Paul warns, invites "eat[ing] and drink[ing] judgment on himself" (1 Cor 11:29). While the children of at least one believer are, by birthright, members of the visible church, they are not entitled to the exercise of all the privileges of that membership until they reach maturation.[54] In this respect, the status of these non-communicant members is comparable to that of under-age citizens of a nation.[55] Each is recognized as belonging to the church or nation. Each has certain duties and responsibilities that follow from membership, and the church or nation has certain obligations toward them. In both cases, the church or nation may withhold the exercise of particular privileges

---

52. Proponents of paedocommunion, the position that all members of the covenant, including children, are entitled to come to the Lord's Table by virtue of their covenant membership, interpret these conditions in such a way as to argue that covenant children are able to meet them. For a response to this position, see George W. Knight, "1 Corinthians 11:17–34: The Lord's Supper: Abuses, Words of Institution and Warnings and the Inferences and Deductions with respect to Paedocommunion," in *Children and the Lord's Supper*, ed. Guy Waters and Ligon Duncan (Fearn, UK: Mentor, 2011), 75–95.

53. "Infants cannot examine themselves, nor discern the Lord's body, nor shew his death, all which … the apostle requires of communicants," Witsius, *Economy of the Covenants*, 2:458. Compare the earlier and concurring opinion of Calvin, *Institutes*, 4.16.30 (=2:1352–53).

54. In Presbyterian church, it is upon making a "credible profession of faith" that one is admitted to the Lord's Supper. As A. A. Hodge observes, "as God has not endowed any of these officers with the power of reading the heart, it follows that the qualifications of which they are the judges are simply those of competent knowledge, purity of life, and credible profession of faith. [By 'credible' is meant not that which convinces, but that which can be believed to be genuine.]" *Outlines of Theology*, 645.

55. Dabney, *Lectures in Theology*, 794. What follows here is indebted to Dabney's analogy.

(voting in elections, for instance) until the young person reaches a certain age or meets certain qualifications.

Prayer PRAYER IS, IN THE WORDS of the Westminster Confession of Faith, a "special part of religious worship" (21.3). Prayer admits of both a "more specific" and a "more general" sense.[56] In its specific sense, prayer "is equivalent to supplication, the act of the soul in presenting its desires to God, and asking God to gratify them and to supply all the necessities of the supplicant"; in its general sense, "prayer is used to express every act of the soul engaged in spiritual intercourse with God," and thus "includes all direct acts of worship."[57]

We may therefore speak, in this latter sense, of prayer as an element of worship. Prayer has been an element of public worship since human beings have gathered to worship God.[58] There is a diversity of prayers that surface in public worship—prayers of adoration, confession, supplication, intercession, and thanksgiving.[59] And, of course, the singing of psalms and hymns are "in their essence only metrical and musically-uttered prayers."[60] Because public prayer is so important to public worship, leading in prayer therefore is indispensable to the work of the minister in the church's worship.[61]

But there is a distinct sense in which the entirety of public worship should be characterized by prayer. That is to say, the worshipers' sense of need for and dependence upon God, and the corresponding cognizance of God's sufficiency and willingness to meet the needs of his people, should mark every element of public worship.[62] Nurturing and promoting such a

---

56. Hodge, *Confession of Faith*, 373.

57. Hodge, *Confession of Faith*, 373.

58. Samuel Miller, *Thoughts on Public Prayer* (Philadelphia: Presbyterian Board of Publication, 1849), 42.

59. Hodge, *Confession of Faith*, 373.

60. Hodge, *Confession of Faith*, 373.

61. Miller, *Thoughts on Public Prayer*, 9, 16. See the remarkably useful work of Hughes Oliphant Old, *Leading in Prayer: A Workbook for Worship* (Grand Rapids: Eerdmans, 1995).

62. Even within prayer, theologians have registered the critical distinction between the "gift" of prayer, and the "spirit" or "grace" of prayer, on which see Miller, *Thoughts on Public Prayer*, 19, 20.

sensibility within the church helps to ensure that the ordinances of public worship do not devolve into mechanical and lifeless forms.

THE DAY OF WORSHIP

God not only dictates what is and is not to be done in the church's worship, but he also dictates the time at which the church is to gather for that sacred duty. The fourth commandment stipulates that Israel was to set apart one day in seven, the last day of the week, to rest from their earthly labors and to gather together for the public worship of God (Exod 20:8–11; Deut 5:12–15). The Sabbath was a day to remember God's work of creation (Exodus) and God's work of redemption (Deuteronomy).[63]

Some have argued that the Sabbath was a command unique to old covenant Israel, abrogated upon the conclusion of that covenant and the inauguration of the new covenant. Under the new covenant, it is said, the Sabbath has found its fulfillment, and the church is therefore no longer bound to observe the weekly Sabbath.[64] Following the practice of the apostles and the earliest centuries of the church, believers gather to worship God on "the Lord's Day" (Rev 1:10). But the Lord's Day, this view maintains, should not be understood as the Christian Sabbath, as the Westminster Confession of Faith does (21.7).

What, then, are the biblical reasons for the Sabbath continuing as a command binding the church under the new covenant? First, the Sabbath, while promulgated under the Mosaic law, is not unique to the Mosaic law. It is an ordinance of the creation. The form of the command in Exodus 20:8–11 grounds the obligation of the Sabbath in God's own pattern of work and rest in Genesis 1:1–2:3, and the text of Genesis 2:1–3 points to God's seventh-day rest as establishing a pattern of a weekly holy resting for human beings.[65]

---

63. For further discussion of these verses and a biblical-theological argument for the perpetuity of a weekly day of rest and worship, see my *The Sabbath as Rest and Hope for the People of God*, SSBT (Wheaton, IL: Crossway, 2022).

64. On the non-obligation of the Sabbath under the new covenant, see D. A. Carson, ed., *From Sabbath to Lord's Day: A Biblical, Historical, and Theological Investigation* (Grand Rapids: Zondervan, 1982) and, more recently, Thomas R. Schreiner, "Good-bye and Hello: The Sabbath Command for New Covenant Believers," in *Progressive Covenantalism: Charting a Course Between Dispensational and Covenantal Theologies*, ed. Stephen J. Wellum and Brent E. Parker (Nashville: B&H, 2016), 159–88.

65. On which, see Gregory K. Beale, *A New Testament Biblical Theology: The Unfolding of the New Testament in the New* (Grand Rapids: Baker Academic, 2011), 775–81. Geerhardus Vos

As an ordinance of the creation, then, the Sabbath predates the Mosaic law and therefore obliges all human beings as bearers of the image of God.

Second, when Jesus teaches about the Sabbath, he neither criticizes nor abolishes the command. His criticisms are reserved for the Jewish leadership's additions to and distortions of the Sabbath commandment (see, for instance, Mark 2:23–3:6). Although Jesus is accused of violating the Sabbath, he breaks only the human traditions that have built up around the Sabbath, never the Sabbath command itself. Furthermore, Jesus speaks only positively about the Sabbath.[66] He affirms it as an ordinance of the creation: "The Sabbath was made for man, not man for the Sabbath" (Mark 2:27). It is a day "to do good ... to save life" (Mark 3:4). Jesus declares himself to be "lord even of the Sabbath" (Mark 2:28). As the divine lawgiver, Jesus has the authority to declare what is and is not proper activity on the Sabbath.

Third, the New Testament testifies to the fact that Jesus Christ rose from the dead on the first day of the week (Luke 23:55–24:1). Furthermore, Jesus meets with his disciples on the first day of the week, speaking to them and bestowing blessing upon them (see Luke 24:13–35; 24:36–43; John 20:11–18, 19–23, 26–29). The apostles lead the church in gathering to worship God in Christ on the first day of the week (Acts 20:7–12; 1 Cor 16:1–4), even as the synagogue continues to gather on the seventh day of the week. As the seventh day of the week commemorated God's work of creation, so the first day of the week commemorates God's work of *new* creation, inaugurated in the resurrection of Christ from the dead (see WLC 116).[67]

The apostle John speaks of "the Lord's Day" (Rev 1:10), that is, the day of the week that is peculiarly the Lord Jesus Christ's.[68] This day can be none other than the first day of the week, Sunday, the day on which Christ rose from the dead. That the New Testament understands the Lord's Day to be

---

notes, furthermore, that "the so-called 'Covenant of Works'" in Genesis 2:15–17 "was nothing but an embodiment of the Sabbatical principle. Had its probation been successful, then the sacramental Sabbath would have passed over into the reality it typified," *Biblical Theology*, 140.

66. "The Sabbath came out of Christ's hands ... not despoiled of any of its authority or robbed of any of its glory, but rather enhanced in both authority and glory," Warfield, "The Sabbath in the Word of God," *Selected Shorter Writings*, 1:318.

67. The change in day does not mean that God has substantially changed the fourth commandment. The fourth commandment stipulates one day in seven as reserved for the worship of God. The particular day of the week is circumstantial and is set by God's own authority.

68. Roger T. Beckwith and Wilfrid Scott, *This Is the Day: The Biblical Doctrine of the Christian Sunday* (London: Marshall, Morgan & Scott, 1978), 36.

the Sabbath under the new covenant appears from a couple of considerations. First, Hebrews speaks of a "Sabbath rest" that "remains ... for the people of God" (Heb 4:9). In context, this "Sabbath rest" describes the entirely future eschatological rest that concludes the church's wilderness pilgrimage.[69] The writer identifies this rest with God's rest of Genesis 2:1–3 (Heb 4:3–4). The Sabbath as an ordinance of the creation, then, continues to bind believers under the new covenant until the end of the world, when the church will enter its eschatological Sabbath rest. Upon the resurrection of Christ from the dead, the Sabbath carries the additional name, "Lord's Day." Second, the apostles continue to point the church to the Decalogue as the rule and norm of Christian duty (Rom 13:8–10; Eph 6:2; Jas 1:25; 2:8–13). Since the Sabbath commandment is among those Ten Commandments, the Sabbath continues to bind the church under the new covenant.[70]

The church, therefore, observes the Lord's Day as a weekly day of rest and public worship. It does so not because of expediency, tradition, antiquity, or ecclesiastical authority.[71] It does so because it is a divine command, given to the church in Scripture. On this day, the church not only meets with one another, but it also meets with the risen Christ for direction, encouragement, and strengthening in grace.

CONCLUSION

Jesus declared in his earthly ministry that the Father seeks people to "worship in spirit and truth" (John 4:24). The people of God worships God only according to the provisions that he has explicitly made known in Scripture, a book authored by the Holy Spirit. In word and sacrament, the church approaches God in Christ by the grace and power of the Holy Spirit. The Holy Spirit, the "Lord and Giver of Life," governs and quickens the church in worship, even as

69. Richard B. Gaffin, Jr., "A Sabbath Rest Still Awaits the People of God," in *Pressing Toward the Mark: Essays Commemorating Fifty Years of the Orthodox Presbyterian Church*, ed. C. G. Dennison and R. C. Gamble (Philadelphia: The Committee for the Historian of the Orthodox Presbyterian Church, 1986), 41–46.

70. Passages that appear to abrogate the Sabbath (Rom 14:5–6; Col 2:16–17; Gal 4:9–11) in actuality abrogate the regular feasts and festivals appointed in the Mosaic law for Israel's gathered worship of God, on which see Waters, *The Sabbath as Rest and Hope for the People of God*, 125–27.

71. Presbyterian writers particularly emphasized the fact that the church has no power to establish holy days and to compel Christians to observe them, on which see, representatively, Samuel Miller, *Presbyterianism*, 73–78.

he ensures the growth and flourishing of the church in all departments of her life and work. The next chapter will explore the gifts that the Spirit has given to the church, and the discipline that he has appointed for the church.

FURTHER READING

Calvin, John. "On the Necessity of Reforming the Church." In *John Calvin: Tracts and Letters*, 123–234. 7 vols. Reprint, Edinburgh: Banner of Truth, 2009. The Genevan Reformer's concise defense of the Protestant Reformation. Calvin argues that the church's worship was one of the leading considerations driving the Reformation of the church in the sixteenth century.

Clowney, Edmund P. "Presbyterian Worship." In *Worship: Adoration and Action*, edited by D. A. Carson, 110–22. Grand Rapids: Baker Academic, 1993. A brief and concise exposition and defense of the Regulative Principle of Worship. Clowney offers exegetical, biblical-theological, and systematic theological arguments in support of the biblical doctrine.

Ferguson, Sinclair. "Infant Baptism View." In *Baptism: Three Views*, edited by David F. Wright, 77–112. Downers Grove, IL: InterVarsity Press, 2009. An irenic and biblical defense of the doctrine of paedobaptism. In advancing his case, Ferguson helpfully probes the implications of this question for one's understanding of the nature and composition of the church.

Ryken, Philip Graham, Derek W. H. Thomas, and J. Ligon Duncan, III, eds. *Give Praise to God: A Vision for Reforming Worship*. Phillipsburg, NJ: P&R, 2003. A collection of essays by Reformed pastors and theologians addressing the subject of worship in the church. The authors defend a Reformed understanding of worship and engage trends and practices within the contemporary evangelical church.

XII

THE LIFE OF THE CHURCH

MEMBERS OF THE CHURCH, BY virtue of their union with Christ, are bound not only to Christ, but also to one another. As members of the one body of Christ, they "have one common life."[1] The Westminster Confession of Faith summarizes the biblical testimony well.

> All saints, that are united to Jesus Christ their Head, by his Spirit, and by faith, have fellowship with him in his grace, sufferings, death, resurrection, and glory: and, being united to one another in love, they have communion in each other's gifts and graces, and are obliged to the performance of such duties, public and private, as do conduce to their mutual good, both in the inward and outward man. (WCF 26.1)

The life of the church consists, in no small measure, in believers' participation in one another's "gifts and graces." In this chapter we will explore in particular the nature and place of gifts in the life, growth, and well-being of the church. Since the church presently exists in a state of eschatological imperfection, sin remains in every believer. The life of the church is necessarily affected by such remaining sin. This state of affairs is the occasion for the system of discipline that Christ has instituted in his church. We will also give attention to the nature, workings, and ends of church discipline.

---

1. A. A. Hodge, *The Confession of Faith*, 324.

GIFTS IN THE CHURCH

WHILE ONE MAY SPEAK OF "gifts" (*charismata*) "in a broad sense" to encompass "the benefits of grace imparted to all believers (Rom 5:15–16; 6:23)," the term more frequently denotes "those special gifts that are granted to believers in a variable measure and degree for each other's benefit."[2] The risk attendant to giving concerted attention to gifts in the church is to neglect the Giver of those gifts, the Holy Spirit, who is himself the preeminent Gift of Christ to the church.[3] Any discussion of gifts in the church must therefore first address the Spirit as both Gift and Giver of gifts. The Acts of the Apostles speaks of the Spirit as "Gift" to the church. The phrase "the gift of the Holy Spirit" is once used in reference to a Jewish audience, and, on another occasion, to a gentile audience (Acts 2:38; 10:45). The whole church, then, is the recipient and beneficiary of the Father's and the Son's bestowal of the Spirit.[4]

It is this point that Paul underscores at the commencement of his instruction on gifts in 1 Corinthians 12–14, "for in one Spirit we were all baptized into one body—Jews or Greeks, slaves or free—and all were made to drink of one Spirit" (1 Cor 12:13).[5] What Paul is describing characterizes every believer by virtue of the believer's union with Jesus Christ.[6] The Spirit is "the gift in which all participate by virtue of their belonging to the one body of Christ," such that "the sequence in this conception is ...

---

2. Bavinck, *Reformed Dogmatics*, 4:299.

3. "And so on the day of Pentecost [the Spirit] communicated himself with all his charismata to the church of Christ," Bavinck, *Reformed Dogmatics*, 4:299.

4. Of course, Christ, the Baptizer of the Spirit, was himself baptized with the Spirit at the commencement of his public ministry, on which see Ferguson, *The Holy Spirit*, 45–52, and Graham Cole, *He Who Gives Life: The Doctrine of the Holy Spirit* (Wheaton, IL: Crossway, 2007), 156–59.

5. The expression "baptize in the Spirit" appears in the New Testament six other times, each of which refers indisputably to Pentecost (Matt 3:11; Mark 1:8; Luke 3:16; John 1:33, Acts 1:5;11:16). Paul's statement in 1 Corinthians 12:13, therefore, should be taken to refer to the gift of the Spirit at Pentecost. Furthermore, the Greek text presents a syntactical difficulty. The phrase ἐν ἑνὶ πνεύματι may be rendered "by the Spirit" (agency) or "in the Spirit" (medium). Because Christ is the one who gives the Spirit to the church, and because Paul's expression in 1 Corinthians 12:13b ("and all were made to drink of one Spirit") speaks of the Spirit as "the gift granted to all by virtue of their being in the body," the latter option, followed by the ESV, is preferable, Gaffin, *Perspectives on Pentecost*, 29; compare Ridderbos, *Paul*, 373.

6. Gaffin, *In the Fullness of Time*, 142–43. Note Donald Macleod's forceful concluding summary of the point, "without 'baptism in the Spirit' we are not Christians at all; and that to have had it is to have received the Spirit in His fulness," *The Spirit of Promise* (Fearn, Ross-shire, UK: Christian Focus, 1986), 10.

Christ → the body-in-Christ → the Spirit."[7] Thus, Paul argues, "all in the church are in possession of the gift of the Holy Spirit as the foundation of their Christian life and experience."[8]

It is within this framework of the common, present possession of the Gift of the Spirit within the church that Paul addresses the manifold gifts of the Spirit to the church in 1 Corinthians 12–14. Here, Paul underscores the Spirit as the one who not only gives all gifts to the church but also makes them effective in the church (1 Cor 12:11).[9] Gifts, furthermore, are given to and for the body of Christ (1 Cor 12:7).[10] While no one person has all the gifts (1 Cor 12:29–30), every gift is given for the benefit of all believers. In particular, gifts are bestowed for the purpose of edifying the body (1 Cor 14:3, 12, 17, 19; Eph 4:7–16). In their orientation, gifts, then, are not self-referential, but other-referential. Their primary concern is the maturity and establishment of one's fellow believers.

The gifts of the Spirit, nevertheless, must be distinguished from the graces of the Spirit.[11] The saving graces of the Spirit are "a far greater privilege than any" spiritual gift.[12] This distinction informs Paul's argument in 1 Corinthians 13:1–13. Having discussed spiritual gifts in 1 Corinthians 12:1–31a, Paul turns to "a still more excellent way" (12:31b). In 1 Corinthians 13, Paul celebrates the grace of love. Without love, the most extravagant gift is "nothing" and "gain[s] nothing" (13:2, 3). Unlike such gifts as "prophecies," "tongues," and "knowledge," "love never ends" (13:8). Among the abiding graces of "faith, hope, and love ... the greatest of these is love" (13:13).

This distinction comes into clearer focus when one defines "gifts" according to their New Testament usage. Although the New Testament never proffers a formal definition of "gifts," one may nevertheless define

---

7. Ridderbos, *Paul*, 373, 372.

8. Gaffin, *In the Fullness of Time*, 143.

9. Paul accents the Trinitarian shape of the giving of gifts of the church at 1 Corinthians 12:4–6. The Father, in Christ, gives each gift by the Spirit to the church.

10. "Properly speaking, the charismata are given to the *churches*, not to individual persons," Kuyper, *The Work of the Holy Spirit*, 181. Compare Anthony C. Thiselton, *The Holy Spirit—In Biblical Teaching, through the Centuries, and Today* (Grand Rapids: Eerdmans, 2013), 71.

11. See at length the discussion of John Owen, *The Works of John Owen* (1850–1853; repr., Edinburgh: Banner of Truth, 1967), 4:425–38.

12. Jonathan Edwards, *Ethical Writings*, WJE 8, ed. Paul Ramsey (New Haven: Yale, 1989), 157. For the whole of Edwards's sermon on 1 Corinthians 13:1–2 ("Love More Excellent Than Extraordinary Gifts of the Spirit"), see WJE 8, 149–73.

"gifts" as "certain capacities, bestowed by God's grace and power, which fit people for specific and corresponding service."[13] Gifts may be natural or acquired, but in every case they are the provision of God the Spirit.[14] Gifts, furthermore, may be possessed by persons who are not regenerate (Matt 7:21–23).[15] Judas Iscariot exercised the same gifts of teaching and miracles that the other eleven disciples exercised, but Jesus pronounced him a "devil" in the midst of his public ministry (John 6:70–71). Ideally, gifts and graces together indwell the same person and, as such, "are exceedingly helpful to each other."[16] But gifts may exist in the absence of grace and still accomplish their God-appointed purposes.

The New Testament offers exemplary lists of gifts, lists that appear to be "selective and illustrative rather than exhaustive" (see 1 Cor 12:8–10, 28–30; Rom 12:6–8; Eph 4:11; 1 Pet 4:11).[17] But if these lists are not comprehensive, neither are they scattershot. The gifts in these lists coalesce around one central idea—"the revelatory word through apostle and prophet is foundational (Eph 2:20), while all else is informed by and flows from this."[18] Thus, in Ephesians 4:7–16, Paul argues that the ascended Christ has gifted the church with "the apostles, the prophets, the evangelists, the shepherds, and teachers" (Eph 4:11) in order "to equip the saints for the work of ministry, for building up the body of Christ" (4:12). These word-gifts present the truth of God to their fellow believers who then, "speaking the truth in love ... grow up in every way into him who is the head, into Christ" (4:15).[19] Word-officers instrumentally equip all believers with the truth so that, by that same truth, the church may mature in Christ.

---

13. John R. W. Stott, *Baptism & Fullness: The Work of the Holy Spirit Today*, 2nd ed. (Downers Grove, IL: InterVarsity Press, 1975), 87. Compare Kuyper, "the charismata or spiritual gifts are the divinely ordained means and powers whereby the King enables His Church to perform its task on the earth," *The Work of the Holy Spirit*, 184.

14. See Owen, *Works*, 4:518–20; Bavinck, *Reformed Dogmatics*, 4:299; Stott, *Baptism & Fullness*, 90–94.

15. Edwards, WJE 8, 152–53, 165–66.

16. Owen, *Works*, 4:438.

17. Ronald Y. K. Fung, "Ministry in the New Testament," in *The Church in the Bible and the World*, ed. D. A. Carson (Grand Rapids: Baker Academic, 1983), 156.

18. Ferguson, *The Holy Spirit*, 208–9. It is important to recall that certain gifts entail the entrance into and exercise of church office, considered in a previous chapter. Note Fung's helpful rejoinder to Ernst Käsemann's dichotomization of spiritual gifts and office, "Ministry," 163–77.

19. See here the comments of Fung, "Ministry," 160–61.

One question that surfaces in connection with the gifts in the church is whether any of the gifts and associated offices within the apostolic church has ceased in the post-apostolic church. To frame the question differently, is the theological distinction between "extraordinary gifts" and "ordinary gifts" a biblically defensible one?[20] We may begin by noting that certain offices in the apostolic age were foundational and, by design, not intended for the duration of the church's existence. These offices include the offices of apostle and of prophet. Paul describes "apostles and prophets" as constituting "the foundation" of the church (Eph 2:20; compare Matt 16:18; Rev 21:14).[21] They laid this foundation as they delivered new covenant revelation from Christ, by the Spirit, to the church.[22] Christ having laid the complete and sufficient revelatory foundation for the new covenant church through his apostles and prophets, the need for these offices—and the offices themselves—has come to an end.[23]

Correspondingly, the gifts of tongues and miracles have ceased with the death of the apostolic generation. Tongues were given by the Spirit to the church on the day of Pentecost (Acts 2:4), at Peter's visitation to the household of Cornelius (Acts 10:43, 44–46), and were in exercise in

---

20. See, representatively, Edwards, WJE 8, 153; Owen, *Works*, 4:474–86; George Smeaton, *The Doctrine of the Holy Spirit* (Edinburgh: T & T Clark, 1882), 244; Witherow, *The Form of the Christian Temple*, 46–52; Kuyper, *The Work of the Holy Spirit*, 187–89; B. B. Warfield, *Counterfeit Miracles* (New York: Scribner's, 1918), 1–31.

21. For a survey of exegetical discussion surrounding these verses, see Gaffin, *Perspectives on Pentecost*, 93–97.

22. See particularly John 14:25; 16:12–15; 1 Corinthians 14:37; and 2 Thessalonians 3:14, and the discussion of these passages at Guy Prentiss Waters, *For the Mouth of the Lord Has Spoken: The Doctrine of Scripture* (Fearn, UK: Christian Focus, 2020), 89–96.

23. Wayne Grudem has influentially argued for two kinds of prophetic activity in the New Testament. The first (the "apostle-prophet") brings verbal revelation to the church and, in this respect, is identical with the prophets of the Old Testament. The second (the "prophet") is the recipient of infallible revelation that this prophet fallibly utters to the church. The former has ceased, but the latter continues in the church today, *The Gift of Prophecy in the New Testament and Today*, rev. ed. (Wheaton, IL: Crossway, 2000); *Systematic Theology*, 2nd ed. (Grand Rapids: Zondervan, 2020), 1293–1313. For a response, see my *For the Mouth of the Lord Has Spoken*, 192–200 and the literature cited at 195n144. In brief, Grudem's proposal is objectionable for at least three reasons. First, it argues for a syntactically dubious reading of Ephesians 2:20, on which see Harold W. Hoehner, *Ephesians: An Exegetical Commentary* (Grand Rapids: Baker Academic, 2002), 399–403, and Clowney, *The Church*, 261–63. Second, God's revelation to his people, according to the New Testament, is limited to the foundational, apostolic generation of the church. Third, Grudem's doctrine of "prophecy mixed with error" poses insuperable textual and theological problems, Thomas R. Schreiner, *Spiritual Gifts: What They Are & Why They Matter* (Nashville, TN: B&H, 2018), 101–22.

the church in Corinth (1 Cor 14:1–40). In Acts, the same word "tongue" is used to refer to the languages spoken by the multi-national audience gathered in Jerusalem (Acts 2:8, 11). What is communicated to this audience in these "tongues" are "the mighty works of God," a Septuagintal phrase denoting "God's mighty acts in delivering his people" (Deut 11:2; Pss 71:19; 105:1; 106:21).[24] These tongues are "the fulfillment of Joel's prophecy (Joel 2:28–32)," and thus are "a form of prophecy."[25] What Luke is describing, then, is the conveyance of divine revelation to these hearers in Jerusalem, revelation of which the apostle Peter's sermon (Acts 2:14–36) is a specimen. The same pattern inheres at 1 Corinthians 14:1–40. An interpreted tongue, according to Paul, is the "functional equivalent" of prophecy (1 Cor 14:5).[26] The content of tongues in Corinth was "mysteries" (14:2), a technical term in the New Testament denoting revelation.[27] Tongues and prophecy, then, for all their differences, "both are revelatory word-gifts."[28] As revelatory gift, tongues (like prophecy) have ceased with the close of the New Testament canon in the apostolic age.

A similar rationale informs the position that the gift of miracles has ceased in the church.[29] Miracles served as the way in which Christ confirmed and credentialed his apostles as divine messengers (Acts 14:3; Rom 15:18–19; 2 Cor 12:12; Heb 2:3–4). Across redemptive history, miracles appear alongside new revelation that God gives to the church.[30] The justification for miracles, in other words, is the grant of divine revelation to the people of God. Once special revelation ceases, there is no continuing warrant for

---

24. C. K. Barrett, *A Critical and Exegetical Commentary on the Acts of the Apostles*, 2 vols., ICC (Edinburgh: T&T Clark, 1994, 1998), 1:124.

25. Gaffin, *Perspectives on Pentecost*, 82.

26. Ferguson, *The Holy Spirit*, 214.

27. Gaffin, *Perspectives on Pentecost*, 79.

28. Gaffin, *Perspectives on Pentecost*, 80.

29. This is not to say that God is not free to work a miracle when, where, how, and upon whom he wishes. It is to say that the gift of exercising miracles, on display in the apostolic period in the New Testament, has ceased. On this point, see Richard B. Gaffin, Jr., "A Cessationist View," in *Are Miraculous Gifts For Today? Four Views*, ed. Wayne A. Grudem (Grand Rapids: Zondervan, 1996), 41–42.

30. Warfield, *Counterfeit Miracles*, 25–26. Note on these and the following pages the corroborating quotes that Warfield furnishes from Calvin, Kuyper, and Bavinck.

the giving of miracles to the church. The gifting of miracles ceases because special revelation has ceased.[31]

It would be a mistake to leave the impression that the Spirit no longer gifts the church. The extraordinary gifts, having served their purpose in redemptive history, have ceased. But the Spirit continues to furnish the church richly with ordinary gifts and to make these gifts effective in their use. Chief among these, we have observed above, are the gifts of proclaiming the finished revelatory word of God. "God's way of teaching in today's church is not by fresh revelation but by exposition of his revelation completed in Christ and in Scripture."[32] It is the plentiful and unending supply of such word gifts that ensures that the people of God individually are equipped to exercise the gifts that the Spirit has given to them, and that the people of God corporately mature into their living head, Jesus Christ (Eph 4:7–16).

DISCIPLINE IN THE CHURCH

It may seem incongruous to follow a discussion of the Spirit's gifts to the church with a discussion of the church's discipline. But on closer inspection, the two are connected in a couple of important ways. First, central to the gifts of the ascended Christ to the church is the word of God. In the church today, gifted men read, proclaim, and enforce the Scripture. Discipline is one important way that the word is brought to bear on the lives of God's people. In particular, when professing Christians sin in violation of Scripture, discipline is one means that Christ has appointed to draw them to repentance and to restore them to obedience to the word. Second, the goal of the gifts is the edification and maturation of the body of Christ. Two goals of discipline, we shall see, are the recovery of the offender and the purity of the church. Both of these goals subserve the church's edification and maturation. In this respect, discipline is a complement to the gifts that Christ has given to the church.

---

31. This is certainly not to deny that while "God, in his ordinary providence, maketh use of means," he "yet is free to work without, above, and against them, at His pleasure" (WCF 5.3). But it is to say that the Scripture affords no expectation that God will work miracles in the post-apostolic church.

32. Stott, *Baptism & Fullness*, 102.

In addressing the church's discipline, it is important to rehearse two matters addressed in a previous chapter. First, the church's discipline is a lawful exercise of the power (*potestas diacritica*) that Christ has given to the church. Second, the power of discipline is exercised jointly by the elders, and not by the congregation.

> To these [church] officers the keys of the kingdom of heaven are committed; by virtue whereof, they have power, respectively, to retain, and remit sins; to shut that kingdom against the impenitent, both by the Word, and censures; and to open it unto penitent sinners, by the ministry of the Gospel; and by absolution from censures, as occasion shall require. (WCF 30.2)

Congregationalists, however, frequently press the congregation's right to exercise discipline. There is a plausibility to this claim from Jesus's words in the foundational New Testament passage for discipline in the church, "If he refuses to listen to them, tell it to the church. And if he refuses to listen to the church, let him be to you as a Gentile and a tax collector" (Matt 18:17). Here, it is argued, "the church" (ἐκκλησία) refers to the local congregation as such. The congregation, then, is the body that directly handles matters of discipline in the church.

In reply, it must be stressed that Jesus's words "the church" do not require the congregation as such exercising the power of discipline. For one thing, the New Testament consistently identifies the church's elders as the ones tasked with the exercise of power in the church. As we saw in chapter 10, power resides in the church as a whole, but, apart from the church's election of its officers, is exercised only through the church's officers. As Witherow has argued, while "the power of rule is given to the church in the first instance ... the authority given is exercised through the officers. The officers, instituted by the command and with the approval of Christ, are the organs through which the Church acts."[33]

33. Witherow, *The Form of the Christian Temple*, 147. Witherow, as does his contemporary Thomas E. Peck, employs the analogy of the human body, "these powers are always exercised through one or other particular organ to which a special function is assigned," *The Form of the Christian Temple*, 147–48; compare Peck, *Notes on Ecclesiology*, 85, 170. Both Witherow and Peck reference in this connection James H. Thornwell, "Church Boards and Presbyterianism,"

That "church" in Matthew 18:16–18 denotes not the "assembly of all believers" but the "governors of believers" is supported by the context.[34] Matthew's Gospel has one other reference to binding and loosing (Matt 18:18), namely, Matthew 16:19, "I will give you the keys of the kingdom of heaven, and whatever you bind on earth shall be bound in heaven, and whatever you loose on earth shall be loosed in heaven." Readers are meant, then, to understand the process described in Matthew 18:16–18 in terms of the exercise of the keys that Christ bestows upon the apostles, "the only Church rulers appointed during the public ministry of the Lord."[35] This association, coupled with the fact that "bind" and "loose" is "judicial language," commends "church" in Matthew 18:17 not as the congregation of all believers, but as the assembly of the ruling officers of the church.[36] The New Testament subsequently tells us that the apostles have "committed ... the authority of rule" to elders.[37] The exercise of discipline, therefore, belongs not to the congregation as such, but to "the Church act[ing] through its officers appointed to rule, that is, through its eldership or presbytery."[38]

To define discipline strictly in terms of judicial process, however, is to define the church's discipline too narrowly. Broadly speaking, "discipline is systematic training under the authority of God's Scripture." It "is the exercise of authority given the church by the Lord Jesus Christ to instruct and guide its members and to promote its purity and welfare."[39] As such, discipline carries the broad sense of "the whole government, inspection, training, guardianship and control which the church maintains over its members, its officers, and its courts," and the "restricted and technical

---

in *Collected Writings of James Henley Thornwell*, 4 vols., ed. John B. Adger and John L. Girardeau (1871–1873; repr., Edinburgh: Banner of Truth, 1974), 4:272–73.

34. T. David Gordon, "When 'Church' Is a Judicial Assembly," unpublished paper.

35. Witherow, *The Form of the Christian Temple*, 150.

36. Witherow, *The Form of the Christian Temple*, 150. See Gordon's discussion of the judicial language throughout this passage. Given that judicial process was the task of Israel's elders under the old covenant, Witherow further observes, judicial process by the church's rulers is precisely what we would expect in this passage, *The Form of the Christian Temple*, 150.

37. Witherow, *The Form of the Christian Temple*, 151. Compare Cunningham, "Church Power," in *Discussions of Church Principles*, 242–43.

38. Witherow, *The Form of the Christian Temple*, 151. Compare the argument of Macpherson, *Presbyterianism*, 106–10.

39. *BCO* 27-4, 27-1.

sense" of "judicial process."[40] Christ tasks the elders of the church to "teach" the people of God "to observe all that I have commanded you" (Matt 28:20). Elders, then, do not simply teach the contents of Christ's commands, but offer practical guidance and direction to the people of God. Individual members of the church bear personal responsibility for obeying Christ's commands. The New Testament roots discipline in each Christian's call to self-governance. Among the fruit of the Spirit is "self control" (Gal 5:23). When self-discipline fails, the fellowship of believers in the local church helps to bring needed instruction and correction in that person's life (see Rom 15:14; Col 3:16; 1 Thess 5:11).[41] When this level of discipline fails, then elders, as undershepherds, must be prepared to pursue the formal discipline of the offender. It is this formal process that Jesus legislates in Matthew 18:15–20, and that we see implemented under apostolic supervision in the churches of Corinth (1 Cor 5:1–13), Thessalonica (2 Thess 3:6–14), Ephesus (1 Tim 5:20), and Crete (Titus 3:10).

Discipline is common to all human societies, as Calvin observed.[42] It is not the existence of discipline that is unique to the church, but the nature, exercise, and purposes of discipline that are unique to the church. In the first place, discipline, whether considered in its general or in its more restricted sense, takes its definition and point of departure from the word of God to which it is inseparably attached—"as the saving doctrine of Christ is the soul of the church, so does discipline serve as its sinews, through which the members of the body hold together, each in its own place."[43] For this reason, discipline in the church may only proceed when a church member's belief or conduct is "contrary to the Word of God."[44]

---

40. *BCO* 27-1.

41. So Bavinck, *Reformed Dogmatics*, 4:421.

42. "If no society, indeed, no house which has even a small family, can be kept in proper condition without discipline, it is much more necessary in the church, whose condition should be as ordered as possible," *Institutes* 4.12.1 (=2:1229–30). Compare Turretin, *Institutes*, 18.32.9 (=3:296–97). Compare also Bavinck's argument for the necessity of discipline in the church from the various metaphors that the New Testament uses of the church, *Reformed Dogmatics*, 4:421.

43. Calvin, *Institutes*, 4.12.1 (=2:1230).

44. *BCO* 29-1. Ramsay, observing that many matters that come before the church courts that are "at the same time political or civil and ecclesiastical." Since church courts may only address ecclesiastical matters, what, then, is an ecclesiastical matter? Ramsay concludes his answer to that question by stating, "That question is ecclesiastical which the church cannot expound and apply the whole Scripture without answering; and that is not

The church's practice of discipline is limited to and by the word of God. As such, discipline in the church is "exclusively a spiritual power."[45] Because all church power is only "ministerial and declarative," the courts of the church are to declare the will of God revealed in Scripture. The church has no right to "exercise force" as the civil magistrate exercises force, that is, to "inflict temporal pains and penalties," because the church's "authority is in all respects moral or spiritual."[46]

Positively, the church's discipline must be understood in the context of what the church is authorized to grant to people. The church admits qualified persons into the membership and offices of the church.[47] In discipline, the church may "exclude the disobedient and disorderly from such offices and sacramental privileges," up to and including the removal of a member from the fellowship of the church.[48] Critically, the church is authorized to remove from an offender only what it has first bestowed upon an offender, whether membership, admission to the Lord's Table, or office.[49] Even so, its declarations and actions are not infallible. The "Church is merely acting according to its views of how Christ would in the circumstances act. ... [In so acting,] it may have erred also, having misapplied the law of Christ; and if so, the act done, although it may wrongfully give or withhold outward privileges, has no spiritual efficacy or virtue to throw open or to close the door of sacred privilege."[50]

There are several interrelated purposes of discipline in the church, summarized in WCF 30.3, "Church censures are necessary, for the reclaiming and gaining of offending brethren, for deterring of others from like offenses, for purging out of that leaven which might infect the whole lump, for vindicating the honour of Christ, and the holy profession of the gospel, and for preventing the wrath of God." The first of these concerns

---

ecclesiastical which may be differently answered by men that agree in their understanding of the Scriptures," *An Exposition of the Form of Government*, 68, 69.

45. Bannerman, *The Church of Christ*, 2:197.

46. *BCO* 3-4, 11-1.

47. A crucial implication of this point is that only church members are subject to the discipline of the church. The church has no authority to administer discipline to persons outside the church's membership.

48. *BCO* 11-2. Compare the discussion at Bannerman, *The Church of Christ*, 2:186-89.

49. Witherow, *The Form of the Christian Temple*, 159.

50. Bannerman, *The Church of Christ*, 2:196.

the reclaiming and restoration of the offender. Discipline, Jesus teaches, is a means of bringing a sinning church member to repentance of his sin and to restoration in the fellowship of the church (Matt 18:15–20). The second concerns the purity of the church as a holy society that treats sin with the seriousness that it merits (1 Pet 2:9; 1 Cor 5:1–13; 1 Tim 5:20). The third concerns the glory of God and the honor of Christ, which is to have preeminence in everything that is done within the church (1 Cor 10:31).

Given these ends or purposes, church discipline may never be retributive in its practice. This is the case partly because discipline is designed to reclaim the offender, not to punish him. As Peck notes, the church's "discipline is not the punishment of an avenging judge, asserting the unbending majesty of the law, but the discipline of a tender mother, whose bowels yearn over the wayward child, and who inflicts no pain except for the child's reformation and salvation."[51] But it is also the case because church discipline is not eschatological justice. God alone is the judge and arbiter of men and angels. The last judgment awaits the consummation of all things at the end of the age. Church discipline is an eschatological signpost of the judgment to come. It is not God's final verdict upon a person, but it does point that person to the tribunal before which God's final verdict will one day be pronounced.[52] The church's pronouncements and censures in discipline are ordered precisely so that the offender "may be saved in the day of the Lord" (1 Cor 5:5).

A thorough discussion of the steps, procedures, and censures of formal discipline is beyond the scope of this chapter. We may, however, offer four general reflections on the Scripture's testimony to these concerns. First, there are different kinds or classes of offenses. Sometimes sins are directed against a particular person (Matt 18:18), but sometimes sins are general in the harm or offense they bring, as when the Judaizers preached another gospel in the churches in Galatia (Gal 1:8, 9). Sometimes, sins are private and known only to a few people, but sometimes sins are public and are

51. Peck, *Notes on Ecclesiology*, 150.

52. Note Calvin, "although excommunication also punishes the man, it does so in a way that, by forewarning him of his future condemnation, it may call him back to salvation. But if that be obtained, reconciliation and restoration to communion await him," *Institutes* 4.12.10 (=2:1238).

known more widely. The church's elders must take into account these distinctions of sin as they undertake the discipline of an offending member.

Second, discipline follows an orderly, set process, as Jesus details in Matthew 18:15–20. The exercise of discipline, then, necessarily requires procedural integrity for discipline to accomplish its divinely-appointed ends.[53] Furthermore, according to Matthew 18:15–20, what typically propels discipline to more advanced stages is the impenitence of the offender, and what often arrests the process of discipline is the genuine repentance of the offender. Because, however, the restoration of the offender is not the sole end of discipline, the goals of the church's purity and Christ's honor may dictate the imposition of a church censure upon someone who professes repentance for a particular sin.

Third, the censures of the church are the solemn withdrawals of privileges that the church has previously granted. The greatest censure that the church may inflict is excommunication, "exclu[sion] from the communion of the church."[54] Jesus authorizes the church to excommunicate persons from her fellowship, and the apostle Paul commands the church in Corinth to take just this step (Matt 18:17; 1 Cor 5:11, 13). To be put out of the fellowship of the church is a pointer to the final, eschatological exclusion from Christ and his people that befalls the impenitent (Matt 25:31–46). A penultimate censure is the suspension of a person from the Lord's Supper. This censure, termed *excommunicatio minor* ("lesser excommunication") in the Dutch Reformed tradition, bars the offender from receiving the elements of bread and wine in the Supper.[55] Because the Lord's Supper is an ordinance of fellowship with Christ and with his people (1 Cor 10:16, 17), excluding an offender from the Lord's Supper serves to impress upon this person the gravity of his offense, to communicate the breach that stands between the impenitent offender and the church, and to call the offender to repentance and reconciliation. If an offender is an officer of the church, then among the censures that may be imposed are removal or suspension

53. For this reason, denominations frequently adopt disciplinary procedures to ensure that process is conducted in biblical, orderly fashion, including the preservation of the rights of accused persons.

54. Turretin, *Institutes*, 18.32.1 (=3:293). "The excision of an offender from the communion of the Church," *BCO* 30-4.

55. Vos, *Reformed Dogmatics*, 5:49; J. L. Schaver, *The Polity of the Churches*, 2 vols. (Chicago: Church Polity Press, 1947), 1:213.

from office. As the church has admitted a person into office, it maintains the right to remove that person from office.

Fourth, ecclesiastical censures are not ends in themselves. They are designed, rather, to draw persons to repentance. Jesus anticipates such an outcome in his instruction on discipline, "If [your brother] listens to you, you have gained your brother" (Matt 18:15). Paul expects that discipline will be administered with a view to the sinner's restoration (Gal 6:1; 2 Cor 2:7). The criterion for restoration is the sinner's repentance. Repentance is not merely a declaration of sorrow or regret, but is accompanied by visible changes in one's life (2 Cor 7:10–11). Jesus's words to the apostles in John 20:23 ("If you forgive the sins of anyone, they are forgiven") authorize the church to declare publicly the restoration of a penitent offender.

CONCLUSION

Christ, by his Spirit, has given his church a government, a pattern for worship, gifts, and discipline. Each of these serves to build up and to mature the church while simultaneously glorifying the church's head and king. The church no less has a divinely-appointed mission in this world. Christ not only grows his church upward, but also outward. That mission is the subject of the next chapter.

FURTHER READING

Gaffin, Richard B. *Perspectives on Pentecost*. Phillipsburg, NJ: P&R, 1979. Gaffin sets the New Testament's teaching about gifts within the context of the events of Pentecost. This work offers an irenic and clear Reformed engagement of charismatic understandings of spiritual gifts.

Owen, John. "A Discourse of Spiritual Gifts." *The Works of John Owen*, 4:420–520. 1850–1853. Reprint, Edinburgh: Banner of Truth, 1967. A Puritan treatment of the nature and purpose of spiritual gifts. Owen concisely explains and defends the distinction between extraordinary and ordinary gifts.

Warfield, B. B. *Counterfeit Miracles*. New York: Charles Scribner & Sons, 1918. Warfield's classical argument for the cessation of some spiritual gifts. Much of the work addresses the claims to extraordinary gifts that have surfaced over the course of the church's history.

Calvin, John. *Institutes of the Christian Religion*. Edited by John T. McNeill. Translated by Ford Lewis Battles. 2 vols. 1211–40 (= IV.XI.1—IV.XII.13). Philadelphia: Westminster, 1960. A brief exposition of the church's power of discipline by the Genevan Reformer. Calvin's discussion is foundational to subsequent Reformed reflections on discipline in the church.

XIII

THE MISSION OF THE CHURCH

Christ, the head and king of his church, has given his people a form of government, has directed them in how to worship God, and provides them with gifts and standards for discipline. Christ has also given his people a mission to undertake between his resurrection and his return in glory. In this chapter, we will explore that mission from the vantage point of the commissions that the risen Christ gave to his apostles, and of the implementation of those commissions in the ministry of the apostles. We will further address proposals that conceive the church's mission in terms of temporal relief or cultural engagement.

THE CHURCH'S MISSION—TO GATHER AND PERFECT THE SAINTS

The Westminster Confession of Faith offers a concise statement of the church's mission.

> Unto this catholic visible church Christ hath given the ministry, oracles, and ordinances of God, for the gathering and perfecting of the saints, in this life, to the end of the world: and doth, by his own presence and Spirit, according to his promise, make them effectual thereunto. (WCF 25.3)

Westminster affirms that the church has not chosen its own mission. The church, rather, has been assigned a mission by Christ. This mission follows from the "ministry, oracles, and ordinances of God" that Christ has committed to the church. Christ has furnished his people with these gifts "for the gathering and perfecting of the saints."[1] The "gathering and perfecting of the saints" is a comprehensive summary of the church's mission. It is to occupy the church until Christ returns, and the sole guarantee of success in this mission stems from "[Christ's] own presence and Spirit."

Christ's Commissions IN A PREVIOUS CHAPTER, WE gave brief and initial consideration to the commissions that the risen Christ gives to the apostles (Matt 28:18–20; Luke 24:44–49; Acts 1:8; John 20:19–23), highlighting the continuity (though not identity) between Jesus's own mission in his earthly ministry and the mission of his church in the window between his resurrection and return. Looking at these commissions together, we may identify the tasks that Christ assigns to the church. In Matthew's account, the church is to "go," that is, to "all nations" (Matt 28:19; compare Luke 24:47; Acts 1:8). The command to "go" does not have independent significance. Rather, it expresses "attendant circumstance" with respect to the command, "make disciples" (Matt 28:19).[2] The church will only "make disciples" if goes out to the nations. The means by which the church is to "make disciples" are "baptizing" people in the Triune name of God and "teaching them to observe all that I have commanded you" (Matt 28:19, 20). Baptism describes the terminus of a person professing faith in Jesus Christ (Acts 2:38, 41) ("gathering ... the saints"). Teaching characterizes the ongoing life of the professing disciple ("perfecting the saints").

---

1. The language "gather and perfect the saints" has made its way into American Presbyterian books of order, and, contemporaneously to the Westminster Standards, appeared in the 1645 *The Form of Presbyterial Church Government, The Westminster Confession* (Edinburgh: Banner of Truth, 2018), 588. Ramsay comments on the clause "gather and perfect the saints"—"For it is not the office of the Church to do all good in human society, nor even to work upon all men except so far as it does this in working upon a class, the saints. For them it has two things to do: first, to gather them, that is, out of the world into the Church; and second, to perfect them. The Church works upon men not already saints in their own consent in order to make them such, not in order to other ends, and upon saints, in order to make them perfect. By saints is meant persons that belong to Christ in sacred covenant," *An Exposition of the Form of Government*, 13.

2. For the underlying Greek syntax, see the discussion at Daniel Wallace, *Greek Grammar Beyond the Basics: An Exegetical Syntax of the New Testament* (Grand Rapids: Zondervan, 1996), 645.

In Luke's account, Christ's commission highlights the apostles as "witnesses," particularly of Christ's finished work bringing the Old Testament Scripture to its intended fulfillment (Luke 24:48 with 24:44–47; Acts 1:8). Here, Jesus underscores the response required of those who hear that apostolic witness, "repentance," and the blessing that they receive, "forgiveness of sins" (Luke 24:47). But, as Acts clarifies, the tasks of Luke 24:44–49 are not limited to the initial evangelization of the nations. To be sure, the duty of "witness" in Acts primarily concerns testifying to Christ and pressing his claims upon unbelieving audiences. But "witness" surely encompasses "the apostles' teaching" to which disciples were devoted (Acts 2:42), even as repentance (and faith) comprehend the way in which disciples are to respond to that teaching (Acts 20:21).[3]

In John's Gospel, the risen and ascended Jesus commissions his apostles, "Peace be with you. As the Father has sent me, even so I am sending you" (John 20:21). As the Father has "sent" the Son into the world, so the Son "send[s]" his disciples into the world. The church's sending by the Son is analogous to the Son's sending by the Father, but not identical with it.[4] The prefatory benediction, "Peace be with you," points to the reconciliation of these disciples to the Father by virtue of the death and resurrection of Jesus Christ. It prepares the disciples for Jesus's command that follows, "If you forgive the sins of any, they are forgiven them; if you withhold forgiveness from any, it is withheld" (John 20:23). Jesus is not entrusting the church with power to forgive sin in his name.[5] He is, rather, authorizing the church's elders to declare the forgiveness of sins to those who have

---

3. On the latter text, see J. A. Alexander, *A Commentary on the Acts of the Apostles*, 2 vols. (1857; repr., Edinburgh: Banner of Truth, 1963), 2:244.

4. Roman Catholic theologians have appealed to John 20:21 (and John 17:18) in order to argue that "Christ founded the Church in order to continue His work of redemption for all time," Ludwig Ott, *Fundamentals of Catholic Dogma*, trans. Patrick Lynch, 4th ed. (Rockford, IL: Tan Books, 1960), 274. Since, it is argued, "Christ's mission was the eternal salvation of man," and "Christ bequeathed his mission to the Apostles," therefore Christ has "given the Church [his] teaching office, [his] pastoral office, [and his] sacerdotal office. Ott, *Fundamentals*, citing Leo XIII, *Satis Cognitum* (1896). "What did Christ the Lord achieve by the foundation of the Church; what did He wish? This: He wished to delegate to the Church the same office and the same mandate which He had himself received from the Father in order to continue them (i.e., the three-fold office, the teaching office, the pastoral office, and the sacerdotal office)." But Christ argues for an analogy, not an identity, between his mission and that of his church. Furthermore, Christ calls the church "to be a *witness*; it is neither designed nor adapted to be a *substitute* for Christ." Bannerman, *The Church of Christ*, 1:84, emphasis original.

5. *Pace CCC* §1441.

responded with repentance and faith to the apostolic witness to Christ.[6] The church, then, not only bears witness to Christ and calls human beings to repentance and faith in the gospel, but also declares the remission or withholding of sins to those who receive or reject the gospel of Christ.

Apostolic Implementation

ACTS AND THE EPISTLES TESTIFY to a church that was faithful to implement the commission that Christ had given to it, and that was careful neither to add nor to take from it. The first public act of the apostles is to proclaim Jesus Christ, crucified and raised, and to offer him to sinners as Savior from sin and Lord of all (Acts 2:14–39). The first recorded accession to the church is of persons professing faith and submitting to baptism (Acts 2:41). Luke then gives a cameo portrait of the church as committed to apostolic teaching, to worship, and to common life in fellowship with one another (Acts 2:42–47).

Throughout the remainder of Acts, the apostles publicly preach Christ, call men and women to repentance and faith, and gather professing disciples into worshiping communities under the supervision of the apostles. Luke reinforces this message formally through several summarizing passages that punctuate the narrative of Acts and highlight the way in which the word of God brought growth to the church both quantitatively and qualitatively (Acts 6:7; 9:31; 12:24; 13:48–49; 16:5; 19:20; 28:30–31).[7] Therefore, both the contents and the structure of Acts establish the same point—the church was obedient to Christ's commission to the church to gather and perfect the saints.

Importantly, the church of Jerusalem and, later, of Antioch, emerge as bases of support for the apostles and their itinerant evangelistic ministry. The gospel not only comes to Samaria from Jerusalem (Acts 8:1), but its

---

6. See Calvin's comment on John 20:23, "Now, when Christ gives the apostles a mandate to forgive sins, He does not at all transfer to them what is His own. It belongs to Him to forgive sins. Inasmuch as this honour is peculiar to Himself, He does not yield it to the apostles; but he commands them to declare in His name the forgiveness of sins, that He may reconcile men to God through them. In short, He alone, properly speaking, forgives sins, through his apostles," *Calvin's Commentaries: The Gospel According to St. John, Part Two (11-21) and The First Epistle of John*, trans. T. H. L. Parker (1959; repr., Grand Rapids: Eerdmans, 1974), 207. See also Calvin, *Institutes*, 3.4.12, 14 (=1:636, 638–39).

7. See further Richard Longenecker, "Acts," in *The Expositor's Bible Commentary, Volume 10: Luke-Acts*, rev. ed. (Grand Rapids: Zondervan, 2007), 696.

reception receives apostolic confirmation from Jerusalem (Acts 8:14–15). A similar pattern transpires in the founding of the church in Antioch (Acts 11:19–30). Antioch, in turn, sends the apostle Paul and his colleague, Barnabas, to undertake the work to which the Spirit has called them (Acts 13:1–3). Paul and Barnabas complete this mission by returning to the church in Antioch (Acts 14:26–28). Paul departs the church in Antioch twice again to undertake campaigns of missionary preaching (Acts 15:36–41; 18:23b). As the apostle Paul, toward the end of his public ministry, contemplates the conclusion of his labors in the Eastern Mediterranean, he looks to the church in Rome as a future base of support for an anticipated ministry in Spain (Rom 15:19–29).

But such ecclesiastical commitment to the work of evangelization was not restricted to the support of the apostles. Paul commends the churches in Thessalonica and Philippi for their own initiative and participation in the work of evangelizing their neighbors (Phil 2:12–18; 1 Thess 1:8; 2:13–16; 2 Thess 3:1).[8] Wherever the apostles proclaimed the gospel and established churches, they appointed elders to provide government and teaching for the church—for the gathering and perfecting of the saints (Acts 14:23; Titus 1:5). Whereas the labors of the apostles were foundational and therefore unique to the founding generation of the church, the ecclesiastical endeavors that Paul commends are to characterize the life of the church in every age. Building upon the once-for-all foundation laid by the apostles, the church in every age proclaims Christ to the nations.[9]

The picture that emerges from Acts and the New Testament letters, then, is a consistent one. The church is committed to proclaiming the gospel of Jesus Christ, receiving into her membership those who profess faith in

---

8. Kevin DeYoung and Greg Gilbert, *What Is the Mission of the Church? Making Sense of Social Justice, Shalom, and the Great Commission* (Wheaton, IL: Crossway, 2011), 61, summarizing Robert L. Plummer, *Paul's Understanding of the Church's Mission: Did the Apostle Paul Expect the Early Christian Communities to Evangelize?* (Eugene, OR: Wipf & Stock, 2006). Other passages adduced by Plummer include Ephesians 6:15; 1 Corinthians 4:16, 11:1; 2 Corinthians 6:3–7; 1 Thesselonians 2:5–12; Titus 2:1–10. The pattern of these instances confirms that Paul expected the church to participate in the work of proclaiming the gospel to the nations.

9. As Gaffin has noted, "In the light of Acts 1:8, Acts documents a *completed, universal, apostolic* task. Acts records the *finished founding* of the 'one holy catholic' church as also 'apostolic' (the Nicene Creed)," *In the Fullness of Time*, 54. Recognizing that Acts documents the laying of such a foundation in no way militates against "the worldwide missionary mandate of the church today," as envisioned in Matthew 28:18–20, *In the Fullness of Time*, 55.

Christ, and pursuing as a community the worship of God and holy living. These commitments stem from the apostles who, in turn, are implementing the commissions of the risen Christ for his church in every age.

MISSION AS WORD AND DEED?

FEW EVANGELICAL AND REFORMED THEOLOGIANS would deny that the Lord Jesus Christ has called the church to take up these tasks until his return at the end of the age. Some, however, have argued that the scope of endeavor reflected in the "gathering and perfecting of the saints" is too narrow. The evangelical Old Testament scholar, Christopher J. H. Wright, for instance, has influentially pled for "recovering the wholeness of the gospel."[10] Wright alleges that what the "gospel integrates ... we so often tend to polarize," namely, the "individual and cosmic," "believing and living," and "proclamation and demonstration."[11] With respect to this last pairing (proclamation and demonstration), Wright argues that the apostles communicated the gospel in word and deed.

> Peter summarizes the ministry of Jesus as *both* telling the message that God sent to Israel—the good news of peace—*and* that, anointed and empowered by the Holy Spirit, "he went around doing good" (Acts 10:36–38). The same combination is found in Paul's own practice: in Romans 15 he reflects on his whole missionary work and speaks of "what Christ has accomplished through me in leading the nations to *obey* God by what I have *said* and *done*—by the power of signs and wonders, through the *power of the Spirit of God*" (Rom. 15:18–19, italics added). Words, works, and wonders, as some have said."[12]

By "demonstration," Wright has in mind the miracles that Jesus wrought in his earthly ministry, and that Paul wrought in his apostolic ministry. Wright does not argue that the church performs such miracles today as part of her presentation of the whole gospel to the world. To these miracles,

10. Christopher J. H. Wright, *The Mission of God's People: A Biblical Theology of the Church's Mission* (Grand Rapids: Zondervan, 2010), 273.

11. Wright, *The Mission of God's People*, 273, 274.

12. Wright, *The Mission of God's People*, 275.

rather, correspond deeds of love and mercy, particularly to those in need.[13] To be sure, Wright insists upon the "centrality" of "evangelism within mission," and is clear that he does not intend demonstration to displace proclamation.[14] But, within this framework, Wright is uncomfortable with the language even of proclamation's "primacy."[15]

Wright is by no means alone in advancing this understanding of the church's mission.[16] Nor is the way in which Wright defines the church's mission the only concern that has been raised concerning his understanding of mission.[17] But it is a decided theological challenge to the narrower

13. Wright terms this conception of mission "integral mission." Citing approvingly "The Micah Declaration on Integral Mission," Wright defines integral mission as "the proclamation and demonstration of the gospel. ... As in the life of Jesus, being, doing and saying are at the heart of our integral task," *The Mission of God's People*, 278.

14. Wright, *The Mission of God's People*, 278. And yet, as one critic has observed, in the ways in which Wright articulates what he understands to be the integration of word and deed in biblical mission, Wright's formulations "veil important distinctions we find in Scripture which should lead us to place a unique emphasis on making disciples of Jesus Christ," Bobby Jamieson, review of *The Mission of God's People*, *9Marks Journal* (October 27, 2010).

15. Wright, *The Mission of God's People*, 279, 280. See further on this point, Wright, *The Mission of God: Unlocking the Bible's Grand Narrative* (Downers Grove, IL: InterVarsity Press, 2006), 316–23.

16. Wright references approvingly the work of John R. W. Stott, who led the drafting committee that produced The Lausanne Covenant (1974) (*The Mission of God*, 316n18), and who led the Consultation on the Relationship between Evangelism and Social Responsibility (1982) (*The Mission of God's People*, 276). For Stott's own articulation of the church's mission, with its affinities to Wright's later formulations, see John R. W. Stott, *Christian Mission in the Modern World* (Downers Grove, IL: InterVarsity Press, 1975), 15–57. For a brief but thoughtful critical engagement of Stott's understanding of mission, see DeYoung and Gilbert, *What Is the Mission of the Church?*, 53–58.

17. There are at least three further concerns. (1) The way in which Wright enfolds missions into what he terms "God's mission" virtually "identif[ies]" the two. DeYoung and Gilbert, *What Is the Mission of the Church?*, 41. Wright argues that "mission" is "all that God is doing in his great purpose for the whole creation and all that he calls us to do in cooperation with that purpose," while "missions" describes "the multitude of activities that God's people can engage in, by means of which they participate in God's mission," *The Mission of God's People*, 25. Such a pairing fails to respect what we have argued are the biblical delimitations on the work of missions. (2) There is the sheer breadth and scope of "God's Mission." For Wright, God's mission is "a vast, comprehensive project of cosmic salvation," *The Mission of God's People*, 46. Consequently, the mission of God's people includes "*ecological* mission," *The Mission of God's People*, 62, emphasis original. "A comprehensive redemptive response to human need," including "political injustice, economic exploitation, social oppression and spiritual bondage," *The Mission of God's People*, 112. But such endeavors go well beyond the church's missional mandate to "gather and perfect the saints" (WCF 25.3). (3) Wright places so much emphasis upon the Old Testament materials in his treatment of mission that the New Testament testimony to the church's mission is effectively attenuated, on which see Mike Gilbert-Smith, review of *The Mission of God*, *9Marks Journal* (October 25, 2010); John A. Wind, "Does the Old Testament 'Authorize' a Creation Care Mission of the Institutional Church? Examining

conception of mission reflected in the Westminster Confession of Faith. Wright's challenge rests in no small measure (although by no means exclusively) upon the missiological implications that he draws from the miracles of Jesus and the apostles.[18]

To respond to Wright's understanding of the church's mission, we need to take up the significance and place of these miracles in the New Testament, asking whether Jesus's and the apostles' miracles warrant the inclusion of activities addressing the temporal needs, wants, and suffering of individuals and peoples within the church's mission proper.[19] To answer this question, one must first address the purpose for which Jesus (and the apostles after him) performed miracles. Although each of Jesus's miracles (except one) was a demonstration of benevolence toward human beings, the relief of human suffering or provision for human want was not these miracles' most basic meaning.[20] Like the miracles performed by the canonical prophets before him, Jesus's miracles had a fundamental "sign" character.[21] That is to say, each of Jesus's miracles pointed beyond itself to some eternal, spiritual reality.[22] That reality, as Ridderbos observes, is the kingdom of God.

Christopher Wright's Claims," *Journal of Global Christianity* 2, no. 1 (February 2016), 33–47; and DeYoung and Gilbert, *What Is the Mission of the Church?*, 42–45.

18. For additional critical engagement of Wright's proposal, see I. Macleod, "The Mission of God's People: A Biblical Theology of the Church's Mission," *PRJ* 6, no. 2 (2014): 377–81; and John A. Wind, "The Church's Mission Constrained by the Covenants: Engaging Christopher Wright's Conception of the Bible's Covenantal Structure," *SBJT* 23, no. 3 (2019): 61–75.

19. This is not to deny that Christians ought to be abundant in good works, not least to commend the gospel to their neighbors (Titus 2:10), nor that those who are called to engage in the missionary proclamation of the gospel may and ought to serve those in physical need around them. The question is whether such actions and services comprise or constitute the church's mission as such.

20. Vos notes a single exception to the fact that each of Jesus's miracles were "beneficent miracles," *The Teaching of Jesus Concerning the Kingdom of God and the Church* (Phillipsburg, NJ: P&R, 1979), 54. Jesus's cursing of the fig tree (Matt 21:18–22; Mark 11:12–14, 20–25) was a sign of eschatological judgment to come upon impenitent Israel. And yet, even Jesus's miraculous cursing of the fig tree was intended for the good of the disciples who observed it. This action "was an eloquent prophecy of the punishment that would come on" God's people for their "unrepentance, which was revealed so glaringly during His final days in Jerusalem," Ridderbos, *Matthew*, 390. This miracle was not only a reminder of the remaining window for the impenitent to turn to God in repentance, but a call to faith in and prayer toward God.

21. On the prophetic miracles as "sign," see Vos, *Biblical Theology*, 231–33.

22. This is not to deny, of course, that miracles carried with them—as all presentations of the word of God carry with them—a summons to respond to the miraculous, saving work of God in faith, on which see Vos, *The Teaching of Jesus*, 95.

> [Jesus' miracles] confirmed the truth of His words (see, e.g., [Matt] 9:6; John 14:11) [and] formed proof that in Him the kingdom of heaven had arrived in principle. The coming of this kingdom brings deliverance, not only for the soul, but also for the body. It embraces nothing less than the re-creation of heaven and earth. In His miracles Jesus gave the signs, the prelude, and the pledge of this complete renewal (see, e.g., [Matt] 11:1–6, 12:28). The wonders that He performed thus already were a visible and tangible manifestation of the kingdom of heaven.[23]

In fact, such is the relationship between miracles and the kingdom that Jesus's "miracles can only be viewed within the scope of the coming of the kingdom."[24] They not only confirmed the presence and inbreaking of the kingdom in the life and ministry of Jesus, but they were, like Jesus's "preaching," "a revelation of the kingdom of God."[25]

Jesus's preaching and miracles together comprised the substance of Jesus's public ministry (Matt 4:23; 9:35). But Jesus's preaching has priority over his miracles within his public ministry. This priority surfaces in several ways in the Gospels. First, Jesus himself testifies to this priority at the outset of his ministry. Jesus's disciples press him to return to Capernaum, pleading, "Everyone is looking for you" (Mark 1:37). The unstated reason for this intense public interest in Jesus lies in the miracles that Jesus had performed in Capernaum the evening before (Mark 1:32–34). Jesus, however, has other plans: "Let us go on to the next towns, that I may preach there also, for that is why I came out" (Mark 1:38). Consequently, Jesus "went throughout all Galilee, preaching in their synagogues and casting out demons" (Mark 1:39). While still performing miracles in other Galilean towns, Jesus affirms that he was sent to preach, a priority reflected in the sequence of Jesus's activities in Mark 1:39 (compare Matt 4:23; 9:35).[26]

Next, Jesus's miracles, as "signs," brought no lasting benefits. The beneficiaries of miracles experienced the restoration of health from sickness

---

23. Ridderbos, *Matthew*, 79.

24. Ridderbos, *The Coming of the Kingdom*, 69.

25. Ridderbos, *The Coming of the Kingdom*, 70.

26. Some interpreters justifiably argue that the verb translated "came out" (1:38) refers to Jesus's having been sent by his Father into the world, that is, to the "purpose of his messianic mission," Ridderbos, *The Coming of the Kingdom*, 117.

or disease, bodily wholeness from disability, liberation from demonic possession, or in a few instances life from the state of death. But none of these persons was preserved from further sickness, injury, or death itself.[27] This state of affairs confirms the transitory character of miracles as signs. By design, miracles display—but do not constitute or necessarily effect—the redemptive realities of the kingdom.

Finally and relatedly, Jesus often couples miracles with faith. Because of the "unbelief" of the inhabitants of Nazareth, Jesus "could do no mighty work there, except that he laid his hands on a few sick people and healed them" (Mark 6:5). The persons' unbelief is not a force externally constraining Jesus from what he was otherwise inclined to do. Their unbelief, rather, is "an impossibility within the scope of Jesus's task and activity," in that it would render any miracle wrought a mere "deed of power," "lack[ing] the background from which miracles derive their significance and against which they can only be understood."[28] Unbelief stood at cross purposes with the meaning of miracles in Jesus's earthly ministry.

In summary, the miracles of Jesus complemented his preaching by confirming the truth of his teaching and by signifying the presence and power of the kingdom that Jesus was proclaiming. As such, miracles took a necessarily subordinate role to his preaching. It was only by repentance and faith in the kingdom proclamation of Jesus that one could have entrance into the kingdom of God (Mark 1:14–15).

The same pattern obtains with the apostles, those men whom the risen Christ commissioned to be his witnesses (Acts 1:8). Throughout Acts, the apostolic miracles are conjoined with apostolic preaching, the former signifying the kingdom realities declared in the latter.[29] Acts speaks of mir-

---

27. Note Jesus's statements at Luke 11:24–26, that even a person from whom a demon had been cast out could subsequently suffer an even worse demonic habitation. "Jesus's point ... is that it does no good to be delivered of an evil spirit for a time if the Holy Spirit does not take its place. Unless this change of occupants occurs, the exorcism has no positive, lasting value." Ridderbos, *Matthew*, 248.

28. Ridderbos, *The Coming of the Kingdom*, 118. Ridderbos continues by noting that this point is not to say that Jesus's miracles were self-explanatory, nor that many or most of those attending his public ministry understood the kingdom significance of his miracles. The point rather is the incongruity of performing a miracle in the presence of manifest unbelief.

29. "[Miracles'] primary purpose is indeed to show us the power and grace of God, but since we are bad and perverse interpreters of them, God hardly ever allows them to be detached from His Word, lest they should be drawn into abuse and corruption. If miracles have at any time been wrought apart from His Word, in the first place it was a rare occurrence,

acles, furthermore, as the Lord Jesus Christ bearing "witness to the word of his grace" (Acts 14:3; compare Rom 15:18–19, 2 Cor 12:12).

The mission of the post-apostolic church consists of the preaching of the word of God but does not consist of the working of miracles. Paul's charges to Timothy and Titus, for instance, consistently reference the preaching of the word (1 Tim 4:13; 2 Tim 4:1–5; Titus 2:1, 15), but make no mention of the working of miracles. This silence points to the fact that miracles have served their purpose in authenticating the ministries of Jesus and of the apostles, and in signifying the spiritual realities of the kingdom. Nor are good works, including deeds of mercy and compassion to those who are suffering or in want, ever presented as analogous to the apostolical miracles. Henceforth, the church proclaims the word, inviting sinners to enter the kingdom in the way of faith and repentance.

CONCLUSION

To MAKE THIS CASE IS in no way to deter Christians from serving their neighbors through good works. It is to say, however, that such deeds do not comprise the mission of the church. The word of God prevents the church in her organized capacity from undertaking activities that are entirely permissible to individual Christians or associations of Christians.[30] Just as the word regulates the worship and government of the church, so also the word regulates the mission of the church. The church is authorized and tasked with the preaching of the word of God and the ingathering and training of all who profess faith in Christ.[31] Beyond the boundaries assigned to the church and her mission in Scripture, the church may not go. But the very purpose of the church confining herself to these boundaries is to ensure that the word of God is preached and enforced in its full biblical integrity to human

---

and secondly a very meagre result followed from them. For the most part, however, God has wrought miracles, so that by them the world might know Him, not simply or in His bare majesty but in the Word." Calvin, *The Acts of the Apostles 14–28*, trans. John W. Fraser (1966; repr., Grand Rapids: Eerdmans, 1973), 3.

30. David VanDrunen, *Living in God's Two Kingdoms: A Biblical Vision for Christianity and Culture* (Wheaton, IL: Crossway, 2010), 159. Compare Bryan Estelle, *The Primary Mission of the Church* (Fearn, UK: Mentor, 2022), 131.

31. The diaconate, it must be stressed in this connection, is an office intended to serve the genuine temporal needs of the people of God. It is not an ecclesiastical arm whose purpose is to bring relief to the physical wants of the world's poor. On the theological relationship between the communion of the saints and the diaconate, see Peck, *Notes on Ecclesiology*, 206–10.

beings. Believers, equipped by the church's elders with the teaching of Scripture, are to live answerably to Scripture's teaching by the doing of the good works commanded by Scripture. The beneficiaries of those good works are not merely their fellow believers but all kinds of people. Seen in this light, the church's mission ("the gathering and perfecting of the saints") is engineered to unleash a force of good upon every sphere and sector of the world, as believers, informed by the teaching of Scripture, pursue their various callings in the world to glorify God in the service of others.

FURTHER READING

DeYoung, Kevin, and Greg Gilbert. *What Is the Mission of the Church? Making Sense of Social Justice, Shalom, and the Great Commission.* Wheaton, IL: Crossway, 2011. A contemporary statement of and argument for the church's mission as the gathering and perfecting of the saints. DeYoung and Gilbert interact with challenges from within evangelicalism to that understanding of mission.

Köstenberger, Andreas and Peter T. O'Brien. *Salvation to the Ends of the Earth: A Biblical Theology of Mission.* NSBT. Downers Grove, IL: InterVarsity Press, 2001. A biblical-theological survey of mission that encompasses both the Old Testament and the New Testament. The work offers concise studies of mission across the various epochs of redemptive history.

VanDrunen, David. *Natural Law and the Two Kingdoms: A Study in the Development of Reformed Social Thought.* Grand Rapids: Eerdmans, 2009. A historically rich survey of the way in which Reformed churches since the Reformation have understood the mission of the church, particularly in relation to the kingdoms of this world.

PART 3

TRUTH FOR LIFE AND MISSION

XIV

THE CHURCH IN THE WORLD: CHURCH AND CIVIL GOVERNMENT

The church has scarcely known a day when it has not had to negotiate its relationship with the civil powers of this world. The nature and dynamics of the relationship between the church and the civil magistrate are simultaneously theological and practical. Whether or how the church should be active in the public square requires careful reflection upon the nature, government, and mission of the church. One's answer to this question has wide-ranging implications for the church's day-to-day engagement with the world, and particularly the temporal authorities in this world.

In this chapter, we will first chart some of the primary positions that Christians throughout the centuries have staked with respect to the relationship between the church and civil government. In doing so, we will particularly explore the way in which Reformed theologians in Scotland and the United States articulated this relation. We will give specific attention to some of the practical implications that this doctrine has for the church's engagements with the governments of this world.

CHURCH AND STATE—A BRIEF SURVEY

Any survey of positions within the church's history regarding the relationship between church and state must be selective and brief. We may look to some of the leading positions within the Protestant churches of the Reformation. An important question concerned whether the civil magistrate had authority with respect to the worship and discipline of the church, and, if so, the extent of that authority. Many in the sixteenth and seventeenth centuries affirmed that the civil magistrate had some responsibility with respect to either or both of these. The sixteenth-century Continental Reformed writer, Thomas Erastus, argued that the state had a proper role in aspects of the church's government, particularly in matters of church discipline.[1] What came to be known as "Erastianism" in fact denoted a constellation of positions that advocated generally for "state control of religion."[2] Such divines as John Lightfoot and John Selden advocated (unsuccessfully) for Erastian views of church and state at the Westminster Assembly.[3] The Church of England, from its founding, acknowledged the crown to be that church's head. The king or queen of state possessed and exercised wide-ranging powers with respect to the doctrine, worship, and government of the Church of England.[4]

Within the broader Reformed tradition, however, a more circumscribed view of the powers of the civil magistrate with respect to the church became increasingly prominent. The late seventeenth-century Genevan theologian, Francis Turretin, denied that the civil magistrate had authority to "make new articles of faith or institute and enjoin new worship," or to "exercise ecclesiastical discipline by the authority of the ecclesiastical keys."[5] The principle of the delimitation of the magistrate's authority with respect to the church was one that Calvin had earlier articulated.[6] Even so, Calvin positively affirmed the lawful authority of the civil magistrate

---

1. On the life and thought of Erastus, see Charles D. Gunnoe, Jr., *Thomas Erastus and the Palatinate: A Renaissance Physician in the Second Reformation*, BSCH 48 (Leiden: Brill, 2010).

2. Alan D. Strange, *The Doctrine of the Spirituality of the Church in the Ecclesiology of Charles Hodge*, RAD (Phillipsburg, NJ: P&R, 2017), 21.

3. On the debates relating to church and state in the Westminster Assembly, see Robert S. Paul, *Assembly of the Lord: Politics and Religion in the Westminster Assembly and the 'Grand Debate'* (Edinburgh: T&T Clark, 1985).

4. See the survey of the powers of the crown with respect to the Church of England at Charles Hodge, "Relation of the Church and State," *Discussions in Church Polity* (New York: Scribner's Sons, 1878), 110–11. In different circumstances, Lutheran churches experienced the oversight and even control of German princes. Decisive in this regard for formalizing this practice was on the Continent was the principle of *cuius regio, eius religio* ("whose territory, his religion") in which the prince of a realm had the authority to determine the religion of his realm, whether Roman Catholic, Lutheran, or Reformed.

5. Turretin, *Institutes*, 18.34.12, 13 (=3:319).

6. Calvin, *Institutes*, 4.20.1–2 (=2:1485–88).

with respect to some aspects of "religion and divine worship," a point that Turretin would later reiterate and develop.[7] In the middle of the seventeenth century, the Westminster Assembly forcefully affirmed this delimitative principle in expansive and comprehensive terms.[8]

> *The civil magistrate may not assume to himself the administration of the word and sacraments, or the power of the keys of the kingdom of heaven:* yet he hath authority, and it is his duty, to take order, that unity and peace be preserved in the church, that the truth of God be kept pure and enter, that all blasphemies and heresies be suppressed, all corruptions and abuses in worship and discipline prevented or reformed, and all the ordinances of God duly settled, administered, and observed. For the better effecting whereof, he hath power to call synods, to be present at them, and to provide that whatsoever is transacted in them be according to the mind of God. (WCF 23.3, emphasis added; compare WCF 30.1)[9]

The material that follows the colon in this paragraph would have been unobjectionable to many seventeenth-century Protestants (yet, as we will note below, it was substantively rewritten by the eighteenth-century American Presbyterian church). But the initial statement (italicized) "was a

7. Calvin, *Institutes*, 4.20.9 (=2:1495); Turretin, *Institutes*, 18.34.1–51 (=3:316–36), esp. 18.34.14 (=3:320). In the course of this question, Turretin denies that the magistrate "can or ought to compel his subjects to religion and faith," while arguing that the civil magistrate may "coerce and ... inflict some punishment upon contumacious and obstinate heretics," even to the point of capital punishment (18.34.21, 32, 44 [=3:323, 328, 333]).

8. A critical antecedent to Westminster's doctrine of the independence of the church's government from the civil magistrate is found in the Scottish Second Book of Discipline (1578), on which see Strange, *The Doctrine of the Spirituality of the Church*, 25–30, and "Second Book of Discipline," *Dictionary of Scottish Church History and Theology*, ed. Nigel S. Cameron (Downers Grove, IL: InterVarsity Press, 1993), 765–66. The author of the SBD, Andrew Melville, is famous for his 1596 declaration to King James VI of Scotland, "There are two kings and two kingdoms in Scotland; there is King James, the head of the commonwealth, and there is Christ Jesus, the King of the church, whose subject James the Sixth is, and of whose kingdom he is not a king, nor a lord, nor a head, but a member," Thomas M'Crie, *The Life of Andrew Melville*, 2 vols. (Edinburgh: William Blackwood, 1824), 1:391–92. For a discussion of this doctrine in the writings of the Scottish Commissioners to the Westminster Assembly, Samuel Rutherford and George Gillespie, see Fesko, *The Theology of the Westminster Standards*, 304–12.

9. Unless otherwise indicated, references to the Westminster Confession of Faith in this chapter are to the original edition of 1647.

radical proposal for the times," not least within the Church of England.[10] Furthermore, while the Westminster Confession later affirms the right of the civil magistrate to "call a synod of ministers, and other fit persons, to consult and advise with, about matters of religion," such a call was not required for an assembly of ministers to convene (WCF 31.2). Whatever the circumstances of these assemblies' convening, Westminster affirmed their right "ministerially" to address matters of doctrine, order, and discipline, and declared that the authority of their "decrees and determinations" derived entirely from Scripture (WCF 31.3). The deliberations, conclusions, and authority of such assemblies are therefore expressly said to be independent of the civil magistrate.

The confession's articulation of the fundamental integrity of the church's government and its essential independence from the authority of the civil magistrate received development and refinement within the American Presbyterian Church.[11] The American Presbyterian Church, in adopting the Westminster Confession of Faith a little less than a century after the confession's drafting, proceeded to modify some of the confession's articles pertaining to the church's relationship to the governments of this world.[12] In the judgment of the American Presbyterian Church, the original Westminster Confession had not adequately safeguarded the church's

10. Letham, *The Westminster Assembly*, 312. Note the assessment of Alexander F. Mitchell, "Some, I know, will have it, that though the limits of civil obedience are rightly defined in this chapter, too much is allowed to the magistrate in connection with religion. But such should consider that what is here allowed is less than was claimed for him in the old Scotch and other early reformed confessions, and far less than what was conceded in the English and the Irish Articles." Alexander F. Mitchell and John F. Struthers, eds., *Minutes of the Sessions of the Westminster Assembly of Divines* (1874; Edmonton, AB: Still Waters Revival Books, 1991), lxix, as cited in Barker, "Lord of Lords and King of Commoners: The Westminster Confession and the Relationship of Church and State," in *The Westminster Confession into the 21st Century: Essays in Remembrance of the 350th Anniversary of the Westminster Assembly*, vol. 1, ed. J. Ligon Duncan III (Fearn: Christian Focus, 2003), 418–19.

11. The Scottish Church maintained its adherence to the Westminsterian Doctrine, even as it upheld the doctrine of the state's establishment of the church, on which see, representatively, George Smeaton, "The Scottish Theory of Ecclesiastical Establishments" (1875), in *Sermons and Addresses of George Smeaton*, ed. John W. Keddie (Edinburgh: Banner of Truth, 2022), 193–235; James Bannerman, *The Church of Christ*, 1:94–185, 2:345–51; and William Cunningham, *Historical Theology*, 2:557–87. See in particular the surveys, "Church and State (Legal Questions)" and "Church and State (Theological Questions)," ed. Nigel M. de S. Cameron, *Dictionary of Scottish Chruch History & Theology* (Downers Grove, IL: InterVarsity Press, 1993), 179–80, 180–82.

12. The material in the remainder of this paragraph and in the following paragraph has come from my "Westminster and Church Government," ed. Kevin Bidwell, *The Westminster*

independence from the civil magistrate. To this end, the American church in 1788 amended portions of WCF 20.4, 23.3, and 31.1. This effort was complemented by the drafting of eight, prefatory "Preliminary Principles" to the new church's "Form of Government," in which care was taken to reaffirm the independence of the church's government from the civil magistrate.[13]

When read alongside the original text of the Westminster Confession, the American Presbyterians' modifications should not be seen as a repudiation of the original confession's doctrine. On the contrary, the American modifications were advanced in the interest of clarifying, refining, and maturing the confession's original statements.[14] The amendment of WCF 20.4 categorically prohibited any involvement of the civil magistrate in the workings of ecclesiastical discipline.[15] The revision of WCF 23.3 clarified that the civil magistrate's obligations and commitments to a particular Christian denomination extended no farther than its obligations and commitments to any other particular Christian denomination. It added the provision that the civil magistrate could not "in the least interfere in matters of faith," and omitted lines from the original confession that affirmed the civil magistrate's duty "that all blasphemies and heresies be suppressed; all corruptions and abuses in worship and discipline prevented or reformed, and all the ordinances of God duly settled, administered, and observed." The revision of WCF 31.1 removed from the civil magistrate the right "lawfully [to] call a synod of ministers, and other fit persons, to consult and advise with, about matters of religion," leaving it to the officers of the church alone to call ecclesiastical synods and councils. In summary, the American revisions served to remove what were regarded as inconsistencies within the Westminster Confession by affirming with greater clarity

---

Standards for Today: Recovering the Church and Worship for Everyday Christian Living (Darlington, UK: EP Books, 2018), 154–55.

13. Lewis S. Mudge, ed., *Digest of the Acts and Deliverance of the General Assembly of the Presbyterian Church in the U.S.A.* (Philadelphia: General Assembly of the PCUSA, 1938), 73–75, as cited at Barker, "Lord of Lords and King of Commoners," 425–26.

14. So, rightly, A. A. Hodge, *The Confession of Faith*, 427–29. This also was the view of Charles Hodge, so Strange, *The Doctrine of the Spirituality of the Church*, 42–48. The American Presbyterian Church also removed "tolerating a false religion" as a sin against the second commandment from Westminster Larger Catechism 109.

15. For a listing of the original Westminster Confession and the American revisions in parallel columns, see A. A. Hodge, *The Confession of Faith*, 22–23.

the very biblical principles that the Westminster Divines had expressed in the Westminster Confession.[16]

BASIS AND NATURE OF THE CHURCH'S RELATIONSHIP WITH THE STATE

This "Scoto-American Theory" of the relationship of church and state finds its basis in the teaching of Scripture, particularly Jesus's teaching regarding the kingdom of God and the church.[17] Jesus declared to Pilate that his "kingdom is not of this world" (John 18:36). His kingdom is "in origin and nature of another order than the kingship of which Pilate has spoken."[18] Jesus elsewhere affirms the legitimacy of civil government, even as he affirms it to be distinct from the kingdom of God (Matt 22:21). Specifically, disciples have obligations to the governments of this world—they are to "render to Caesar the things that are Caesar's" (compare Rom 13:1–7; Titus 3:1; 1 Pet 2:13–14). But disciples no less have obligations to God and to his kingdom, "render ... to God the things that are God's" (Matt 22:21). The kingdom and the state, then, represent distinct spheres of authority

16. That this was the intent of the American Presbyterian Church is suggested by a declaration of the Synod of New York and Philadelphia in 1786, "The Synod of New York & Philadelphia adopt, according to the known and established meaning of their Terms, the Westminster confession [*sic*] of faith as the confession of their faith; save that every candidate for the gospel Ministry is permitted to except against so much of the twenty third Chapter as gives authority to the Civil Magistrate in matters of Religion. The Presbyterian Church in America considers the Church of Christ as a spiritual Society intirely distinct from the Civil Government; & having a right to regulate their own ecclesiastical policy independently of the Interposition of the Magistrate," *Minutes of the Presbyterian Church in America: 1706–1788*, ed. Guy S. Klett (Philadelphia: Presbyterian Historical Society, 1976), as cited by Leah Farish, "The First Amendment's Religion Clauses: The Calvinist Document that Interprets Them Both," *Journal of Religion & Society* 12 (2010): 3–4.

17. The expression is that of Stuart Robinson, *Discourses of Redemption*, 474. This doctrine has gone under various names. A common one is that of the "Spirituality of the Church," a label that can carry liabilities, on which see the discussions of Strange, *The Doctrine of the Spirituality of the Church*, 3–5, and Preston D. Graham, Jr., *A Kingdom Not of This World: Stuart Robinson's Struggle to Distinguish the Sacred from the Secular during the Civil War* (Macon, GA: Mercer University Press, 2002), 169–73. What has come to be known as the "Two kingdoms Doctrine" substantially overlaps with the doctrine under review here, on which see David VanDrunen, *Natural Law and the Two Kingdoms: A Study in the Development of Reformed Social Thought* (Grand Rapids: Eerdmans, 2010). The extensive biblical-theological framework of the Two Kingdoms Doctrine, however, is unique to it, on which see David VanDrunen, *Living in God's Two Kingdoms: A Biblical Vision for Christianity and Culture* (Wheaton, IL: Crossway, 2010), and the review of Michael N. Jacobs, "The Resurgence of Two Kingdoms Doctrine: A Survey of the Literature," *Themelios* 45, no. 2 (2020): 314–32.

18. Ridderbos, *The Gospel of John*, 594, referencing in addition John 8:23, 38.

that respectively command the allegiance of every disciple. Because God has appointed each sphere and commands people's allegiance, as an act of obedience to God, to each, the kingdom and the state therefore do not overlap in their spheres of authority. Each possesses "autonomy in reference to the other" and possesses inherent "freedom from intrusion on the part of the other" with respect to "function and ... sphere."[19] "They are as planets moving in concentric orbits."[20]

The kingdom comes to visible and fullest expression in the church that Jesus establishes.[21] To the church Jesus assigns a government that is separate from the government of the state. The "rock" upon which Jesus builds his church is Peter as the representative of the twelve, and as the apostolic recipient of revelation from Jesus's heavenly Father (Matt 16:17–18).[22] For this reason, the state has no authority to instruct the church on which doctrines or teachings that the church must embrace, teach, inculcate, propagate, and enforce. The authorized teachers of the church—the "elders"—are elected by the church upon the church's satisfaction that they possess the requisite qualifications for that office set forth in Scripture. When Jesus speaks of the church's discipline a little later in Matthew's Gospel, the persons and procedures entailed in discipline comprise a closed system within the church (Matt 18:15–20). The state plays no role in determining how the church should discipline or whom the church should discipline, and its agents in no way participate in the church's disciplinary proceedings. It is the church's elders and they alone who are tasked with implementing discipline within the church.

The New Testament, however, does not teach the immunity of church members or officers from due punishments lawfully administered by the civil magistrate. The apostle Paul informed the Roman official, Festus, that he was willing to face the death penalty for any capital crimes that he had committed (Acts 25:9–11). The independence of church and state is

19. John Murray, "The Relation of Church and State," *The Collected Writings of John Murray: One Volume*, 254.

20. *BCO* 3-4, employing language originally drafted by the nineteenth-century American Presbyterian, James Henley Thornwell.

21. "The visible Church ... is the kingdom of the Lord Jesus Christ" (WCF 25.2). For an exegetical argument in support of this particular identification, see Vos, *The Teaching of Jesus Concerning the Kingdom of God and the Church*, 77–90.

22. See further my *How Jesus Runs the Church*, 36–37.

not, therefore, altogether absolute. Each, after all, is an ordinance of God. It may help, then, to consider more precisely how it is that church and state (and their respective governments) differ from one another.[23] First, both church and state look to "God as the source of power" for each, but in distinct ways.[24] Civil government is an ordinance of the creation and looks to God as the Creator, Preserver, and Judge of all human beings. The church's government is instituted by God as the Redeemer of his chosen people.[25] Second and relatedly, the state's government concerns human beings as created in the image of God, whereas the church's government concerns human beings as sinners in need of redemption through Christ. "The state is for the whole race of man, the church consists of that portion of the race which is really, or by credible profession, the mediatorial body of Christ."[26] Third, as "the state is ordained for man as man, [it] is ordained to realize the idea of justice."[27] It is for this reason that the apostle Paul characterizes civil government through the symbol of a sword (Rom 13:4). The state is not the implement of eschatological justice, but its infliction of penalties and punishments is an expression of "God's wrath on the wrong-doer" (Rom 13:4) and, thus, a pointer to the judgment of the last day.[28] The church's government, however, is not punitive or retributive. It is disciplinary, seeking the "reformation and salvation" of the church's members.[29] As such, it does not employ force or intimidation and has no right to impose

---

23. The order and observations of what follows is particularly indebted to Peck, *Notes on Ecclesiology*, 145–52.

24. Peck, *Notes on Ecclesiology*, 145.

25. This distinction underlies the related distinction between "essential" and "mediatorial" reigns of Christ, the former concerning his sovereignty as the Second Person of the Godhead over all the works of his hands, and the latter concerning his authority over all things for the sake of his church, on which see James Fisher, *The Westminster Assembly's Shorter Catechism Explained by Way of Question and Answer*, 3rd ed. (repr., Philadelphia: Presbyterian Board of Christian Education, 1925), 138.

26. Peck, *Notes on Ecclesiology*, 145. And, of course, the children of at least one professing member of the church are also subject to the church's government.

27. Peck, *Notes on Ecclesiology*, 145.

28. Peck observes that civil government, as an ordinance of creation, would have been a feature of human society even had Adam not fallen into sin. In such a case, it would have been "simply a directing power," coordinating the efforts of many human beings to "fulfil … love of self and love of neighbor." Given the fall, however, civil government necessarily assumes the added function of "restraining and punishing" people for their evil activities. *Notes on Ecclesiology*, 147.

29. Peck, *Notes on Ecclesiology*, 150.

this-worldly or bodily sanctions upon its members. Because "the church ... moves in the sphere of the spirit," it "appeal[s] to the judgment, the faith, the conscience of its members," and employs "only ... argument, exhortation, admonition, [and] censure."[30] It is "not a kingdom of force, but of persuasion, founded upon the conviction of the truth."[31] Finally, both church and state are accountable to God and regulated by the truth of God. But "the constitution of the church is a divine revelation; the constitution of the state must be determined by human reason and the course of providential events."[32] The state is bound to observe general revelation, and the church is bound to observe special revelation. Because the state is an ordinance of creation, civil magistrates have no authority, as officers of the state, to pronounce the Bible, or any other text, to be revelation from God—"God has given no commission to the state to testify to the truth of Christ's revelation, or to interpret it."[33] This is solely the prerogative of the church.

FOUNDATIONS FOR RELIGIOUS LIBERTY

This Scoto-American understanding of the relationship between the church and the state yields at least two particular benefits, each of which serves not only members of the church but all human beings who come into contact with the church. The first benefit is the provision made for the basis of and guarantee for the divinely-guaranteed religious liberty of all human beings, particularly in the face of attempts by civil government to abridge or to usurp that authority.

Although the Protestant Reformation laid the foundations for religious liberty, it was not until the seventeenth-century that Protestants began to articulate the doctrine.[34] In contrast with the philosopher Thomas Hobbes (1588–1679), who claimed that the civil magistrate had complete authority over the church even in doctrinal matters, the philosopher and theologian John Locke (1632–1704) drew clear delineations between the authority,

30. Peck, *Notes on Ecclesiology*, 149–50.

31. Peck, *Notes on Ecclesiology*, 155.

32. Peck, *Notes on Ecclesiology*, 151, citing the General Assembly of the Presbyterian Church in the United States (1861).

33. Peck, *Notes on Ecclesiology*, 152.

34. See VanDrunen's brief but incisive treatment of Calvin on this point, *Politics after Christendom: Political Theology in a Fractured World* (Grand Rapids: Zondervan, 2020), 195–96.

scope, and power of the commonwealth and that of the church.[35] Locke argued for the "duty of toleration" within civil society, a duty especially incumbent upon the civil magistrate.[36] "Men [are] freed from all dominion over one another in matters of religion," and "these religious societies I call churches ... these I say the magistrate ought to tolerate."[37] In particular, Locke denied that the civil magistrate had any authority to regulate the worship and doctrine of particular churches.[38]

In the American colonies, Roger Williams (1603–1683) is widely recognized as a pioneer in the doctrine of religious liberty.[39] Williams pled not only for the Christian citizen's liberty of conscience, but for liberty of conscience as a right belonging to all people, at least since the dawn of Christianity.

> It is the will and command of God that (since the coming of his Son the Lord Jesus) a permission of the most pagan, Jewish, Turkish, or Antichristian consciences and worships be granted to all men in all nations and countries, and they are only to be fought against with that sword which is only (in soul matters) able to conquer, [that is], the sword of God's Spirit, the word of God.[40]

---

35. Thomas Hobbes, ed. Richard Tuck, *Leviathan* (Cambridge: Cambridge University, 1996), chapter 39; John Locke, "A Letter Concerning Toleration," in *Two Treatises of Government* and *A Letter Concerning Toleration*, ed. Ian Shapiro (New Haven: Yale University Press, 2003), 214–25. Note his statement later in *A Letter Concerning Toleration*, "But there is absolutely no such thing, under the Gospel, as a Christian commonwealth," 239. For a recent survey of John Locke's understanding of religious freedom, see Joseph Loconte, *God, Locke, and Liberty: The Struggle for Religious Freedom in the West* (Lanham, MD: Lexington, 2014).

36. Locke, "A Letter Concerning Toleration," 223, 228. Whereas Locke speaks of "toleration," that is, the permission granted by the civil magistrate to citizens to exercise religious freedom, later writers will speak of "liberty," that is, the inherent right of an individual to believe and act according to the dictates of his conscience.

37. Locke, "A Letter Concerning Toleration," 232.

38. Locke, "A Letter Concerning Toleration," 233–40, 240–44. On Locke's qualifications to this principle, see "A Letter Concerning Toleration," 244–46.

39. For Williams's writings, see representatively, *On Religious Liberty: Selections from the Works of Roger Williams*, ed. James Calvin Davis (Cambridge, MA: Belknap, 2008). For a treatment of Williams's views, see Timothy L. Hall, *Separating Church and State: Roger Williams and Religious Liberty* (Urbana, IL: University of Illinois Press, 1998).

40. Roger Williams, "The Bloody Tenent of Persecution," in *On Religious Liberty*, 86. Williams subsequently argues that the Israelite civil order is only "figurative and ceremonial, and [is] no pattern nor precedent for any kingdom or civil state in the world to follow," "The Bloody Tenent of Persecution," 86.

Williams furthermore argued that "true civility and Christianity may both flourish in a state or kingdom, notwithstanding the permission of diverse and contrary consciences, either of Jew or Gentile."[41] That is to say, not only must the gospel advance by persuasion and not by the sword, but Christianity may and has flourished in a pluralistic society in which the civil magistrate gave no legal preferment to Christianity.

American Presbyterians, particularly in Virginia, took a leading role in advancing the cause of religious liberty in the late eighteenth century.[42] It is for this reason that we may characterize the doctrine of religious liberty in the modern West as particularly indebted to American Presbyterianism. To be sure, Thomas Jefferson and James Madison emerged as leading figures championing the cause religious liberty in the Revolutionary era and the early Republic.[43] Even so, one may not discount the influence of American Presbyterianism, even upon Jefferson and Madison, with respect to this particular question of the relationship between church and state.[44] Importantly, the Memorial of Hanover Presbytery (1776), which petitioned the General Assembly of Virginia, pled for religious liberty and against religious establishments by appeal to what was common to all human beings—the rights of conscience before the Creator.

> Therefore we rely upon this Declaration, as well as the justice of our honorable Legislature, to secure us the *free exercise of religion according to the dictates of our consciences*. ... But that *the duty which we owe our Creator, and the manner of discharging it, can only be directed by reason and conviction; and is no where cognizable but at the tribunal of the universal Judge.*[45]

---

41. Roger Williams, "The Bloody Tenent of Persecution," in *On Religious Liberty*, 87.

42. See Thomas Cary Johnson, *Virginia Presbyterianism and Religious Liberty in Colonial and Revolutionary Times* (Richmond, VA: Presbyterian Committee of Publication, 1907); Charles F. James, *Documentary History of the Struggle for Religious Liberty in Virginia* (Lynchburg, VA: J. P. Bell, 1900).

43. See, representatively, "The Virginia Statute for Religious Freedom" (1786), authored by Jefferson, and James Madison's "Memorial and Remonstrance Against Religious Assessments" (1785). For discussion of the views of each, see Daniel L. Dreisbach, *Real Threat and Mere Shadow: Religious Liberty and the First Amendment* (Westchester, IL: Crossway, 1987), 99–158.

44. Johnson, *Virginia Presbyterianism and Religious Liberty*, 80, 84.

45. "Memorial," in William Henry Foote, *Sketches of Virginia, Historical and Biographical* (Philadelphia: William S. Martien, 1850), 323, emphasis original.

The memorial advanced several arguments against establishments and for religious liberty. Absent the possession of "a chair of infallibility," the civil magistrate is not competent "to adjudge the right of preference among the various sects that profess the Christian faith."[46] Not only are "religious establishments ... highly injurious to the temporal interests of any community" in multiple respects, but "the gospel" has no "need [of] any such civil aid."[47] Establishments transgress "the only proper objects of civil government," namely, "the happiness and protection of men in the present state of existence; the security of the life, liberty and property of the citizens; and to restrain the vicious and encourage the virtuous by wholesome laws, equally extending to every individual." [48]

Religious liberty, then, is tied to a number of theological and political realities—the rights of the conscience of every image-bearer; the prerogatives of God, the Creator and Judge, over each man and woman; the competencies, concerns, and limitations of civil government; and the corrupting influences of state establishment upon both the commonwealth and the church. Significantly, American Presbyterians' arguments for the rights of religious liberty safeguarded the rights of all human beings—not merely Presbyterians or Christians—with respect to the civil magistrate. This is not to say that American Presbyterians have uniformly or consistently advocated for these principles in the public square.[49] But it is to say that these arguments will serve well Christians who live in many different kinds of societies. They will help Christians to plead for liberties that are inherent to the humanity of every person, to encourage civil government that stays within its proper bounds, and to strive for the church to steer clear of compromising entanglements with the state.

---

46. "Memorial," 324.

47. "Memorial," 324.

48. "Memorial," 324.

49. See, for instance, Darryl Hart's discussion of John Witherspoon's 1776 sermon, "The Dominion of Providence over the Passions of Men," in *A Secular Faith: Why Christianity Favors the Separation of Church and State* (Chicago: Ivan R. Dee, 2006), 50–52. Even Hanover Presbytery, in its actions during and after the Revolution, was not entirely consistent with its Memorial of 1776, on which see David VanDrunen, *Natural Law and the Two Kingdoms: A Study in the Development of Early Reformed Social Thought* (Grand Rapids: Eerdmans, 2010), 212–75; and P. C. Kemeny, "Eighteenth-Century Virginia Presbyterians and the Long Road to Religious Liberty," Westminster Theological Journal 84, no. 2 (Fall 2022): 216–20.

PRINCIPLES OF THE CHURCH'S ENGAGEMENT OF THE STATE

The Scoto-American understanding of the relationship between church and state yields a second benefit. It affords principles for the way in which the church, in its organized capacity, may and may not engage the state in matters that concern both the church and the state. The Westminster Standards address this subject forthrightly.

> Synods and councils are to handle, or conclude nothing, but that which is ecclesiastical: and are not to intermeddle with civil affairs which concern the commonwealth, unless by way of humble petition in cases extraordinary; or, by way of advice, for satisfaction of conscience, if they be thereunto required by the civil magistrate. (WCF 31.4)

The Westminster Assembly makes clear that the courts of the church are neither to "handle" nor "conclude" anything except what is "ecclesiastical." They are forbidden from taking up "civil affairs which concern the commonwealth." For this reason, "the charge of danger [i.e., posed by the church] to government, as in the case of an *imperium in imperio,* is unfounded."[50] Westminster, however, recognizes two exceptions to this general rule. In one case, the church may approach the state. In the other, the state may approach the church. In the first instance, "in cases extraordinary," the church may humbly petition the civil magistrate. Such situations are "extraordinary," that is to say, uncommon, and they must be such that "the interests of the Church are immediately concerned."[51] In the second instance, the state may solicit the church for advice on some matter of state, and the church "for satisfaction of conscience" may comply with that request.

Underlying this paragraph of the Westminster Confession is the doctrine of church power as exclusively ministerial and declarative (WCF 31.3). The church has neither authority nor competency to pronounce anything save what God has revealed in his word. The church, however, has "no right

---

50. MacPherson, *Confession of Faith*, 164.

51. A. A. Hodge, *Confession of Faith*, 377.

to presume to give advice to, or to attempt to influence, the officers of the civil government in their action as civil officers," except for the two instances noted above.[52] In the words of the 1845 General Assembly of the Presbyterian Church in the United States of America, "The church of Christ is a spiritual body, whose jurisdiction extends only to the religious faith, and moral conduct of her members. She cannot legislate where Christ has not legislated, nor make terms of membership which he has not made."[53]

This doctrine came to particularly full expression in the Southern United States, before, during, and after the American Civil War.[54] But it is not unique to the Southern Presbyterian Church, nor may it be dismissed as an instrument of Southern ecclesiastical resistance to postbellum Reconstruction.[55] Charles Hodge, who would serve within the Northern Presbyterian Church after the Church's geographical division in 1861, was a firm supporter of the Union and a firm adherent of the church's spirituality, both before and after the Civil War. His protest of Gardiner Spring's 1861 Resolution to the General Assembly of the Presbyterian Church illustrates his commitments to the doctrine. Spring's Resolution sought the Assembly's "expression of their devotion to the Union of these States, and their loyalty to the Government."[56] After the assembly adopted that resolution, Hodge offered a protest. His protest opens with a statement of the doctrine of the church's spirituality and its application to the question at hand.

---

52. A. A. Hodge, *Confession of Faith*, 377.

53. As cited at Strange, *The Doctrine of the Spirituality of the Church*, 198.

54. In addition to the work of Peck, cited above, see the writings of James Henley Thornwell, especially "Address to all the Churches of Christ upon Earth," in *Collected Writings of James Henley Thornwell*, 4 vols. (1871–1873; repr., Edinburgh: Banner of Truth, 1974), 4:446–52; and Samuel R. Wilson, "Declaration and Testimony against the Erroneous and Heretical Doctrines and Practices, which have been obtained and propagated in the Presbyterian Church in the United States during the past five years" (1865), repr. in John S. Grasty, *Memoir of Rev. Samuel B. McPheeters* (St. Louis: Southwestern Book and Publishing Co., 1871), 316–27.

55. Jack P. Maddex has argued that the Southern church received the doctrine of the spirituality of the church from border-state Presbyterians, and then adopted and employed it during Reconstruction for self-serving ends, "From Theocracy to Spirituality: The Southern Presbyterian Reversal on Church and State," *Journal of Presbyterian History* 54 (1976): 438–57. Compare E. T. Thompson, *The Spirituality of the Church: A Distinctive Doctrine of the Presbyterian Church in the United States* (Richmond, VA: John Knox Press, 1961).

56. "The Gardiner Spring Resolutions," *PCA Historical Center*, https://www.pcahistory.org/documents/gardinerspring.html.

> We make this protest, not because we do not acknowledge loyalty to our country to be a moral and religious duty, according to the Word of God, which requires us to be subject to the powers that be; nor because we deny the right of the Assembly to enjoin that, and all other duties, on the ministers and churches under its care; but because we deny the right of the General Assembly to decide the political question, to what government the allegiance of Presbyterians as citizens is due, and its rights to make that decision a condition of membership in our Church.[57]

The assembly, Hodge argued, was within its rights to demand loyalty to country and obedience to the civil magistrate, both of which are taught in Scripture. But the political question that was being agitated in 1861 concerned whether one's allegiance should be with his state government or with the federal government. Through this resolution, Hodge argued, the Church was attempting to settle that political question. In doing so, it was binding the consciences of its members, going beyond the testimony of Scripture and requiring as a condition of church membership adherence to a particular political viewpoint.

Hodge's Protest clarifies that the doctrine of the spirituality of the church in no way prevents the church from speaking to moral issues of contemporary importance.[58] The doctrine critically establishes certain parameters around such speech. The issue must be one that is expressly

---

57. "The Gardiner Spring Resolutions."

58. As becomes evident from even a casual survey of the acts and deliverances of the General Assemblies of the American Presbyterian Church. See, representatively, Samuel J. Baird, *A Collection of the Acts, Deliverances, and Testimonies of the Supreme Judicatory of the Presbyterian Church ...*, 2nd ed. (Philadelphia: Presbyterian Board of Publication, 1855), and G. F. Nicolassen, *A Digest of the Acts and Proceedings of the General Assembly of the Presbyterian Church in the United States* (Richmond, VA: Presbyterian Committee of Publication, 1923). Note the testimonies against "foeticide" (abortion) of the 1869 General Assembly (Old School), reaffirmed by the 1874 General Assembly, "Nor can we shut our eyes to the fact that the horrible crime of infanticide, especially in the form of destruction by parents of their own offspring before birth, also prevails to an alarming extent." "[We view this] with abhorrence, as a crime against God and against nature; and as the frequency of such murders can no longer be concealed, we hereby warn those that are guilty of this crime that except they repent they cannot inherit eternal life." "All who seek to avoid the responsibilities and cares connected with bringing up children not only deprive themselves of one of the greatest blessings of life, and fly in the face of God's decrees, but do violence to their own natures, and will be found out of their sins even in this world," as cited by J. Aspinwall Hodge, *What Is Presbyterian Law*, 106–7.

raised in Scripture. The church's declaration on the matter must not venture into the arena of public policy, and thus bind the consciences of any of its members. The church must recognize that Christians may concur with respect to biblical beliefs and morals, and yet disagree as to their prudential implementation in the public square. It is the task of the church to inform people of the revealed will of God so that the people of God may undertake the application of the word of God in their various callings.

CONCLUSION

Understanding these principles is critical to the life and well-being of the church in the twenty-first century. Faithfulness to them will help to preserve the peace and unity of the church. It will help to safeguard the liberty of the Christian and to respect the bounds that Christ has set for his church. It will also help to ennoble and to encourage Christians' engagement in the culture, particularly the public square. And it will especially help the church to remain faithful to her calling to proclaim the gospel of Christ, making known the whole counsel of God.

FURTHER READING

Johnson, Thomas Cary. *Virginia Presbyterianism and Religious Liberty in Colonial and Revolutionary Times*. Richmond, VA: Presbyterian Committee of Publication, 1907. A historical account, by a nineteenth-century American Presbyterian, of the role that Presbyterians in Virginia played in the development of religious freedom in the American colonies and in the early American republic. One valuable feature of this work is that it contains a number of extracts from important primary sources.

Peck, Thomas Ephraim. "The Church and State." In *Miscellanies of Rev. Thomas E. Peck, Volume II*, edited by Thomas C. Johnson, 266–89. Richmond, VA: Presbyterian Committee of Publication, 1896. An extensive survey of the relationship between church and state by a late nineteenth-century American Presbyterian. Peck's work provides an overview of different understandings of church and state that have surfaced in the church's history.

Strange, Alan D. *The Doctrine of the Spirituality of the Church in the Ecclesiology of Charles Hodge.* RAD. Phillipsburg, NJ: P&R, 2017. A survey of the doctrine of the church and its relationship to the governments of this world in the writings of one of the nineteenth century's preeminent Reformed theologians, Charles Hodge. Strange shows the ways in which Hodge's views were in continuity with earlier Reformed reflection on the subject.

David VanDrunen. *Politics after Christendom: Political Theology in a Fractured World.* Grand Rapids: Zondervan, 2020. A leading Reformed political theologian and ethicist, VanDrunen reflects on Christian political engagement in contemporary, pluralistic societies.

CONCLUSION

SEVEN THESES ON THE CHURCH

THE CHURCH OF JESUS CHRIST is, indeed, "one, holy, catholic, apostolic church." The church is one across the ages and across the world. The church is holy, set apart by God for himself and indwelt by the Holy Spirit. The church is catholic, that is, universal and not parochial. The church is apostolic, founded upon the doctrine transmitted to the people of God by Christ through his apostles.

And yet, in so many ways, the church falls short of this affirmation. As Samuel J. Stone's hymn, "The Church's One Foundation," leads us to confess, "Though with a scornful wonder men see her sore oppressed / by schisms rent asunder, by heresies distressed." Persecution, division, and heresy (to name only three threats) appear to jeopardize or call into question the church's unity, holiness, catholicity, and apostolicity. But it is here, Stone reminds us, that we remind ourselves, "Yet saints their watch are keeping, their cry goes up, 'How long?' / And soon the night of weeping shall be the morn of song." The church—like the Christian—has not yet arrived. We are not yet what we will be. The day will come when the church will pass from her state of militancy to her state of triumph. The church will enter her Sabbath rest (Heb 4:9), but in the meantime we are called to make the arduous, dangerous trek in the wilderness between Egypt and Canaan.

As the church is on pilgrimage, the following seven propositions help her to remember who she is and what she is called to do:

1. The biblical accounts of the creation establish a critical foundation for the biblical doctrine of the church.
2. The church traces its origins to the garden of Eden, following Adam's fall into sin.
3. The Old Testament is an account of God growing and preserving his people, whom he has called into being and into his service.
4. Jesus Christ eschatologically reconstitutes the people of God around himself and establishes that people upon a single apostolic foundation.
5. The one, holy, catholic, apostolic church is identified and defined by the written word of God.
6. The Bible is a sufficient norm for the government, discipline, and worship of the church.
7. The church's mission is to glorify the Triune God by gathering and perfecting the saints.

SEVEN THESES

1. The biblical accounts of the creation establish a critical foundation for the biblical doctrine of the church.

The church, as the body of the redeemed, does not come into existence until after the fall of humanity into sin. Even so, the opening chapters of Genesis testify to realities that underlie the nature and mission of the church. We read here that human beings are created in the image of God and, therefore, are in relationship with God and with one another. In the context of these relationships, human beings are to undertake God-assigned tasks for the good of humanity and the glory of God. The covenant that God makes with Adam (and, in him, with his all ordinary posterity) in the garden points to the eternal life and fellowship with God that is the intended goal for the human race.

2. The church traces its origins to the garden of Eden, following Adam's fall into sin.

In the fall, Adam—and all who descend from him by ordinary generation—turns his back upon God and the callings assigned to him at the creation. God, in his infinite mercy, declares his purpose to redeem a people to himself through the work of a promised offspring of Eve. This people, called into being by the Spirit and word of God, gathers to worship and to serve their Redeemer, and suffers persecution from unredeemed humanity. God advances his redemptive purposes by a single gracious covenant through which he preserves his people and prospers his people through the promises he grants to them.

3. The Old Testament is an account of God growing and preserving his people, whom he has called into being and into his service.

The foundational redemptive event of the Old Testament is the exodus—God's deliverance of his people from Egypt. God delivers his people *from* oppressive bondage and *for* the worship and service of their Creator and Redeemer. The covenant that God makes with Israel at Sinai serves to order the life of the redeemed community and to foreshadow the person and work of the promised offspring (Jesus Christ). In this way Israel was to bear witness of their God to the nations. Israel lamentably failed in this calling. God sends the prophets to declare not only forthcoming judgment for Israel's violation of its covenant with God but also the coming of the Messiah (Jesus Christ), the dawn of the new covenant, and the renewal and expansion of God's people at his coming.

4. Jesus Christ eschatologically reconstitutes the people of God around himself and establishes that people upon a single apostolic foundation.

Jesus Christ is the promised offspring of Eve, by whom redemption is accomplished for the people of God in every age. In light of Christ's incarnation and public ministry, the people of God undergoes transformation—in its definition, response to God, outward form, worship, and mission. Through his apostles, Jesus emphasizes that this people, transformed with the arrival of the new covenant, is one and the same with the people of

God under the old covenant. Through his apostles, Jesus orders the life, government, worship, and mission of the church under the new covenant.

5. The one, holy, catholic, apostolic church is identified and defined by the written word of God.

The church bears the attributes of unity, holiness, catholicity, and apostolicity. The church's *mark* (that which defines the church) is the truth of God set forth in Holy Scripture. As such, the church evidences itself to be the church through the pure preaching of the word of God, the biblical administration of the sacraments of baptism and the Lord's Supper, and the biblical administration of discipline. In keeping with the centrality of the Scripture to the church, the church formally confesses biblical truth through creeds and confessions.

6. The Bible is a sufficient norm for the government, discipline, and worship of the church.

The norming authority of the Bible for the church is evident in three departments of the church's life and ministry. Christ, the only king and head of his church, appoints for his people a form of government, a system of discipline, and a pattern of worship. Each of these three areas is set down in the Scripture, and, in each, the Bible constitutes a sufficient guide to the church. In this way, the authority, wisdom, and goodness of Christ to his people are made evident.

7. The church's mission is to glorify the Triune God by gathering and perfecting the saints.

Christ commissioned his apostles and, through these apostolic commissions, the church after the apostles. In these commissions, Christ assigns specific tasks for the church until he returns in glory. The church is to go out into the world and to gather sinners through the preaching of the gospel. Through the same proclamation of the word of God, the church is to be built up and matured. The church is in the world, but the church's mission is not of the world. That mission is spiritual and not temporal or secular. Furthermore, the government and mission of the church is altogether separate from the governments of this world. In these ways, the church equips the saints to be faithful in their callings everywhere in the world.

The church's hope for Sabbath rest (Heb 4:9)would be sheer presumption but for the fact that Christ has promised us that he "will build [his] church, and the gates of hell shall not prevail against it" (Matt 16:18). Christ, who has "the keys of Death and Hades" (Rev 1:18), will never let his people perish. The church is the "apple of [God's] eye" (Zech 2:8), precious and protected. The Father who chose his people, the Son who died and rose again for his people, and the Spirit who preserves and sanctifies his people will keep them to the very end.

While tremendous blessing awaits the church at the consummation, God has blessing in store for his people, now and on the way. God gives us foretastes of the feast that awaits us. In "The Church's One Foundation," Stone captures this beautifully.

> Yet she on earth hath union with God the Three in One,
> and mystic sweet communion with those whose rest is won:
> O happy ones and holy! Lord, give us grace that we,
> Like them, the meek and lowly, on high may dwell with thee.

In the present, we have access to the Father, in Christ, by the Spirit. Union and communion with the Triune God is something that we experience now. Furthermore, the saints who have gone before us stand as a "great ... cloud of witnesses" that stirs and prods us to "lay aside every weight, and sin which clings so closely, and ... run with endurance the race that is set before us" (Heb 12:2). We look, as they looked, to "Jesus, the founder and perfecter of our faith" (Heb 12:2). As Christ passed from humiliation to exaltation, so he leads his people to "suffer with him in order that [they] may also be glorified with him" (Rom 8:17). We have every assurance that, as the bridegroom has entered into glory, so he will lead his bride into glory.

This present blessing and future hope does not leave us idle. There is much work that Christ has given his church to do. But what the church does, the church does in full knowledge that the Father's love to his people is from everlasting to everlasting, that the Son's union with his people is unbreakable, and that the Spirit's commitment to indwell, support, preserve, and sanctify his people is unshakeable. Standing on this foundation, we labor on until Christ returns and the Triune God completes the good work that he has already begun.

GLOSSARY

Anthropology: in systematic theology, a term that refers to the doctrine of humanity.

Apostle: Greek, "sent one." The term that the New Testament uses to describe Jesus's twelve disciples as the authoritative and commissioned witnesses of his life, death, and (especially) resurrection. The apostles constitute the foundation of the church under the new covenant.

Attributes of the Church: those features of the church that characterize but do not define or distinguish the church from other societies or organizations. Reformed Protestants understand unity, holiness, catholicity, and apostolicity to be attributes of the church.

Biblical theology: a discipline that studies the Bible in terms of its unfolding narrative, from creation to consummation. Biblical theology explores either the whole of that narrative or particular themes or motifs within that narrative.

Christology: in systematic theology, a term that refers to the doctrine of the person and work of Jesus Christ.

Circumstance: a detail attending an action that does not belong to the substance of that action. Such a category surfaces, in discussions of both public worship and church government, in distinction from what are termed "elements." Circumstances are *circum sacra* (Latin, "about/around sacred things"), whereas elements are *in sacris* (Latin, "in sacred things").

Common Grace: in distinction from saving grace, which refers to the grace of God in Christ for the salvation of sinners, common grace describes God's non-redemptive favor to all human beings.

Confession: a non-inspired statement that aspires to provide a faithful and orderly summary of the leading teachings of Scripture. Confessions are sometimes distinguished from creeds, which refer to such early, ecumenical statements of Christian faith as the Apostles' Creed and the Nicene-Constantinopolitan Creed.

Covenant: a bond between two parties that serves to formalize those parties' relationship with one another.

Covenant of Grace: the covenant that God instituted after the fall with Christ as the last Adam and, in Christ, with all the elect. God promised salvation to his elect solely on the basis of the obedience and satisfaction of Jesus Christ.

Covenant of Redemption: the eternal covenant among the three persons of the Godhead to secure the salvation of the elect. The Father sends his Son into the world to save the elect; the Son agrees to undertake all that is necessary for the salvation of the elect; the Spirit agrees to apply to the elect in time the salvation purchased by the Son.

Covenant of Works: the covenant that God instituted in the garden with Adam as a representative man and, in Adam, with all human beings ordinarily descending from Adam, before Adam fell into sin. God promised confirmed, eschatological life to Adam upon condition of perfect and continued obedience to God's commandments. When Adam sinned, he brought death upon himself and upon all whom he represents.

Deacon: an office of service in the people of God under the New Testament. In the apostolic age, deacons were particularly entrusted with the care of needy, qualified widows in the church.

Ecclesiology: in systematic theology, a term that refers to the doctrine of the church.

Ekklēsia: Greek, "assembly, church." The word that Jesus and the apostles use of the people of God under the new covenant and that the Septuagint (the Greek translation of the Old Testament) uses of Israel.

Elder: an office of rule or government in the people of God under both the Old and New Testaments. Under the New Testament, some elders serve as teachers or pastors of the church.

Episcopacy: a form of church government characterized by the rule of monarchical bishops.

Eschatology: in systematic theology, a term that refers to the doctrine of the four last things (death, judgment, heaven, and hell); in biblical theology, a term that refers to the arc and movement of human history toward a divinely appointed goal, namely the glory of God in Christ.

***Excommunicatio minor*:** Latin, "lesser excommunication." A term used historically within Dutch Reformed churches to describe the ecclesiastical censure of suspension from the Lord's Supper. This phrase refers to the fact that this censure may be immediately followed by the censure of excommunication.

Ex nihilo: Latin, "from nothing." Theologians use this phrase to express the fact that, when God created the world, he did not use preexisting materials.

Gift: in the context of the church, an endowment of the Triune God (preeminently the Holy Spirit) upon a person which is intended for the spiritual edification of the church.

Image of God: a biblical phrase that expresses the unique resemblance that human beings bear to God. Classically, the image of God (Latin, *imago Dei*) expresses three points of similarity between a human being and his or her Creator—knowledge, righteousness, and holiness.

Immanuel: Hebrew, "God with us." The title used of Jesus in the New Testament to denote the gracious and abiding presence of God with his people in fulfillment of the promises of the covenant of grace.

Independency: a form of church government characterized by the governmental independence of congregations from one another.

Invisible Church: the whole number of the elect that have been, are, or will be gathered to Jesus Christ as their Mediator.

***Jure divino*:** Latin, "by divine right." With respect to church polity, the doctrine that the Scripture is a sufficient rule for the government of the church. Contrast *jure humano* (Latin, "by human right") church government, which allows for custom, tradition, human authority, expediency, or other such considerations to contribute to the elements of the church's polity.

Kingdom of God: the redemptive rule and reign of God over all things and particularly over his people. Although the kingdom of God is present under the Old Testament, the kingdom breaks into history powerfully and climactically in the public ministry of Jesus Christ.

***Media gratiae*:** Latin, "means of grace." Instruments or channels in the church through which God is ordinarily pleased to convey saving grace to his elect. Examples include the reading and preaching of the word of God, the sacraments of baptism and of the Lord's Supper, and prayer.

Mediator: one who stands between two parties and undertakes the work required to bring those two parties together. In the covenant of grace, Jesus Christ is the sole Mediator between God and human beings.

Messiah: Hebrew, "Anointed One" (cf. Greek, *Christos*, "Anointed One"). The title used of Jesus both in the Old Testament and in the New Testament. It captures the fact that he was anointed with the Holy Spirit to undertake the work of a prophet, priest, and king of his church.

***Munus triplex*:** Latin, "three-fold office." A technical theological phrase denoting the three-fold office of Christ as prophet, priest, and king of his church.

New Covenant: the final and climactic administration of the covenant of grace. The prophet Jeremiah announced the new covenant in Jeremiah 31, and the New Testament confirms that the new covenant was inaugurated with the death and resurrection of Jesus Christ (Luke 22; 2 Cor 3). The new covenant is particularly characterized by the outpouring of the Holy Spirit in fullness, and the extension of the blessings of salvation to the nations.

***Notae ecclesiae*:** Latin, "marks of the church." That which serves to define the church as the church, in distinction from other societies and organizations.

Office: a position that entails the exercise of authority. In the church, according to the New Testament, office presupposes a man's possession and exercise of requisite gifts; the church's recognition of those gifts and call to that man to exercise those gifts in office; and ordination.

Old Covenant (Mosaic Covenant, Sinaitic Covenant): the administration of the covenant of grace inaugurated at Mt. Sinai and concluded at the resurrection of Jesus. The primary purpose of this administration was to portray the coming Messiah to the people of God through its promises, prophecies, types, ordinances, sacrifices, and sacraments.

Ordination: the solemn admission into office, by the elders of the church, of a man who has been called by the church to ecclesiastical office.

Pentateuch: the first five books of the Bible (Genesis, Exodus, Leviticus, Numbers, Deuteronomy).

Pneumatology: in systematic theology, a term that refers to the doctrine of the person and work of the Holy Spirit.

Power: the ability to do something (compare "authority," the right to do something). In discussions of church government, church power is understood along three lines—doctrine (dogmatic power), order (diatactical power), and discipline (diacritical power). Dogmatic power is the church's power to teach the word of God. Diatactical power is the church's power to order the affairs of the church under the word of God. Diacritical power is the church's power to enforce the word of God among the membership of the church.

Presbyterianism: a form of church government characterized by the rule of a plurality of elders serving in graded courts.

Protoevangelium: Latin, "first announcement of the gospel." A term that the church has used to describe God's words in Genesis 3:15—the initial promise to sinners of salvation to be accomplished by the work of Christ.

Redemptive History: a term describing the period of human history from the fall to the consummation (i.e., the return of Christ), during which God is saving sinners through the work of Jesus Christ.

Regulative Principle of Worship: the doctrine that public worship is so limited by Scripture as to forbid in public worship whatsoever is not expressly authorized in Scripture.

Sabbath: Hebrew, "rest." The term "sabbath" preeminently describes the one day each week that God sets apart for human beings to devote to his worship. God appointed this day at creation as a perpetual commandment for all humanity.

Sacerdotal: of or pertaining to a priest (Latin, *sacerdos*).

Sacrament: an ordinance, appointed by Christ for his church, to signify and to confirm to those within the covenant of grace the benefits of Christ's mediation.

Servant: the individual featured in four "Servant Songs" in Isaiah's prophecy (Isaiah 42, 49, 50, and 53). The Servant is characterized by his obedience to God and his righteous suffering on behalf of sinners. The New Testament confirms that the Servant is the Lord Jesus Christ.

Sola scriptura: Latin, "Scripture alone." A phrase capturing the Reformation's commitment to the Scripture as the only rule of faith and practice.

Son of Man: the individual person featured in Daniel 7. He enters into the heavenly presence of the Ancient of Days and receives an eternal kingdom that will displace all earthly kingdoms. People from all nations will serve the Son of Man. The New Testament confirms that the Son of Man is the Lord Jesus Christ.

Soteriology: in systematic theology, a term that refers to the doctrine of salvation and, particularly, its application to human beings by the Holy Spirit.

Subscription: the embrace, usually by an officer of the church, of a particular church's confessional standards.

Successio Verbi aut doctrinae: Latin, "succession of the word or of doctrine." A phrase that expresses how Protestants understand apostolic succession. The church is apostolic in that the doctrine committed to the church by the apostles is both preserved and faithfully transmitted from one generation to another.

Torah: (a) the first five books of the Bible (Genesis, Exodus, Leviticus, Numbers, Deuteronomy); (b) in particular, the legislation of the first five books of the Bible.

Visible Church: the society consisting of all those who profess faith in Christ, and of their children.

BIBLIOGRAPHY

Aalders, G. Ch. *Genesis*. 2 vols. BSC. Grand Rapids: Zondervan, 1981.

Adger, John B. "Inaugural Discourse on Church History and Church Polity." *Southern Presbyterian Review* 12, no. 1 (April 1859): 140–81.

Alexander, J. A. *Essays on The Primitive Church Offices*. New York: Charles Scribner, 1851.

Allison, Gregg R. *Sojourners and Strangers: The Doctrine of the Church*. Wheaton, IL: Crossway, 2012.

The Apostolic Fathers: Greek Texts and English Translations. 3rd edition. Edited and translated by Michael W. Holmes. Grand Rapids: Baker Academic, 2007.

Baird, Samuel J. *A Collection of the Acts, Deliverances, and Testimonies of the Supreme Judicatory of the Presbyterian Church*. 2nd ed. Philadelphia: Presbyterian Board of Publication, 1855.

Bannerman, Douglas D. *The Scripture Doctrine of the Church, Historically and Exegetically Considered*. 1887. Reprint, Grand Rapids: Baker Academic, 1976.

Bannerman, James. *The Church of Christ: A Treatise on the Nature, Powers, Ordinances, Discipline, and Government of the Christian Church*. 2 vols. Edinburgh: T&T Clark, 1868.

Barclay, Robert. *An Apology for the True Christian Divinity: Being an Explanation and Vindication of the Principles and Doctrines of the People Called Quakers*. 9th ed. London: Thomas Tegg, 1825.

Barker, William. "Lord of Lords and King of Commoners: The Westminster Confession and the Relationship of Church and State." In *The Westminster Confession into the 21st Century: Essays in Remembrance of the 350th Anniversary of the Westminster Assembly*. Vol. 1. Edited by J. Ligon Duncan III. Fearn: Christian Focus, 2003.

Barnett, Paul. *The Second Epistle to the Corinthians.* NICNT. Grand Rapids: Eerdmans, 1997.

Barth, Karl. *Church Dogmatics.* Vol. 3.1. Translated and edited by G. W. Bromiley and T. F. Torrance. Edinburgh: T&T Clark, 1960.

Bavinck, Herman. *Reformed Dogmatics.* 4 vols. Translated by John Vriend. Grand Rapids: Baker Academic, 2006.

Beale, G. K. "Eden, the Temple, and the Church's Mission in the New Creation." *JETS* 48 (2005): 5–31.

———. *A New Testament Biblical Theology: The Unfolding of the Old Testament in the New*. Grand Rapids: Baker Academic, 2011.

———. *The Temple and the Church's Mission: A Biblical Theology of the Dwelling Place of God.* NSBT 17. Downers Grove, IL: InterVarsity Press, 2004.

Beckwith, Roger. *Elders in Every City: The Origin and Role of the Ordained Ministry.* Waynesboro, GA: Paternoster, 2003.

Beckwith, Roger T., and Scott, Wilfrid. *This Is the Day: The Biblical Doctrine of the Christian Sunday.* London: Marshall, Morgan & Scott, 1978.

Belcher, Richard P., Jr. "The Davidic Covenant." In *Covenant Theology: Biblical, Theological, and Historical Perspectives*, ed. Guy Prentiss Waters, J. Nicholas Reid, and John R. Muether. Wheaton, IL: Crossway, 2020.

———.*The Fulfillment of the Promises of God: An Explanation of Covenant Theology.* Fearn, UK: Christian Focus, 2020.

———. *Prophet, Priest, and King: The Roles of Christ in the Bible and Our Roles Today.* Phillipsburg, NJ: P&R, 2016.

Berkhof, Louis. *Systematic Theology*. Grand Rapids: Eerdmans, 1996.

Berkouwer, G. C. *Man: The Image of God.* Translated by Dirk W. Jellema. Grand Rapids: Eerdmans, 1962.

———. *The Church.* Translated by James E. Davison. Grand Rapids: Eerdmans, 1976.

———. *Studies in Dogmatics*. Grand Rapids: Eerdmans, 1952.

Blaising, Craig R., and Bock, Darrell L. *Progressive Dispensationalism: An Up-to-Date Handbook of Contemporary Dispensational Thought.* Wheaton, IL: Victor, 1993.

Block, Daniel I. "Eden: A Temple? A Reassessment of the Biblical Evidence." In *From Creation to New Creation: Biblical Theology & Ex-*

egesis. Essays in Honor of G. K. Beale, edited by Daniel M. Gurtner and Benjamin L. Gladd, 3–30. Peabody, MA: Hendrickson, 2013.

The Book of Church Order of the Presbyterian Church in America. Lawrenceville, GA: The Office of the Stated Clerk of the General Assembly of the Presbyterian Church in America, 2021.

The Book of Church Order of the Presbyterian Church in the United States. Richmond, VA: Presbyterian Committee of Publication, 1879.

Bradshaw, Paul F. *Reconstructing Early Christian Worship.* London: SPCK, 2009.

———. *Search for the Origins of Christian Worship.* 2nd ed. Oxford: Oxford, 2002.

———. Bray, Gerald. *The Church: A Theological and Historical Account.* Grand Rapids: Baker Academic, 2016.

Calvin, John. *Commentaries on the First Book of Moses Called Genesis.* Translated by John King. 2 vols. Grand Rapids: Baker Academic, 1996.

———. *Institutes of the Christian Religion.* Edited by John T. McNeill. Translated by Ford Lewis Battles. 2 vols. Philadelphia: Westminster, 1960.

———. "On the Necessity of Reforming the Church." In vol. 1 of *John Calvin: Tracts and Letters.* Translated by Henry Beveridge. 1844. Reprint, Edinburgh: Banner of Truth, 2009.

Calvin, John. Translated by Henry Beveridge. 1844. *Institutes of the Christian Religion: 1541 French Edition.* Reprint, Grand Rapids: Eerdmans, 2009.

Cameron, Nigel S., ed. *Dictionary of Scottish Church History and Theology.* Downers Grove, IL: InterVarsity Press, 1993.

Carson, D. A. *From Sabbath to Lord's Day: A Biblical, Historical, and Theological Investigation.* Grand Rapids: Zondervan, 1982.

Catechism of the Catholic Church, with Modifications from the Editio Typica. New York: Doubleday, 1997.

"Church and State (Legal Questions)" and "Church and State (Theological Questions)." In *Dictionary of Scottish Chruch History & Theology,* edited by Nigel M. de S. Cameron, 179–80, 180–82. Downers Grove, IL: InterVarsity Press, 1993.

Clowney, Edmund P. "Corporate Worship: A Means of Grace." In *Give Praise to God: A Vision for Reforming Worship.* Edited by Philip Graham Ryken, Derek W. H. Thomas, and J. Ligon Duncan III. Phillipsburg, NJ: P&R, 2003.

———. "Interpreting the Biblical Models of the Church: A Hermeneutical Deepening of Ecclesiology." In *Biblical Interpretation and the Church: Text and Context*, edited by D. A. Carson. Grand Rapids: Eerdmans, 1987.

———. "Presbyterian Worship." In *Worship: Adoration and Action*, edited by D. A. Carson, 120–22. Eugene, OR: Wipf and Stock, 2002.

———. "The Biblical Theology of the Church." In *The Church in the Bible and the World: An International Study*, edited by D. A. Carson, 13–87. Grand Rapids: Baker Academic, 1987.

Coffin, David F. Jr. "The Justification of Confessions and the Logic of Confessional Subscription." In *The Practical Calvinist: An Introduction to the Presbyterian and Reformed Heritage, In Honor of Dr. D. Clair Davis on the Occasion of His Seventieth Birthday*, edited by Peter A. Lillback. Fearn, UK: Christian Focus, 2002.

Cole, Graham. *He Who Gives Life: The Doctrine of the Holy Spirit*. Wheaton, IL: Crossway, 2007.

Crowe, Brandon D. *The Obedient Son: Deuteronomy and Christology in the Gospel of Matthew*. BZNW 188. Berlin: De Gruyter, 2012.

Cullmann, Oscar. *Early Christian Worship*. Philadelphia: Westminster Press, 1953.

Cunningham, William. *Historical Theology*. 2 vols. 1862. Reprint, Edinburgh: Banner of Truth, 1960.

———. *The Reformers and the Theology of the Reformation*. Edinburgh: T&T Clark, 1862.

Curtis, Byron G. "Hosea 6:7 and the Covenant-Breaking like/at Adam." In *The Law Is Not of Faith: Essays on Works and Grace in the Mosaic Covenant*, edited by Bryan D. Estelle, John V. Fesko, and David VanDrunen. Phillipsburg, NJ: P&R, 2009.

Dabney, Robert L. "The Doctrinal Contents of the Confession." In *Memorial Volume of the Westminster Assembly, 1647–1897*. Richmond, VA: Presbyterian Committee of Publication, 1897.

———. *Lectures in Systematic Theology*. Grand Rapids: Baker Book House, 1972.

———. *Systematic Theology*. 2nd ed. Edinburgh: Banner of Truth Trust, 1985.

———. "What is Christian Union." In *Discussions: Evangelical and Theological*. Richmond, VA: Presbyterian Committee of Publication, 1891.

Dagg, J. L. *Manual of Theology, Second Part: A Treatise on Church Order*. 1858. Reprint, Harrisonburg, VA: Gano, 1990.

Davis, James Calvin, ed. *On Religious Liberty: Selections from the Works of Roger Williams*. Cambridge, MA: Belknap, 2008.

DeYoung, Kevin, and Gilbert, Greg. *What Is the Mission of the Church? Making Sense of Social Justice, Shalom, and the Great Commission*. Wheaton, IL: Crossway, 2011.

Dreisbach, Daniel L. *Real Threat and Mere Shadow: Religious Liberty and the First Amendment*. Westchester, IL: Crossway, 1987.

Dunlop, William. *The Use of Creeds and Confessions of Faith*. London: Hamilton, Adams, & Co., 1867.

Edwards, Jonathan. "East of Eden" (Sermon on Genesis 3:24). Vol. 17 of *The Works of Jonathan Edwards*, edited by Mark Valeri. New Haven, CT: Yale University Press, 1999.

———. *A History of the Work of Redemption*. Vol. 9 of *The Works of Jonathan Edwards*, edited by John F. Wilson. New Haven: Yale, 1989.

———. *The "Miscellanies": Entry Nos. 501–832*. Vol. 18 of *The Works of Jonathan Edwards*, edited by Ava Chamberlain. New Haven, CT: Yale University Press, 2000.

Estelle, Bryan D. *The Primary Mission of the Church: Engaging or Transforming the World?* Fearn, UK: Mentor, 2022.

Fairbairn, Patrick. *The Typology of Scripture*. 2 vols. New York and London: Funk and Wagnalls, 1911.

Farish, Leah. "The First Amendment's Religion Clauses: The Calvinist Document that Interprets Them Both." *Journal of Religion & Society* 12 (2010): 3–4.

Ferguson, Sinclair B. *Devoted to God: Blueprints for Sanctification*. Edinburgh: Banner of Truth, 2016.

———. "Infant Baptism View." In *Baptism: Three Views*, edited by David F. Wright, 77–112. Downers Grove, IL: InterVarsity Press, 2009.

———. *The Holy Spirit*. Downers Grove, IL: InterVarsity Press, 1996.

Fesko, J. V. *The Need for Creeds Today: Confessional Faith in a Faithless Age*. Grand Rapids: Baker Academic, 2020.

———. *The Theology of the Westminster Standards: Historical Context and Theological Insights*. Wheaton, IL: Crossway, 2014.

———. *Word, Water, and Spirit: A Reformed Perspective on Baptism.* Grand Rapids: Reformation Heritage, 2010.

Fisher, James. *The Westminster Assembly's Shorter Catechism Explained by Way of Question and Answer.* 3rd ed. Philadelphia: Presbyterian Board of Christian Education, 1765, 1925.

Foote, William Henry. *Sketches of Virginia, Historical and Biographical.* Philadelphia: William S. Martien, 1850.

"The Form of Presbyterian Church Government ... Agreed Upon by the Assembly of Divines at Westminster." In *The Westminster Confession.* Edinburgh: Banner of Truth, 2018.

Fung Ronald Y. K. "Ministry in the New Testament." In *The Church in the Bible and the World,* edited by D. A. Carson. Grand Rapids: Baker, 1983.

Gaffin, Richard B., Jr. "A Cessationist View." In *Are Miraculous Gifts for Today?*, edited by Wayne A. Grudem, 25–64. Grand Rapids: Zondervan, 1996.

———. *In the Fullness of Time: An Introduction to the Biblical Theology of Acts and Paul.* Wheaton, IL: Crossway, 2022.

———. *Perspectives on Pentecost: New Testament Teaching on the Gifts of the Holy Spirit.* Phillipsburg, NJ: P&R, 1979.

———. "The Redemptive-Historical View." In *Biblical Hermeneutics: Five Views,* edited by Stanley E. Porter and Beth M. Stovell, 89–110. Downers Grove, IL: InterVarsity Press, 2012.

———. "A Sabbath Rest Still Awaits the People of God." In *Pressing Toward the Mark: Essays Commemorating Fifty Years of the Orthodox Presbyterian Church,* edited by C. G. Dennison and R. C. Gamble. Philadelphia: The Committee for the Historian of the Orthodox Presbyterian Church, 1986.

Gentry, Peter J., and Wellum, Stephen J. *Kingdom through Covenant: A Biblical Theological Understanding of the Covenants.* 2nd ed. Wheaton, IL: Crossway, 2018.

Gibson, David. "Sacramental Supercessionism Revisited: A Response to Martin Salter on the Relationship between Circumcision and Baptism." *Themelios* 37, no. 2 (2012): 191–208.

Gilbert-Smith, Mile. Review of *The Mission of God*, *9Marks Journal* (October 25, 2010).

Gillespie, George. *A Dispute Against the English-Popish Ceremonies Obtruded on the Church of Scotland*. 1662. Reprint, Edinburgh: Ogle, Oliver, and Boyd, 1844.

Gladd, Benjamin L. *From Adam and Israel to the Church: A Biblical Theology of the People of God*. Downers Grove, IL: InterVarsity Press, 2019.

Glodo, Michael J. "Dispensationalism." In *Covenant Theology: Biblical, Theological, and Historical Perspectives*, edited by Guy Prentiss Waters, J. Nicholas Reid, and John R. Muether, 525–50. Wheaton, IL: Crossway, 2020.

Goswell, Greg. "What Makes the Arrangement of God with David in 2 Samuel 7 a Covenant?" *ResQ* 60, no. 2 (2018): 87–98.

Graham, Preston D., Jr. *A Kingdom Not of This World: Stuart Robinson's Struggle to Distinguish the Sacred from the Secular during the Civil War*. Macon, GA: Mercer University Press, 2002.

Grudem, Wayne. *The Gift of Prophecy in the New Testament and Today*. Revised edition. Wheaton, IL: Crossway, 2000.

———. "The Meaning of *Kephalē* ('Head'): An Evaluation of New Evidence, Real and Alleged." In *Biblical Foundations for Manhood and Womanhood*, edited by Wayne Grudem, 145–202. Wheaton, IL: Crossway, 2002.

———. *Systematic Theology*. 2nd ed. Grand Rapids: Zondervan, 2020.

Gunnoe, Charles D., Jr. *Thomas Erastus and the Palatinate: A Renaissance Physician in the Second Reformation*. BSCH 48. Leiden: Brill, 2010.

Hall, David W., ed. *Jus Divinum Regiminis Ecclesiastici* or *The Divine Right of Church-Government*. Revised and edited by David W. Hall. 1646. Reprint, Dallas, TX: Naphtali Press, 1995.

———. *The Practice of Confessional Subscription*. Oak Ridge, TN: Covenant Foundation, 1997.

Hall, Timothy L. *Separating Church and State: Roger Williams and Religious Liberty*. Urbana, IL: University of Illinois Press, 1998.

Haykin, Michael A. G. *Amidst Us Our Belovèd Stands: Recovering Sacrament in the Baptist Tradition*. Bellingham, WA: Lexham, 2022.

Heppe, Heinrich. *Reformed Dogmatics Set Out and Illustrated from the Sources.* Translated by G. T. Thomson. 1950. Reprint, Grand Rapids: Baker, 1978.

Hobbes, Thomas. *Leviathan.* Edited by Richard Tuck. Cambridge: Cambridge University, 1996.

Hodge, A. A. *Outlines of Theology.* 1879. Reprint, Edinburgh: Banner of Truth, 1972.

———. *The Westminster Confession: A Commentary*. Edinburgh: Banner of Truth Trust, 2002.

Hodge, J. Aspinwall. *What Is Presbyterian as Defined by the Church Courts?* 7th ed. Philadelphia: Presbyterian Board of Publication and Sabbath-School Work, 1894.

Hoehner, Harold W. *Ephesians: An Exegetical Commentary.* Grand Rapids: Baker Academic, 2002.

Hoekema, Anthony A. *Created in God's Image*. Grand Rapids: Eerdmans, 1994.

Horton, Michael Scott. *The Christian Faith: A Systematic Theology for Pilgrims on the Way*. Grand Rapids: Zondervan, 2011.

Hugenberger, Gordon. *Marriage as a Covenant: Biblical Law and Ethics as Developed from Malachi.* VTSup 52. Leiden: Brill, 1994.

Hünermann, Peter, Helmut Hoping, Robert L. Fastiggi, Anne Englund Nash, and Heinrich Denzinger, eds. *Compendium of Creeds, Definitions, and Declarations on Matters of Faith and Morals*. 43rd ed. San Francisco, CA: Ignatius Press, 2012.

Jacobs, Michael N. "The Resurgence of Two Kingdoms Doctrine: A Survey of the Literature." *Themelios* 45, no. 2 (2020): 314–32.

James, Charles F. *Documentary History of the Struggle for Religious Liberty in Virginia.* Lynchburg, VA: J. P. Bell, 1900.

Jefferson, Thomas. "*The Virginia Statute for Religious Freedom.*" 1786.

Johnson, Thomas Cary. *The Life and Letters of Benjamin Morgan Palmer.* Richmond, VA: Presbyterian Committee of Publication, 1906.

———. *Virginia Presbyterianism and Religious Liberty in Colonial and Revolutionary Times.* Richmond, VA: Presbyterian Committee of Publication, 1907.

Kaiser, Waler C., Jr. "The Blessing of David: The Charter for Humanity." In *The Law and the Prophets*, edited by John H. Skilton. Phillipsburg, NJ: P&R, 1974.

Kemeny, P. C. "Eighteenth-Century Virginia Presbyterians and the Long Road to Religious Liberty." *Westminster Theological Journal* 84, no. 2 (Fall 2022): 216–20.

Knight, George W., III. "1 Corinthians 11:17–34: The Lord's Supper: Abuses, Words of Institution and Warnings and the Inferences and Deductions with respect to Paedocommunion." In *Children and the Lord's Supper*, edited by Guy Prentiss Waters and Ligon Duncan. Fearn, UK: Mentor, 2011.

———. "Two Offices and Two Orders of Elders." In *Pressing Toward the Mark: Essays Commemorating Fifty Years of the Orthodox Presbyterian Church*, edited by C. G. Dennison and R. C. Gamble. Philadelphia: The Committee for the Historian of the Orthodox Presbyterian Church, 1986.

———. *The Faithful Sayings in the Pastoral Letters.* Grand Rapids: Baker Book House, 1979.

Köstenberger, A. J. "Mission." In *New Dictionary of Biblical Theology: Exploring the Unity and Diversity of Scripture*, ed. T. Desmond Alexander, Brian S. Rosner, D. A. Carson, and Graeme Goldsworthy, 663–68. Downers Grove, IL: IVP Academic, 2000.

———. "Was the Last Supper a Passover Meal?" In *The Lord's Supper: Remembering and Proclaiming Christ Until He Comes*, edited by Thomas R. Schreiner and Matthew R. Crawford, 6–30. Nashville, TN: B&H, 2010.

Köstenberger, A. J., and P. T. O'Brien. *Salvation to the Ends of the Earth: A Biblical Theology of Mission.* Downers Grove, IL: InterVarsity Press, 2001.

Kuiper, R. B. *The Glorious Body of Christ.* Grand Rapids: Eerdmans, 1967.

Kuyper, Abraham. *The Work of the Holy Spirit*. London: Funk & Wagnalls Company, 1900.

Letham, Robert. *The Westminster Assembly: Reading Its Theology in Historical Context*. The Westminster Assembly and the Reformed Faith. Phillipsburg, NJ: P&R, 2009.

Litton, Edward Arthur. *The Church of Christ in Its Idea, Attributes, and Ministry.* 3rd rev. ed. Philadelphia: Smith & English, 1863.

Locke, John. "A Letter Concerning Toleration." In *Two Treatises of Government* and *A Letter Concerning Toleration*, edited by Ian Shapiro, 211–56. New Haven, CT: Yale University Press, 2003.

Loconte, Joseph. *God, Locke, and Liberty: The Struggle for Religious Freedom in the West.* Lanham, MD: Lexington, 2014.

Machen, J. Gresham. "The Creeds and Doctrinal Advance." In *God Transcendent and Other Selected Sermons*, edited by Ned B. Stonehouse. 1949. Reprint, Edinburgh: Banner of Truth, 1982.

MacLeod, Donald. *The Spirit of Promise.* Fearn, UK: Christian Focus, 1986.

MacPherson, John. *Presbyterianism.* Edingburgh: T&T Clark, 1882.

———. *The Westminster Confession of Faith, with Introduction and Notes.* Edinburgh: T&T Clark, 1911.

Maddex, John. "From Theocracy to Spirituality: The Southern Presbyterian Reversal on Church and State." *Journal of Presbyterian History* 54 (1976): 438–57.

Madison, James. "Memorial and Remonstrance Against Religious Assessments." In *10 March 1784–28 March 1786*, vol. 8 of *The Papers of James Madison*, edited by Robert A. Rutland, William M. E. Rachal, Barbara D. Ripel, and Fredrika J. Teute. Chicago: University of Chicago Press, 1973.

Marshall, I. Howard. *Last Supper and Lord's Supper.* Grand Rapids: Eerdmans, 1980.

———. *The Pastoral Epistles.* ICC. London: T&T Clark, 1999.

Martin, R. P. *Worship in the Early Church.* 2nd ed. Grand Rapids: Eerdmans, 1974.

Mason, John Mitchell. *Essays on the Church of God: In Which the Doctrines of Church Membership and Infant Baptism Are Fully Discussed.* 1843. Reprint, Taylors, SC: Presbyterian Press, 2005.

M'Crie, Thomas. *The Life of Andrew Melville.* 2 vols. Edinburgh: William Blackwood, 1824.

———. *Two Discourses on the Unity of the Church, Her Divisions, and Their Removal.* 1821. Reprint, Dallas: Presbyterian Heritage Publications, 1989.

McDowell, Catherine L. *The Image of God in the Garden of Eden: The Creation of Humankind in Genesis 2:5–3:24 in Light of the* mīs p. pīt p. *and* wpt-r *Rituals of Mesopotamia and Ancient Egypt*. Siphrut: Literature and Theology of the Hebrew Scriptures 15. Winona Lake, Indiana: Eisenbrauns, 2015.

McGill, Alexander T. *Church Government: A Treatise Compiled from His Lectures in Theological Seminaries*. Philadelphia: Presbyterian Board of Publication and Sabbath Work, 1888.

McKelvey, Michael G. "The New Covenant as Promised in the Major Prophets." *Covenant Theology: Biblical, Theological, and Historical Perspectives*, edited by Guy Prentiss Waters, J. Nicholas Reid, and John R. Muether, 191–210. Wheaton, IL: Crossway, 2020.

Miller, Samuel. *An Essay on the Warrant, Nature, and Duties of the Office of The Ruling Elder in the Presbyterian Church*. Philadelphia: Presbyterian Board of Publication, 1832.

———. *Presbyterianism the Truly Primitive and Apostolical Constitution of the Church of Christ*. Philadelphia: Presbyterian Board of Publication, 1835.

———. *Thoughts on Public Prayer*. Philadelphia: Presbyterian Board of Publication, 1849.

———. *The Utility and Importance of Creeds and Confessions*. 1839. Reprint, Dallas, TX: Presbyterian Heritage Publications, 1989.

Mitchell, Alexander F., and Struthers, John F., eds. *Minutes of the Sessions of the Westminster Assembly of Divines*. 1874. Reprint, Edmonton, AB: Still Waters Revival Books, 1991.

Moule, C. F. D. *Worship in the New Testament*. 2nd ed. Bramcote: Grove, 1977–1978.

Murray, John. "The Church: Its Definition in Terms of 'Visible' and 'Invisible' Invalid." In *The Claims of Truth*, 663–68. Vol. 1 of *The Collected Writings of John Murray*. Edinburgh: Banner of Truth, 1976.

———. "The Nature and Unity of the Church." In *Select Lectures of Systematic Theology*, 321–35. Vol. 2 of *The Collected Writings of John Murray*. Edinburgh: Banner of Truth, 1977.

———. "Office in the Church." In *Select Lectures of Systematic Theology*, 321–35. Vol. 2 of *The Collected Writings of John Murray*. Edinburgh: Banner of Truth, 1977.

———. *Principles of Conduct: Aspects of Biblical Ethics*. Grand Rapids: Eerdmans, 1957.

———. "The Relation of Church and State." In *The Claims of Truth*, 253–39. Vol. 1 of *The Collected Writings of John Murray*. Edinburg: Banner of Truth, 1977.

Nicolassen, G. F. *A Digest of the Acts and Proceedings of the General Assembly of the Presbyterian Church in the United States*. Richmond, VA: Presbyterian Committee of Publication, 1923.

O'Brien, P. T. *Gospel and Mission in the Writings of Paul: An Exegetical and Theological Analysis*. Grand Rapids: Baker Academic, 1995.

Oliphant Hughes. *Leading in Prayer: A Workbook for Worship*. Grand Rapids: Eerdmans, 1995.

Ortlund, Raymond C., Jr. *God's Unfaithful Wife: A Biblical Theology of Spiritual Adultery*. NSBT. Downers Grove, IL: InterVarsity Press, 2003.

Ott, Ludwig. *Fundamentals of Catholic Dogma*. 4th ed. Translated by Patrick Lynch. Rockford, IL: Tan Books, 1960.

Owen, John. "A Discourse Concerning Liturgies and Their Imposition." In vol. 15 of *The Works of John Owen*, edited by William H. Goold, 1–57. 1850–1853. Reprint, Edinburgh: Banner of Truth, 1965.

———. "A Discourse of Spiritual Gifts." In vol. 4 of *The Works of John Owen*, edited by William H. Goold, 420–520. 1850–1853. Reprint, Edinburgh: Banner of Truth, 1967.

———. "Meditations and Discourses on the Glory of Christ." In vol. 1 of *The Works of John Owen*, edited by William H. Goold, 418–61. 1850–1853. Reprint, Edinburgh: Banner of Truth, 1965.

———. "The True Nature of a Gospel Church," In vol. 16 of *The Works of John Owen, The Works of John Owen*, 16 vols., edited by William H. Goold, 1–209. 1850–1853. Reprint, Edinburgh: Banner of Truth, 1965.

Paul, Robert S. *Assembly of the Lord: Politics and Religion in the Westminster Assembly and the 'Grand Debate.'* Edinburgh: T&T Clark, 1985.

Pearson, John. *An Exposition of the Creed*. 5th ed. Revised by E. Burton. 5th ed. Oxford: Clarendon, 1864.

Peck, Thomas E. "The Action of the Assembly of 1879 on Worldly Amusements, or the Powers of Our Several Church Courts." In vol 2 of *Miscellanies of Rev. Thomas E. Peck*. Edited by Thomas C. Johnson, 331–60. Richmond, VA: Presbyterian Committee of Publication, 1896.

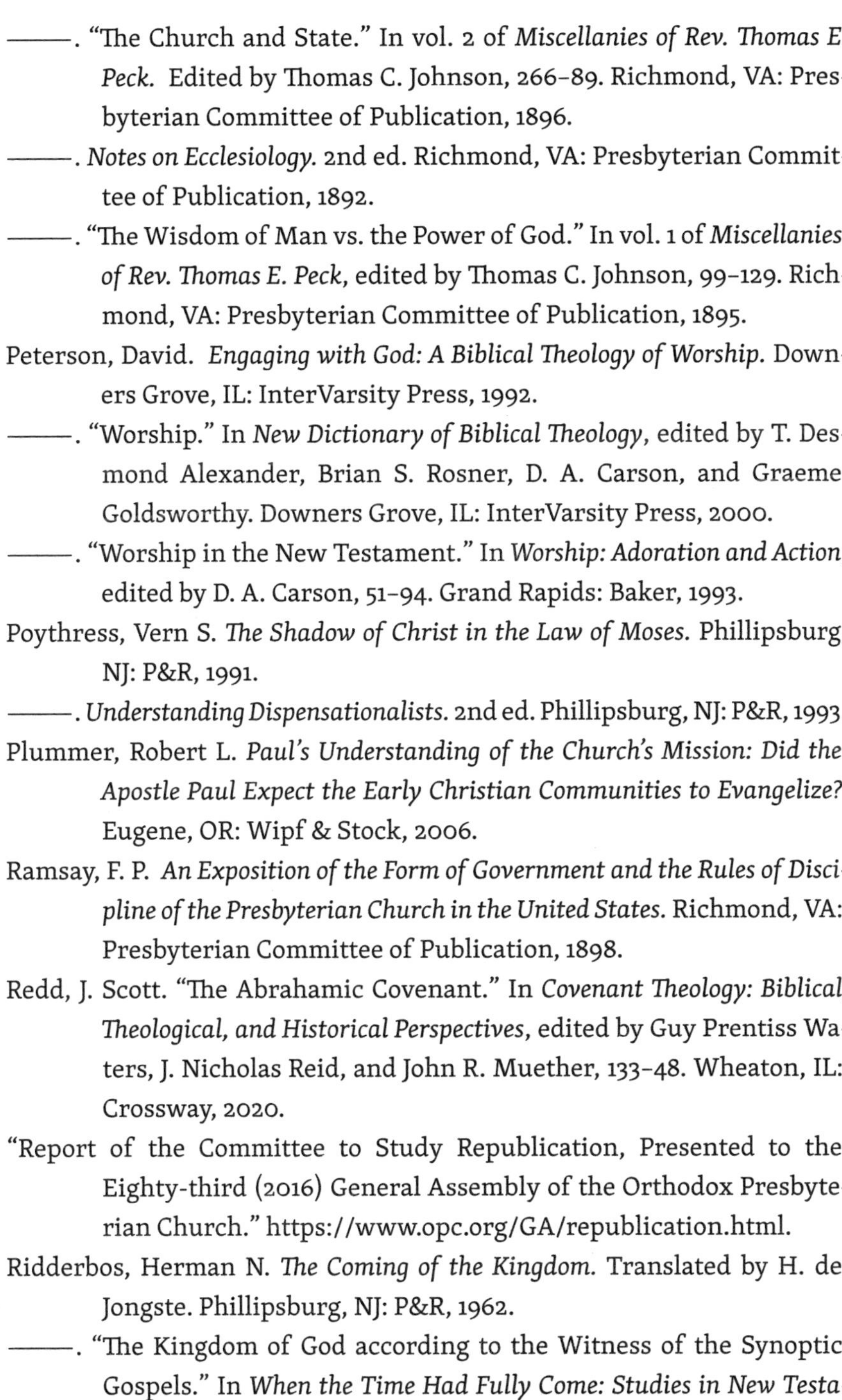

———. "The Church and State." In vol. 2 of *Miscellanies of Rev. Thomas E. Peck.* Edited by Thomas C. Johnson, 266–89. Richmond, VA: Presbyterian Committee of Publication, 1896.

———. *Notes on Ecclesiology.* 2nd ed. Richmond, VA: Presbyterian Committee of Publication, 1892.

———. "The Wisdom of Man vs. the Power of God." In vol. 1 of *Miscellanies of Rev. Thomas E. Peck,* edited by Thomas C. Johnson, 99–129. Richmond, VA: Presbyterian Committee of Publication, 1895.

Peterson, David. *Engaging with God: A Biblical Theology of Worship.* Downers Grove, IL: InterVarsity Press, 1992.

———. "Worship." In *New Dictionary of Biblical Theology,* edited by T. Desmond Alexander, Brian S. Rosner, D. A. Carson, and Graeme Goldsworthy. Downers Grove, IL: InterVarsity Press, 2000.

———. "Worship in the New Testament." In *Worship: Adoration and Action,* edited by D. A. Carson, 51–94. Grand Rapids: Baker, 1993.

Poythress, Vern S. *The Shadow of Christ in the Law of Moses.* Phillipsburg, NJ: P&R, 1991.

———. *Understanding Dispensationalists.* 2nd ed. Phillipsburg, NJ: P&R, 1993.

Plummer, Robert L. *Paul's Understanding of the Church's Mission: Did the Apostle Paul Expect the Early Christian Communities to Evangelize?* Eugene, OR: Wipf & Stock, 2006.

Ramsay, F. P. *An Exposition of the Form of Government and the Rules of Discipline of the Presbyterian Church in the United States.* Richmond, VA: Presbyterian Committee of Publication, 1898.

Redd, J. Scott. "The Abrahamic Covenant." In *Covenant Theology: Biblical, Theological, and Historical Perspectives,* edited by Guy Prentiss Waters, J. Nicholas Reid, and John R. Muether, 133–48. Wheaton, IL: Crossway, 2020.

"Report of the Committee to Study Republication, Presented to the Eighty-third (2016) General Assembly of the Orthodox Presbyterian Church." https://www.opc.org/GA/republication.html.

Ridderbos, Herman N. *The Coming of the Kingdom.* Translated by H. de Jongste. Phillipsburg, NJ: P&R, 1962.

———. "The Kingdom of God according to the Witness of the Synoptic Gospels." In *When the Time Had Fully Come: Studies in New Testament Theology,* 9–25. Grand Rapids: Eerdmans, 1957.

———. *Paul: An Outline of His Theology*. Translated by John Richard De Witt. Grand Rapids: Eerdmans, 1975.

———. *Redemptive History and the New Testament Scriptures*. 2nd rev. ed. Translated by. H. de Jongste. Phillpsburg, NJ: P&R, 1988.

Robertson, O. Palmer. *The Christ of the Covenants*. Phillipsburg, NJ: P&R, 1980.

Robinson, Stuart. *Discourses of Redemption*. 4th ed. Richmond, VA: Presbyterian Committee of Publication, 1866.

———. "The Churchliness of Calvinism: Presbytery *Jure Divino* Its Logical Outcome." In *Report of Proceedings of the First General Presbyterian Council*, edited by J. Thomson, 60–68. Edinburgh: Thomas and Archibald Constable, 1877.

———. *The Church of God as an Essential Element of the Gospel*. 1858. Reprint, Willow Grove, PA: The Committee on Christian Education of the Orthodox Presbyterian Church, 2009.

Ross, Mark. "Baptism and Circumcision as Signs and Seals." In *The Case for Covenantal Infant Baptism*, edited by Gregg Strawbridge, 85–111. Phillipsburg, NJ: P&R, 2003.

Ross, Philip S. *From the Finger of God: The Biblical and Theological Basis for the Threefold Division of the Law*. Fearn, UK: Mentor, 2010.

Ryken, Philip Graham, Derek W. H. Thomas, and J. Ligon Duncan, III, eds. *Give Praise to God: A Vision for Reforming Worship*. Phillipsburg, NJ: P&R, 2003.

Ryrie, Charles C. *Dispensationalism Today*. Rev. ed. Chicago: Moody, 1995.

Sailhamer, John H. *The Meaning of the Pentateuch: Revelation, Composition and Interpretation*. Downers Grove, IL: InterVarsity Press, 2009.

Salter, Martin. "Does Baptism Replace Circumcision? An Examination of the Relationship Between Circumcision and Baptism in Colossians 2:11–12." *Themelios* 35, no. 1 (2010): 15–29.

Schaver, J. L. *The Polity of the Churches*. 2 vols. Chicago: Church Polity Press, 1947.

Schreiner, Thomas R. "Good-bye and Hello: The Sabbath Command for New Covenant Believers." In *Progressive Covenantalism: Charting a Course Between Dispensational and Covenantal Theologies*, edited by Stephen J. Wellum and Brent E. Parker, 159–88. Nashville, TN: B&H, 2016.

———. *Spiritual Gifts: What They Are & Why They Matter.* Nashville, TN: B&H, 2018.

Smeaton, George. *The Doctrine of the Holy Spirit.* Edinburgh: T & T Clark, 1882.

———. "The Scottish Theory of Ecclesiastical Establishments (1875)." In *Sermons and Addresses of George Smeaton*, edited by John W. Keddi, 193–235. Edinburgh: Banner of Truth, 2022.

Smyth, Thomas. *Ecclesiastical Republicanism, or the Republicanism, Liberality, and Catholicity of Presbytery, in Contrast with Prelacy and Popery* in *Complete Works of Thomas Smyth.* Vol. 3. Edited by J. William Flynn. Columbia, SC: R. L. Bryan, 1908.

Stott, John R. *Baptism and Fullness: The Work of the Holy Spirit Today*. 3rd ed. Downers Grove, IL: InterVarsity Press, 2006.

Strange, Alan D. *The Doctrine of the Spirituality of the Church in the Ecclesiology of Charles Hodge.* RAD. Phillipsburg, NJ: P&R, 2017.

Strauss, Mark L. *The Davidic Messiah in Luke-Acts: The Promise and Its Fulfillment in Lukan Christology.* JSNTSS 110. Sheffield: Sheffield Academic, 1995.

Strong, Augustus H. *Systematic Theology.* Philadelphia: Judson, 1907.

Thiselton, Anthony C. *The Holy Spirit—In Biblical Teaching, through the Centuries, and Today.* Grand Rapids: Eerdmans, 2013.

Thomas, Johnson Cary. *Virginia Presbyterianism and Religious Liberty in Colonial and Revolutionary Times.* Richmond, VA: Presbyterian Committee of Publication, 1907.

Thompson, E. T. *The Spirituality of the Church: A Distinctive Doctrine of the Presbyterian Church in the United States.* Richmond, VA: John Knox Press, 1961.

Thompson, James W. *The Church According to Paul: Rediscovering the Community Conformed to Christ.* Grand Rapids: Baker Academic, 2014.

Thornwell, James Henley. "Address to all the Churches of Christ upon Earth." In vol. 4 of *Collected Writings of James Henley Thornwell*, 446–52. 1873. Reprint, Edinburgh: Banner of Truth, 1974.

Trueman, Carl R. *The Creedal Imperative.* Wheaton, IL: Crossway, 2012.

Turretin, Francis. *Institutes of Elenctic Theology.* Translated by George M. Giger. Edited by James T. Dennison, Jr. 3 vols. Phillipsburg, NJ: P&R, 1992–1997.

Ursinus, Zacharias. *Commentary on the Heidelberg Catechism*. Translated by G. W. Williard. 1852. Reprint, Phillipsburg, NJ: P&R, n.d.

Van Dam, Cornelis. *The Deacon: Biblical Foundations for Today's Ministry of Mercy*. Grand Rapids: Reformation Heritage, 2016.

VanDrunen, David. *Living in God's Two Kingdoms: A Biblical Vision for Christianity and Culture*. Wheaton, IL: Crossway, 2010.

———. *Natural Law and the Two Kingdoms: A Study in the Development of Reformed Social Thought*. Grand Rapids: Eerdmans, 2010.

———. *Politics after Christendom: Political Theology in a Fractured World*. Grand Rapids: Zondervan, 2020.

Van Groningen, Gerard. *Messianic Revelation in the Old Testament*. 2 vols. Grand Rapids: Baker, 1990.

Van Pelt, Miles V. "The Noahic Covenant of the Covenant of Grace." In *Covenant Theology: Biblical, Theological, and Historical Perspectives*, edited by Guy Prentiss Waters, J. Nicholas Reid, and John R. Muether, 111–32. Wheaton, IL: Crossway, 2020.

Vitringa, Campegius. *Ancient Roots for Reformed Polity: De Synagoga Vetere and the Ecclesiology of the Early Church—An Annotated Compendium*. Edited by H. David Schuringa. Translated by Joshua L. Bernard. 1685, 1696. Reprint, Monee, IL.: North Star Ministry Press, 2020.

Vos, Geerhardus. *Biblical Theology: Old and New Testaments*. Edinburgh: Banner of Truth, 1975.

———. *The Eschatology of the Old Testament*. Edited by James T. Dennison, Jr. Phillipsburg, NJ: P&R, 2001.

———. *Redemptive History and Biblical Interpretation: The Shorter Writings of Geerhardus Vos*. Phillipsburg, NJ: P&R, 1980.

———. *Reformed Dogmatics*. 5 vols. Edited by Richard B. Gaffin Jr. Bellingham, WA: Lexham, 2016.

———. *The Teaching of Jesus Concerning the Kingdom of God and the Church*. Phillipsburg, NJ: P&R, 1972.

Wallace, Daniel. *Greek Grammar Beyond the Basics: An Exegetical Syntax of the New Testament*. Grand Rapids: Zondervan, 1996.

Waltke, Bruce K. "The Kingdom of God in the Old Testament: The Covenants." In *The Kingdom of God*, edited by Christopher W. Morgan and Robert A. Peterson, 73–94. Wheaton, IL: Crossway, 2012.

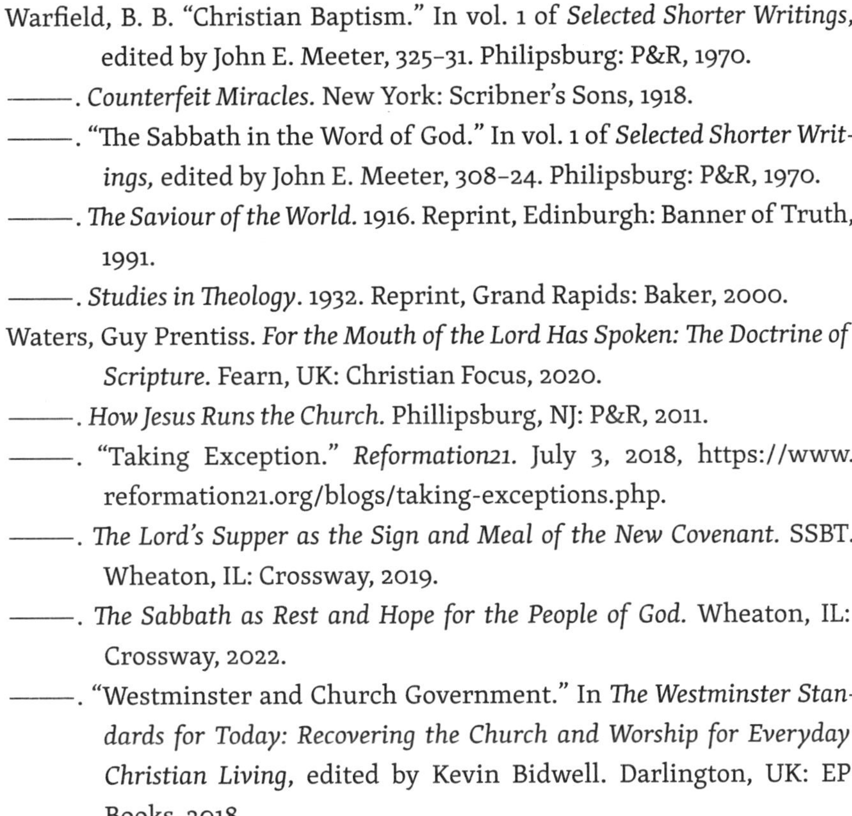

Warfield, B. B. "Christian Baptism." In vol. 1 of *Selected Shorter Writings*, edited by John E. Meeter, 325–31. Philipsburg: P&R, 1970.

———. *Counterfeit Miracles*. New York: Scribner's Sons, 1918.

———. "The Sabbath in the Word of God." In vol. 1 of *Selected Shorter Writings*, edited by John E. Meeter, 308–24. Philipsburg: P&R, 1970.

———. *The Saviour of the World*. 1916. Reprint, Edinburgh: Banner of Truth, 1991.

———. *Studies in Theology*. 1932. Reprint, Grand Rapids: Baker, 2000.

Waters, Guy Prentiss. *For the Mouth of the Lord Has Spoken: The Doctrine of Scripture*. Fearn, UK: Christian Focus, 2020.

———. *How Jesus Runs the Church*. Phillipsburg, NJ: P&R, 2011.

———. "Taking Exception." *Reformation21*. July 3, 2018, https://www.reformation21.org/blogs/taking-exceptions.php.

———. *The Lord's Supper as the Sign and Meal of the New Covenant*. SSBT. Wheaton, IL: Crossway, 2019.

———. *The Sabbath as Rest and Hope for the People of God*. Wheaton, IL: Crossway, 2022.

———. "Westminster and Church Government." In *The Westminster Standards for Today: Recovering the Church and Worship for Everyday Christian Living*, edited by Kevin Bidwell. Darlington, UK: EP Books, 2018.

Wellum Stephen J., and Kirk Wellum. "The Biblical and Theological Case for Congregationalism." In *Baptist Foundations: Government for an Anti-Institutional Age*, edited by Mark Dever and Jonathan Leeman, 47–77. Nashville, TN: B&H, 2015.

Willborn, C. N. "The Deacon: A Divine Right Office with Divine Uses." *The Confessional Presbyterian* 5 (2009): 185–99.

———. "The Gospel Work in the Diaconate: A Ministry 'Proportioned in Number.' " *The Confessional Presbyterian* 10 (2014): 23–32.

Williams, Roger. "The Bloody Tenent of Persecution." In *On Religious Liberty: Selections from the Works of Roger Williams*, 85–156. The John Harvard Library. Cambridge, MA: Belknap Press, 2008.

Williamson, Paul R. *Sealed with an Oath: Covenant in God's Unfolding Purpose*. NSBT 23. Downers Grove, IL: InterVarsity Press, 2007.

Wilson, Samuel R. "Declaration and Testimony against the Erroneous and Heretical Doctrines and Practices, which have been obtained and propagated in the Presbyterian Church in the United States during the past five years" (1865). Reprinted in John S. Grasty, *Memoir of Rev. Samuel B. McPheeters*, 316–27. St. Louis: Southwestern Book and Publishing Co., 1871.

Wind, John A. "Does the Old Testament 'Authorize' a Creation Care Mission of the Institutional Church? Examining Christopher Wright's Claims." *Journal of Global Christianity* 2, no. 1 (February 2016): 33–47.

Witherow, Thomas. *The Form of the Christian Temple: Being a Treatise on the Constitution of the New Testament Church*. Edinburgh: T&T Clark, 1889.

Witherspoon, John. "The Dominion of Providence over the Passions of Men." 1776. Reprinted in Darryl Hart, *A Secular Faith: Why Christianity Favors the Separation of Church and State*. Chicago, IL: Ivan R. Dee, 2006.

Witsius, Herman. *The Economy of the Covenants Between God and Man: Comprehending a Complete Body of Divinity*. Edinburgh: Thomas Turnbull, 1803.

———. *Sacred Dissertations on What is Commonly Called the Apostles' Creed*. Translated by Donald Fraser. 2 vols. 1823. Reprint, Escondido, CA: den Dulk, 1993.

Wooley, Paul. "What Is a Creed For? Some Answers from Church History." In *Scripture and Confession: A Book About Confessions Old and New*, edited by John H. Skilton. Phillipsburg, NJ: P&R, 1973.

Wright, Christopher J. H. *The Mission of God's People: A Biblical Theology of the Church's Mission*. Grand Rapids: Zondervan, 2010.

Wright, Shawn D. "Five Preliminary Issues for Understanding the Ordinances." In *Baptist Foundations: Church Government for an Anti-Institutional Age*, edited by Mark Dever and Jonathan Leeman, 81–90. Nashville, TN: B&H Academic, 2015.

Yeago, D. S. "The New Testament and Nicene Dogma: A Contribution to the Recovery of Theological Exegesis." *ProEcclesia* 3 (1994): 87–100.

Young, William. "The Puritan Principle of Worship." In *Reformed Thought: Selected Writings of William Young*, edited by Joel R. Beeke and Ray B. Lanning, 140–87. Grand Rapids: Reformation Heritage, 2011.

SUBJECT INDEX

AUTHOR INDEX

SCRIPTURE INDEX

Old Testament

Exodus

Jeremiah

Lamentations

Ezekiel

Daniel

Hosea

Joel

Amos

Micah

Habakkuk

Zephaniah

Haggai

New Testament

Colossians

1 Thessalonians

2 Thessalonians

1 Timothy

2 Timothy

Titus

Hebrews

The
LORD
JESUS
CHRIST
The
BIBLICAL
DOCTRINE
of the
PERSON
AND
WORK
of CHRIST
Volume Three
BRANDON D.
CROWE
Series Editors
JOHN McCLEAN &
MURRAY J. SMITH